SUGAR IN THE BLOOD

Andrea Stuart

Sugar in the Blood

A Family's Story of Slavery and Empire

Portobello
BOOKS

Published by Portobello Books 2012

Portobello Books
12 Addison Avenue
London
W11 4QR

A CIP catalogue record is available from the British Library

9 8 7 6 5 4 3 2 1

ISBN 978 1 84627 071 0

www.portobellobooks.com

Typeset by Avon DataSet, Bidford on Avon, Warwickshire

Printed and bound by CPI Group (UK) Ltd, Croydon, CR0 4YY

For my uncle, Trevor Ashby, whose stories started it all

The past is not dead. In fact, it's not even past.

William Faulkner

Contents

Illustrations

A. 'A Corvette, a Brigantin and a Barque', from West India Vessels of the Close of the Seventeenth Century, English School, 20th century (Private Collection/The Bridgeman Art Library).

B. Richard Ligon's map of Barbados, 1657 (courtesy of The Barbados Museum and Historical Society).

C. 'A Prospect of Bridge Town in Barbados', Samuel Copen, engraving by Johannes Kip, 1695 (Private Collection/The Bridgeman Art Library).

D. Sugar cane (courtesy of The Barbados Museum and Historical Society).

E. 'Sir Henry Morgan at Porto Bello', lithograph by Howard Pyle, 1887 (Private Collection/ Peter Newark Pictures/ The Bridgeman Art Library).

F. 'A Representation of the Sugar-Cane and the Art of Making Sugar', from Universal Magazine, 1749 (Private Collection/ The Bridgeman Art Library).

G. *Barbadoes Mulatto Girl*, Agostino Brunias, 1765 (courtesy of The Barbados Museum and Historical Society).

H. Portrait assumed to be of Robert Cooper Ashby (courtesy of John Knox).

I. Title page of a pamphlet calling for the emancipation of African slaves, 1776 (Private Collection/ Peter Newark American Pictures/ The Bridgeman Art Library).

J. Robert Cooper Ashby's will (courtesy of Andrea Ramsey).

K. Sukey Ann's certificate of manumission, 1832 (courtesy of Andrea Ramsey).

L. Photograph of Drax Hall, 1980 (courtesy of The Barbados Museum and Historical Society).

M. Photograph of Edward Everton Barnes Ashby (from the author's family album).

N. Photograph of Muriel Haynes Skinner (from the author's family album).

O. Photograph of Barbara Cecille Ashby (from the author's family album).

P. Photograph of Kenneth Stuart Lamonte (from the author's family album).

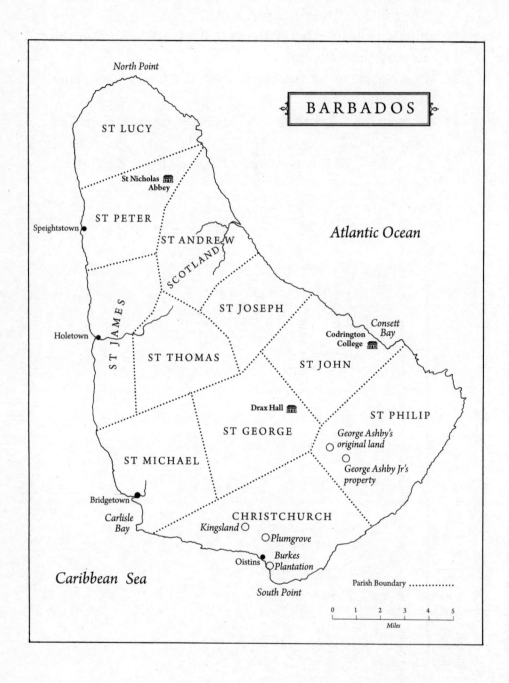

North Point

BARBADOS

ST LUCY

St Nicholas Abbey

ST PETER

Speightstown

ST ANDREW

SCOTLAND

Atlantic Ocean

ST JAMES

Holetown

ST JOSEPH

Codrington College

Consett Bay

ST THOMAS

ST JOHN

Drax Hall

ST GEORGE

ST PHILIP

George Ashby's original land

George Ashby Jr's property

ST MICHAEL

Bridgetown

Carlisle Bay

CHRISTCHURCH

Kingsland

Plumgrove

Oistins

Burkes Plantation

South Point

Caribbean Sea

Parish Boundary ....

0   1   2   3   4   5
Miles

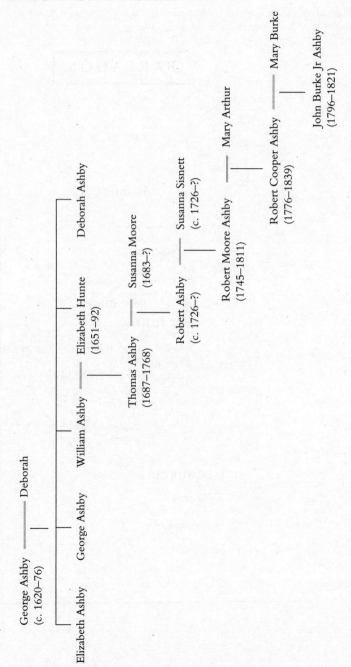

George Ashby
(c. 1620–76) ——— Deborah

Elizabeth Ashby

George Ashby

William Ashby ——— Elizabeth Hunte
(1651–92)

Deborah Ashby

Thomas Ashby ——— Susanna Moore
(1687–1768)   (1683–?)

Robert Ashby
(c. 1726–?) ——— Susanna Sisnett
(c. 1726–?)

Robert Moore Ashby ——— Mary Arthur
(1745–1811)

Robert Cooper Ashby ——— Mary Burke
(1776–1839)

John Burke Jr Ashby
(1796–1821)

(see next page for Robert
Cooper Ashby's slave families)

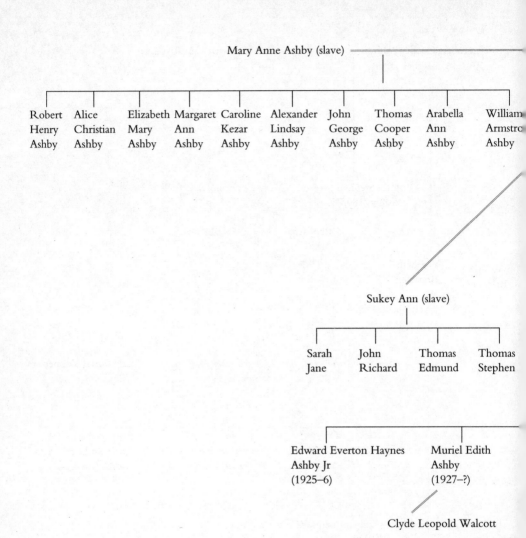

Mary Anne Ashby (slave)

Robert Henry Ashby | Alice Christian Ashby | Elizabeth Mary Ashby | Margaret Ann Ashby | Caroline Kezar Ashby | Alexander Lindsay Ashby | John George Ashby | Thomas Cooper Ashby | Arabella Ann Ashby | William Armstro Ashby

Sukey Ann (slave)

Sarah Jane | John Richard | Thomas Edmund | Thomas Stephen

Edward Everton Haynes Ashby Jr (1925–6) | Muriel Edith Ashby (1927–?)

Clyde Leopold Walcott

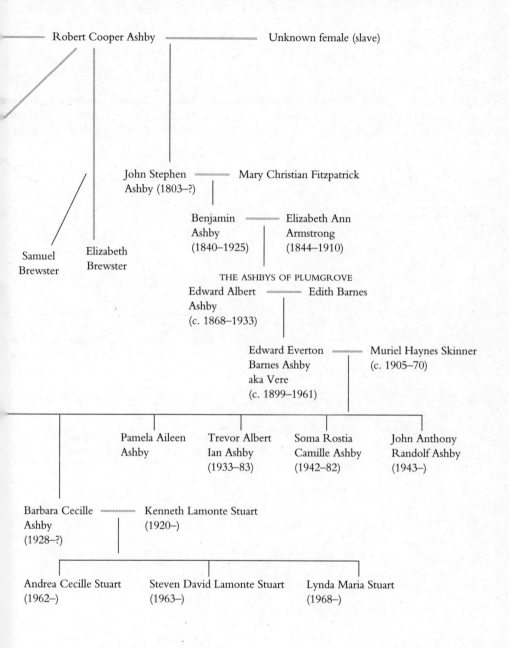

Robert Cooper Ashby ——————————— Unknown female (slave)

John Stephen ——————— Mary Christian Fitzpatrick
Ashby (1803–?)

Samuel   Elizabeth
Brewster   Brewster

Benjamin ——————— Elizabeth Ann
Ashby   Armstrong
(1840–1925)   (1844–1910)

THE ASHBYS OF PLUMGROVE
Edward Albert ——————— Edith Barnes
Ashby
(c. 1868–1933)

Edward Everton ——————— Muriel Haynes Skinner
Barnes Ashby   (c. 1905–70)
aka Vere
(c. 1899–1961)

Pamela Aileen   Trevor Albert   Soma Rostia   John Anthony
Ashby   Ian Ashby   Camille Ashby   Randolf Ashby
                 (1933–83)   (1942–82)   (1943–)

Barbara Cecille ——————— Kenneth Lamonte Stuart
Ashby   (1920–)
(1928–?)

Andrea Cecille Stuart   Steven David Lamonte Stuart   Lynda Maria Stuart
(1962–)   (1963–)   (1968–)

Preface

My family is just one of millions across the globe that were forged by sugar and slavery. Virtually all our stories began the same way: some English or European migrant abandoned the Old World for the New, eventually to become enriched by the production of sugar, which became known as 'white gold'. During this process, their bloodlines inevitably became intermingled with that of the slaves imported to farm and service this new economy. Yet, despite the ubiquity of this tale, I could not recollect a non-fiction book that tried to tell it; one which explored how the epic forces of sugar, slavery and settlement made and shaped the life experiences of our ancestors, and our world today. So I have written that book myself.

The narrative of the book is organized around the particular genealogy of the Ashby family, my maternal ancestors. It begins with my first identifiable ancestor and continues to the present day. This approach caused me some heartache, since it has meant focusing the initial section of the story largely around its white progenitors, whose experience is definitively documented. That doesn't feel comfortable, but it allows a more representative story to be told, since the Caribbean was a European world in the early years of settlement, with blacks in the minority for several decades. And this methodology also demonstrates a fundamental truth about the region's families, which overwhelmingly started as ethnically white and over time became predominantly black.

So, historical veracity triumphed. But that has meant that my African ancestors do not enter the picture until they are confirmed on the family tree. The unknowability of their past is one of the many terrible by-products of slavery, when people, reduced to chattels, are written out of history and deprived of a personal past. Ghosts haunt this tale, small men whose lives leave only very faint footprints and slaves whose sufferings leave no mark at all. My debt of honour has been to try to reconstruct their stories, black and white, and bring them to vivid life, using the scraps and fragments of information available to me. In doing so, I have been very aware of the tensions between helping stories to be told without abusing the limitations of historical record, and allowing myself to interpret and comment while acknowledging the silences of the undocumented past.

The completion of *Sugar in the Blood* would not have been possible without the support and encouragement of a great number of people. My first debt is to my editor, Laura Barber, whose passion for the book, unfailing encouragement and editorial prowess have made this the book it is; and then to everyone else at Portobello for producing and publicizing it with such enthusiasm and energy. In America I am grateful to Sonny Mehta's team at Knopf, with a special mention to Diana Cugolianese, for taking this project to their hearts and backing it so unequivocally. My wonderful agent, Clare Alexander, 'got' this project immediately and went in to bat for it with panache and passion. My profound gratitude also goes to the Wingate Foundation, without whose financial support this book could not have been written.

My research has taken me on interesting journeys. In Barbados, where much of my primary research was undertaken, I was met with great kindness. My dear friend Alissandra Cummins, director of the Barbados Museum, has been invaluable: introducing me to the right people, tracking down useful sources, recommending useful texts. Huge thanks are due to Robert

Morris and my newly discovered cousin John Knox, who have guided me through the maze of Ashby-related sources, and whose unstinting generosity with their research, time and superior local knowledge have been invaluable. Thanks are also due to Sir Hilary Beckles, Dr Pedro Welch, Dr Karl Watson and Dr Tara Iniss, who in different ways have contributed to this project. Cynthia Cummerbatch and Patricia Stafford both shared their precious work with me. The library staff at the Barbados Museum and the Barbados Archives were always patient and helpful. In England I particularly wish to thank Bill Schwarz at Queen Mary, University of London, for his vital input in thinking through the research process. Staff at the London Library were always willing to help me source material, and I would like to thank the Athenaeum for granting access to their collection of pamphlets on the slave trade.

My special gratitude goes to Tara Kaufmann, who has walked the entire way with me, helping with research and reading and editing sections; and to my daughters Ava and Georgie, whose cries of 'Is it finished yet?' have spurred me to the finishing line. My siblings, Lynda and Steven, have been unstinting in their support, while my parents, Kenneth and Barbara Stuart, have been wonderful in every way: finding material, reading samples and providing feedback. My wider family – especially my uncle John and aunts Muriel and Dottie – have provided me with pictures and other family material. And, to end, I offer a special salute to all the new relatives whom I have uncovered in researching this book, especially Andrea Ramsey, Diana Miller and Robert Wuulf. To them and all the other Ashbys I have spoken to or heard about, from Australia to America, Canada to Trinidad, France to Holland, this book belongs to you.

AS
February 2012

Introduction

In every conceivable manner, the family is link to our past, bridge to our future.

Alex Haley

I happened upon the name of my earliest known ancestor while sitting in a brutally air-conditioned library at the Barbados Museum, poring over a seventeenth-century census. There he was: George Ashby, an Englishman, my maternal grandfather eight times removed. I knew how unusual it was for family research to reach back that far and I felt utterly exhilarated: my stomach lurched and my eyes filled with tears. This sense of elation lingered for a long time and my previously vague interest in genealogy suddenly sharpened. I decided to find out more.

The journey that followed wasn't always joyful. There were unpleasant shocks as well as happy surprises, perhaps the most painful being the discovery of one of my ancestors on a slave return (a register of slaves held on an individual plantation): just another commodity, listed like pigs and cows and farm machinery. My sorrow and fury were tempered only by my gratitude that I had found him, as if somehow he could draw comfort – as I did – from having his life noticed and honoured by a free descendant.

Eventually I built up an unbroken family tree reaching back to 1620. I was initially triumphant, but as time went on a sense of anticlimax overwhelmed me. What did my neatly formatted family tree really mean? It was, after all, just names on a page. Genealogical research has its limitations: it yields the skeleton, not the body. But between the bones I had, nonetheless, glimpsed something intriguing: a story of migration, settlement, survival, slavery and the making of the Atlantic world. I realized that there was a book here, struggling to emerge. I continued investigating, but now focusing on secondary sources that brought to life the context and detail of the period. Over time, my maternal line began to gain both shape and colour. I followed George Ashby from seventeenth-century England, where he, alongside thousands of others, turned his back on his homeland and migrated to the Caribbean island of Barbados in search of a new life. I tracked the lives of his descendants as they became enmeshed in the sugar industry and the Atlantic slave system. And I followed the offspring of those descendants, myself included, as they migrated back to the cold winters of England, the US and Canada.

Although this book is not about me, the story is of course my own. It forced me to revisit my own Caribbean childhood: the holidays spent at the family plantation, Plumgrove, where we could look out of the bedroom windows and watch the fields of waving sugar cane being harvested by other, poorer Barbadians. At the time, I had no idea how privileged this life was; that understanding came later, after I had grown up and made my home in England and had come to see that the cane fields in which I played had once been drenched in exploitation, grief and death. And I had recognized something else: that my family's story is at once very specific, very particular, but also wholly typical and representative. It is a story that belongs not just to me but to many, many others.

My family, like the families of those others, is the product of sugar and of its siblings, settlement and slavery. This book is the story of how those forces shaped the minutiae of the Ashby family's intimate relationships – and how, in turn, those family relationships rippled outwards, transforming the societies in which they lived. It is, then, more than a family history: it is a global story, too – one that fixes its gaze on the connections between continents, between black and white, men and women, the free and the enslaved – demonstrating that the individual is not just a victim of global history, but an author of it as well.

Part One
THE PIONEER

1

There was a wind over England, and it blew.
(Have you heard the news of Virginia?)
A west wind blowing, the wind of a western star,
To gather men's lives like pollen and cast them forth,
Blowing in hedge and highway and seaport town,
Whirling dead leaf and living but always blowing,
A salt wind, a sea wind, a wind from the world's end,
From the coasts that have new wild names, from the
huge unknown.

Stephen Vincent Benét, 'Western Star'

George Ashby's story began as all migrants' stories do: with a journey.

Some time in the late 1630s, when George Ashby was finally given notification that his ship was ready to sail, he must have been afraid. He was a blacksmith, a young man in his late teens, about to leave behind everything he had ever known. Though the voyage carried the seeds of his dreams he, like most of the population, had probably never undergone a long sea journey before and had no real idea of what to expect when he arrived in the Americas.

Those who chose to undertake the fearsome Atlantic crossing in search of a new life were generally tough – or else dangerously foolish. But what else can we know about George Ashby? Was he fleeing from a family or seeking a new one? Did he dream of religious freedom or of wealth? Was he ambivalent about leaving England or were his life experiences so bitter that he believed nothing in the Americas could be worse? As he set sail for the adventuresome world of the Caribbean he would have had no idea how heavily the odds were stacked against him. (According to one historian, men like him were 'pursuing a will-o'-the-wisp', since very few of them ever achieved the better life they longed for.) He could not know that he would be one of the lucky ones: that he would not just survive but found a dynasty that endures to this day, built on sugar and forged by slavery.

The first sight of the ship would have done nothing to allay his trepidation. The typical merchant vessel that plied the route between the Caribbean and Britain was rated at around 200 tons (meaning that it could accommodate 200 casks or tuns of wine). Trussed against the stone walls of the dock, the ship looked like a gigantic gutted carcass afloat upon the water. The gaunt ribs of the wooden hull curved menacingly into the sky and the base was coated with a shaggy pelt of seaweed and barnacles. It would have been hard for George to countenance that he would be confined in the belly of this behemoth for almost two months, with the real possibility that his journey would end, like that of so many before him, in massacre by pirates or drowning at sea.

After unpacking and settling in, the passengers were summoned on deck to present their documents to the 'searchers'. These officials administered the oath of allegiance to the king, stamped each traveller's ticket with the crucial 'Licences under their hands and seals to pass the seas', and then cleared the vessel for departure. Since every passenger had to undergo this process, no matter what their individual circumstances or where they came from, it represented their first rite of passage, one that made their new status as migrants starkly real.

Still gathered on the bridge, the passengers chatted among themselves or waved to family and friends gathered portside to wish them bon voyage. Then, all of a sudden, a flurry of activity: the sailors scrambling across the deck, busying themselves with a series of tasks that were inexplicable to most of the passengers, the screeching of the anchor as it was winched aboard, the screaming of the hoisted sails, the shouting of the master and the sailors, all combined in a violent auditory assault. As the crew worked furiously in the bows, stern and dock, the passengers jostled to be as near the rails as possible.

Despite the noise and bustle of the ship, most of the migrants would have been as hushed as worshippers in a church, fearful of what the voyage might hold or trying to imagine what lay at the other end. They were aware that the journey was, in all probability, final. Some may have dreamt of returning to their homeland enriched, perhaps even ennobled, but most rightly sensed that they would not be coming back.

To truly grasp what this sea journey meant, what bravery and audacity it required, one must understand how the world was seen and known at that time. Though George Ashby and his contemporaries had been born in the Age of Discovery (1500–1700), most of the world was still *terra incognita* for Europeans. Maps were often sketchy and inaccurate. Two continents, Australia and Antarctica, had not been traced at all, and vast areas were still blank. The interiors of South America, Africa and Asia had scarcely been explored. Beyond the eastern fringe of North America, which George's fellow pioneers had begun to document, were millions of square miles of uncharted wilderness.

In England, a country poised between the medieval and the modern, most people's lives played out within a narrow radius around their birthplace, and their beliefs were characterized by superstition and ignorance. It was an age in which magic still played a large part in the lives of ordinary people and many

firmly believed in witches and fairies, that butterflies were the
souls of the dearly departed, and that churchyards swarmed with
souls and spirits. In the absence of real information about far-
off lands, fantasies abounded: that the east was populated with
dog-headed men and basilisks, that Africa had tribes with no
heads at all – just eyes and mouths in their breasts – and that the
Caribbean was peopled by cannibals, amazons and giants. Some
believed that the oceans were full of strange creatures such as
mermaids and sea dragons. In 1583 Sir Henry Gilbert professed
to have encountered a lion-like sea monster on his return from
claiming St John's, Newfoundland, for England. In a world
that was as yet so immeasurable, frightening and inexplicable,
George and his fellow travellers must have feared that they were
not just crossing the map, but falling off the edge of it.

Yet by the seventeenth century, many thousands of Britons,
beguiled by the much-vaunted possibilities of the 'New World',
were willing to take that leap into the unknown, and left their
homeland to start a fresh life in the Americas. The migration
had begun as a trickle in 1607 with the settling of Jamestown,
the first permanent colony in what is now the United States. It
had increased to a recognizable stream by 1629 and became a
veritable flood in the 1640s, when over 100,000 people left a
country with a population of just under five million. (Between
1600 and 1700 over 700,000 people emigrated from England,
about 17 per cent of the English population in 1600.) At the
rate of one ship departing from England every day, these
pioneers arrived to 'settle the Americas', fanning out from
Newfoundland for three thousand miles, via Virginia and the
Caribbean, to Guiana on the South American mainland. All the
way they fought, worked and died to establish themselves in
new and terrifying lands.

The English weren't the only nation on the move. The
Spanish were the pioneers of colonization of the Americas,
and the Portuguese, French and Dutch swiftly became essential

players in the region. But just over a century after Christopher Columbus's discovery of the New World (which the historian Germán Arciniegas described as being 'so momentous a development in human history that it was like the passing from the third to the fourth day in the first chapter of Genesis'), it was the small nation of England that emerged as Europe's greatest colonizing power. This was particularly surprising for a people who were 'wedded to their native Soile like a Snaile to his shell'. What motivated these patriotic and insular people to abandon the world as they knew it and move halfway across the globe?

The why of George Ashby's departure is something I will never know; my great-great-great-great-great-great-great-great-grandfather was most likely typical of the men who settled much of the New World, a man of action, not reflection, who did not take time out to write letters or keep journals; nor was he important enough for others to write about him. But certainly some of the wider reasons that stirred migrants to risk the New World would have applied to him. Historians have summarized Europe's motivation for the conquest of the Americas with the pithy phrase 'God, gold and glory'. This formula is slightly reductive – and certainly doesn't allow for the large number of migrants who had no say in their transfer – but it does convey the positive pull of the opportunities represented by the New World.

It was not only the much-persecuted Puritans who went to settle New England for whom God was important. The vast majority of those who migrated to colonies south of Maryland were what the historian Carl Bridenbaugh has dubbed 'non-separating puritans'. They may not have moved together as a religious community led by a minister, but they did share the Puritans' profound unease with the old ways of worship and were questioning of the ancient, ceremonial doctrines of the established church. They too had looked on at the risible spectacle of 'the typical Sunday service in England, where parishioners stared dumbly at a minister mumbling incomprehensible phrases from the Book of Common Prayer' and recognized 'how far most people were from a true engagement with the word of God'. So while they had not been impassioned enough to make their faith the prime motivation for their migration, their religious leanings meant that they were that bit more likely to be disillusioned – and therefore to contemplate migration – than their fellow Englishmen.

The Bible was, in fact, a potent recruiter for colonization. In an age where the scriptures permeated everyday life, there were numerous passages that would have resonated with those tempted by the 'Western Star'. Great orators such as the Anglican priest Robert Gray, or John Donne, the Dean of St Paul's, or the Puritan preachers Thomas Hooker and John Cotton thundered from Genesis: 'Get thee out of thy country, and from thy kindred, and from thy father's house, unto a land that I will shew thee: And I will make of thee a great nation,' or from II Samuel 7:10: 'I will appoint a place for my people Israel, and will plant them, that they may dwell in a place of their own, and move no more: neither shall the children of wickendess afflict them any more, as beforetime.'

The dream of building a City on the Hill for the perfection of the human spirit, so inspirational to the Puritans, was also an attractive one for many other migrants, as was the entire project of spreading the word. Captain John Smith, the era's most famous adventurer turned planter, declared:

If hee have any graine of faith or zeale in Religion, what can he doe less hurtfull to any, or more agreeable to God, then to seeke to convert those poore Savages to know Christ and humanity, whose labours with discretion will triple requite thy charge and paine; what so truly sutes with honour and honesty, as the discovering things

unknowne, erecting Townes, peopling Countries, informing the ignorant, reforming things unjust, teaching
vertue and gaine to our native mother Country a
Kingdome to attend her.

But rhetoric about taking Christianity and civilization to the
heathen (so lavishly exploited by the Spanish conquistadors),
or giving European creativity and imagination space to grow,
was a smokescreen for the economic imperatives that drove the
majority of migrants. They hungered for gold; or at least the
chance to acquire land, their own little piece of paradise.

Most seventeenth-century English settlers were in flight from
terrible poverty. In the late sixteenth and early seventeenth
centuries, rapid population growth and periodic agricultural
depression, culminating in a series of terrible famines, caused
genuine hardship. In the countryside large numbers of people
had been deprived of their ancient rural security. The lack
of land to cultivate frustrated many, while unemployment
threatened agricultural labourers as well as village artisans. The
rise in the cost of living and the simultaneous fall in the value
of wages meant that many people were surviving on the very
margins of existence. Housing was inadequate at best; in cold or
wet weather fuel was scarce and expensive. Health scares were
frequent, with regular outbreaks of tuberculosis and plague.
Effective medical treatment was almost non-existent and so the
mortality rate – already high – rose even higher.

Resentment against these conditions focused and crystallized
on a lavish, self-indulgent monarch: Charles I. His resistance
to parliamentary challenge meant that, from 1629, the people
had been governed by arbitrary monarchical rule. His decision
to levy various taxes to obtain revenue and his exploitation of
press-gangs who forced unwilling souls into the navy, meant
greater financial strain for his already beleaguered subjects and
generated a real sense of bitterness. ('Thus was the king's coffers

filled with oppression,' concluded one pamphlet in 1649.) His popularity was eroded further by his religious affiliations: not only had he displayed a preference for the High Anglican worship that would so alienate the Puritans and others of that ilk, he had also married a Catholic queen, Henrietta Maria, and allowed her to observe her faith publicly.

The wider political situation also contributed to the depressed mood of the country and the general suffering endured during this period. The Thirty Years War (1618–48), which had seen warring Protestant and Catholic forces reduce much of Europe to a corpse-strewn battleground, further depleted the nation and contributed to profound collective dissatisfaction with the status quo. The decades from the 1630s through to the end of the 1650s were, according to the historian Peter Bowden, 'probably amongst the most terrible years through which the country had ever passed'. He goes on: 'It is probably no coincidence that the first real beginnings of the colonisation of America dated from this period.' Facing poverty, hunger and actual starvation at home, the English were more than usually attentive to the pedlars of tales told in taverns of the lands across the sea, where everyone could have a full belly and their own property.

One such economic migrant was Richard Ligon. A cultured, educated English gentleman of 'above sixty years' who had served at Charles I's court, he sailed for Barbados in 1647. Ligon was untypical of most migrants to the Caribbean by virtue of his age and class. But his reasons for migrating – essentially economic – would have resonated with most of his contemporaries. Though in the 'last scene of my life', he had 'lost (by a Barbarous Riot) all I had gotten by the painful travels and cares of my youth . . . and left destitute of a subsistence'. In this desperate condition he looked about for friends to support him, found none, and therefore considered himself 'a stranger in my own Countrey'. As a result, he 'resolv'd to lay on the first opportunity that might convey me to any other part of the World, how far distant soever, rather than abide here'.

But the impetus towards the west was also a romantic one. Though the 1600s were still primarily a 'listening age', England, by virtue of its high literacy rates (over half the males in London could read by 1640), had a great many subjects who were able to disseminate the seductive mythology of the New World. This story, which had been evolving ever since Columbus, was a dream of Shangri-La, a completely inviolate and untouched world. In Richard Eden's *A Treatyse of the Newe India* (1553), the first book about the Americas printed in England, the author writes about the new lands, beautiful and rich, where there was much gold and a mountain whose sand sparkled with 'pearls and other such riches'. He also talks of 'strange new peoples, some antagonistic, some friendly, all essentially rude and barbarous', 'beastly and fierce'. This frightening yet bewitching fiction was heightened in the sixteenth century by the widely read tales of Spanish conquistadors like Antonio de Berrio and the English adventurers Walter Raleigh and John Hawkins, who swashbuckled their way across the 'torrid zone' in search of El Dorado. If these heroic quests came to naught, it did not dent the public appetite for images of America as a place where an adventurous man could fulfil his destiny.

From the publication of the *Treatyse* in 1553 until the departure of Newport's ships for Virginia in 1606, there were literally scores of books published about the New World. In subsequent years Eden's book was thrice reprinted and was joined by Peter Martyr's *Decades of the Newe Worlde* (1530), Richard Hakluyt's seminal *Principal Navigations of the English Nation* (1598–1600) and Samuel Purchas's *His Pilgrims* (1625). Over time the information in these works was supplemented by first-hand accounts of European voyages to the New World (many of which were published in English) as well as the numerous catalogues of people and fauna that had been generated from journeys that swept from Newfoundland to the Amazon. Maps of the Americas (including the one that Shakespeare refers to in *Twelfth Night*) also enhanced geographical knowledge of the region. The curios that English sailors brought home to England were acquired by shopkeepers, who titillated their customers with displays of American treasures, genuine as well as fake. The fascination with the New World was even evident in popular entertainment: the public could now go and see curiosities from the region in the form of artefacts and real humans, such as men dressed as 'savages', at places like London's annual Bartholomew Fair.

Many great writers of the age depicted the Americas in gendered terms as 'a succulent maiden to be seduced, deflowered, and plundered by a virile Europe, which shall bask in her treasures'. John Donne, who was closely connected to many of those in the Virginia Company and at one point planned to go to America as the company's official recorder, thoroughly eroticized the colonial conquest:

> Licence my roaving hands, and let them go,
> Before, behind, between, above, below.
> O my America! my new-found-land,
> My kingdome, safeliest when with one man mann'd,
> My Myne of precious stones, My Emperie,
> How blest am I in this discovering thee!

Andrew Marvell's poem 'The Emigrants' celebrated the bravery and fortitude of those who had followed the 'Western Star', while Shakespeare – whose two patrons, the successive Earls of Pembroke, were great colonizers and adventurers – was fascinated by those daring enough to chase the dreams associated with the New World. In *Two Gentlemen of Verona*, he declaimed:

He wondered that your lordship
Would suffer him to spend his youth at home
While other men, of slender reputation,
Put forth their sons to seek preferment out –
Some to the wars, to try their fortune there,
Some to discover islands far away.

The message was clear. There was no longer any room for noble endeavours in England; the future lay in places of danger and profit, delight and possibilities – the Americas.

Henry Colt, a young ex-soldier turned gentleman adventurer who arrived in the Caribbean in 1631, was typical of such men. He clearly saw himself and his fellows as the descendants of heroes like Raleigh and Hawkins: 'they could not rest' until they too had 'done some thinges worthy of ourselves, or dye in the attempt'. These men's decision to go to the West Indies was not as surprising as it now seems. The Caribbean was, according to the historian Richard Dunn, 'the Wild West of the sixteenth and seventeenth centuries, promising far more in the way of excitement, quick profit and constant peril, than the prosaic settlements along the North American coast'. It was in these 'provinces of El Dorado' that the more romantic yarns had been spun, it was here that the gold and pearls could be found, it was here that English pirates made their base, it was here that Hawkins and Raleigh had flirted with glory.

Migration to the New World was also actively promoted by those who stood to profit from it. The shipping companies that transported people to the west had a vested interest in selling this dream, as did the companies that financed the early settlements across the region. These groups took it upon themselves 'to educate the English public in the wonders of the New World and the possibilities there for a new and better life'. Many of these promotional tracts played on the sense of disillusion that already existed among ordinary Britons. One, written in 1624 to promote migration to Newfoundland, implored: 'Bee not too much in love with that countrie, wherein you were borne . . . which bearing you, yet cannot breed you, but seemth and is indeed, weary of you.' These tracts were supplemented by excited letters home from the recently departed, as well as sermons, broadsides and ballads. Depictions of the New World tended towards the hyperbolic. One critic described the company, which had disseminated a tract designed to promote Virginia, as 'varnishing their owne actions with colourable schemes and Cozzening ballads', filled with 'we know not what imaginarie success of plenty and prosperitie'.

The English, then, had a vivid – if not entirely accurate – image of the New World to fuel their dreams of a different and better life. And so they went, hundreds upon hundreds, on ships with heroic names like the *Achilles* or the *Alexander* or the *Invincible*. These emigrants were unrepresentative of the population of the British Isles in that they were overwhelmingly young, male and unmarried. While history has highlighted the stories of ambitious adventurers and the privileged second and third sons who made their reputations in the New World, the vast majority were, in fact, ordinary people. As the passenger manifests of the day attest, it is men of modest means who are listed page after page: rope-makers and butchers, masons and farmers. Their numbers were swelled by the streams of involuntary migrants who went to the Americas in chains: indentured servants who were tricked aboard ship by 'spirits' (agents paid by the settlement companies to recruit labourers by any means necessary); political prisoners who were exiled as punishment; vagrants and orphans and criminals who had been deposited there like so much rubbish.

Whether travelling by choice or by compulsion, all of these individuals flooding into the New World were part of a historical epic that had consequences its participants could not begin to foresee. Those who survived would become the hub of the

British Empire and help Britain to become the dominant world power of the day. Along with their European counterparts, they would enrich the European subcontinent and extend the tentacles of its power virtually across the globe, westernizing the great bulk of humanity, imposing its institutions and beliefs, its languages and cultures across the world. Their collective migration would also precipitate the vast redistribution of life across the globe, most notably the millions of Africans who were forcibly transplanted to the Americas to work as slaves on their plantations. And it would transform the world's entire eco-system, destroying numerous species and moving innumerable others, to create a world that would be entirely different from what had been before.

Of George Ashby's life in England, I could find no historical trace, but the name Ashby was initially associated with the county of Leicestershire and has now spread throughout the Midlands. It is a combination of the Anglo-Saxon word '*aesc*' (ash tree) and the Danish word '*bye*' (town) and has numerous spellings: Ashby, Ashbee, Ashbey, Ashbye. In an English context, the name goes back to the thirteenth century, when a Frenchman, Richard de Ashby, arrived from Normandy with William the Conqueror and settled in Leicestershire. The ancient castle of Ashby is mentioned in the Domesday Book, and was held by the Countess Judith, a niece of William's. Nearby Quenby Hall, for many successive centuries the county seat of the Ashbys, is a Jacobean jewel set in 1,400 acres of rolling woods and hills. It was built in 1627 by another George Ashby, and its claim to fame is that it is the place where Stilton cheese was first made.

We cannot know exactly what motivated George Ashby's departure, but if each migrant's motives were singular – a complex web of religious, economic, political and personal incentives – the preparations for relocation usually followed a predictable pattern. It was a process that could take several months as the would-be wayfarer bounced backwards and forwards between shipping agents, grocers, hardware suppliers, lawyers and factors. The first act for many was to make a will in recognition of the hazards posed by the voyage. Another task was to liquidate their English estates. The well-to-do, who could afford to maintain property at home, rented it out or placed it in the care of relatives or agents. The less wealthy sold their homes, alongside virtually everything else, in order to fund the trip. But many were young men who didn't own homes, or much of anything else, and it is a testament to their determination that they managed to make their passage to the New World. The only thing they held on to were the tools of their trades, since 'plantation skills' were much prized in the Americas, and they counted on exploiting them to supplement their living. With virtually all their material possessions gone, reduced to a sum of ready money, the travellers entered a curiously vulnerable state – one that would be familiar to any migrant today. Everything that anchored them to their previous existence had gone and now they were in limbo, nowhere people, exiled from their old life but as yet unable to begin their new one.

Beyond their means of livelihood, migrants received variable levels of guidance about how to prepare for their new lives. One contemporary neatly summed up their new role:

> The West Indian Colonist of the Seventeenth Century was at all times a fighting farmer . . . It is no figure of speech to say that he went to his daily toil with his sword at his side and with pistols at his belt. At any time he might be called to throw down the hoe and defend himself against the Caribees, the Buccaneers, the Spaniards, the French, the Dutch and the vindictive treachery of his Negro slaves.

Because the Caribbean was the most popular American destination in the early decades of the seventeenth century, there were fewer pamphlets 'selling' life in the region, so the migrants planning to move there tended to be far less well informed than those destined for the American mainland. New England, in particular, offered its prospective residents more detailed guidance:

> Before you come be careful to be strongly instructed on what things are fittest to bring with you for your more comfortable passage at sea, also for your husbanding occasions when you come to the land. For when you are once parted with England you shall meet neither with . . . butchers nor grocers nor apothecaries shops or markets or fairs to help [provide] what things you need, in the midst of the great ocean, nor when you come to land . . . Therefore be sure to furnish yourself with things fitting to be had before you come.

Even for those without such sensible admonishments, certain purchases were unavoidable for any migrant. One of the most expensive of these was the ticket, which averaged the astronomical sum of five pounds (almost two years' wages for the average labourer) for berth and victuals. Many travellers, aware of the unreliable quality of ship food, carried their own provisions: oil, peas, oatmeal, vinegar, spices, butter, bread, beef, cheese, codfish, beer, wine and mustard seed. They also took bedding, kitchen equipment, clothing and tools such as hatchets, axes and hammers. Men were also advised to bring a musket, sword or bandolier, and a purse that they could affix directly to the body to keep their money safe. Once the cost of these goods was added up, the exorbitant rates for storing them on board had to be factored in: this alone could double the price of passage.

There were other expenses to deplete the migrant's nest egg, beginning with the journey from home to the dockside. Then there were the costs precipitated by the almost inevitable delays that occurred with seventeenth-century sea travel, such as contrary winds that confined their ship to the harbour long after they should have been at sea. In these cases, every shilling spent on lodging or food was that much less to spend in the New World. By the time the travellers boarded ship they were often frazzled, tired and substantially poorer than they had hoped to be.

And so, finally, the enormous ship carrying George Ashby and his fellows manoeuvred itself, inch by steady inch, away from the wharf; and the cacophony of departure gave way to a new sound – the rhythmic slapping of water against the sides of the ship. Some of the passengers drifted away from the rails. Others stayed on deck, their eyes glued to the horizon as the English coastline faded from view. This sometimes occurred a few hours after the ship left the dock, but it could take up to a couple of days, depending on the caprices of the wind. Then, as one traveller remarked, 'having tasted much of God's mercy in England and lamenting the loss of our native country when we took our last view of it, one and all betook them to the protection of the Lord on the wide ocean.' When all that they had known was out of sight and there was nothing to measure themselves against but the endless expanse of water, they realized that they were no longer just passengers but migrants, cut adrift from the past, and set forth into an unknown future.

2

The real voyage of discovery consists not of seeking new landscapes but in having new eyes.

Marcel Proust

The route that George Ashby's ship would almost certainly have taken to the Caribbean was the one that Columbus had pioneered a century and a half before: working south past Portugal, Madeira and the Canaries, picking up the trade winds and heading west across the Atlantic. Despite the proximity to England at the start of the voyage, it was still an anxious time, since the Channel was menaced by men-of-war from hostile nations. The captain's first task therefore was usually the appointment of men to watches, then assessing the number of men who were fit to fight and assigning them their place on deck in the event of a struggle.

In the first days of the passage, George Ashby had a lot to get used to. Most migrants were astonished and intimidated by the scale of the ship on which they were now confined. It was an epic sight: huge masts towered high overhead against the sky, yards and yards of undulating sails and shrouds whipped into the wind, the shifting deck was be-snaked with tangles of ropes used to train and check the sails. Passengers had to creep over these lines warily as they rose and sank and jerked across the wood. Indeed, the entire network of cloth, mast and rope that made up the sailing apparatus was a hazard: a giant spider's web in which the passenger was in perpetual danger of being ensnared.

The accommodation too was daunting. It was divided roughly into three categories. The best cabins were reserved for the 'gentlemen' (there were few or no ladies) who could 'finish' them as they pleased: with their own bedding, linen, wax lights, even their own beds. The worst were assigned to the servants for whom the cost of the passage was exchanged for their commitment to labour on arrival. These people endured terrible conditions. As the transportee John Coad recounted, they were taken aboard ship and immediately confined below deck 'in a very small room where we could not lay ourselves down without lying upon one another'. The crew gave them no water, provided no heat, and placed only one receptacle in the middle of the room for the use of them all. They were only allowed on deck after the halfway mark of the journey was passed. The captain, eager to save money, kept them on short rations during the entire trip. Inevitably disease broke out: smallpox, calentures, plagues and ailments accompanied by 'Frightful Blotches'. Others, according to Coad, 'were devoured with lice till they were almost at death's door'. One-fifth of these pitiable souls died on the crossing.

Situated between the hold and the top deck were the berths for what today we would call steerage passengers. They were not as abject as those allocated to the servants but they were still wretched. The first thing to assail those who descended ''tween decks' would have been the smell: a horrible commingling of old food, sweaty bodies and salt. Then there was the curious quality of light: because of its position on the ship, life here was carried on in a perpetual twilight. The only source of direct light and fresh air was a hatch that was opened and closed at the whim of the sailors.

In this dank, airless space, as many as one hundred passengers

– mainly young men like George – lived cheek by jowl. They tried to claim their own bit of territory by looping blankets over ropes or piling trunks and boxes atop one another to create makeshift cabins. They arranged their meagre possessions – casks of food, bedding, cooking pans and chamber pots – in as homely a manner as they could. Since steerage passengers were only allowed on deck at the captain's discretion, these men spent most of their time here, preparing food to supplement the ship's limited rations, talking to their fellow passengers, trying to sleep, counting down the hours until arrival. It was no wonder that Samuel Johnson famously remarked that 'Being on a ship is being in jail, with the chance of being drowned.'

It took some time to become accustomed to being at sea. Richard Ligon wrote about the perils of the ocean, its 'operation and the several faces that watery Element puts on, and the changes and chances that happen there, from Smooth to Rough, from Rough to Raging Seas, and High going Billows (which are killing to some Constitutions)'. In the early days of Ligon's journey the ship suffered from 'scant' and 'slack' winds, 'the weather being very calm and almost no wind at all'. But later on there were storms so severe that he and his shipmates feared for their safety. In contrast, Henry Colt found that in the first few days of his trip the ship was carried along by 'a prosperous gale' only to have the winds diminish to so 'niggardly' a degree that 'the breath the ayre gives us, is noe other butt like the languishinge motions of a dyinge man'. For both men, the unpredictability of the weather only added to the *longueurs* of the journey. The voyage could be completed in six weeks but often stretched to months. Tales of terribly protracted Atlantic crossings reached the status of legend: the *Virginia Merchant*, for example, took twenty-two tempest-tossed weeks to arrive at its destination in Virginia in 1649. When its food supplies were exhausted the passengers had started eating rats, and when those ran out they turned to cannibalism. 'The living fed upon the dead,' declared one lurid narrative.

There were other trials. Seasickness affected almost everyone at the beginning of the journey, until they found their sea legs. George Ashby was unlikely to have escaped its symptoms: dry mouth, headache, vomiting and dizziness. There were no effective remedies against it, despite the myriad quack potions sold by apothecaries. The tossing and turning of the ship also caused injuries: bruises and broken bones were frequent as unwitting passengers were thrown against the hull of the ship. Deaths on board were common. There were plenty of accidents: one unfortunate passenger bound for New England, attempting to fish for mackerel, managed to get tangled in the ship's rigging and fell overboard to his death. There were frequent outbreaks of smallpox and 'ship fever'. And the longer the journey, the greater the the risk of scurvy. In the seventeenth century its cause was unknown, and it was often ascribed to bad air, thickening of the blood or melancholy. The ships carrying servants to the Chesapeake and the West Indian colonies provided the poorest accommodation, so they often had the worst health problems. One passenger on such a voyage wrote: 'Our ship was so pestered with people and foodes that were so full of infection that after a while, we saw little but throwing folks over board.' Many also went hungry as unscrupulous suppliers maximized their profits by delivering second-rate goods to ships: musty oatmeal, rotten cheese and rancid butter, the state of which would only be discovered after departure.

But perhaps the most unexpected annoyance was the noise: the tramping sounds of the sailors as they thudded across the decks, as well as their constant shouting, in particular that of the captain, whose ability to be heard for miles around seemed the primary requirement of the job. There was the creaking of the wood, the whining and sawing of the ropes and the whipping and flapping of the sails. And then there were the

animals: the average seventeenth-century vessel was a cacopho-
nous floating menagerie of dogs, pigs, horses and poultry.

Worse than these daily nuisances was the very real danger of
pirates. Even while still in the English Channel, 'Dunkirkers'
often boarded ships. In one notorious case in 1637, the English
ship *Elizabeth* was surprised by warships from the Spanish
West India fleet while sailing the southern route to America.
All 120 of her passengers were captured and transported to
Spain, where they were still languishing in prison more than
twenty years later. The waters around the Caribbean were
also dangerous. The West Indies was 'beyond the line' – that
is, outside the jurisdiction of existing treaties – and so was
effectively lawless. Therefore pirates, largely untroubled by
the authorities, combed through the azure waters for bounty,
while marauding fleets of all colours battled one another for
gold and territory.

Describing a skirmish which 'had well nigh putt an end to
this my Journall & to my whole voyage', Henry Colt illustrated
the constant peril of the tropical waters. While en route from
Barbados to Dominica in 1631, the crew of his ship, the
Alexander, noticed they were being pursued by two vessels.
Recognizing that the ships were part of a larger Spanish fleet
which had hidden itself away on the coast of Dominica, they
took flight. (England was then officially at peace with Spain,
but the Spaniards regarded the West Indies as their private
preserve and therefore would attempt to punish any incursion
into their territory.) Laden down by the timber it had taken
on board in Barbados, the *Alexander* was handicapped and a
fight became inevitable. Fortified by 'Hott Water' (alcohol),
the *Alexander*'s crew confronted their pursuers and musket shots
were exchanged. It was only the realization that the *Alexander*
had a large contingent of fighting men on deck that saved it
from being boarded and sacked. Colt, an ex-soldier, relished the
prospect of a fight, concluding that 'Death is better to happen

once than to fear itt always; even those that fear it most must
still come unto it.'

Despite the difficulties and worries, most passengers attempted
to maintain some kind of familiar daily routine. Daylight and
darkness regulated their behaviour at sea as much as on land; so
did the rituals of preparing and partaking of meals. These took
a bit more planning and time because of the limited food stocks
and lack of equipment and space. They fished to supplement
their meagre rations and occasionally butchered the livestock
they had brought on board. And there were entertainments.
The passengers would get together to sing, play backgammon
or cards and gamble in the moonlight.

Life on board was strictly stratified, replicating the class
divisions of life on land. (These hierarchies operated alongside
the social world of the sailors, who formed a fraternity of their
own, with a different language and code of conduct, largely
impenetrable to the other passengers.) Henry Colt, for example,
marked out his privileged position by insisting on wearing the
uniform of an English gentleman at all times: 'a long sleeved
shirt reaching to the knees, a suit of jerkin and hose (that is,
a sleeveless jacket and puffed knee breeches), a handkerchief
around the neck, a feathered hat, beads, boot hose, stockings
and shoes'. He also wore a stomacher – the seventeenth-century
equivalent of a sweater – to guard against the wind. The only
concession he made to the rigours of the sea journey was to
discard his quilted doublet, because they rotted in the humidity.

As the journey progressed, George would have become
familiar with his fellow passengers, forging the kind of friendships
that were only possible on a passage as long and significant as
this one. Those berthed between decks had a certain amount in
common, since they were largely of the same estate: small and
middling men. But beneath the similarities in their backgrounds
were any number of individual stories and colourful personalities.

Some travellers were bold and ambitious, others merely curious; some were in flight from debtors or angry relatives, others were broken-hearted or bereaved. These men were brought together by a common goal: all dreamt of improving their fortunes. At the very least they desired 'a competency' – a popular seventeenth-century term that indicated 'a sufficiency, although not an abundance, of worldly goods'. But the word also signified 'independence, the possession of property sufficient to free oneself from reliance on others'. Since only one in seven English heads of households owned freehold land and almost all of them owed at least token payments to a manorial lord, for most men the prospect of a 'competency' – and the security and respectability it represented – was alluring.

And the journey did have its consolations: many travellers were enthralled with the sea itself, 'sometimes rough with mighty mountains and deep valleys, sometimes smooth like a level meadow'. As the days passed and the ship moved nearer to the Tropic of Cancer, a perceptible change in climate occurred and a balmy quality filled the air. The passengers could not help but be bewitched by the changing hues of the ocean: the dark petrol bleeding into beautiful bright blue and creamy foam. As they entered Caribbean waters, they were joined by wondrous creatures: leaping shoals of flying fish, schools of dolphins swimming alongside the ship, their silvery skins shimmering like gossamer in the sunlight. Colt marvelled that his ship was surrounded by porpoises and fish called grampuses, which were blackish-coloured and much bigger than 'our greatest bullocks of England, and they spout out water like the whale'.

Richard Ligon was fascinated by the birds: great gulls that 'attend the rising of the fishes and if they be within distance, seldom fail to make them their own', and by the turtles that 'lye and sleep upon the waves, for a longtime together'. As time passed, however, he recognized that the sea's pleasures were often 'mixt with Cruelties': 'I have seen 20 Porpisces very large of that kind, Cross the Prow of our Ship one behind another in so steady and constant a course, in chase of some other fishes; as I have seen a kennel of large Hounds, In Windsor Forrest in the chase of a Stag; one following directly in a track.'

Even the skies were different from anything they had seen before. Ligon wrote of the pleasures of viewing 'the heavens and the beauty of them, which were objects of so great glory, that the Inhabitants of the world from 40 degrees to either pole can never be witness of'. The sunsets delighted him, the 'sun then there being far brighter than with us here in England, caused such glorious colours to rest upon those clouds, as 'tis not possible to be believed by them that hath not seen it, nor can imagination frame so great a beauty'. He noted that though the stars seemed much more brilliant in the tropics, they also seemed disordered: a particular star that appeared large and bright in England was hardly visible in this hemisphere. There were also celestial phenomena that he had never encountered before: for example, when a perfect confluence of moon shining onto clouds produced a rainbow in the night sky.

The length of the voyage also meant that George Ashby and his fellow travellers would have had the time to acclimatize to the profoundly alien conditions of the tropics: the sun so dazzling they couldn't look at it directly and so hot that it burnt their pale skins. 'One might almost believe,' wrote one startled traveller, 'that the puny sun that peeps out upon Old England, is not the same refulgent orb that glows within the Tropics.'

But these wonders aside, there came a point in every journey when the travellers' spirits began to sag. As the days turned into weeks and the weeks into months, boredom became the defining characteristic of the passage, and the two months at sea often seemed as long as two years. Even swashbuckling Henry Colt found himself lamenting, 'Surely the Journey is as great and further by a 1000 miles than ever I supposed it to be.' The challenge of a journey like this transcended mere discomfort and became almost existential. Whatever order and routine were observed on board ship, they were mocked by the untameable vastness of the surrounding sea. As Ligon wrote gloomily, 'There is no place so void and empty.' Confined for weeks within a small space, afloat on the great wilderness of the ocean, every traveller became aware of his frailty and insignificance.

Eventually, though, they neared the island. The ship's master proceeded warily. Barbados is the easternmost island in the Caribbean and lies somewhat apart from its neighbours, which made its longitude difficult to calculate. Sir Henry Colt described the challenge of locating the island as being like finding 'sixpence throwne downe upon New Market heath'. This problem had dogged sailors throughout the century, and many ships had inadvertently overshot the island. But it was a mistake that was strenuously avoided because once a ship found itself leeward of any Caribbean island it was extremely hard to tack back against the wind and recover position.

It was said that landfall was always made at night, leaving passengers awaiting daylight like 'the woman with childe for her good hour'. And so the ship's inmates' first glimpse of their destination was often a shadowy one, blurred outlines of the land and buildings only barely illuminated by flickers of candlelight, the water lit by the rays from the moon and stars.

That George Ashby should choose to settle in Barbados was in many ways predictable. If the Caribbean was considered more desirable than the American mainland for most seventeenth-century English migrants, then Barbados was the most popular choice among the islands. One of the earliest colonizing expeditions in the area noted that Barbados resembled England, was 'more healthful than any of hir neighbours' and therefore 'better agreeing with the temper of the English Nacon'.

Barbados is geographically and geologically different from its neighbours because it is not part of the long volcanic mountain range in which the Caribbees are rooted. Instead it is a coral island which has fortuitously worked its way out of the sea. Shaped like a leg of mutton, Barbados feels like two islands rolled into one. The eastern coast, which borders the Atlantic, is wild and steep, dotted with huge, sculptural limestone outcrops, while the Caribbean coast is as tame and smooth as a turquoise rug. In 1690, Governor James Kendall described it as 'the beauty-fullst spot of ground I ever saw'.

Barbados has a complex history. Columbus did not actually land on the island during any of his four visits to the Caribbean, but Spanish and Portuguese conquistadors reported a number of visits there during the sixteenth century. It was one of the first islands settled by the English, claimed in 1625 when Captain John Powell landed there on his way back to England from Brazil. The party erected a wooden cross at the site of what would become St James Town, later known as Holetown, and inscribed on a nearby tree: 'James King of England and this island'. After inspecting the south and west coasts, the party realized what a promising prospect for 'planting' the island offered. It was lush, with rich open land, and entirely uninhabited: the Amerindian population that had once lived there had long since deserted the island. The settlers of Barbados, therefore, would avoid the years of tumultuous and bloody battles that their brethren on the American mainland, and nearby islands such as Martinique, endured in order to settle their colonies.

Two years after Powell's reconnaissance mission, a colonizing expedition led by his brother Henry and funded by two London merchants – Peter and William Courteen – set out for the island. Their ship set sail with eighty settlers and managed to capture eight African slaves en route, stolen from another ship. Their numbers were supplemented by thirty-two Indians from Maine who had been 'hired' to teach the settlers how to plant, and were promptly enslaved as soon as they landed. The two groups, Africans and Indians, were the first slaves to land on an English settlement. These original settlers had a simple plan for life in Barbados: they were going to make a living cultivating tobacco and cotton and they would sustain themselves with the unfamiliar crops they had brought with them – cassava, yams, Indian corn, potatoes, plantains, bananas, oranges, lemons, limes, pineapples and melons. Over the next decades, more pioneers – including George Ashby – would swell the ranks of this first wave and the island would emerge as the most important in the region.

As George Ashby saw his new home for the first time, he would have had no idea what a tumultuous story he had been catapulted into. As well as being caught up in the more quotidian dramas of the region – hurricanes, rebellions and famine – he would also survive an outbreak of plague and a civil war with his own homeland, which would see Barbados besieged for months by Cromwellian forces. But most significantly, he would be a witness to a seismic shift in world events, when his little island successfully pioneered the production of sugar through the industrial exploitation of enslaved human beings.

But for now, morning dawned and the excited immigrants rushed from their berths, clambered on deck and crowded against the rails, pushing and jostling for a view. The first sight of the island evoked rhapsodies in Ligon: 'The nearer we came, the more beautiful it appeared to our eyes.' Indeed, Barbados approached by sea was a wonderful sight, as the ship cut through the water and the seafarers were first assailed by the fresh, tangy air. The land was lush and green, covered by 'high, large and lofty trees, with their spreading branches and flourishing tops'. As the ship moved on, sailing through the turquoise waters, George Ashby would have been able to see, clustered around the shoreline, several plantations – small and large – carved out of the woods.

When the ship arrived at the entrance to Carlisle Bay, it fired its guns to salute the fort and manoeuvred gingerly to accommodate its tricky entrance. On that morning it would have taken George Ashby some time to appreciate what was around him. Now that the ship was becalmed in the bay, the sun reflected off the sea and the deck would have made him squint. Shading his eyes with his hand, he would have taken in the body of blue glittering water and the curves of land coated with the green forest that embraced the bay.

He must have felt that all the stories and letters home had understated the awe-inspiring freshness of this new world with its vivid brushstrokes of greens, blues and gold. Directly surrounding him were the azure waters of the bay, which despite the youth of the colony, were busy with English and Dutch vessels of various kinds. These small and large craft – sloops, ketches, barques and brigantines – decorated the bay with their rigging, casting fantastic shapes against the iridescent sky. And beyond, he would have seen the wharves, crowded with men rolling and handling hogsheads of merchandise.

Aboard ship, the travellers would have been busy packing up their belongings and queuing to be ferried to the port by watermen, whose job it was to ply backwards and forwards moving goods and passengers between the ship and the shore. Stepping onto the wharf, George would have staggered and swayed as his feet, so long accustomed to the motion of the ship, adjusted to this new stillness. And, from the wharf, he would have been able to take in the town. George may not have realized it, but he was lucky. In contrast with New England, where the Puritans had disembarked to be confronted with nothing but rough country, Bridgetown was bustling with many of the amenities the traveller needed to refresh his weary body and supplement his waning stores.

Founded the year after Barbados was settled in 1627, Bridgetown was then more commonly known as 'The Bridge',

'The Indian Bridge' or 'Indian Bridge Town'. It had emerged as the island's major port because of certain natural advantages: an abundant water supply and a convenient harbour. But the site also had its drawbacks. 'Their main oversight,' according to Richard Ligon, 'was to build their Towne upon so unwholesome a place where there remains a kind of Bog or Morass, which vents out so loathsome a savour, as cannot but breed ill-blood and is (no doubt) the occasion of much sickness to those that live there.' Ligon was correct: the town's position resulted in terrible smells, and outbreaks of fever were a constant problem for its inhabitants.

A fetid, scrambling sort of place, Bridgetown had developed in a higgledy-piggledy manner. It was both a residential and a mercantile district, so houses great and small were interspersed with brothels and taverns. It even had its own cage for containing riotous sailors as well as a ducking stool, situated in the horse pond, to cool the ardour of ladies condemned as common scolds. The town swiftly built up its reputation as the island's economic centre because of its role of provisionary and supplier to the streams of English immigrants who arrived to plant the land. Its importance grew when Governor Henry Hawley established his Courts of Law and built the Session Houses there in the early 1630s. As a result, 'The Bridge' became not just the administrative but the political centre of the island; it emerged as the pivotal port in the entire region, positioned alongside Boston to dominate the commerce of the British West Indies in the Western Atlantic colonies.

The population was incredibly cosmopolitan. It was a stopping-off point for Portuguese and Dutch traders, Virginia merchants and French planters, sailors, employees of the Crown, scholars, pirates, priests and other travellers, who gathered here to carry out their business or indulge their leisure under the sweltering heat of the tropical sun. Some of the town's populace would have been startling to George: he had certainly never seen any Amerindians in the flesh before, and probably no Africans. Both groups had been brought here as slaves, even though the slave trade was not yet a significant part of the Barbadian economy. But still, in these early days of settlement, white faces were in the majority and the planters saw themselves simply as 'Englishman transplanted'.

George Ashby's first task would have been finding somewhere to stay. He would probably have been directed to the taverns on Cheapside like the Rose or Three Tunns or Cook's Arms. These places were the commodity, financial and information exchanges of the period where visitors could not only take up lodging and enjoy a bite to eat but also find out more about the new society they had come to join. Here, George would have been given advice about the best places to obtain any goods he needed such as machetes and axes.

But the most significant purchase was, of course, the land, which required George to make an appointment with the island's 'fire-eating' governor, Captain Henry Hawley. Hawley had been appointed governor of the island in 1630 with the power invested in him by the Earl of Carlisle to establish a council and depose Sir William Tufton, his mild-mannered predecessor, by force if need be. Hawley proceeded to do just that, arresting Tufton for 'mutiny' and putting him to death. Most of the islanders felt that Hawley had been too harsh, concluding that 'Sir William Tufton had Severe Measure'. Hawley's belligerence continued; he fell out with the son of the Earl of Carlisle, who had inherited the colony from his father, and then arbitrarily imposed a poll tax upon the unwilling islanders. It was widely believed that he had men locked up merely because 'they would not submit to his yoke'.

With such a fearsome reputation, George must have felt some trepidation at the thought of meeting him but, if he wanted land, there was no alternative. Hawley, who had received a grant from the first Earl of Carlisle for 1,000 acres, was busy making a fortune by selling on plots in variable sizes to aspiring planters. The encounter between George and Hawley probably took place at the Session House, where Hawley did most of his official business. I can just picture my ancestor being presented to him there, his hat twisting in his hands and his hair limp with sweat and plastered to his skull, while Hawley sat resplendent in his coat and stockings, intermittently scratching his periwig as his scalp itched in the heat. After the customary exchange of pleasantries, a certain amount of haggling inevitably ensued, and Hawley – for a consideration (that little something extra that eased the bureaucratic wheels and made the relevant documents appear more swiftly) – eventually agreed to sell George Ashby a nine-acre plot in the parish of St Philip. My first known ancestor had finally acquired his longed-for property, later to become known as 'Ashby Land'.

3

Be not afeard. The isle is full of noises,
Sounds, and sweet airs, that give delight, and hurt not.
Sometimes a thousand twangling instruments
Will hum about mine ears, and sometimes voices
That if I then had waked after long sleep
Will make me sleep again; and then in dreaming
The clouds methought would open and show riches
Ready to drop upon me, that, when I waked
I cried to dream again.

William Shakespeare,
The Tempest, Act III, scene ii

At some point on the journey to his new plot of land, George Ashby must have cursed the duplicity of this small island. The tangerine sunsets, the cooing doves, which had seduced him as they did all newcomers, had deceived him into believing in the island's benign felicity. But now as he moved inland, the orderly vistas of Bridgetown gave way to a nightmarish jungle.

During a brief stay in 1634, Father Andrew White found the island 'growne over with trees and undershrubs without passage, except where planters have cleared'. There were only a few roads outside the capital and those that did exist were poor: muddy and slippery in rainy weather and full of the stumps of recently felled trees. Early settlers relied on the narrow tracks made by stock such as sheep, donkeys and even camels that had been specially imported to cope with the island's terrain. In many places there were no tracks at all, so for some of the thirteen-mile trip to St Philip, George, his guide and their pack-mule had to fight their way through dense undergrowth, slashing their path with machetes. As they slogged their way up and down gullies, their shirts sticking to their bodies, dazed by humidity and heat and weighed down by supplies, the pair would have fought for every yard of progress.

I wonder how George felt when he finally arrived at his acreage, the blank canvas onto which he was going to paint his new life. Was he elated, as only someone who had never had the chance to own anything substantial would be on becoming a man of property? Or was he overwhelmed and dismayed, as so many early settlers were, when first confronted by the untamed wilderness that was to be their new home? To many it seemed impossible that they could make an impression on the unruliness of this place; a world older than Genesis, labyrinthine, virtually untouched by the hand of man.

The nine acres that George Ashby had purchased are cradled in a gorgeous valley in St Philip, the easternmost parish on the island, where it borders neighbouring St George. (The island only had six parishes until 1645, so the boundaries are different from today.) Three centuries on, the area, which is verdant and green with breathtaking views, still has a preternaturally peaceful feel to it. To the east lies one of the most beautiful beaches on the island, the Crane, with wide expanses of talcum-fine white sand; to the west the vista is dominated by rustling cane fields bordered by huge palms. Just visible in the distance are the Jacobean walls of Drax Hall, the oldest and most famous plantation on the island. Built in the early 1650s, several years after George's arrival, it is a place that came to encapsulate the dreams of the later generations of immigrants: the legacy of a humble man, like them, who built one of the greatest sugar fortunes ever made.

Today George Ashby's land is part of a working sugar plantation called Edgecombe. His plot alternates between a functioning field covered with a sea of sugar cane and a piece of 'resting' land waiting to be replanted later in the year. Perched atop the dark brown soil is a triumvirate of dilapidated but pretty wooden chattel houses, in sherbet shades of green, coral and purple. The land, which abuts a number of famous plantations, is still directly connected to the family. It is known as Peacocks, taken from George Ashby's daughter's married name. Here the loamy earth is good – not the best on the island, but good. George had been lucky.

On the day he arrived, his good fortune was covered in a vast swathe of forest populated with indigenous trees: fustic and redwood, cedar and ironwood. Everywhere he looked was the vivid green of tree canopies, the ornate drapery of moss, the tangle of vines climbing up to the sun and the thick carpet of fallen leaves that covered the ground. Small, unidentifiable creatures scuttled through his woods, each crackling twig sharpening his awareness that he was out of his element, coping with an unaccustomed landscape.

That first night, when the sun had set and the light was fading from the sky, George Ashby would have pitched his tent and made a fire more for light than heat. Beyond the circle of illumination cast by the flames, the darkness was full of strange noises. The music of the Caribbean night – that orchestra of sounds made by cicadas, frogs and rustling leaves – which seemed so charming when accompanied by the bustle of Bridgetown, now seemed menacing in the context of this great, dark, breathing wilderness, and George must have slept fitfully if he managed to sleep at all.

Dawn brought relief, and new challenges. The first task was to find water: not easy on an island with so few rivers. The second task was to create a makeshift shelter, probably some palm leaves propped up on saplings. Then on to the logistical problem of how to start clearing this promised land. Every square inch of the nine acres was covered in plants and thick undergrowth. In an age before diggers, cranes and power saws, it took enormous effort for a man to level one of these huge trees. And once they had been felled, they had to be hacked into pieces and carried away. It was truly formidable work. Richard Ligon learned from some of the early settlers that 'the woods were so thick, and most of the Trees so large and massive, as they were not to be fallen by the few available colonists'. When they did fell them, 'the branches were so thick' only the 'strong and active men' could 'lop and remove them off the ground'. Many of the big planters resorted to clearing their land as the Indians did, by slashing and burning. Henry Colt was shocked to see charred tree trunks, weeds and brush and desolate stumps six feet high standing or lying in the fields.

Two decades after the first settlement, Ligon noted that many farmers still planted potatoes and corn 'between the boughs, the Trees lying along on the ground; so far short was the ground of being cleared'. So the first few weeks of George Ashby's time were devoted to digging up roots, grubbing out bushes, and hacking at saplings. Like most of the settlers, he was not a farmer by trade, so half an hour of bending and slashing with the machete or crouching with the hoe, in the unfamiliar heat, would have made his back ache and his face stream with sweat. Still he persevered, working feverishly in the hope of clearing enough land to plant a crop and start a small vegetable patch.

There was so much to adjust to in this New World. As an Englishman, George Ashby was used to a palette permanently tinged with grey; here, the world was suffused with light and brightness, bursting into vibrant greens, yellows, blues, reds and pinks, like a painting by Gauguin or the unruly splashes of a Jackson Pollock. The night was different here: the constellations disordered, the stars brighter and more prolific above him.

The smell of the tropics was also novel: the intense perfume of flowers and spices mingled with the salty sea air and the warm fermenting smell of the earth.

For a man accustomed to winter's shortening days – the turning of the leaves, the occasional flurry of white snow, cold nights spent huddled around heat-giving fires – this place would have been a revelation. Here the days were divided equally all year round and the change of seasons was punctuated by a shorter series of notes, hot and wet, cool and dry: the relative coolness of November till April, the torrid heat of summer from May to September, which overlapped with a wet season that began in July and culminated in the fearsome hurricane season of September and October.

Rain too had a new character: instead of the persistent cold drizzle of England, in Barbados it fell unheralded from the sky, often so copiously and forcefully that it etched deep grooves into the ground and stung the skin of those who were caught in it. 'It was,' wrote one visitor, 'as if the whole Atlantic ocean was pouring down through a sieve.' Then the island's modest rivers swelled to impassable torrents, roaring and foaming down the hills and steeps of the gullies with irresistible fury, hurrying rocks and trees before them. When the moisture and heat combined, they produced a humidity so fierce that, as one traveller noted, it rusted all things metal: knives, buckles and swords.

Most new arrivals were amazed by the tropical vegetation, which seemed to thrive in a state of glorious frenzy. They were instantly impressed by its confident abundance, a ceaseless explosion of energetic, throbbing plant life, in which all the component parts grew together, creating a solid, almost impenetrable knot of vegetation.

There was beauty too. Richard Ligon was beguiled by the plants and noted one dubbed 'the flower of the moon', a purple blossom with black seeds 'that opens when all else close, when the Sun goes down', and the calabash, with its incomparably bright green leaves and circular fruit that the settlers made into bowls and plates. Most impressive of all was the Royal Palm. This elegant plant, which sometimes grew to over 200 feet tall, with a long, elegant trunk topped by wide green fronds and bunches of yellow and purple berries 'about the bigness of French grapes', was, he noted, 'as graceful as a woman'. There was also a new world of birds to enjoy: ground doves, Antillean bullfinches and – 'the last and strangest of them all' – the tiny, shimmering hummingbird, no bigger than a man's thumb.

Fugitives from temperate climes also found themselves having to adjust to an entirely different diet. Instead of the 'beef, bread and beer' that made up the traditional English menu, they had to develop a taste for new dishes, like turtle stew. The wild hogs that had so prodigiously populated the island had been nearly hunted out of existence, and there was little meat available. Fish was popular, but they had difficulty keeping it fresh. Staples were sweet potatoes, the 'Staffe and Support' of the settlers, which were boiled, fried or used to make a drink called 'mobby'; and cassava, another root vegetable, which was used to make beer and bread. The settlers enjoyed plantain, the starchy cousin of the banana, and ate it baked, fried or stewed. They quickly added a host of local fruits to their menu: custard apples, melons, papaya and guavas. The most popular was the pineapple, which Sir Henry Colt described as tasting like a 'great white ripe strawberrye'. It was, concluded another, 'the Prince of all fruits!'

George Ashby's land swarmed with creatures he had never seen before: lizards, snakes, scorpions and insects of vibrant colour and unexpected size. At first every rustle or sudden movement must have startled, even frightened him. Most were harmless; but not all. Because so many islanders went barefoot, every-one agreed on the mischief caused by chiggers. According to

Ligon, these minuscule insects easily slipped unnoticed into the skin or under the nails, or both, and if this happened the victim experienced 'a smarting pain' and was sometimes rendered lame.

At night the islanders were often tormented by gnats and mosquitoes. Just as the traveller starts to fall asleep their demonic whine begins, and on many nights George Ashby must have lain furious and miserable as they buzzed around him. Cockroaches posed another threat to slumber. If they 'find you sleeping', noted one visitor, they will 'bite your skin, till they fetch blood'. Yellow land crabs were so prolific that in some spots they covered the highways. Their pincers were strong enough to bite right through shoes. The early settler Thomas Verney told a story, no doubt exaggerated, about drunken men collapsing on the beaches and in their stupor being eaten by these crustaceans.

But the most difficult thing to cope with was the climate. While Barbados was not as hot as other Caribbean islands, it was still described as 'a scorching island', where the 'sun is so great, that it will melt a ship's pitch and shrink her planks'. The heat worked on new arrivals gradually but inexorably, slowing them down, forcing them to become more languid and unhurried, or else perish.

It was an assault of newness. And so, even if George Ashby was the sort of man who longed for the strange and unfamiliar, this transition to a life in the tropics must have been profoundly challenging. His was the perennial plight of the migrant. He expected things to be different but had no idea how cope with this world which was so unfamiliar and hard to comprehend. Then there was the discrepancy between the dream and the reality; for none of this was quite what he thought it would be. His sense of disorientation was compounded by the loss of everything that had been left behind: loved ones, favourite foods, habitual pastimes. This overwhelming sense of homesickness would grow day by day as he realized how far he was from all that he knew and how difficult it would be to return there. As George Ashby passed his days drenched with sweat, his hair plastered to his scalp, tormented by ceaseless thirst and feelings of despondency, he could not help but feel like a stranger in this world, an intruder.

Adapting to tropical conditions was not George Ashby's only challenge; he also had a new profession to master. He dreamt of becoming a planter, and since most of those who came to Barbados were expecting to cultivate tobacco, he had to learn how to handle this new crop. Tobacco was introduced to England by dashing New World adventurers like Walter Raleigh in the late 1500s; by the end of that century one contemporary noted that 'tobacco shops are now as ordinary as taverns and tippling houses'. Paul Hentzner, a German visitor to England in 1597, declared while attending a bear baiting that at 'all these spectacles, and everywhere else the English are constantly smoking the Nicotian weed'. Considered simultaneously to be an exotic extravagance, a medication (particularly useful in treating the pox) and a stimulant, smoking became known as 'dry drinking' and its fearless practitioners as 'tobacconists'. Though many found smoking offensive, only the far-sighted philosopher Francis Bacon seemed to anticipate the issues of addiction that would preoccupy our modern age: 'In our time the use of tobacco is growing greatly and conquers men with a certain secret pleasure, so that those who have once become accustomed thereto can later hardly be restrained therefrom.'

Planters in Virginia made vast profits from supplying this new drug in the 1620s and 1630s, and their success was inspirational for neophyte planters in Barbados. Tobacco was a perfect crop for 'men of modest means': it required very little initial investment – just the cost of the plants, a few hoes and some Indian digging sticks to make holes in the ground. Its plants came to maturity quickly, offering a crop to sell within the first year. And there were no economies of scale associated with production, so even those with little acreage could compete with larger planters.

This early commercial success sowed the seeds of its own destruction, however. The tobacco market proved so attractive that there was soon a glut of providers. As other colonies – including Virginia, Bermuda and St Christopher – joined the party, prices began to plummet. Barbados struggled to hold its own, particularly since the quality of its tobacco was often inferior: John Winthrop, who was trying to sell his son's tobacco crop in London, described it as 'very ill-conditioned, foul and full of stalks and evil-coloured'. This was partly due to the planters' lack of experience, since they did not appreciate the meticulous daily care demanded by the crop. It was also because tobacco has a devastating impact on soil quality, which could only be mitigated by regular rotation. Barbados, a small island, lacked the vast tracts of land available to planters in places like Virginia, and so could not develop a proper land rotation system. By the early 1640s, the richest Barbados planters were already beginning to look for a new crop with which to make their fortune, while small planters, such as George Ashby, struggled to eke a living out of their unbiddable portions of land.

The daily life of small planters like George Ashby was a study in monotony and discomfort. Rising with the sun, he would most likely have begun the day with nothing more than a cup of sweetened water, and would have gone to the fields in the clothes in which he had slept – a linen shirt and pantaloons – and a wide-brimmed hat. There he would labour, probably barefoot, till around midday, when there would be a break for a starchy meal: loblolly, a cornmeal paste, or some sweet potatoes, eaten out of calabash gourds. He would return to the fields till sundown, when he would endure another dull and stodgy meal prepared in an iron pot over an open fire – he would be lucky if he tasted meat twice a week. The day would end as it had begun, alone, with only the flicker of the fire for company. One contemporary, defending these men from the charge that tobacco planting was easy money, confirmed this desolate picture: 'Anyone who has seen them bent double in the tobacco fields, expos'd the greatest part of the day to the scorching heat of the Sun, and spending one half of the night reducing it to that posture wherein it is transported to Europe,' could not help but change their minds about 'the sweating and labours of so many miserable creatures'.

George Ashby may have long cherished the dream of being a landowner and an independent planter, but this first year must have been a cruel and demoralizing one. It was also a lonely existence. The only thing that most planters could see of their neighbours was the sight of their cook-smoke rising. George Ashby's new parish of St Philip, though eventually one of the more populous on the island, was then still sparsely settled. The new arrivals, who in England may have lived in overcrowded cities or in the community of a rural village, endured profoundly isolated lives. Until George's tobacco crop was harvested, his only income was from the smithing work he did in his spare time. What he couldn't afford to buy would have to be foraged, bartered or done without. As an inexperienced planter he had to learn each new task like a child: the planting, weeding, pruning, harvesting, drying and packing were tough, repetitive tasks. All the while the heat beat on relentlessly, day after day after day, occasionally sluiced through by torrential rain. At night, besieged by biting insects, he would find scant comfort in a rough rope hammock. Many newcomers, adventurers by temperament, could not develop the patience that is the lifeblood of farming, and some simply abandoned their fields and sought their fortune in more adrenalin-fuelled occupations like soldiering and piracy.

Those who did stick it out soon gained a reputation for being scrawny and ill-looking. When a shipload of Frenchmen arrived at the colony of Cayenne in 1664, to take over from those already there, the ghastly countenances of the Dutch settlers provoked some to return to their ships and refuse to land. (Dr Hans Sloane remarked that 'a yellowish sickly look was the badge of the rank and file of the inhabitants of the Lesser Antilles'.) The lack of food and the relentless physical labour of planting had made the colonists vulnerable to the host of new diseases that beset them in the tropics: malaria, yellow fever, dysentery, yaws and hookworm. The absence of medical care in the region, or any real understanding of how these new diseases were transmitted or could be treated, guaranteed that the settlers succumbed in droves. George Ashby would not have been human if he did not sometimes dream of what he had left behind in England. In order to make a new life rise out of the Caribbean wilderness, he was being forced to push himself to the limits of endurance, beyond the boundaries of anything he had experienced before.

The work of transforming each patch of anarchy into viable farmland did not fall to planters alone: they needed labourers. Although the region would later become synonymous with black slaves, at this point they made up only a small minority of the workforce. Instead the early Barbadian settlers mostly used white indentured servants, known as *engagés* in the French territories. George Ashby was typical of the island's other planters in that he relied on white labour. He had one servant, and would probably have bought this poor man (only 1 per cent of the servants were female) right off the wharf. The process went something like this: as soon as a ship carrying servants arrived at the port, eager planters would collect at the dockside. They watched as the men, mostly aged between fifteen and twenty-four, were shepherded down the plank onto the wharf. Confined below decks for most of the voyage, many had suffered terribly on the journey and emerged bruised, depleted and unnerved. The pale, scabby servants were lined up in ragged rows. The healthiest men – and those with useful trades, like masons, smiths and shoemakers – were creamed off by the rich planters, while smaller men like George scrabbled to get the best of the rest. Then for the sum of around six to ten pounds, the befuddled servants signed or put their mark on a document that sold their time – anywhere from four to seven years.

Agricultural workers were the most important element in a successful plantation. As early as 1638 one planter explained that 'a plantation in this place is worth nothing unless there be a good store of hands upon it'. At least 2,000 servants arrived on the island every year until 1666, but even this was not enough: the planters lobbied the authorities incessantly for more workers. Over time the English planters established a system that loosely reflected the social order back home, the key difference being that indentured servants were compensated in advance, rather than receiving wages. The indenture system was first trialled in 1620, by a Virginia planter who began purchasing the labour of servants for a specified period in return for paying their passage to the colony. The system had spread rapidly across the Americas, only dying out when these same colonies embraced African slavery.

Of the servants who found themselves on Barbados, some were volunteers, some were felon or prisoners of war; some were English, others Scottish or Irish. (Indeed, so many people were dispatched to the island that the term 'to be Barbadosed' swiftly gained popular currency.) The Irish were particularly plentiful because of the frequent food shortages, high unemployment and English military disruption in their homeland. In the 1650s their numbers were swollen further by a huge number of Irish prisoners of war; indeed, nearly 7,000 Irishmen were transported to the island during the Cromwellian period. But in the context of the traditional hostilities between the English and Irish, the large numbers of indentured servants who were arriving from Ireland provoked particular alarm among the planters. According to one historian they were regarded as 'a principal internal enemy, at times more dangerous and feared than Africans'. As early as 1644 English planters sought to create legislation to limit their numbers. It was unsuccessful and tensions continued to grow. Irish servants who misbehaved were treated horribly by the authorities; in 1656 Cornelius Bryan was sentenced to '21 lashes on the bare back' for remarking, while refusing a tray of meat, that 'if there was so much English blood in the tray as there was meat, he would eat it all'. After he had recovered from his punishment, Bryan was arrested and deported for his anti-English remarks.

A new plan by the legislature to control the Irish made it an offence to sell them firearms and decreed that any Irish servant found travelling without a pass could be conveyed by any English person to the nearest constable, who was empowered to whip him and return him to his plantation. Over the years, the government adopted wave after wave of measures to curb recalcitrant Irish servants who had caused 'great damage to their masters' by their 'unruliness, obstinacy and refractoriness'. None of these measures was effective, and the Barbadian authorities' fear of 'that profligate race' would later prove justified after a number of Irish rebellions occurred, sometimes in partnership with African slaves.

It wasn't only the Irish who inspired distrust, however. Servants of all nationalities caused alarm. Those who remained on the island after the completion of their indentureship were considered an especial threat to public order. Unable to afford land, many turned to crime, drink and disruptive behaviour. But the servants who did leave the island, whether in search of pastures new, on military expeditions or even to join the pirate 'brotherhood', were also a worry. Later, when the black slave population had increased, the haemorrhaging of white servants threatened to create an imbalance of black men over white, sparking paranoia in the planters, who feared the slaves would become so numerous they could not be controlled.

Wherever they came from, it is fair to say that indentured servants had no idea of the conditions under which they would live and work, or how vulnerable and powerless they would be. Although they had signed a contractual document – the indenture – that set out mutual obligations, the reality of bound service was a highly unequal power relationship. Servants found themselves constrained by repressive local legislation that imposed severe punishments for the slightest infractions and provided them with very little redress under the law. If they stole, left their plantations without permission or did anything that impeded their ability to work – such as break a limb – they were penalized. Masters could corporally punish their servants, or trade them without consultation. Richard Ligon noted that it was common for planters to 'sell their servants to one another for the time they have to serve; and in exchange receive any commodities that are in their island'. Servants also found that their masters could extend their length of service if they misbehaved; some had their original term stretched into infinity, when a series of misadventures – often under the influence of rum – led them to wander off or become too drunk to find their way home.

There are few surviving accounts of the lives of indentured servants in Barbados. One of these rare reports was provided by Heinrich von Uchteritz, a German mercenary captured after the Battle of Worcester in 1651. Motivated by 'the urge to try something noble' and seek his fortune, von Uchteritz 'chose war as the most fitting means to achieve this'. He entered employment in the cavalry under the command of Count Ogilvy and was part of the Royalist army who dreamt of recapturing the kingdom taken by 'the brutes and murderers' of Charles I. After the defeat at Worcester, he and his fellows were taken prisoner by Cromwell's personal regiment. From there they went to London, where Cromwell himself sharply questioned them, remarking that 'he had in mind to give us sugar to eat'. They were duly sent to Barbados, where von Uchteritz was sold, for 800 pounds of sugar, to an English planter who had a workforce of 'one hundred Christians, one hundred Negroes and one hundred Indians'.

Von Uchteritz was put to work immediately, with no opportunity to recover from his journey. On the first day he spent his time 'sweeping the plantation yard, on another day I fed the pigs'. Thereafter he had to do 'the kind of work usually performed [by] the slaves'. The only possessions that unskilled indentured servants were provided with was a single change of ill-fitting clothes: linen shirt and drawers, a pair of shoes and a flat round Monmouth cap totally unsuited to labour in the tropics. When these were wet from the rain or soaked in perspiration, the servant had nothing else to wear.

In contrast to the plantation houses, which were made of cedar and 'located in beautiful meadows', the servants lived in small huts dotted around the plantation yard. These, von Uchteritz related, were 'made of inferior wood, looked almost like dog-houses', and 'were covered with the leaves of trees that they call plantain'. Their diet was limited and extremely poor, consisting only of roots: sweet potato and cassava. However, von Uchteritz acknowledged that even he was fortunate compared to the black slaves and Indians who worked alongside him. Their food was worse and they were not provided with anything to wear. 'They go about completely naked except for a cloth tied around their privates.'

Von Uchteritz spent 'sixteen to eighteen weeks of my miserable life in such difficult bondage that it is easy to see with what desire I longed for my beloved fatherland and for my precious freedom'. Believing that he would die in Barbados, he had all but lost hope when an influential relative intervened and had him freed. To his knowledge, he was the only one of his party to survive indentureship.

Historians have debated which indentured servants suffered the most: those bound to small planters like George Ashby, who were desperate to get the best out of their investment and were known to exploit them mercilessly; or those who laboured on larger plantations, where their masters regarded their workers as so many anonymous drones, and frequently inflicted terrible physical abuse. But it is clear that, whichever the type of master, an indentured servant led a terrible life. According to Ligon: 'Truly I have seen such cruelty there done to servants, as I did not think one Christian could do to another.'

Antoine Biet, a French priest who visited the island in 1654, was also disturbed by the treatment of English servants. 'The masters are obliged to support them,' he wrote, 'but God knows how they are maintained. All are very badly treated. When they work, the overseers, who act like those in charge of galley slaves, are always close by with a stick with which they often prod them when they do not work as fast as is desired.' Though the treatment was not dissimilar to that on the French islands, Biet concluded: 'It is an unhappy state of things to treat with such great severity creatures for whom Jesus Christ shed his blood. It is true that one must keep these kinds of people obedient, but it is inhuman to treat them with so much harshness.'

Servants could only hope and pray that they would survive their indenture and that, if they did, their 'freedom fee' would be enough to buy them a small plot of land on the island. For most, this was a vain hope: as Barbados converted to sugar, land prices rose, and the freed servants were actively encouraged to leave the island. A broadsheet written by the Earl of Carlisle explained: 'Each freeman who is unprovided of land and shall therefore desire to go from Barbados shall have a portion of land allotted to him in my islands of Nevis, Antigua, or any other island in my command.' Those who remained in Barbados would be lucky if the fee was sufficient to buy them a horse or set them up in trade. But many servants were too destroyed by their experiences of indentureship to be able to take advantage of even these little amenities after they were set free. Physically broken by the years of relentless labour and nutritional deprivation, and psychologically affected by depression, anxiety and despair, they were permanently damaged men.

As captive victims of their employers, the indentured servants may have suffered particular cruelty, but their treatment was also symptomatic of the wider culture of violence and disorder that characterized Barbados during these early years. In fact, dissent and conflict had permeated the island from the moment it was claimed in 1627. Charles I had issued not one but two patents for the island: one to Sir William Courteen, the head of a powerful syndicate, and another to James Hay, the Earl of Carlisle. So both men sent their own people to colonize the island, and for ten years the contesting claimants battled against each other on Barbados and in the English courts. Though it was Courteen who had financed the first settlement, it was Carlisle who eventually won out, in what would become known as the 'The Great Barbados Robbery', leaving posterity to conclude that the island's initial colonization was itself a crime.

Barbados was also destabilized by the constant tensions in neighbouring islands. The struggles between North American settlers and the Native Americans have been the most mythologized in the New World, but the Caribbean colonists also fought long and brutal battles to subdue indigenous peoples. In nearby Martinique, the early French colonists under the command of Guillaume d'Orange engaged in a long and bitter campaign against the island's Caribs. Jamaica endured a similar and equally bloody conflict. On St Christopher, the first year of that island's settlement was devoted to the genocide of its original inhabitants, the Kalingo. But the native people of the region did not succumb without a fight. Charles de Rochefort wrote of the Caribs before 1658, 'there hardly passes a year but they makes one or two irruptions, in the night time unto some one of the islands, and then, if it be not timely discovered and valiantly opposed they kill all the men they meet, ransack the Houses and burn them and carry off all the women and children with their booty.'

Amidst these contested beginnings and the pervasive atmosphere of fear, the settlers nonetheless tried to establish some sense of order. When Charles I granted the charter to the Earl of Carlisle he gave him power to make laws in Barbados, but only with the consent of the free men who settled the colony. The laws were to be 'agreeable, and not repugnant unto reason; nor against, but as convenient and agreeable as may be to the laws, statutes, customs, and rights, of our kingdom of England'. Carlisle delegated his authority to a governor, who was to act with a council, some of whom were elected from England and the rest provided by those on the island. The settlers agreed to pay Carlisle 'the twentieth part of all profits arising and accruing from the island'; and Barbados adopted the English model of government: a parliament in which the governor corresponded to the Crown, the Council to the House of Lords, and the House of Assembly (instituted in 1639) to the House of Commons.

But despite the colonists' desire to transfer English institutions and traditions as quickly as possible, the early years of the colony were anarchic. New arrivals to Barbados in the 1630s entered a settlement where the rule of the strongest prevailed over the rule of law. This was epitomized by the men who governed the island. Working from the premise that only exceptionally rough men could be expected to control the island's unruly colonists, the authorities employed a series of governors who were renowned for their viciousness and cruelty. Hawley, the man George had already encountered, ruled with an iron fist, but his successor was even more formidable. Henry Huncks was characterized by one of his contemporaries as 'a drunken, vindictive tyrant', who was accused of raping a female colonist and threatened to make one of his opponents 'shorter by the heade'. Far from being a solution to the problems of these volatile early colonies, men like Huncks often contributed to their discord. Their aggressive and arbitrary behaviour drove some colonists to leave the islands while provoking others into violent resistance.

The situation was only worsened by the fact that heavy drinking was an intrinsic part of the social life of the colony. It was considered a mortal insult for a planter to visit a fellow without taking a glass. There was little else to do and the consumption was prodigious: indeed, one visitor described the settlers as 'such great drunkards' that they 'will find the money to buy their drink all though they goe naked'. In this culture of excessive drinking it is likely that George Ashby too found himself imbibing more than he had previously. Certainly this was true of Henry Colt, who was no mean drinker at the best of times; he found his consumption of alchohol increased more than tenfold during his stay on the island.

Bridgetown was the centre of debauchery, with the highest concentration of the island's 'houses of entertainment'. It became so disorderly that for a time a curfew was imposed on visiting sailors. Fighting was a particular problem: the colonists were an explosive lot who resorted to violence with frightening speed, especially when they had been drinking. 'They settle their differences by fist fighting,' wrote the French priest Antoine Biet. 'They give each other black eyes, scratch each other, tear each other's hair, and do similar things. The onlookers let them do this and surround them so as to see who will be victorious. If they fall down they are picked up, and they fight until they can no longer do so and are forced to give up.'

Barbados was, in short, an illustration of what was happening right across the New World, from the French islands of Martinique and St Dominique to the Dutch settlements in Surinam and Curaçao and the mainland colonies in Virginia or the Chesapeake. These early American societies were made up almost exclusively of young men. Of those who departed from London in 1635 for Barbados and St Christopher, only 1 per cent were female, and only slightly more than 1 per cent were aged over thirty. Suddenly, these ill-educated youngsters found themselves in a frontier town, marooned together in an unfamiliar and threatening wilderness with a bizarre new selection of people of different national and cultural background, class, religious belief, skin colour and language. There was plenty of alcohol, but none of the usual social norms and constraints. And, according to contemporaries, every kind of deviance was recorded: incest, bestiality, sodomy. The institutions that had ordered their societies of origin had also been left behind. The church was marginal, judicial systems in their infancy, and wives, parents and elders were absent. Theirs was a society of orphans, in which men became almost feral. They formed a new community that was volatile, transient, hyper-masculine, and intoxicated with its own mythology, that of a land where the young and fearless could build their own paradise.

The historian Richard Pares described these early colonists as 'tough guys': rough, unschooled, physically robust men, given to neither self-doubt nor rumination. They did not make a good impression on visitors to the island: 'This Island is the Dunghill whereupon England doth cast forth its rubbish,' wrote Henry Whistler, 'rogues and whores and such like people are those which are generally brought here.' He concluded, 'A rogue in England will hardly make a cheater here.'

The islanders' lack of moral restraint was attributed by one historian to 'the weak conditions of the Church of England' in the colony. In spite of the scriptural writings that justified the colonial project overall, religion had not been established as the centre of life in Barbados, as it was for the Puritans who settled in New England. Many of the islanders neglected their religious commitments, failing to attend church and observe regular prayers. One prominent planter, typically more interested in money than his immortal soul, excused these lapses by declaring wryly that 'it is enough to believe that there is a God, and that Jesus Christ died for us'. In 1652, the Assembly of Barbados, in the hope of generating greater religiosity in the unruly islanders, took special measures to clamp down on anti-social behaviour on the Sabbath, such as rioting, drunkenness, swearing, whoring, shooting at marks, gaming, quarrelling, 'and many other vicious and ungodly courses'. But the problem was not solved and, five years later, a proclamation by the governor blamed 'the continual abounding of cursing and drunkenness, as the root and foundacion of many other crimes and offenses and the disabling and overthrow of divers manual tradesmen, labourers or workmen and the impoverishing (if not ruine) of many families, together with public disorder'.

Many felt moved to admonish the island's inhabitants about their unruly behaviour. In a diatribe against the immorality of its white inhabitants, John Rous attacked the inhabitants of Barbados 'who live in pride, drunkenesse, covetousnesse, oppression and deceitful dealings'. The Quaker Richard Pinder wrote a tract entitled 'A Loving Invitation (to Repentance and Amendments of Life) unto all the inhabitants of the island Barbados'. In it he labelled the island's whites as 'sinners' and criticized their 'cruel usage' of their indentured servants and slaves, reminding them that 'they are of the same blood and mould you are off'. He also bitingly condemned their behaviour and a way of life 'given to the lusts and pleasures of this evil world'.

The colonists' rowdy conduct often masked profound unhappiness. For what these men had not fully anticipated, and had little skills to cope with, were the feelings of loneliness, homesickness and fear that overwhelmed them on arrrival in the Caribbean; feelings only exacerbated by the deprived conditions in which they lived. According to Ligon:

The hard labour and want of victuals had so much

depress'd their spirits, as they were come to a declining
and yielding condition. Nor can this be called slothfulness
or sluggishness in them, as some will have it, but a decay
of their spirits, by long and tedious hard labour, slight
feeding, and ill lodging, which is able to wear out and
quell the best spirit of the world.

The human price paid in colonizing the Caribbean was breathtaking: historian Carl Bridenbaugh calculates that around half of
the white men who settled the colonies died in the undertaking.
Richard Ligon was shocked to learn upon his arrival that in a
decade and a half each island had undergone an almost total turnover in population: most of the Barbadians were 'new men, for
few or none of them that first set foot there, were now living'.

But George Ashby beat the odds: he not only survived, he
adapted. And he also managed to find a wife. We cannot be sure
he did not arrive with her, but it is extremely unlikely – cases of
married couples travelling to the island in these early years were
very rare. To get married in Barbados was also an achievement:
the earliest passenger lists in 1627 show no women at all, and
only 8 per cent of the servants arriving in the years up to 1640
were female. By the late 1650s, the proportion had risen to just
over 25 per cent.

Since women were scarce, they were highly sought after.
Colonies across the Americas faced the same problem in the
nascent days of settlement. In some parts of North America,
colonial promoters formed joint-stock companies to send 'girls
for sale to the planters as wives'. In places were there was no
official strategy to recruit female migrants, planters sometimes
resorted to contracting for wives, pre-paying their passage and
giving their family a sum of money as a sort of dowry. But most
brides were selected from the small pool of women who had
completed their indentures.

Many of these women had been recruited from whorehouses and prisons. In 1656, for example, the Venetian envoy to Britain, Francesco Giavarina, claimed that 'The soldiers of the London garrison visited various brothels and other places of entertainment where they forcibly laid hands on over 400 women of loose life, whom they compelled to sail for the Barbados islands.' Richard Ligon, en route to Barbados, recalled travelling with such a group: when an attempt was made to assault them at a stop in the Cape Verde islands, the women easily repelled their attackers, being 'better natur'd than to suffer such violence'. Hundreds of women (including the fictional Manon Lescaut of Abbé Prévost's classic novel) were also dispatched from the *Hôpital*, a notorious Parisian prison, to the French colonies. These were throwaway women with rough lives. Some were prostitutes, some were criminals, some were mentally ill, some were just victimized or unlucky – but mad or bad, virtuous or fallen, once these girls arrived in the New World they were in demand. Despite their colourful reputation, the real defining characteristic of these women's lives was not their immorality but their powerlessness. Many were desperate – discarded by family, abandoned by husbands, broken by poverty and abuse.

My first known female ancestor would have shared many of the terrifying and transformative experiences as George Ashby. Virtually the only thing I know about her is a name: Deborah. But some of the rest is possible to surmise. By working backwards from the birth of her children, she must have married George Ashby in the early 1640s, and therefore was born in England. In all likelihood, she too would have been assigned a steerage berth on one of the transatlantic ships that sailed from Britain to the Americas almost daily. She would have staked out her tiny piece of territory between decks with her meagre pile of possessions, amid a sorority of indentured, disgraced or disposable women. On disembarking in Barbados, many of the women were hired as domestic servants in the larger plantation households, but some were expected to work the land alongside the men. Unsurprisingly, in these placements the women were vulnerable to physical and sexual abuse and had little redress under the law. It was only once her term of indenture was finished that Deborah would have been able to contemplate a future of her own.

One of the few positive aspects of migration for women like Deborah was the opportunity it provided to reinvent themselves. As Henry Whistler acerbically noted, after his brief visit to the island in 1655: 'a Baud brought ouer puts on a demur comportment, a whore if handsome makes a wife for sume rich planter'. Despite Whistler's disapproval, in this respect the women were no different from their men. They too had crossed an ocean with dreams of beginning again. This was the opportunity this untamed world offered them all, a chance to carve a new life out of the wilderness.

And so George Ashby made preparations for his wedding. Alongside tending the tobacco crop, the vegetable garden and the stock, he needed to build a house fit for a bride. Together with his servant, and with the customary help of neighbours, he constructed a simple wooden cottage with two rooms and dirt floors. Here the newly married couple settled down to begin their family. Richard Ligon, who had a great interest in architecture, felt that the houses of planters, particularly those of 'a meaner sort' like George Ashby, were poorly adapted to local conditions. Their small timber houses had 'roofs so low, as for the most part of them I could hardly stand upright with my hat on, and no cellars at all'. In an effort to keep rain from driving through the windows, the houses were typically designed to be closed on the east and open to the west. But since the breezes blew the other way, this effectively prevented 'the cooling flow of wind' that would give them 'the greatest comfort'. As a result, the rooms were 'like Stoves, or heated Ovens'. Richard Ligon concluded that the reason the houses were designed like this was not ignorance but poverty; the colonists couldn't afford glass or shutters to keep out the driving rain.

The interior of the house was probably furnished only with the bare essentials. A 1643 inventory of the possessions of John Higgingbotham, a blacksmith like George, mentions only 'sieves, lamps, pewter platters, tubs, trays, two runlets' and some 'smythes tooles'. For the ordinary planter, life was very primitive; it took very hard labour merely to survive.

Starting a family was a fraught enterprise in many parts of early colonial America. It was not only adults who tended to have the short and brutish lives in Barbados; the infant mortality rate was devastating. So it is almost inevitable that George and Deborah would have suffered the grief of losing a child. In the end there were three surviving offspring: the eldest, christened George after his father, a middle child called William, and a daughter named Deborah after her mother. Their childhood, despite its difficulties and discomforts, would have had an entirely different texture from that of their parents: savouring the sweet tangy taste of pink-fleshed guavas; feeling the darting surprise of tiny shoals of mercurial fish that flashed silver past their feet as they swam in the clear Caribbean water. At dusk they watched the molten sunsets, chased fireflies and fell asleep to the sound of the cicadas and tree frogs whose symphony accompanied the day's descent into darkness.

In 1647, when George's family was still young, Barbados was decimated by 'plague' – more likely an epidemic of yellow fever, a disease that was poorly understood by the early planters. According to Ligon, the outbreak – which spread swiftly throughout the region – was well under way when he arrived in the September of that year and it raged for several months. Whether the contagion arrived from abroad or was brought on by the islanders themselves because of 'the ill dyet they keep, and drinking strong waters', the 'sickness', according to Ligon, 'raign'd so extremely, as the living could hardly bury the dead'.

Richard Vines, a landowner in St Michael, saw the plague as an admonishment from a vengeful God: 'We have felt his heavy hand in wrath, and yet I feare are not sensible of it, for here is little amendment or notice taken of his great punishments. The sickness was an absolute plague; very infectious and destroying, in so much that in our parish there were buried 20 in a weeke, and many weekes together, 15 or 16.' The outbreak surprised Vine, because 'It first seized on the ablest men both for account and ability of body. Many who had begun and almost finished greater sugar works, who dandled themselves in their hopes but were suddenly laid in the dust, and their estates left to strangers.' During the epidemic, the capital, Bridgetown, was transformed into a charnel house, with bodies piled up in all available buildings and corpses littering the roadside. By its end the outbreak claimed the lives of an estimated 6,000 people (some put the figure as high as 10,000). Hard on the heels of the epidemic came famine, since the sick planters had fatally neglected the subsistence crops that they depended on for sustenance, which pushed the death toll even higher.

The two years that followed were hard. Food shortages continued, further undermining the health and morale of an already vulnerable community. Unsurprisingly, the worst affected were the poorest, and in 1649 the island had its first recorded rebellion. Ligon's description of the event is dramatic:

> Their sufferings being grown to a great height, and their daily complainings being to one another (of the intolerable burdens they labour'd under) being spread throughout the Island; at the last, some amongst them, whose spirits were not able to endure such slavery, resolved to break through it, or dye in the act; and so conspired with some others . . . to fall upon their

> Masters, and cut all their throats, and by that means, to
> make themselves [not] only free men, but Masters of
> the Island.

The reality was more prosaic. This first uprising, an uneasy
partnership between enslaved Africans and indentured labourers,
was, according to another historian, a 'small-scale affair', more
of a food riot born out of hunger and desperation. It was
nonetheless put down with some ferocity. As Ligon reported:
'the greatest part of the plotters were put to death' as an example
'to the rest'. Though the rebellion was unsuccessful, it was a
harbinger of things to come; over the centuries the island's slave
society would continue to resist their enslavement on both an
individual and a collective level, provoking a growing mistrust
in their masters which often led to terrible excesses of brutality.

In 1650 George Ashby officially stepped into the island's history.
There he is in that year's census, the first held on the island. In
this he was typical of most of his peers on the island; men and
women whose past before their arrival on the island is shadowy
and elusive, and whose story only begins to be documented
when they arrive in the New World and gain a foothold on the
economic ladder. The census lists George among the returns for
the parish of St Philip. Comprised of 12,158 acres, St Philip was
– along with the neighbouring parish of St George – one of the
most populous areas on the island. Most of the white population
of the parish were categorized as smallholders, possessing ten to
twenty acres. Their lives were in striking contrast to those of
the great planters of the same parish: men like the aristocratic
Christopher Codrington, who had 618 acres in 1679, and Jon
Pearse, the largest landholder on the island, who is credited with
owning 1,000 acres in 1673.

The census divided the planters into four categories, which
assessed their worth according to a combination of the acreage

held and the size of their slave holdings. Those with sixty or more slaves were all large landowners, while those with between twenty and fifty-nine slaves were classified as middling planters. The owner of twenty slaves had a force large enough to operate a sugar plantation, but not a very sizeable one. Most of the middling planters held significantly smaller tracts of land than the big planters, ranging from thirty to a hundred acres. Landholders with ten or more acres and fewer than twenty slaves were classified as small planters. These people qualified in Barbados law as freeholders, and were therefore eligible to vote in the colony elections (unless they were minors, women or Quakers). Lastly, landholders with fewer than ten acres were classified as freemen, indicating that they were not servants but were not entitled to vote.

As the possessor of only nine acres and one white servant, George Ashby would have fallen into the last category and would not have been able to claim the title 'planter'. It meant the difference between having some role in the island's political life and none at all. For the want of a single acre George Ashby was excluded from the privileges that these small planters held, the right that was shared by 25 or 30 per cent of the white adult males on the island, to elect or be elected assemblymen, vestrymen and jurors. Those below the ten-acre threshold were near the bottom of the social pile, only one rung above indentured servants and slaves. Maybe his lack of status gnawed at George. But maybe, after the dramas and deprivations of his life thus far, he felt it enough that he and his wife had survived, and so had some of his children. For despite everything, George Ashby had succeeded in making a life.

4

Too much sugar is bitter.

Nepalese proverb

While George Ashby and his family were struggling to stay afloat in the embryonic years of Barbados settlement, the winds of change were blowing through his island home. This process of transformation became known as 'the sugar revolution' because of its speed and impact. This 'noble condiment' would have a dramatic effect on the island's fortunes and on those of the Ashby family. The rise of sugar also coincided with one the bloodiest periods in Britain's history: the events that led up to and would follow the regicide of Charles I. The prosperity that this commodity would generate made the island of greater significance to the British Empire and would lure a new set of émigrés to the island, who would in turn drag the island into the motherland's civil war.

Humans have always craved sweetness and sought methods of sweetening their food. The ancient inhabitants of the Middle East used fig and date syrup; the Romans distilled must from grapes; the Chinese extracted the sap of the sugar palm. Others used grape juice, raisins, honey or manna from branches or leaves. But it is refined sugar that is the most famous sweetener of them all. It is a substance that doesn't occur in nature, but has to be distilled methodically from the juice of sugar cane or, more recently, sugar beet. It is the only chemical substance that is consumed in almost pure form as a staple food.

The rise of sugar has been remarkable. For many centuries few Europeans even knew it existed, then it metamorphosed into one of the most coveted commodities in the world. Now it is so ubiquitous, abundant and easy to procure that we can barely imagine life without it. Our consumption of sugar is prodigious; its only rival, in both ubiquity and symbolic value, is the substance we often classify as its opposite: salt. But it is sugar that represents tenderness, comfort and love in many languages. It saturates our cultural references, and is invested with a significance far exceeding its innate properties. More than any other commodity in human history, sugar has shaped our tastes, transformed our landscape and influenced our politics.

Indigenous to the South Pacific, sugar cane is a giant grass, part of the *Gramineae* family that includes maize, rice and sorghum. There are numerous species of cane, but the one that dominated cultivation in the Americas was known as the 'Creole'. It thrives in hot and humid places, flourishing in a range of soils including the coral limestone of Barbados. It often grows to twelve feet in height, and sometimes exceeds twenty feet. Its stalks can be green or yellow or rust-red, and divide into joints or nodes from which extrude the leaves, long narrow blades of green.

Some of the earliest linguistic references to sugar are from northern India, where the cultivation of cane is likely to go back to 500 BC. From there the crop migrated to China some time around 300 BC, when cane juice or 'sugar liquor' became a popular fermented drink. By the third century AD, cakes or loaves of hard sugar, made by drying the juice of the cane in the sun and then forming the paste into the shape of men or animals, were known as 'stone honey'. But the Chinese were slow to master the process of sugar manufacture, and in 640 the Emperor Tai Tsung sent a mission to Bihar in the Ganges valley to find out more about Indian distilling techniques. The resulting report invigorated the Chinese industry and sugar production flourished there down the years. In the thirteenth century, writing about the region around the mouth of the Yangtze, the trader and explorer Marco Polo noted that 'the production of sugar is immense in this province, much greater than all the rest of the world, and it brings in a huge revenue'.

While sugar flourished in India and China it was, according to the historian W. Aykroyd, unknown to the ancient Egyptians, Hebrews and Greeks. There is no mention of sugar in the Bible, the Talmud or the Koran, in contrast to the frequent appearances of honey, and there are only a few vague references to sugar in the classical literature of Greece and Rome. The Arab conquests that followed the death of Mohammed in AD 632 saw the crop travel to Persia, Mesopotamia and the Lower Nile. There are numerous references to sugar in the *Arabian Nights* and, by the fifth century, it was cultivated on a large scale in Baghdad. By the tenth century it was being planted along the coast of East Africa, Zanzibar and Madagascar.

It was in Palestine and Syria, between the thirteen and fifteenth centuries, that the Crusaders developed a taste for sugar and brought it home to Western Europe, where it became a highly prized commodity, in the same category as musk and pearls. Sugar was so precious it was bought by the ounce instead of the pound. It was used as a spice, alongside cinnamon and nutmeg, to enliven savoury dishes, and was also used for medicinal purposes. Its value as a drug during this period explains the tag 'an apothecary without sugar', which was a popular way of describing someone who lacked the essential materials for their trade.

In November 1565 a sculpture was unveiled at the wedding of Alexander Farnese to Princess Maria of Portugal depicting the voyage of the Portuguese princess. It consisted of tableaux of all the cities she had passed through, complete with models of palaces, theatres and ships. Each one was so large it had to be carried by three or four men. Every part of this extravaganza was made from sugar, one of the greatest status symbols of the sixteenth century.

Sugar cane arrived in the New World with Columbus. But as a crop for cultivation, it crossed the Atlantic with the Portuguese and the Spanish: the former took it to Brazil and the latter to their colonies in Hispaniola. Realizing the ideal match between territory and crop, they began to invest in cane heavily and by the late 1500s the Spanish and Portuguese held a virtual monopoly on the supply of sugar to Europe. As the scale of production grew, prices fell and sugar began to appear not only on the tables of princes but on those of the merely rich.

From its inception, sugar in the New World was reliant upon slave labour, but for the first 150 years of production in Iberian America, African slaves were only used sporadically. This was because it was easier to exploit local labour. The Portuguese first developed the sugar plantation model in Pernambuco, Brazil, around 1580. Their *engenhos* (plantations) relied on a mix of local, African and indentured servants. But the death rate of the indigenous population across the New World was dreadful. In many parts of the region the collapse of the native population was so extreme that it was described as genocide. As one Spanish planter remarked about the Arawaks in Hispaniola and Cuba, whom the colonists had attempted to enslave, 'They died like fish in a bucket.'

This unanswerable reaction to 'forced labour and the lash' meant that the Iberians were swiftly in need of a new source of labour. Their first response was to bring workers from home, but the Spanish population was too small to provide a consistently large enough pool of workers. African slaves proved both more hardy and more cost effective than indigenous labour. From the early 1600s African slavery became increasingly intertwined with the world of sugar production. In the 1630s Father Antonio Vieira conjured up a Dantesque vision of a plantation in Bahia, Brazil:

> People the colour of the very night, working briskly and moaning at the same time without a moment of peace or rest, whoever sees all the confused and noisy machinery and apparatus of this Babylon, even if they have seen Mt. Etna and Vesuvius will say that this indeed is the image of Hell.

As time passed sugar became an increasingly important food commodity. Though still expensive, it was the crucial ingredient in conserving fruits and making jam, pastimes which became popular in the households of wealthy merchants. In Portugal and Spain sugar was used to sweeten rice and conserve everything from chestnuts to Brazilian pumpkins. These sweets were given evocative names: 'celestial lard', 'heaven's marrow', 'angelic Adam's Apples'. In Europe, sugar also starred in a particular genre of paintings which depicted visions of plenty with sugar as their centrepiece.

The watershed moment in Atlantic sugar production took place in Barbados during the period when George Ashby was settling into the colony. Sugar cane had arrived on the island with the first colonists in the late 1620s, but they did not know how to exploit it, so they used it only to make a sweet drink, as the ancients had. But by the 1640s, smarting from the failure of their earlier crop experiments – tobacco, cotton, ginger, indigo – and under pressure from their merchant financiers, who were anxious to make a profit, the colonists were looking for a new opportunity. They chose sugar, for which there was still a strong demand on the international markets. Their timing was good: the sugar industry on the Spanish island of Hispaniola had collapsed and that of Brazil was increasingly vulnerable to competition.

The precise date of the establishment of Barbados's first sugar factory is contested: some claim that it was built by Captain Holdip in 1641, but in September 1647 Richard Ligon wrote: 'At the time we landed on this island, we were informed that the great work of sugar making was but newly practised here.' He went on to explain the process:

> Some of the most industrious men have gotten plants from Fernambrock [Pernambuco], made tryall of them, and finding them grow they planted more and more, until they had such a considerable number as to set up a very small ingenio [sugar mill], and to make tryall what sugar could be made on that soyl.

But, he continued, 'The secret of the work is not being very well understood, the sugars made were very inconsiderable, and ... barely worth the bringing home to England.'

Getting the cultivation process right was an arduous, expensive and frustrating task. Sugar was an altogether more demanding crop than tobacco or cotton; it required a much bigger workforce, investment and level of expertise. So it was only a handful of the bigger planters, such as Holdip and his partner James Drax, who were in position to follow it through. It required a unique combination of farm and factory, where brute strength was combined with a chemist's precision and judgement. The land had to be prepared just so: the right soil, freshly weeded; and the new shoots had to be protected from any number of diseases and pests. The cane had to be cut at exactly the right moment, during the cooler, dry months from January to June, and once the cane was cut it had to be transported immediately and processed swiftly or it would ferment. Then the distilled mixture had to be 'struck' at just the right time, before being moved into a cooling cistern. It would be a number of years and many costly mistakes later before these sugar pioneers got it right. But when that finally happened at the end of the 1640s, they swiftly became rich men.

The Dutch played a pivotal role in the fledgling industry. Their ships carried sugar from the colonies to Amsterdam for refining, and to markets in northern Europe. They became the industry's financiers and the disseminators of technical knowledge. In particular, a community of Dutch Sephardic Jews facilitated the shift of the cane industry to Barbados. Originally from Portugal themselves, they escaped the Inquisition and settled in Amsterdam and Brazil, then fled to the Caribbean when the Dutch settlement in Brazil, Pernambuco, was defeated by the Portuguese. In both places they became involved in the sugar industry as financiers and merchants. In the final years of the 1640s, one anonymous source declared they 'taught the English the Art of making Sugar' and used their international trading contacts to make sugar cane a viable option for planters on the island.

In truth, Barbados discovered sugar just in time. The early 1640s had been so financially precarious on the island that many settlers had gone bankrupt, while others had fled its shores in search of greener pastures. Meanwhile, its merchant backers were beginning to worry that the island would never be financially viable. Then everything came together: civil war in Brazil meant that the Atlantic sugar market crashed, so the Dutch merchants who had supported it needed new ventures to finance and a new place to establish commercial networks. They provided the Barbados planters with cheap credit, procured slaves on good terms and, most importantly, provided the information on the technology of sugar cultivation that was needed to kick-start the industry. Sugar had found a new home. By the mid–1650s the industry was flourishing. After three decades of searching, the islanders had finally struck gold. No one cared that it was not the molten ore from below the ground but instead the 'white gold' that grew above it.

Almost immediately, Barbados saw an influx of prospective planters from Britain, eager for a share in the bounty. Quite apart from a desire to enrich themselves, many of these new migrants were also in flight from one of the greatest convulsions in the mother country's history: the English Civil War. This had begun in 1642 when Charles I began his protracted battle with Parliament for authority over the Commonwealth of England, Scotland and Ireland. Despite his defeats, Charles would not accept Parliament's demands for a constitutional monarchy, and the course was set for a cataclysmic ending. So from the late 1640s Barbados attracted a flood of political exiles who were desperate to escape the violent upheavals back home and were acutely aware of the potential of this new commodity.

In particular, a growing number of English Royalists, or Cavaliers, washed up on the island in the hope of repairing their fortunes. Though most of the earliest planters like George Ashby could roughly be described as Parliamentary sympathizers – Roundheads – there had always been a group of Royalists on the island. Both parties had fled Britain at least partly to escape the troubles and had no desire to replay them in their new home. So the two factions coexisted relatively peaceably, united in the determination not to be distracted from the pursuit of profit. According to Ligon, in order to discourage any sectarian quarrels the planters made a law among themselves that anybody who used the epithet 'Roundhead' or 'Cavalier' should, as forfeit, feed all witnesses a young hog and a turkey. A costly breach, then, and one best avoided.

But as time passed and divisions in the mother country

intensified, it became harder for the islanders to remain detached. This was especially so since ever more Royalists were arriving on the island, embittered and traumatized by their experience on the losing side of the conflict. The situation worsened in January 1649 when Charles I was put on trial, accused of being a 'tyrant and murderer; and a public and implacable enemy to the Commonwealth of England'. At the heavily policed trial, presided over by John Bradshaw, the charges read out against Charles included the accusation that he had attempted 'out of a wicked design, to erect and uphold himself in unlimited and tyrannical power to make according to his will, and to overthrow the rights and liberties of the people of England'. Charles refused to accept the authority of the court and only began to engage with charges after he was convicted. But by then it was too late and he was sentenced to death 'by severing his head from his body'. The nature of his execution only inflamed people further; apparently spectators, for a fee, were allowed to approach the scaffold and dip their handerchiefs in the king's blood. Parliament abolished the monarchy on 6 February 1649, and issued a statement which read: 'The office of the king in this state is unnecessary, burdensome and dangerous to the liberty, society and public interest of the people.'

When news of the regicide reached Barbados, the outraged islanders – now predominantly Royalists – proclaimed his son, Charles II, their lawful sovereign. Six months later, the Council of State back in England wrote to inform the plantations of the change of government and required them to continue their 'obedience' to the Commonwealth if they expected its continued protection. Thus the beginning of 1650 found the colonists in a state of open division, as men of both political persuasions thundered up and down on horseback, traversing the island's roads and byways, delivering pamphlets espousing their cause. George Ashby could not have missed them; these inflammatory leaflets were thrust into the hands of planters as they laboured on their land, or were nailed conspicuously to the fencing of their property.

St Philip's parish, where George lived, was at the centre of the political struggle. Populated with prominent planters of both political persuasions, it saw some of the most heated altercations. It was no longer just alcohol that prompted the islanders' infamous brawls; now, with cries of 'God and the Cause!' and 'God and the King!', they rushed to blows, according to one historian, 'with nought to win and all to lose'. We do not know whether George Ashby was an enthusiastic participant in these conflicts or if he kept his head down, cursing all distractions from his pursuit of an honest income. But whatever the strength of his allegiances, he must have been worried about the prospect of military action against the island. Not only would it endanger his family, but as a white freeman he was obliged to serve in the militia, and would therefore be forced to fight, as well as being separated from his wife, his children and his land.

George Ashby's likely party, the Parliamentarians, was in a minority, even if it did include some of the island's oldest and most influential planters. The Royalists on the opposing side were now more numerous and more vociferous. According to one historian: 'They did not see why they should not repair their fortunes in Little England by sequestering the Estates of Roundheads there, as the Parliament had done to their own property in Old England.' These men found passionate leadership in the persons of Colonel Humphrey Walrond and his brother Edward, who for many months worked steadily and covertly, organizing a vigorous propaganda campaign that alleged there was a plot by the Parliamentarians to overthrow the Assembly, where the island's politicians met. In particular they claimed that the prominent Parliamentarian James Drax, whom they described as being 'that devout Zealot of the deeds of the devil', was, along with his followers, 'determined to put all who were for the king to the sword'.

On the second birthday of the establishment of the Commonwealth, Oliver Cromwell asserted his right to govern 'all the dominions and Territories'. The Barbadians, alongside other rebel colonists in Virginia, Bermuda and Antigua, retaliated by once again proclaiming 'Charles Stuart, Son to the late king' as their sovereign. This act of defiance became known as the 'Horrid Rebellion', and had wide-ranging repercussions. In the name of protecting the rights of freeborn Englishmen, the Barbadian Royalists pushed through 'An Act for the Unity of the Inhabitants of the Islands'. This demanded absolute obedience to the government of the island over allegiance to the London Parliament. The 'Disturbers of the Peace' were targeted and the triumphant king's men disarmed those unwilling to pledge an oath to church and king, while the prominent Parliamentarian planters were forced to either pay a huge indemnity or face exile.

Unsurprisingly, many leading Parliamentarians fled to England, where they appealed for protection from Cromwell. Some had suffered terribly: John Webb had had his tongue bored through with a hot iron, while two other members of the delegation had had the letter 'T' for traitor branded on their cheeks. Predictably, this pitiable contingent was sympathetically received by the Commonwealth, which was already displeased with the Barbadians for continuing to trade with the enemy Dutch. In October a new law forbade commerce with the islanders, and a vast fleet was requisitioned to deal with 'the Barbados business'.

This news, delivered by a passing Dutch ship, reached the island in February 1651. It was a terrible shock to the inhabitants: not only had they been proclaimed 'rebels' by an Act of

Parliament, they were also faced with an invasion designed to force them into submission. Defiant, the colonists vowed to fight for their self-preservation and the General Assembly called on the governor to prepare for war. Men and horses were amassed into an army; fortifications were built, and the property of the departed Parliamentarians was sequestered: 'the profits of the said Estates to be disposed of by his Lordship, towards the defraying of the great charges, which this their unnatural opposition hath already, and will force us to undergo'.

The following month, the spirits of the Royalist islanders were buoyed by news brought by another Dutch ship that the Prince of Wales had led a force into England, and had killed Cromwell. The report was untrue, but the islanders had no way of knowing this and, overjoyed, they held a huge feast, enlivened by many toasts to 'church and crown'. But before the celebrations were even fully under way, a rider pulled up to inform the revellers that the Commonwealth fleet under Sir George Ayscue had arrived in their harbour to blockade the island. According to one historian: 'There must have been mounting in hot haste then, and much firing off of muskets, which in the absence of Telegraphs and Telephones was the manner of sending warnings of danger up and down the Island.' As swiftly as possible an intial force of horse and foot soldiers assembled to dispute the Parliamentarian landing. The long-expected military action, which they had for a brief period thought averted, had commenced. (The subsequent conflict would captivate the broadsheets back in Britain even if many of the accounts, such as one entitled 'Bloody News From Barbados', were both lurid and woefully inaccurate.)

Ayscue's fleet, comprising seven ships, 236 guns and 820 sailors, had made Barbados on the night of 15 October. Ayscue immediately sent forward three of his ships to surprise the vessels anchored in the bay; they successfully seized all fourteen ships, mostly Dutch traders. Ayscue, who had been lying back in Oistins Bay, then sailed the rest of the fleet into Carlisle Bay. They instantly came under fire from the fort. Two sailors were wounded and one killed in the onslaught. Then all resistance died down and the ships anchored in the bay. That night Parliamentarian sympathizers swam stealthily across the bay to inform Admiral Ayscue about the island's defences. He was told that once the entire island was rallied he would be confronted by 6,000 foot soldiers and 400 cavalry. Realizing that he could not match this force on land, Ayscue decided to blockade the port, and his ships prowled the water around Barbados, capturing the supplies of ships destined to dock there.

An exquisitely worded and gentlemanly correspondence between Admiral Ayscue and the island's governor, Lord Willoughby, documented the entire affair. Willoughby declined to return Ayscue's deputy, who had been taken prisoner in the first sally, while Ayscue demanded the surrender of the island in exchange for his departure. He also had leaflets distributed surreptitiously around the island by his sympathizers, in which he reassured the Barbadians of his friendly sentiments towards them and his hope of avoiding the destruction of 'their long-laboured-for estates'. But he also reminded them of the Parliamentarians' many military successes and their inability, as a small colony, to survive without the trade and protection that the Commonwealth could give them. Willoughby responded with a proclamation that was signed by the entire Assembly.

> Despite those Loose and scandalous papers with much Industry scattered up and down our Island to poison the allegiance of the good People . . . We the Representative Body of this whole Island do hereby declare, Resolve and unanimously profess that we will even at the utmost hazard to our Lives and fortunes defend his Majesty's interest and Lawful Power in and on this Island.

The matter came to a head in the third week of November, when the news of Cromwell's victory against Charles II at Worcester was relayed to the islanders in order to persuade them to capitulate. Willoughby predictably refused, and on 22 November Ayscue dispatched a force of 200 men, who swiftly breached the island's defences and took about thirty prisoners without sustaining any fatalities. Ayscue's forces were then joined by fifteen more of Cromwell's ships that were en route to Virginia to reduce the Royalists there. Ayscue now had more than forty vessels under his command. Emboldened, he sent yet another message to Willoughby, offering him a last opportunity to surrender.

As Willoughby was still unwilling to submit, Ayscue attacked again, landing a force of around 500 men on 7 December. They were resisted, but nevertheless managed to take and raze the fort and burn down a number of houses. Thirty islanders were killed and eighty taken prisoner. The latter were released on the proviso that they told their compatriots the truth about Royalist losses in England. Two of the prisoners who did so were hanged, and the governor issued an edict that made it a capital offence to speak against the ruling party on the island.

This protracted conflict took its toll on all the islanders. Households like the Ashbys had lived in fear for many weeks, foodstuffs were scarce and their crops went uncultivated. More and more there were whispered discussions about abandoning the fight. After all, Cromwell was now the undisputed master of England, Scotland and Ireland; and nothing had been gained by the colonists, who felt that they had lost a fortune in trade and suffered continuous deprivation because of the blockade. Finally a prominent colonist, Colonel Modiford, declared for the Parliament. Although he was dubbed a traitor by the governor, it was the beginning of the end. Fearful that the island would be 'utterly ruined', the Barbadians submitted to the will of the Commonwealth. On 10 January peace talks took place at the Mermaid, a hostelry in Oistins. The following day 'The Charter of Barbados' was signed. Its provisions included an act of indemnity that protected the islanders from prosecution for previous utterances or acts, and restored the property of those whose estates had been sequestered. The island's civil war was over.

5

Slavery is theft, theft of a life, theft of work, theft of any property or produce, theft even of the children a slave might have borne.

Kevin Bales

More significant than any political ramifications, the emergence of sugar and the prosperity it promised transformed the racial balance of the island, as African labour came to be regarded as essential for the successful cultivation of the new crop. Although the first black slaves in Barbados had arrived at the very beginning of the colony's history – the eight men captured as bounty from another ship by Henry Powell's colonizing expedition of 1627 – their numbers remained small for the next few years. By 1629, it was believed that there were only about fifty enslaved Indians and Africans on the island. The Barbadian historian Hilary Beckles estimated that there were 800 blacks on the island in the 1630s, when George Ashby arrived, most of whom had been seized by Portuguese and Dutch traders; but some historians suggest that the number was more like 2,000.

These demographic changes would affect George Ashby in a very personal way. In the decade that he had settled on the island, he had been an Englishman among Englishmen, with a sprinkling of other Europeans thrown in for good measure. Even their servants were overwhelmingly white. So in these early days of settlement black faces on the island were an exotic minority, who were a source of ambivalence, even possible disdain, but were not considered a threat. But as time passed, and the island converted to sugar, the situation began to change. Moving around the island, George Ashby and his contemporaries noticed that there were more and more black faces. In the years between 1641 and 1650 the DuBois Voyages Database – the most comprehensive index of slave voyages, named in honour of the African-American scholar W.E.B. DuBois – puts the number of slave arrivals on the island at more than 4,500, though again the real figure was probably higher. Indeed, the historian J.H. Galloway says that there were already 6,000 slaves on the island in 1643. And in the tippling houses and taverns that George Ashby frequented, he noticed that his contemporaries were discussing the purchase of black slaves with almost the same avidity with which they debated the conversion to sugar. By 1655, when sugar reigned supreme and the commodity had become the currency with which goods were valued and exchanged, there were 20,000 slaves on the island.

The perceived threat of being outnumbered by blacks was heightened by the fluctuations in the white population of the island. Though Barbados was still an attractive destination for aspirational white migrants, many were also leaving the island in search of greater opportunities, as less and less land was available for purchase and what was available was inflated in value in comparision to the other colonies. In the 1640s Barbadians went to Surinam, Demerara and nearby Trinidad. In the 1650s they left for other English colonies like Antigua, Montserrat and Nevis, while others went to French islands such as Martinique and Guadeloupe. Then a couple of thousand set off for Virginia. But the biggest exodus was in 1655, when 3,000 islanders volunteered to join the ill-fated Penn–Venables expedition, initiated by Cromwell as part of his Western Design, to seize Spanish territories in the region.

While Barbados seemed to be perpetually haemorrhaging white settlers, the black population continued to grow relentlessly. Soon the African workers in Barbados were in danger of out-numbering the 'white slaves' who had previously been relied upon to farm the land. And as the balance between black and white shifted inexorably against them, George Ashby and his contemporaries became increasingly paranoid and fearful; their 'Britain in miniature', their home away from home, was feeling very alien indeed. By the middle of the 1660s Governor Willoughby wrote to the mother country complaining that if the numbers of white colonists were not replenished, 'wee shall be soe thinned of Christian people . . . I fear our negroes will growe too hard for us'. But the flood would not be reversed – not while sugar was yielding such riches. So whether he liked it or not, George Ashby's island was in transition from being a European world to a black one.

Of course, the New World colonists did not invent slavery; the institution was already thousands of years old and most societies have, at some time in their history, exploited slave labour. Slavery flourished in Africa, the Americas, and Europe. Indeed the term 'slave' comes from 'Slav' because of the many Eastern Europeans who were enslaved in the early modern world. Some people were born into servitude, many others were subjugated later in their lives. Some sold themselves into bondage, others were sold by their families. Some were captured in warfare or kidnapped as they went about their ordinary lives, while others were enslaved as punishment for their crimes, or because of debt. Though most slaves were anonymous drones working unrewarded in households or labouring in fields, there were some who achieved considerable status and power, explains the historian Hugh Thomas. Roman emperors like Augustus frequently promoted his slaves to important offices, while a black eunuch named Kafur became master of both Egypt and

Syria during the tenth century. Slaves were involved in the construction of some of the great wonders of the world, from the Egyptian pyramids to the Great Wall of China. It has been estimated that during the first two centuries of the Roman Empire, one out of three persons living on the Italian peninsula were slaves: approximately two million people. But these slaves were of various cultures and colours, and enslavement was not a condition that was associated with a particular race or skin colour.

Even though slavery had all but disappeared from Western Europe by the end of the fifteenth century because of the new ideas of nationhood and more progressive attitudes to the labouring classes that had emerged from the Renaissance and the Reformation, in the New World slave labour was exploited virtually from the moment that Europeans arrived. Indeed, the beginnings of the slave trade are usually dated to 1502, when the first references to enslaved Africans appeared in Spanish colonial documents. And by 1514 the DuBois index indicates that the Portuguese were carrying out regular slave voyages. On arrival in the Americas, these Africans worked alongside indigenous populations, often cutting cane in the Iberian territories of South America. The Dutch and the Spanish were soon slave traders. Initially England was hostile to the trade. On hearing of the first slave-running voyage by John Hawkins from Guinea to the Caribbean in 1563, Queen Elizabeth I remarked: 'If any Africans were carried away without his free consent it would be detestable and call down the vengeance of Heaven upon the undertaking.' But once the English became aware of the profits associated with the trade, they soon became involved; and, in time, Britain would become the greatest slaving nation in the world.

What explained this volte-face? After all, slavery had not been a feature of English life for more than a century, and by the early seventeenth century the English were more likely to be victims of slavery – purchased in the Mediterranean ports of North Africa – than they were to be slavers. It was particularly surprising for a nation that so valued its own freedom that it was enshrined in their most popular patriotic song. (Written at the high point of the slave trade in 1740, the lyrics to 'Rule, Britannia!' defiantly declare: 'Britons never will be slaves'.) Some have suggested that the reason was an implacable racism. But this explanation is somewhat simplistic. The English settlers had been perfectly content with white workers in the early years of settlement; and in the Australian colonies a couple of centuries later, white convicts were considered appropriate to work in conditions similar to those of the Caribbean.

The real reasons were both numerous and more complex. The early European settlers had not gone to the New World with the expectation of being the mass enslavers of Africans. Instead the very first colonists in the region had relied on the labour of indigenous peoples. But since there were simply not enough local tribesmen available, and those who were accessible had proved so vulnerable to ill health and death, they weren't considered to be a good bet. So many planters, particularly those in the English territories, turned to white indentured servants, occasionally supplementing them with a few African slaves if they came across them. In the early years, therefore, black and white toiled alongside each other; and the planters made little distinction between either group, brutalizing both as the inclination took them.

It was the arrival of sugar, however, that changed everything. Sugar demanded large amounts of capital, and a vast and steady stream of expendable labour to make the crop commercially viable. The flow of indentured servants to the island was finite, and was drying up as time went on, no doubt partly because people at home had begun to become aware of the terrible conditions under which they toiled. Thus it came down to a question of simple mathematics: in the late 1640s an indentured servant cost £10 for a five- to seven-year indenture, while an African could be bought for around £20 but served for life. As the trade in Africans grew more widespread, so the cost of shipping the slaves fell and the numbers available for purchase increased. In addition, the journey from Africa to the Caribbean, which became known as the Middle Passage (so named because of its position in the triangular trade from Britain to Africa, on to the Caribbean, and back to Britain), was somewhat easier than that from Britain. In the end, therefore, the introduction of mass slavery to Barbados was driven largely by economics: acquiring an African labour force was more convenient and cost effective. It is important to remember that Barbados, like most of the American settlements, was set up as a commercial enterprise, financed by merchants and patrons who hoped, and expected, to make money from their investment; and it was settled by chancers intoxicated by dreams of prosperity, unsentimental men who had few scruples about how their fortunes were made. In this context the decision to exploit black people was both an explicable and predictable one.

But if it is clear that racism was not the catalyst for slavery and the slave trade, it is also true that the English nation's attitude to race made it easier for them to justify the enslavement of Africans. Though Richard Ligon was both more educated and more sympathetic to the enslaved population than many of his planter contemporaries, his observations about Africans is nonetheless revelatory about how they were regarded in the period when the expansion of sugar took place. It is a contradictory account. Ligon clearly had many of the prejudices of his era, but was also fascinated and appreciative. He admired the slaves' physiques: 'the men are very well timbered, that is broad between the shoulders, full breasted, well filleted and clean leg'd'. And he was entranced by the women, who 'when young' had 'large hard jutting breasts' that were so firm that 'no leaning, jumping or stirring will cause them to shake', even though he lamented that when 'these women grow old their breasts do hang below their navels'. He was impressed with the athletic skills of both sexes in running, swimming and even fencing when well trained; and he enjoyed their singing and musicality. His opinions only reinforced the stereotypes that black males were designed for physical exploitation and the black female, as a result of her attractiveness, deserved her sexual exploitation.

Ligon was more ambivalent about black people when it came to their philosophies and behaviour. He was impressed by their 'attachment to their wives and their beliefs' and noted that they measured time by the moon; but he also recorded with derision 'that arithmetic fails them'. He presented the slaves sometimes as clever and resourceful and at other times stupid and without initiative. Slaves were 'intrinsically treacherous' but also loyal and 'protective' of their master's well-being, but he concluded that he and the other islanders regarded the slaves as 'a bloody people . . . as near beasts as may be' and that there 'be a mark set upon these people, which will hardly ever be wip'd off, as of their cruelties when they have advantages and of their fearfulness and falseness'. He also went on to say that he had 'strong motives' to make him believe 'that there are as honest, faithful, and conscionable people amongst them, as amongst those of Europe or any other part of the world'. This was not a sentiment shared by most of his planter-hosts, as another of Ligon's anecdotes unwittingly reveals.

In trying to explain the blacks' religious beliefs and illustrate their superstitious nature, Ligon relates how, on an estate owned by Colonel Walrond, a number of slaves had committed suicide, believing they would be resurrected in their 'own country'. After a having lost three or four of his best blacks this way, Walrond organized for 'one of their heads to be cut off, and set upon a pole of a dozen foot height'. Arguing that the body couldn't 'go onto the next life without its head', the remaining slaves became convinced that this would prevent them from being reincarnated and stopped committing suicide. Of course, the story tells us as much about the planters as it does about the slaves, and demonstrates how ruthless they were from the outset, in order to ensure maximum productivity in their cane fields, as well as how desperately enslaved Africans dreamt of escaping the abuse and toil of plantation life and finding a way back home.

Though the English cannot be credited with being the first nation to restrict bondage to peoples of African descent – that honour goes to the Iberians – there is no doubt that the attitudes Ligon and his contemporaries held helped them to feel comfortable with the idea of exploiting Africans. This same combination of ignorance, stereotype and naked racism was shared by the other nations operating in the region, including the French, Dutch, Spanish, and Germans, and marked the slave out as 'the other' or 'the stranger'. In this ideology, their difference – of appearance, beliefs and behaviour – made them somehow deserving of being treated inhumanely. And so in the colonies, Africans' skin colour quickly became their manifest destiny. Not only did the Europeans who settled the New World give the institution of slavery what the historian David Eltis calls 'a new scale and intensity', they also established a particularly noxious form of slavery: one in which race established a hierarchy of human life and decided which people were expendable and which were not, those who could be transformed into commodities and those who could never be. For in the Atlantic world, though not all blacks were slaves, all slaves were black; and no white person could ever become one.

Not only would the American colonists develop a type of slavery that had never existed before, the demands of the New World would prompt the largest forced migration in recorded history, as twelve and a half million souls (some historians believe the number to be closer to fifteen million) were transported from Africa to the Atlantic world. W.E.B. DuBois has called this 'the most magnificent drama in the last thousand years of human history', but of course this 'drama' was in fact a tragedy, not least because between 9 and 20 per cent of the captives died en route. Hence the fact that the slave trade, sugar's sickening by-product, would eventually claim its place alongside the Gulag, the killing fields and the concentration camps as one of the greatest atrocities in human history.

The slave trade worked thus. When a planter decided he needed more 'stock', he would commission an agent to obtain them. This man then employed a ship's captain, with whom he agreed the size of the cargo and negotiated the size of the commission, and who in turn gathered a crew, outfitted a ship, and set sail to Africa to fulfil the order. (Many of the richer planters, like James Drax, also had interests in slave ships, so they could make a profit from every aspect of the trade.)

The ordeal of most slaves began long before they even saw a slave ship. Spirited away from their communities, many as a result of inter-ethnic conflicts, they joined a dusty convoy across Africa in the company of others captured before them, as well as goats and horses, black traders and the occasional white slaver. The men were bound together into coffles, linked by wood and rope and chain, with the women and children straggling alongside, free of shackles but ever vulnerable to violence and opportunistic sexual abuse by the armed men who chaperoned them. They would have had no idea where they were destined to end up; all they knew for sure was that every day they became weaker, hungrier and more dispirited. And so they trudged on, mile after painful mile, watching the land that they knew disappear, to be replaced by strange new vistas and a gabble of unfamiliar tongues. En route any number of measures – amulets and herbs, potions and incantations – were attempted to make the captives forget their past and render them more pliable. Even the Europeans hired medicine men to make concoctions to erase memories of home. But it was to no avail, and the captives, trudging along often for up to seven months, kept on grieving and remembering.

Throughout this reluctant march the prisoners were forced to carry the supplies that were to be traded: textiles and jewellery, pottery and cowhides. They were accompanied always by the incessant sound of clinking irons, swishing rods made of plaited reeds and cat-o'-nine-tails, as well as the cries and groans of their unfortunate companions. As the expedition progressed they watched helpless as those who were too weak to keep up were flogged or killed on the spot. Now the captives understood why people said that the slave routes to the coast were littered with the bones of the abandoned.

Along the way, the captives themselves were probably sold and resold many times, in exchange for any number of commodities: guns and brandy, beads and bracelets, pots and felt caps, knives and cowrie shells, gold dust and bolts of cloth. By the time the dejected caravan finally arrived at the coast, often after trekking hundreds of miles and passing through the hands of numerous African and European traders, its victims were instantly recognizable, by their dull eyes and emaciated bodies, bruises and ulcers, as condemned souls.

The next stage of their journey was just as terrible. For the 'Slave Coast' that served the trade – Togo, Dahomey and western Nigeria – was covered with markets, pens, and forts in which they would next be incarcerated, often for several months. Some were held in prisons called barracoons located on the beach. A little further inland, there were markets in which the spectacle of brutalized captives was there for all to see, their skin shining with palm oil and their bodies stripped of everything except neck collars and chains connecting one to the other;

while traders and ships' captains forced open their mouths and inspected their orifices for disease. Many others ended up in forts like Elmina in modern Ghana, founded by the Portuguese. Once purchased, as William Bosman, a factor who worked there, noted, the slaves were numbered and the name of the trader who delivered them was recorded. 'In the meanwhile, a burning Iron, with the arms or names of the companies, lyes in the Fire; with which ours are marked on the breast. This is done that we may distinguish them from the slaves of the English, French or others; (which are also marked with their mark) and to prevent the Negroes exchanging them for worse.' The death rate at Elmina was as high as 15 per cent, and when the fort was finally cleaned in 1972, it had accumulated on its floors a foot and a half of debris: a noxious mixture of blood and food waste, shit and sloughed-off skin.

Its English counterpart was the Cape Coast Castle, also in modern Ghana, which was built in 1674 as the headquarters of the Royal Africa Company and its successor, the company of Merchants Trading to Africa. The slaves there would endure similar treatment. The English called it a 'factory', but in reality it was a mausoleum where people were buried and were reborn as products. Deprived of everything that defined their lives and made them meaningful – friends and family, homeland and traditions – the captives were reminded that they were no longer people but commodities: things to be used and abused, sold and bartered.

When the time finally came to depart the African continent, most captives had already been enslaved for several months; and yet the Atlantic voyage – the infamous Middle Passage – was still in front of them. As they were grouped together on the shore, awaiting transportation to the huge and unfamiliar 'wooden worlds', with their imposing sails and masts, one can only imagine the sounds of the slaves' grief, and the miasma of fear that surrounded them. A terrible end awaited them, of that they were certain. Paul Isert, a surgeon stationed at a Danish slave fort neighbouring Cape Coast Castle, remarked that the slaves didn't believe the future could possibly 'hold anything good in store for them, when the Europeans use such violent measures to secure them'. But there were no concessions made to their feelings, as they were thrown, like so many bolts of cloth, one by one, into the swampy bottom of a canoe, then ferried across the harbour to be manhandled aboard by rough white hands, and tossed onto the deck of the 'floating dungeon', the label which the historian Joseph Miller gave the slave ship. The uplifting and devout names inscribed across their bows – Christ the Redeemer, Blessed, and The Lord Our Saviour – belied the chaos and hell unfolding on board.

Here, after a cursory examination by a doctor, the slaves who were deemed unfit – often because of temporary illnesses like stomach disorders or fevers – were dispatched back to the coast to die in the market, or they were thrown into the sea. Those who were approved were divided by gender. The women were left sitting on deck, grateful initially for the light and fresh air, only to discover that they were vulnerable once again to the lust of the sailors. To their profound shame, some women were raped there in front of everyone; others were taken to the men's quarters. Meanwhile, the male slaves were shackled and transported below deck, into a space that the sailors had converted into a prison. Partially loaded ships would then wait in the harbour for anything between two and seven months while the captain accumulated his full complement of slaves.

The voyage to the New World would take six to ten weeks, which meant that for many Africans the voyage was often the shortest of the numerous stages of their journey. But the evil reputation of the Atlantic crossing to the New World was none-theless deserved: the Middle Passage was truly a voyage of the damned. For the slave ship, like the gas chamber, was a diabolic innovation. Its talismans were 'instruments of woe', such as manacles and neck rings, locks and chains, cat-o'-nine-tails and the *speculum oris* (designed to prise a slave's mouth open so he could be force-fed), and its rationale was entirely commercial. Despite the traders' constant fretting over the 'perishability' of their cargo, most slavers believed that the loss of 10 per cent of their 'stock' was inevitable, so there was no point in considering their captives' comfort. They opted therefore to use a system they called 'tight packing' (as opposed to 'loose packing') which meant that the slaves were fitted together as closely as 'stones in a wall'.

The ship would have been adapted on the journey over from Britain, when the sailors worked feverishly attaching netting around the deck to contain the slaves on board and building the wooden slave quarters below. Traditionally this area was around five feet in height, which meant that most of the captives could never stand fully upright. The space was organized to hold the maximum number of slaves possible, allowing them less room to move and turn than a corpse would have in a coffin. When the weather was fair, slaves were brought up onto the main deck to consume their scant meals of beans and rice and to 'dance', a horrible euphemism for the enforced jumping and moving that passed for exercise. But most of the time they were locked in the dark and claustrophobic hold, attached to the decking by irons and ringbolts that were fixed along it at intervals. Trapped in the semi-darkness, stewing in their own filth, their wrists would almost inevitably develop ulcerated sores as their shackles chafed their bodies as they rolled around on the rough wooden planks. Held in such dank, unsanitary and painful conditions the detainees were assailed by illnesses: dysentery, fevers, malnutrition and septicaemia. As the journey progressed the smell, a terrible miasma of excrement, sweat and illness, would only thicken. It was no wonder that the sailors went about with handkerchiefs impregnated with perfume or camphor permanently pressed to their faces. Many claimed that the stench of the slave ship was such that it could be smelled five miles away downwind.

One of the few surviving accounts of these fateful voyages told from the perspective of the slave is the one that is left to us by Olaudah Equiano, whose chronicle of his capture in Africa and subseqent years as a slave in the Americas and England would later provide such a potent weapon for the abolitionist movement. Although it was written in the middle of the eighteenth century, Equiano's story provides us with an insight into the experience of the millions of others who had gone before him and would come after.

Born in central Nigeria the 1745, Equiano was eleven years old when he was captured by African raiders, bundled into a sack and taken away from his village. Sold and resold, travelling by land and river, it would be almost seven months before he arrived at the coast, 'all the while oppressed and weighed down by grief at the loss of family and friends'. The first sight of the ship that would transport him away from his homeland filled him 'with astonishment which was soon converted into terror'. Ferried to the vessel by canoe and bundled aboard by the African traders who had last purchased him, he was immediately grappled aboard by the crew members: 'white men with horrible looks, red faces and long hair'. He was then deposited on the main deck, where he sighted a huge copper boiling pot and then nearby 'a multitude of black people of every description chained together, every one of their countenances expressing dejection and sorrow'. Fearing that he had had fallen into the hands of cannibals, the child was 'overpowered with horror and anguish' and promptly fainted.

What made matters worse was the ubiquitous violence of life on a slave ship. When he could not eat the boy was flogged. He also witnessed the fate of a number of slaves who managed to jump off the ship; they were revived and then brutally whipped as an example to the others for preferring 'death to slavery'. And on one occasion he witnessed the ship's captain whip one of his sailors so severely that he eventually died. The shock that the whites could treat one of their own people 'in such a brutal fashion' made the young Equiano fear his captors even more.

But it was the account of the horrors of life below deck that would later mobilize the British population against the slave trade. When he was taken down to his quarters, the stench was so terrible that he was immediately sick. Confined below in the semi-darkness, in the extreme heat, with little light and ventilation, illness was inevitable, and when his companions began to expire, their corpses were not removed immediately, so the living were forced to share their space with the decaying dead.

In this 'hollow world', the only glimpse of light in the endless darkness was provided by Equiano's fellow slaves. Over time these people from their different parts of the African continent found ways to communicate with each other and eventually developed a strong camaraderie. The women mothered the sick and orphaned boy and his companions allayed his fear that he was going to be eaten by his captors, instead reassuring him that he was to be 'carried to these white people's country to work for them'. This news fortified the boy somewhat, and he managed to survive the long sea crossing, while all around him his fellow captives continued to expire.

When they were not dying, the slaves were fighting: for they resisted their captivity fiercely, evading the nets to leap overboard, organizing rebellions, and fighting with the seamen. Although the sailors were free to move about the ship, in many ways they too were damned men. From the earliest days of slaving 'Guineamen', as the slave ships were known, were shunned by many seamen because of the length of the voyages, the high mortality on board, and distaste for 'the trade'. Thus many of the crew were reluctant recruits who had been inveigled aboard by 'crimps'. These unscrupulous labour agents worked hand in hand with tavern keepers to ply the men with drink and whores until they were hopelessly in debt. The poor victims were then forced to either 'sign articles' or face a debtors' prison. Inevitably these resentful and depressed recruits did not make the most conscientious employees and were famous for their hostility to the hard work and fearful conditions of life on a slaver. It was no wonder that the state licensed ships' captains to use corporal punishment to maintain 'subordination and regularity'; or that the commander, intimidated by both his crew and his cargo, often resorted to the most draconian discipline. Thus everyone aboard a slave ship seemed to be in a perpetual state of war with each other, and extensive casualties were suffered on all sides.

The African coasts were often referred to as a 'white man's grave', but on board ship things were even worse, as sailors died almost as readily as the slaves, and a ship's captain who survived four African journeys counted himself extremely fortunate. As the historian Joseph Miller has said, the Middle Passage was a 'way of death'. But, of course, it was the cargo that died most extravagantly, from infection, flogging or despair. The terrible mortality rate would continue when they arrived in the New World, where they would die of overwork in the cane fields, of malnutrition in the quarters, of brutality, trauma and disease everywhere. What made matters worse was that these deaths were not always intentional or even malicious. Slaves were not even significant enough for this: a direct campaign of hate. Instead the captives, whom traders dubbed 'the commodity that dies with ease', perished because they did not matter. The indifference of those involved in the trade meant that they were unwilling to invest any thought, money or care in keeping the slaves alive, and the mass loss of life was regarded merely as the inevitable wastage associated with the transatlantic commerce in the 'black gold'.

6

*Racism rests upon and functions as a kind of seesaw: the
persecutor rises by debasing and inferiorizing his victim.*
                                        Albert Memi

Barbados was important not because it was the first society with
slaves, but because it was the first slave society in the English
Americas: that is, it was the first society that was entirely organized
around its slave system and, as such, it would become the model
for the plantation system throughout the Americas. As Hilary
Beckles has argued, the country's economic structure was totally
based on the labour of enslaved Africans. Its political structure
as well as its system of governance was organized around the
control and management of an enslaved majority, while the
moral, ethical and ideological values of the society were entirely
developed and shaped to reproduce the system of slavery.

The process of becoming a 'slave society' had begun back in
the 1630s, when the then governor, Henry Hawley, had tried
to clarify the length of time a slave should serve; but it wasn't
until the population explosion of the late 1650s that detailed
regulation of the enslaved became a necessity. The result was
the 1661 Act 'For the Better Ordering and Governing of
Negroes'. The historian Richard Dunn has described this as
'the most important surviving piece of legislation in the English
islands during the seventeenth century because it was the first

comprehensive attempt to create a slave law with which to govern the island'. It thus provided both a means for policing the enslaved population and a rationale for instituting special laws. As such it was copied in the rest of the English Caribbean and in the English American colonies. It justified its provisions with racial denigration, declaring blacks to be 'a heathenish, brutish, uncertain and dangerous kind of people'. And since it asserted that the lawmakers 'could find in the body of English law . . . no tract to guide us where to walk nor any rule set as how to govern such slaves', the colonists felt free to both revive old laws and create new ones that they believed were 'absolutely needful for the public safety'.

The management of slave societies was, as this Act indicated, no simple matter. The African captives vigorously and persistently resisted their enslaved condition, so the country's stability rested upon an elaborate system of repression maintained not by consensus but by coercion and cruelty. Drafted by the local slave holders and ratified in Britain by a government that stood to profit from the trade, the laws were then passed in the colonies by elected assemblies dominated by elite slave owners, and enforced on individual plantations by drivers, overseers and planters and in the wider society by a well-financed militia, urban constables and garrisoned soldiers.

The implications of the English slave laws were in stark contrast to some of the other legal frameworks that evolved in the region. The French Code Noir, whose sixty-plus articles were drawn up by King Louis XIV in 1685, guaranteed a slave's right to life and social identity (however poorly this was protected), while the Spanish Siete Partidas, which the historian Franklin Knight described as a 'liberal Code', recognized and accepted the 'personality of the slave' and held aloft 'the idea of liberty'. No such humane ideas were encoded in the laws of the English territories, where the priority was the protection of the planters' property rights and their safety.

The Barbados slave code of 1661 was supplemented over time, with new provisions being added in an ad hoc fashion, often in response to infractions by the black population. In 1676, the year after a slave revolt, an Act was passed which included new capital offences, placed additional restrictions on the movement of enslaved peoples, put strict limits on hiring them out and controlled their involvement in petty trading in places like markets and in their practice of artisan trades like carpentry.

The 1688 Act 'For the Governing of Negroes' was also a response to an earlier revolt in which black slaves and Irish white servants had joined forces. The Act's fateful preamble begins:

> Whereas the Plantations and Estates of this Island cannot be fully managed . . . without the labour and service of great number of Negroes and other slaves and inasmuch as [they] . . . are of a barbarous, wild and savage nature, and such as renders them wholly unqualified to be governed by the Laws, Customes and Practices of our Nation: It therefore becoming absolutely necessary, that such other Constitutions, Laws and Orders, should be in this Island framed and enacted for the good regulating or ordering of them, as may both restrain the disorders, rapines and inhumanities to which they are naturally prone and inclined.

The Act charged every planter with searching the slave cabins on his property weekly and burning any drums or horns, which could be used to call them together; while every fortnight the quarters were also to be searched for fugitives, weapons and stolen goods. No enslaved person could leave the plantation on which he or she lived without a ticket from a white person in authority, specifying the time for his or her return. Any person found without one was to be whipped. Armed posses could be raised to hunt down blacks who had absconded; so the sound and sight of a pack of men and hounds in search of runaways was as familiar in the Caribbean as it was in the American South.

Four years later another conspiracy provoked another rash of Barbadian laws. The death penalty was revived for some categories of runaway slaves. Prohibitions against slaves obtaining strong drink were put in place because 'many enormities were committed' and 'mischief hatched and contrived' under its influence. Those slaves willing to inform on slave rebellions were rewarded with freedom and even relocation.

As well as establishing an elaborate framework of punishment to control slave behaviour, the Barbados slave laws clarified some important ideological issues. One of these was the status of the slave vis-à-vis that of the indentured servant. Slaves were classified in law as 'chattels' or property, meaning that they could be bought and sold, leased or used as collateral. White servants, on the other hand, were only property during the length of their indenture. When it was completed, their rights as human beings were reinstated. And though the behaviour of indentured servants was carefully controlled during the period of their contract, they were also allowed many privileges that were denied their black counterparts. Their food rations, clothing allowances and overall treatment were better. Legally, too, they were better protected. If they were charged with a crime they were entitled to trial before a jury, while the slaves were judged by the planters. Blacks who threatened, assaulted or stole from a white person faced extreme penalties: whipping, the loss of a hand, the loss of an ear; while an indentured servant who killed a slave was potentially merely subject to a fine, like the rest of the white population.

By differentiating so sharply between the rights and treatment of their black and white workers, the Barbadian proprietors set up a legal system in which racism was encoded. Instead of being regarded as a rather unappetizing rag-tag assortment of felons, refractory Irish and rebellious Scots, the indentured servants were now collectively protected as 'white' people. (The latter term was so unfamiliar at the time that one pamphleteer writing for an audience in the mother country felt it necessary to explain that it was used to describe Europeans living in the region.) The impact of this legislation was to separate the interests of the two groups and to stop black and white people fraternizing socially with one another. This, the planters fervently hoped, would make it less likely that the two groups would combine together and so overwhelm their masters.

If the Barbadians helped to invent the concept of 'whiteness' and the privileges intrinsically connected with it, they also by extension helped to invent 'blackness' and its associated dis-advantages. And so the transformation in the make-up of Barbados and the resultant racialization of its laws changed both the island and the world. It also reshaped George Ashby's inner life. He was increasingly aware of himself not just as a man but as a 'white man'. In this society, his colour, which he would have given little thought to in his old life, was becoming the most important determinant of his identity. Simultaneously the island's slaves, who had previously thought of themselves as Kuba or Coromantee or Ibo, now had to accustom themselves to their new identity as 'blacks'. Soon the dichotomy of black and white became the defining factor in every encounter and every conflict on the island.

Another important issue that was thrashed out in Barbados was that slaves would serve for life and in perpetuity, passing their status down to their children and their children's children. This harsh decision profoundly differentiated the black slaves' experience from not just the white servants on the island but many of the enslaved peoples in history; for the Africans in Barbados it was a case of once a slave always a slave, and there was no prospect of escape from this destiny, even for one's children.

The colonists also redefined how slave status would be transmitted. In contrast to the patrilineal tradition of their homeland, the Barbadians decided that status should be taken from the mother. This meant that white men could continue to have sexual relationships with their black female slaves, without worrying that the offspring of these liaisons might claim freedom by means of their paternity. Slave owners could carry on fraternizing with their female workers with impunity, knowing that there would be no unpleasant legal or financial consequences to their behaviour, and they would not have to endure the embarrassment of policing other men's sexual behaviour or their own. White women who transgressed, however, were censured not just for their licentious behaviour but for compromising the entire structure of society.

These slave laws provide an extraordinary mirror of Barbadian society at the time, enabling us to see how slaves lived and the range of activities in which they engaged, as well as the beliefs held by the planters and what they felt about their 'slave property'. Through the development of these laws we can chart not just what the ruling caste thought was happening in this society but also what they feared would happen. We can also see how their attitudes evolved. During these years the Barbados settlers transformed their laws, cultural mores and financial system to make race-based slavery the very foundation of their way of life. Whiteness became associated with social superiority and blackness with poverty and inferiority. Even white indentured servants, who previously might have felt empathy for their fellow black labourers, were now encouraged, by virtue of their shared skin colour, to identify with their oppressors instead. And thus Barbadian society became entirely predicated upon race.

★

As was to be expected, the Ashby family, along with the vast majority of white settlers, became slave owners during this period. One can only imagine the debates around the family table as they discussed the pros and cons of this decision. A modest family like theirs would have had to dig deep in order to find the money. Then there was the fear of sharing their homestead with such a 'barbarous and refractory' people. But whatever reservations they held, George Ashby or one of his sons eventually made the journey to Bridgetown, where the traumatized slaves were being sold, according to Ligon, 'straight from the ship like horses at a market'. In a desperate attempt to make them appear more healthy, the sailors would have shaved the slaves' heads, covered their sores and oiled their skin to remove the ashen hue it had taken on during the long and dreadful Middle Passage. Those who were suffering from dysentery would often have their bottoms plugged to disguise their symptoms. So the slaves stood, arranged in rows, shuddering and silent with shock. Once the auction began, planters examined the slaves like so much cattle, palpating their muscles, checking their orifices, forcing their hands into their mouths to examine their teeth.

Then the bidding started. Prices varied: the highest were for healthy young males and those with plantations skills. The second most desirable category would be the young women who appeared strong enough for field work or who had skills as seamstresses or cooks. Beautiful girls were also dear. Babies were cheap because they were unlikely to survive. For those slaves who were left over, there was what was known as 'the scramble'. After paying an agreed price, the planters would rush around throwing cords with numbers around the necks of the terrified captives they had chosen. Then the purchased slaves were led away. For the islanders, this was a shopping expedition; for the slaves, this was yet another 'moment of rupture', according to one historian, 'this time of the bonds that had been formed among the enslaved on the ship, during the stay on the coast and the Middle Passage . . . [So] as the cords tightened and pulled them away, the enslaved tried to hold fast, to their family members, friends and comrades, without success.' One observer captured the terrible moment in a poem:

> One dreadful shriek assaults th' affrighted sky,
> As to their friends the parted victims cry.
> With imprecating screams of horror wild,
> The frantick mother calls her sever'd child.

Thus the slaves' journey to the New World ended as it had begun: in a welter of grief, fear and horror. For those who were not purchased, because of ill health or old age, the end of the story was even worse. They were often thrown overboard, and some jumped to their deaths in order to avoid further suffering.

It is interesting that a nation that so highly prized and protected its own freedoms found it so easy to reconcile itself to the imprisonment of others. And certainly it can be argued that conditions in the New World placed these Englishmen in a moral quandary to which they were ill equipped to respond. But time and again the colonists adapted their morality to justify their actions, and, prompted by venality and prejudice, forged a system that was a betrayal of natural law and accepted ethics.

Some white colonizers felt disquiet on their first encounter with the slave trade. For example, when the planter John Pinney arrived from Dorset in the late seventeeth century and went to buy slaves in neighbouring St Christopher, he found it an unsettling experience. 'I can assure you,' he wrote home to a friend, 'I was shocked at the first appearance of human flesh exposed to sale.' Immediately, however, he reasons this away. 'But surely God ordained them for the use and benefits of us:

otherwise his divine will would have been made manifest by some particular sign or token.'

Whether George Ashby or his children felt a similar unease is unknown. If so, they, like John Pinney, certainly got over it: by the census of 1680 the family had a total of nine slaves, in addition to one indentured servant, working their land. And most of the surviving records from the Ashby family during this period concern their various slave transactions. These deeds and wills prove that slave holdings, just as much as land, were considered an integral part of the family's wealth, to be bought, sold and exchanged when necessary. In a deed dated 25 March 1687, George Ashby the younger sold his loving mother Deborah Hutton four Negro slaves for the sum of £40. She in turn bequeathed the said slaves – Jack, Betty, Little Jack and Goffe – to her second son, William Ashby, to be transferred to him by deed of gift on her death. In 1690 another deed was lodged, in which 'eight slaves and 2 acres of land' were used as security on a payment Deborah made to her eldest son, George. In 1692 George Ashby the younger, 'for the real love, goodwill and affection' which he had for his wife-to-be Dorothy Nusum, sold six acres of land in the parish of St Philip 'with all appurtenances and one Negro man'; the funds from this sale were to go to providing for Dorothy's maintenance.

Having put aside his scruples, John Pinney was able to congratulate himself on being a compassionate owner, though he was still clearly unable to see his enslaved workers as anything more than possessions: 'It is unnecessary I flatter myself,' he wrote in his standing instructions to his managers, 'to say a word respecting the care of slaves and stock – your good sense must tell you they are the sinews of a plantation and must claim your particular care and attention. Humanity tempered with justice towards the former must ever be exercised, and when sick I am satisfied they will experience every kindness from you, they surely deserve it, being the very means of our support.' The 'latter' he added without a break in the paragraph, 'must be kept clean of ticks'.

While the rules of engagement between blacks and whites were being forged, it was a strange and uneasy time on the island. Just as the early white settlers of Barbados had not gone to the New World with the expectation of becoming slavers, so too their black captives had no idea how to 'be' slaves. The two groups therefore had to invent the rules of this uneven relationship via trial and error over an extended period of time.

For most slaves, the process began with another long and enervating journey to their new owner's plantation, where they arrived disorientated, grief-stricken and brutalized. There, planters like George Ashby stripped them of their African names and assigned them a slave name which must have sounded like gibberish to their ears and rolled uncomfortably off their tongue. The symbolism of this was profound. For a man's name is more than just a way of calling him: it is the verbal symbol of his whole identity, indicating his place in his family and community. To separate a person from his name effectively 'killed' his old self. The new name, chosen by the planter, also carried its own message. The patterns of naming across the Americas were often deliberately insulting and careless. Slaves from one region were given names from another, while many of these African names acquired pejorative meanings: Quarshee, a day-name that originally meant Sunday in Akan, came to signify a stupid, lazy slave; Cudjo, which was the Akan day-name for Monday, came to mean a drunkard. Many slave names in the ledgers of the Jamaican plantation Worthy Park were disconcertingly similar to those of its cattle.

But the slave's new name was only one of the emblems of his transformed position. In many American slave societies, new purchases were routinely branded to make their enslaved status clear. Captives were identifiable in other ways. In most of the sugar islands their clothes, made from cheap cloth such as osnaburg (a type of coarse linen), instantly marked them out as part of the enslaved population. Many sugar societies also had sumptuary laws that forbade slaves from wearing certain things, such as shoes or precious metals like gold. Most significant, of course, was the slaves' colour, for across the Americas being non-white immediately associated one with the slave community.

But the most important transformation that the slave underwent was not material but psychological: the system was designed to transform the way he saw himself and perceived his own interests. From his earliest days on the island, the slave was discouraged from speaking his language, prohibited from practising his religion, and prevented from living in the manner to which he had previously been accustomed. The slave, therefore, had a past but not a heritage. As the historian Orlando Patterson explains: 'Slaves differed from other human beings in that they were not allowed freely to integrate the experience of their ancestors into their lives, or to inform their understanding of social reality with the inherited meanings of their natural forebears, or to anchor the living present in any conscious community of memory.' With such a brutal assault on their physical and psychological self, it was unsurprising that almost a third of slaves died within that first year, expiring because of suicide, abuse or grief.

Communication on the plantations was also a fundamental problem. This first generation of blacks would have known no English, so they would not have been able to speak to their owner nor he to them. They may have fared no better with their fellow captives. The slaves that were brought to Barbados or any other part of the Americas had no understanding of themselves as 'African' or 'black' people. And why should they? The African continent encompasses more than thirty million square kilometres and includes a stupendous variety of peoples with different appearances, beliefs and cultures. To speak of 'African culture' or 'African religion' implies a unity and a uniformity that simply do not exist. Thus the men and women who arrived in Barbados, sometimes taken from very different ethnic groups, often met each other as foreigners, traumatized strangers thrown together in a strange and hostile land.

What an odd, uneasy little household the Ashbys must have been. As the family struggled to raise their children and make enough money to keep them, they shared their living space with people who had neither a common language nor a common backround. Conversation on the farm would have been desultory, difficult and largely one-way, enacted by a series of pantomimes and gestures, and abetted by a few swiftly taught commands and the use of the lash. And then there was the indentured servant, who was neither relative, friend nor slave, and thus had a somewhat ambiguous social place in the domestic unit. These different groups must have circled each other nervously, in a welter of misunderstanding, resentment and misery: lonely as islands.

This unease was exacerbated by the misconceptions each group held about the other. Though there had been a smattering of blacks in England since Elizabethan times, many Englishmen would never have seen a black face before arriving in the Americas and they brought with them a hotchpotch of ideas about blacks that were predominantly negative. Sixteenth- and seventeenth-century English explorers frequently described the Africans they encountered as a 'brutish', 'beastly' and 'savage people'. They regarded their nakedness as a mark of their lewdness and immorality, and their skin colour as a mark of sin, depravity and evil. Religion too played its part: unable to comprehend the complex belief systems of the Africans they encountered, the Europeans dismissed them as 'heathens' and 'devil worshippers'. Indeed many Europeans, particularly the slave owners of the New World, called upon the Bible to justify the practice, citing the 'curse of Ham' passage in Genesis, in which Noah condemns his son Ham to eternal slavery. In their version Ham is understood to be the progenitor of the black line of humanity, so the story justifies the persecution of all black people. But this was an interpretation of convenience, and the same passage has also been used to condemn other groups, including Jews.

In turn, Africans had negative impressions of white people. On first encountering white slavers, many blacks saw them as diabolical figures, dubbing them 'white devils'. They were repelled by the paleness of their skin and the hairiness of their bodies; one chieftain claimed that they looked like 'sea-monsters'. And, as we have seen, Olaudah Equiano firmly believed, along with many of his fellow captives, that whites 'were cannibals who were capturing them in order to eat them'. As well as lamenting Europeans' lack of cleanliness, the slaves associated their pale skins with death, the other world or ghosts (what the slaves called 'duppy spirits').

The sprinkling of American Indians among the body of the enslaved added to this farrago of misunderstanding and hostility and influenced the way Europeans handled their slaves. It was regarded as best to treat the Indians gently as they were 'apt to die out of pure grief if they be put to more than ordinary hardship'. In contrast, it was believed that blacks should be 'kept in awe by threats and blows for if a man grow too familiar with them, they are apt to take advantage of it and abuse that familiarity; but if they be chastised with moderation when they have done something amiss, they will become better, more submissive and more compliant . . . and think better of their masters'. All these stereotypes were of course weapons to justify the subjugation of the slaves and make them even more strange and other to the colonists.

It is impossible to know whether George Ashby was a severe or considerate master, but the island's planters had a poor reputation in this respect. As enthusiastic entrepreneurs they were ever eager to maximize profits and minimize costs. So they were perpetually torn between the need to protect the well-being of their slaves, who represented a sizeable capital investment, and the desire to cut costs for short-term profit. In the end, the latter imperative usually won out, and this, combined with a goodly dash of racial hostility, meant the slaves were fed and housed poorly, and provided with inadequate medical treatment. They were malnourished and vulnerable to disease; their health was so degraded that in these early years of slavery they were largely infertile and their lifespan in captivity was a mere seven to ten years. This inability of most slave populations in the region to reproduce in turn prompted the shipment of even more slaves to take their place.

Father Labat, a French priest seconded to the Antilles who wrote extensively about his travels around the islands, including a stay in Barbados, wrote:

> The English take very little care of their slaves and feed them very badly. The majority give their slaves Saturday to work on their own account so as to satisfy their own needs and their families. The overseers make them work beyond measure and beat them mercilessly for the least fault, and they seem to care less for the life of a Negro than that of a horse.

He continued: 'They are rigorously punished for the least disobedience and more so if they rebel, which does not prevent this happening very often because of the behaviour of their drunken, unreasonable and savage overseers.' On these occasions, 'Those who are captured and sent to prison are condemned to be passed through the mill, burned alive or exposed in iron cages in which they are packed and . . . attached

to the branch of a tree, or, are left to die of hunger and thirst.'
Though Labat admitted that 'these torments were cruel', he
nonetheless cautioned against

> condemning the inhabitants of islands of whatever
> nationality they may be. They are often compelled to
> exceed the limits of moderation in the punishment of
> their slaves so as to intimidate the others and to impress
> fear and dutifulness upon them to prevent them becoming
> the victims of such men, who being usually ten to one
> white man, are always ready to rebel and attempt to
> commit the most terrible crimes to regain their freedom.

The growth of the slave population had not only changed
the face of Barbados, it had also altered the atmosphere of the
colony. With so many different groups struggling to carve out
new identities for themselves – or adjust to the ones that had
been forced upon them – the tension on the island had been
ratcheted up considerably. Barbados had become a place riven by
inequality and teetering permanently on the brink of violence.

7

Sugar is the very Soul of the Place.

Richard Ligon

Within a decade or so of arriving, George Ashby and his fellow settlers found their island not just dominated by sugar, but utterly transformed by it. Across the length and breadth of Barbados, field after field that had once cultivated tobacco was now covered in a sea of rustling green cane. Sugar was now the economic engine of island, the basis on which deals were made and on which goods and services were valued. So when George Ashby traded with his friends or purchased supplies in Bridgetown, he was expected to pay with this new commodity. Most importantly, it permeated the minds of the people who surrounded him, influencing their choices and inflaming their hopes for a more prosperous future. In trading depots and tippling houses, even at church, they debated the relative merits of the crop. They gossiped about who had 'gone over' to sugar and who was going to; above all they speculated about how much money their fellows were making. They could think about little else.

The first to convert had been the big planters. The economies of scale associated with sugar production meant that those with a large acreage and an established workforce were inevitably in a stronger position than small men like George Ashby. Starting up such a venture required at least a thousand pounds (a huge sum at that time) to pay for the mill and its equipment, which included the coppers in the boiling house and the boosts and drips in the cooling house, as well as the carts, hoes, pickaxes and machetes. If they did not have the ready cash personally, the elite planters had the collateral and the contacts to raise it, and sugar soon enriched them beyond their wildest imaginings. Small men could only look on in wonder at the lifestyles of these new sugar magnates as they built beautiful new homes that dominated the vistas of the island. From his modest acreage, George Ashby would have watched as Drax Hall, the first and most enduring paean to sugar, was constructed.

Colonel James Drax was a man who epitomized the aspirations of the neophyte planters. He was the emblematic planter of the age, his meteoric rise fuelling the dreams of more recent arrivals. According to legend, Drax arrived, impoverished and desperate, among the first generation of colonists in the the late 1620s. He and a handful of his fellows sheltered in a cave and supplemented their scant provisions by hunting and fishing. They cleared a piece of land on which they planted tobacco, shipping the crop to England and making a healthy profit because the commodity was at that time scarce. It was a large enough sum for Drax to buy forty or fifty indentured servants who worked the land for him. Aware that Barbadian tobacco was not the best on the market, and that the North American mainland was producing a superior product, Drax experimented with a number of other crops until he plumped for sugar.

His was one of the plantations on which the new crop had first been trialled. After numerous expensive errors, Drax finally got it right. Soon Colonel Drax began to boast that he would not think of returning home to England until he was worth £10,000 a year. He swiftly exceeded even this exalted total. The French priest Antoine Biet noted that Drax was held in such esteem on the island that when he did leave to visit

England in the 1650s, he 'was accompanied to his ship by more than two hundred of the island's most important people . . . all well mounted and marching two by two in a column headed by Drax and the island's Governor'.

According to Biet, the elite sugar planters 'all lived like little princes', driving around in grand coaches and wearing the finest clothes. Since they were able to delegate most of the estate's labour to their servants and slaves, these men led pleasant lives, with ample time to enjoy pursuits like hunting, fishing and paying calls. They were the Russian oligarchs of their day, ludicrously rich and determined to show it.

Their hospitality was legendary. In a feast thrown by Colonel Drax for Richard Ligon (who despite his financial travails was sufficiently the gentleman that he was much feted by the planters), the guests were presented with a menu that included beef – a rarity on the island – served in fourteen different ways. Some cuts were roasted, breaded or boiled, while the tongue and tripe were made into pies 'seasoned with sweet Herbs finely minc'd, Suet, Spice and Currans'. After this course was completed, another was brought in, which featured among its delights a 'shoulder of a young Goat', 'A Kid with a pudding in its belly', as well as 'a loin of veal and eight turtle doves'. The next course included Spanish bacon, pickled oysters, caviar, anchovies and olives. To finish there were desserts such as cheesecakes, tansies and custards, as well as fruit platters that included bananas, guavas, custard apples and prickly pears. All of this was washed down by a dizzying array of beverages: local tipples like mobbie and rum, as well as 'all the drinks available in a privileged home in England' such as brandy, white and Rhenish wine and sherry or 'red sack'. As opulent as these spreads were, the decoration of these planters' homes was often a bit patchy, with touches of great ostentation in the form of Smyrna carpets and rich hangings set in vast but rather neglected rooms. This reflected the rather contingent nature of settlement in the colonies during these years; many planters were loath to spend too much on possessions that were not portable, since they planned to return home once they had made their fortune.

There were just enough tantalizing role models like Drax to sustain the fantasies of the hopefuls now flooding into the island. But in reality it was difficult to succeed in the sugar industry without a certain amount of capital. The great sugar magnates were generally not self-made; they arrived with some funds with which to seed their plantation venture. The most notable of these was the aristocratic Christopher Codrington (1649–98). The scion of feudal magnates of Gloucestershire, he built up one of most profitable estates in these the earliest and most lucrative days of the island's sugar conversion. His son, also called Christopher (1668–1710), followed in his father's footsteps. Educated in Britain, he went on to become an Oxford scholar. On his return to Barbados he became a councillor at twenty-six and was made deputy governor at the youthful age of twenty-nine. He later moved to Antigua to exploit that island's nascent sugar industry. At the time of his premature death in 1710 he was described as 'the richest and most splendid of all early West Indian Grandees'. More philanthropically inclined than his father, he left his two Barbadian plantations, including their slaves, to the Church of England to fund a theological and medical college for young white Barbadian men. The product of this legacy, the immense and graceful Codrington College, remains the most noticeable artefact of the golden age of Barbadian sugar.

The success of the big planters inspired the middling and smaller planters to follow suit and by the 1660s nearly the whole island was covered with sugar cane estates. A sense of desperation bedevilled these men; they had come here to get rich, and now the opportunity to do so had finally presented itself. If they didn't jump on the sugar train now they feared they might be left behind. George Ashby was no exception.

How does one stand by a gold rush and not hunger for gold? But how could he finance this venture? Men like him who relied solely on their own physical toil to amass their fortunes were at a distinct disadvantage, so they had to plan their strategy carefully. George Ashby chose a gradual, rather stealthy entrée into the sugar industry, ploughing his profits back into further land acquisitions, thereby painstakingly extending his holdings, until he had acquired an impressive nineteen acres.

George also found other methods of getting his hands on land to cultivate. A deed registered on 23 May 1660 demonstrates that, in his modest way, he was becoming something of a sugar entrepreneur. It detailed an agreement with Ralph Kersey, 'a tailor', for the seven-year rental of eight and a half acres of Kersey's land. At the end of the contractual period the land would revert to Kersey, but the profits that the land had yielded would go to George Ashby and his business partner. It was a wealth-generating strategy that was exploited by many of those who did not have enough capital to buy new land outright, or could not find properties adjacent to their holdings available for sale.

The success of the sugar crop over the following decade saw the island's status transformed from a beautiful backwater colony to the star of the English overseas possessions. The impact of sugar on the mother country was equally profound. According to the historian Larry Gragg, in 1634 only 5 per cent of London's imports came from the Americas, but from the 1660s the transporting of sugar and tobacco dominated England's overseas trade. Though most of this sugar was earmarked for domestic use, almost 40 per cent was re-exported. In turn this generated profits for English shipping, ports and merchants in the form of freight, commission, and handling charges. Ports in London and Bristol expanded to accommodate this new business. Jobs in shipbuilding boomed, with greater demand for crews as well as skilled tradesmen like shipwrights, carpenters, sail-makers and gun-makers. Sugar refineries opened up and by 1695 there were nearly thirty of them in England processing ten million pounds of muscovado annually. Other trades also expanded – from hat-makers to haberdashers – to meet the needs of the newly enriched planters and merchants.

Thomas Tryon, an Anabaptist who visited Barbados in 1663, summed up sugar's importance to Britain enthusiastically: this 'excellent Juice,' he wrote, 'is of much more importance than all other Fruits and Spices imported to us,' arguing that 'No one could be insensible as to how sugar had enriched the Kings purse.' In addition, he claimed: 'Sugar finds an Employment for many Thousands in England it self, [such] as . . . Sugar-Bakers or Distillers, Coopers, Grocers yea and many Ladies who had more sugar in their kitchen than Confectioner shops had in former days.' It was also extremely useful to apothecaries, 'since more than half of their Medicines are mixed and compounded with Sugar'. In short, he concluded:

> it spreads its generous and sweet influences thro' the whole Nation; and there are but few Eatables or Drinkables that it is not a Friend to, or capable to confederate with: And upon the whole, as there is no Commodity whatever, that doth so much to encourage Navigation, Advance the Kings Customs, and our Land, and is at the same time of so great and Universal Use, Virtue and Advantage as this King of Sweets.

In Barbados, the transformation was not just economic and environmental, but social and cultural too. Bewitched by the financial potential of sugar, the atmosphere in the island became feverish. Prompted by news of what great profits there were to be made out of the crop, new colonists were flooding into the island. In a tumult of desire and expectation they arrived, hoping to cash in on the sugar boom. Blinded by their dreams of what they would do once they had made their fortune, they struggled to gain what toeholds they could in the new industry. It did not matter that sugar planting and its attendant exploitation of black Africans was desperately hard work, full of drudgery and boredom and debasement; they came anyway. If they didn't have the funds to finance a plantation they took jobs as managers; if they didn't have the skills to be managers they became bookkeepers; and if not bookkeepers they became overseers. Others realized that there was a killing to be made in the innumerable businesses that functioned on the periphery of the sugar industry: slave trading, sugar processing and shipping.

There was a new pace to island life and a new intensity to its commerce. Taverns sprang up to provide lodging and libation for those who came to work in the industry, make deals, or visit relatives. Warehouses started up in Bridgetown to sell harvesting equipment and the merchants pitched up to sell them. Physicians arrived to care for their health; lawyers came to litigate their business affairs. Some of the new arrivals had been dispatched by relatives who wanted rid of them; and so the sugar colonies became a repository for footloose second sons, delinquent debtors, legally compromised uncles and unwanted orphans. All came on the chance that they might become rich men. That many of these hopefuls would eventually leave the island disappointed and disillusioned did not at this point matter one jot; they were gamblers all, each convinced that he would be the one to beat the odds and strike it rich.

George Ashby must have been swept up in this frenzy and shared the belief held by almost all the islanders that sugar could transform their fortunes and make *everyone* wealthy. Certainly his plot of land was now a great deal more valuable than it had previously been. For a man like him, it must have felt like such a vindication; at a stroke, his decision to migrate to Barbados and his years of struggle were justified: he was finally in the right place at the right time.

*

But the 'white gold' created unrest as well as wealth across Barbadian society. Men who had previously been content to be tobacco or cotton farmers could no longer countenance such a humble fate. Their beloved plots of land were no longer just 'competences', places that would provide them with sustenance and independence; instead, through the alchemy of sugar, they were transformed into potential gold mines that owed them riches.

In fact, the leisurely and lavish lifestyles of the plantocracy were miles away from those of 'the more inconsiderable of the Inhabitants', like George Ashby, who were still 'forced to earn their bread with the labour of their hands and the sweat of their brows'. For many of these men sugar had improved their finances somewhat but had not radically changed their day-to-day lives. They still rose at dawn and spent their days labouring alongside their bedraggled servants in an effort to make sure their property was yielding as much as it could and therefore provide the best possible future for their families.

Barbados was no longer a society of peasant farmers like George Ashby, struggling alongside one another to stay solvent; it was now a rigidly hierarchical society. At the top were the elite planters, who were reinventing themselves according to an aristocratic model derived from the feudal culture that they remembered from back home, and which shaped their attitudes and behaviour. They dominated the political, military and financial infrastructure of the island, where they held high ranks in the government, militia and Vestry. Beneath them was a middling group of planters and merchants who acted as something of a buffer between the elites and the poorer planters who were struggling to keep their heads above water. The sugar industry was creating extremes of wealth and poverty that would eventually produce a yawning gap between those at the top and those at the bottom, with diastrous consequences. Already, the most successful Barbadians were aware that their new-found riches were increasing the threat from the enemy within their own plantations: that toxic brew of resentful labour made up of disgruntled indentured servants who realized that they would never be able to afford land on the island, and the huge number of exploited and abused slaves, many of them freshly transported from Africa, who carried rebellion in their hearts.

Meanwhile, the rise of sugar not only attracted a flood of migrants into the island; it also prompted another, substantial stream of people to leave it. Some of these were second and third sons with no chance of inheriting the family plantation, but most were ex-indentured servants, without land or prospects, or struggling smallholders who had sold out to bigger planters when they realized that their plots of land simply weren't big enough to make a fortune from sugar. It was no surprise then that Barbados became known as 'the nursery for planting other places'. The islanders sometimes moved to other less populous islands, but most frequently they went to North America; indeed many areas, such as the Carolinas, were largely settled by Barbadians. These migrants took with them knowledge of the plantation system and the blueprint of how to organize and manage a large number of slaves. Thus it could be said that Barbados was 'the laboratory' for the slave and plantation system in many parts of America where cotton, tobacco and rice were later grown.

Not everyone was impressed with the quality of these new arrivals. A Carolinian parish priest wrote: 'They are a perfect medley or hotch potch, made up of bankrupt pirates, decayed libertines, sectaries and enthusiasts of all sorts who have transported themselves hither and are the most factious and seditious people in the whole world.' But these questionable, rather unsavoury migrants kept on coming. By the final decades of the century almost half the whites and considerably more than half of the blacks (slaves brought over by their masters) in the Carolina colony had come from Barbados. A 1685 map of Berkeley County shows that of thirty-three prominent land-holders, twenty-four had connections with Barbados. Their economic and political dominance of the Carolinas was such that contemporaries complained that 'the Barbadians endeavour to rule all'.

The Barbadians' attraction to the mainland was easy to understand. For the small man, according to the historian Richard Dunn, migration to 'Carolina opened possibilities undreamed of in Barbados'. John Collins, for example, found that the sale of his modest plot of land in Barbados allowed him to stake out 290 acres in the Carolinas. He ascended the social ladder swiftly, served on a Carolina grand jury in 1692 and became a captain of the Charleston militia in 1700. John Ladson, another arrival in 1679 of undistinguished Barbados lineage, rose to be a leading figure in the House of Assembly in the 1690s. The descendants of substantial Barbados planters did even better, according to Richard Dunn. All in all, six Barbadians were governors of South Carolina between 1670 and 1730.

The island's imprint on the Carolinas is evident in numerous areas. Some argue that Barbadian derived linguistic influences were taken to South Carolina and are evident in the Gullah dialect. If that idea is contentious, there is no doubt about the Barbadian influence on place names in the region, from Hilton Head, named after the explorer William Hilton, to Colleton County, named after the Barbadian grandee of that name, and Barbados House in Charleston. And when the first slave laws of Carolina were enacted on 16 March 1696, it was clear that they were modelled on those ratified in Barbados in 1688.

George Ashby's own son, also called as George, tried settling in Pennsylvania during this period, probably for the same reasons as other small planters. That he ultimately returned to Barbados does not undermine the allure of migration to the mainland for white settlers from the island. As the historian John Camden Hotten concluded: 'Barbados played a unique role in the settlement of colonial America. Thousands upon thousands of Englishmen, Scotsmen, Welshmen and Irishmen sailed first to that small West Indian Island before immigrating to the mainland colonies.' Whether these immigrants were rich or poor, Quakers or Jews, had lived in Barbados only briefly or came from an established family there, they would later plant deep and lasting roots right across the American mainland, from New England to New Jersey and from Virginia to Georgia.

*Come let us make a hell of our own, and try how long
we can bear it.*

Blackbeard

With no small help from his hard-worked slaves, George
Ashby was beginning to forge a relatively prosperous life. But
he couldn't help feeling somewhat frustrated: the island kept
betraying him. In seventeenth-century Barbados, it seemed as if
some unexpected drama, eruption of violence or natural disaster
was always occuring. And he was not alone in his dismay.
George Ashby and his contemporaries had done their best to
create an orderly and organized society – taming a wilderness,
commissioning imposing public buildings, establishing a
well-run Assembly and Senate, as well as drafting law after
law designed to control everything from fornication to slave
behaviour. And yet, Barbados continued to remain a dangerous
and unpredictable place, threatened perpetually from without
and within.

During this, the first phase of the sugar industry, Barbados
was repeatedly struck by 'Acts of God'. Tropical storms were an
almost yearly occurrence, assaulting the islands in 1657, 1658,
1660, 1665 and 1667. And there were plagues, too. As a hub of
trade, with so many people passing through from such disparate
places, Barbados was, according to one historian, 'a notably

lethal crossroads of contagion, where the velocity of infection was swift'. Then were the follies of man. Barbados would endure three major fires in the second half of the seventeenth century. The first, in 1658, destroyed 200 dwellings and store-houses in Bridgetown, together with the colony's records. The next, which took place two years after the Great Fire of London, in April 1668, was the worst the capital would ever suffer. Purportedly caused by a heedless boy with a candle, the fire would eventually consume between 800 and 1,000 buildings at a value of £400,000. The slow rebuilding of Bridgetown was further impeded when another conflagration broke out in January 1672, consuming more than thirty buildings and much of the island's provisions from North America.

But the most disruptive element was war, which was particularly devastating in a Caribbean context. As one historian explained:

> A few hours' command of the sea, a few hours' liberty to raid and plunder without opposition, could give an invader the power to do damage which could be felt for generations, even if he attempted no permanent conquest. The flimsy timber houses would burn like tinder, and so – which was even for worse – would the canes, indeed it was difficult enough to keep them from catching fire by accident. The negroes, the most important part of the planters' capital, could be carried off quickly, for they had legs to take them where their conquerors bade them go.

In addition, the island's produce could be seized or destroyed at great financial cost, while the crucial supplies that sustained the island's population could be delayed or lost. Hence the incredible sense of alarm that was provoked when even a single enemy squadron was rumoured to be on its way to the Caribbean.

Conflict returned to Barbados in the early part of 1665; this time the antagonist was Holland, which in the early part of that year had dispatched an expedition against the English colonies. It was led by the most famous military figure of the age, Admiral De Ruyter, whose force was made up of twelve battleships, two fire ships and 2,500 troops. He began his offensive by battering the English settlements on the coast of Africa and then moved on to Barbados at the end of April. On the 30th De Ruyter's squadron entered Carlisle Bay. His fleet immediately came under fire, and his own ship, the *Spiegel*, was disabled. After a futile attempt at landing, De Ruyter, who had lost ten men, was forced to withdraw.

But this was not the end of hostilities. At the beginning of the following year the governor of Barbados, Lord Willoughby, dispatched his nephew Francis with a force of 800 men to reinforce the settlers on St Christopher, only to discover that the island had already surrendered. Furious at 'the outrages committed by the French in conjunction with the Dutch upon the British Caribbee islands', Lord Willoughby decided to raise his own expedition to punish the invaders. After gaining Charles II's support, he set sail on 28 July 1666 with seventeen ships and 2,000 men, intitially taking St Lucia and then later Guadeloupe.

The progress of Willoughby's fleet was impeded by a hurricane that started to blow on 4 August. By the time it was over only two of his ships survived. According to one historian, 'the whole coast of Guadeloupe was covered with the wrecks of masts and yards, and a figure from the stern of Lord Willoughby's ship was recognised in the water'. The governor, it seemed, had gone down with his vessel. His brother, Lord William Willoughby, took his place as governor of the islands, and to everyone's relief the English, French and Dutch signed a peace treaty at Breda a year later on 21 July 1667.

★

The volatility of the Caribbean had its roots in the region's collective history of settlement. Many of the islands were founded during the war against Spain, and were intended, in part, to act as bases for privateering. Some islands had first been stumbled upon by pirates or adventurers, who would pass the news of their discoveries on to their patrons or to wealthy merchants who could raise the money to finance a settlement or petition for a patent. These rogues may have been essential to the process of colonization; but they were rogues nonetheless. Indeed, the first trickle of European arrivals could be divided roughly into two categories: the desperate and the damned – people fleeing from justice, vagabonds or sailors who had jumped ship. Unsurprisingly, these first settlers continued to operate on the wrong side of the law, frequently supplementing their meagre income from planting with a bit of buccaneering on the side. And their new home rapidly became a centre of misadventure, smuggling and vice.

If the islands were lawless, the waters that encircled them were even more so. Comparable in size to the Mediterranean, the Caribbean Sea is part of the tumultuous waters of the Atlantic Ocean. It extends in an arc that spans from the chain of islands known as the Greater Antilles – which include Cuba, Haiti and Jamaica – south through to the Lesser Antilles, which extend from the Virgin Islands down to the coast of Venezuela. It was the Caribbean Sea that was the great connector between these 7,000 islands, islets and cays; it transported its variegated population – Amerindians, black slaves, white planters and indentured servants – as they moved, ceaselessly, in all manner of crafts carrying people and supplies.

But the Caribbean waters have long swelled with danger and turmoil. Ever since the late fifteenth century, when Queen Isabella and King Ferdinand had sponsored Christopher Columbus in his perilous enterprise in the Indies, Spain had considered the entire region part of its empire. By treating all the non-Spanish who entered Caribbean waters as pirates, the Iberians united the other European powers against them, and for two centuries the seas reverberated with cries of 'All Against Spain!' But the Spanish were not the only problem. By the early decades of the seventeenth century, virtually all the European nations had colonies in the region, so conflicts in Europe also echoed there. The Caribbean islands lay 'beyond the line' – that is outside the jurisdiction of the European treaties – so were seen as legitimate prizes for European powers tussling for ascendancy in the region. It was no wonder that Henry Colt lamented: 'Suerly the Deuill the spiritt of discord have great poer in America, & loose he is amongst Christians as Infidells; & wonder nott why the natives war so much, one with the other.'

The disputes of Europe continued to have reverberations in the region during the second half of the century, so the beautiful turquoise waters of the West Indies swarmed with vessels flying flags of every colour, roving to and fro on all manner of assignments both legal and illicit, frequently engaging each other in battle or raiding on land. This perpetual fighting meant that islanders like George Ashby lived in a state of constant uncertainty, never knowing when their family and livelihood would be threatened or when their hard-won lands would be seized or their property razed to the ground. The Caribbean had, according to the historian Germán Arciniegas, become an 'international cockpit' in which the players 'in far off Europe . . . [were] watching the fight from a distance, laying bets, egging on the combatants like professional gamblers'.

Pirates and pivateers were an intrinsic part of the region's military strategy. The reasons for this were largely pragmatic: the Caribbean was simply too far away for any of the European colonizing nations to come to their territories' aid when threatened. In the case of England, for example, it would take at least six weeks for the mother country to be notified of an incipient attack, and at least another couple of months before a force could be organized and return to the region. So the pirates and buccaneers of the West Indies became an unofficial army who could intervene at a moment's notice; a politically expedient mercenary force, sanctioned to protect their country's overseas interests, and wage war against their nation's enemies.

Inevitably the pirate became the emblematic figure of the Caribbean during this era. And their histories of murder, violence and shipwrecks came to dominate both the commercial and the military life of the colonies. Clad in their signature garb of leather waistcoat and gold hooped earrings and wielding well-honed machetes, this international cast of reprobates terrorized the daily life of the region and indelibly inscribed themselves on its colourful mythology. These were the glory days of piracy, the most unpredictable and dangerous of times. The 'brethren of the coast' counted among their members Indians and blacks, Jews and Catholics, as well as English, Portuguese, Dutch, French and Spanish. They came from every walk of life: some were disillusioned ex-soldiers, others were Old World pirates who found the balmy air of the Caribbean more appealing, some were escaped slaves and indentured servants for whom life as a pirate represented a step up the social ladder. The brotherhood of the coast was, concluded one historian, the Foreign Legion of the Caribbean: 'a fraternity with stronger, more loyal bonds than those of many more conventional and law-abiding societies'.

They created a style of fighting that had not been seen before, raiding onshore as well as taking prizes at sea, and, when it suited them, they also became involved in poaching, smuggling and other forms of unlawful trade. The 'code' or 'custom of the coast' which governed their behaviour was surprisingly demo-cratic. 'When a buccaneer is going to sea,' wrote the barber-surgeon turned pirate Alexandre Exquemelin, whose book *The Buccaneers of America* was published in 1684, 'he sends word to all who wish to sail with him. When all are ready, they go on board each bringing what he needs in the way of weapons, powder and shot.' Leaders were elected by popular acclaim and retained their position only by maintaining the esteem of their fellows. According to Exquemelin, everything taken — money, jewels, precious stones and goods — had to be shared among them all without any man enjoying a penny more than his share. Those who transgressed this rule were banished from the rovers. They also initiated a form of social security: members who were in financial difficulty were extended credit until they were back on their feet.

Their profligacy was legendary. It was said that they ate their food off plates of silver, and that their horses where shod with gold. 'For that is the way with these buccaneers,' wrote Exquemelin:

> when they have got hold of something, they don't keep it for long. They are busy dicing, whoring and drinking so long as they have anything to spend. Some of them will get through a good two or three thousand pieces of eight in a day — and next day not have a shirt to their back. I have seen a man in Jamaica give 500 pieces of eight to a whore, just to see her naked.

For George Ashby these pirates were more than vibrant folklore about the sea; they were an intrinsic part of daily life on land, threatening the peace and stability of his island. He would have encountered them in the streets and taverns of Bridgetown, where their aggression was notable even in a fist-happy society like that of Barbados. And their presence on the seas meant that George Ashby could never be confident that his exports would reach their market, or that vital imports he needed to carry out his business and sustain his family, such as food and farming equipment, would reach him until the treacherous voyage was over. Pirates flying under one flag felt it was not just desirable but patriotic to raid the cargoes of ships flying under other colours. They could then sell the goods on the region's thriving black market, where everything was traded from sugar and silk to candlesticks and alcohol. For lesser planters, working at the very edge of survival, a pirate raid could spell financial ruin. And they were a constant reminder that despite their best efforts, the society they had built was still precarious and brutal. To make matters worse, men like George Ashby were forced to stand by helpless and enraged as these outlaws' trespasses went unpunished because of their usefulness to the political powers in Europe.

The emblematic figure of the age was 'the Emperor of Buc-caneers', Sir Henry Morgan. According to Germán Arciniegas, his arrival was the 'the most important thing that happened in the West Indies under Cromwell'. His career began in Barbados and, in many ways, it parallelled those of sugar entrepreneurs like James Drax, except that Morgan spent more time on the wrong side of the law. Like Drax, he had fled the Old World in search of new opportunities and was willing to do anything to make his fortune. And both men would display the same initiative, persistence and ruthlessness to progress their New World profession. In truth, the legal and extra-legal elements of the region's life were never very far apart in the Caribbean. The region was settled by chancers who were never over-particular about how they made their money. So criminals swiftly became councillors and pirates like Morgan became public officials.

Born in Glamorgan in 1635, the adolescent Morgan was unhappy with his father's plan to turn him into a farmer, and so fled to Bristol, where he bound himself to Barbados as an indentured servant for four years. He is said to have served his Barbadian master 'with a great deal of fidelity', and at the end of his term he joined the Penn–Venables expedition destined for Jamaica. Still in his twenties, he transformed himself from a mere foot soldier into the boldest pirate of the age. By the time he was thirty, Morgan was famous for his daring raids, adored by women and worshipped by his men. His reputation was fearsome. Never hesitant to utilize torture, he frequently hung his prisoners by their thumbs or crucified them with burning fuses stuck between their fingers and toes. He was even known to 'hang them from their genitals until the weight of the body tore them off'. His prisoners often 'threw themselves from the walls into the sea preferring death to becoming Morgan's prisoner'.

His exploits were chronicled by Alexandre Exquemelin, who served under him for a number of years. Morgan's raid on the Panamanian city of Portobelo in July 1688 was typical of his daring and brutality. His fleet arrived in the waters ten leagues west of the city around dusk. That night his men transferred into small craft and crept along the coast, disembarking on the outskirts of the city. Marching with his men to the city, Morgan demanded that the populace surrender. When they refused, the buccaneers rushed the city and the ensuing battle continued till the following day. Morgan considered retreating but then reinforcements arrived in the form of another pirate vessel, which joined him with cries of 'Victory!' The sight of his brethren rejuvenated Morgan and his men and they redoubled their assault. All the citizens abandoned the fight except the governor, who declared that it was 'better to die an honourable soldier than be hanged as a coward'. His bravery was rewarded with a bullet, and the rovers entered the town.

The following day those who refused to give up their wealth were 'put to the rack and tortured'. All resistance was quelled, and Morgan demanded – and received – a levy of 100,000 pieces of eight to save the city from being torched. His booty from the raid was swelled by vast amounts of jewels and silver, as well as linen, silk and other goods that were stolen from the populace. Astounded that 400 men could have conquered such a strong fortress, the president of Panama sent a messenger to Morgan requesting to see the weapon that gave him such power. Morgan acquiesced, sending him his French musket, with a message that he would be back to collect the weapon in a year or two. In response, the president thanked him for the firearm and sent a present to Morgan: a golden ring with a rosette of emeralds. In his letter he begged Morgan 'not to call on him in the manner he had visited Portobelo, because he might not have such a good reception' as he had found at that place.

But as the seventeenth century grew old, the political mosaic shifted and attitudes towards piracy began to change. Spain was no longer the great collective enemy against which the rest of Europe united. 'Suddenly,' according to Arciniegas, 'the gang began to break up.' As another historian explained: 'England or France might be found in alliance with Spain against each other, or against the Dutch. It no longer suited the European powers to let loose a band of adventurers against the Spanish Empire.' The rise of sugar also played an important part. Once this lucrative enterprise was firmly established, the planters – and the importers back home – realized that their business did not benefit from the presence of a thousand unruly buccaneers in the colony. As long as there was 'no peace beyond the line', trade was upset. The region needed to be policed by more conventional means: national navies or regular army troops.

The ambivalence that had always existed around the buccaneers was now openly expressed. The French Royal Navy officer Jean Baptiste Ducasse lamented the terrible example they set for the young men of the colonies: 'They are very bad subjects who believe they have not been put in the world except to practise brigandage and piracy. Enemies of subordination and authority, their example ruins the colonies, all the young people having no other wish than to embrace this profession for its libertinage and ability to gain booty.' The pirates were no longer seen as the solution to the problems of the region but were seen as the problem itself. By 1671 the English government's official policy was to curb their activity. And men like Morgan, already enriched by buccaneering, started to give up the brotherhood.

Alongside the perpetual threats from the sea during this period, the Barbadians also had home-grown difficulties to deal with, when in the summer of 1675 the harried settlers uncovered a major slave plot. Originating in the Speightstown area to the west of the island, the plot, three years in the planning, was an island-wide conspiracy forged largely by African-born slaves who wanted to instigate a general uprising. To the chagrin of the islanders, despite the length of its gestation and the large number of conspirators involved, this 'damnable design' was not discovered by their own formidable intelligence and policing efforts; instead it came to light through a female slave called Fortuna, eight days before it was due to commence. Apparently, she had overheard a young male slave discussing the details with another conspirator, in which he had expressed grave reservations about the plotters intention to kill the 'white folks'. She persuaded him to tell a local judge, who in turn mobilized the militia.

In a later report Governor Atkins related that the uprising was to begin with the sound of trumpets and gourds to be sounded on various hills. Then the cane fields were to be torched, and slaves were to descend on their masters and slit their throats. A respected elder called Cuffee, a slave born on the Gold Coast on the Gulf of Guinea, was to be crowned king and an exquistely wrought and carved chair was prepared for the ceremony. Scores of slaves were arrested and tried. Some were flogged, others deported or hanged. Those more deeply implicated were beheaded and their bodies were dragged through the streets of Speightstown and burned as a warning to other slaves. The ringleaders were roasted alive by slow fire. The defiance displayed by some of them shook the islanders. One of the condemned men, a sturdy rogue called Tony, is said to have crowed to his tormentors: 'If you roast me today, you cannot roast me tomorrow.'

Fortuna, the slave who brought the planned rebellion to light, was given her freedom. The Crown also reimbursed the planters for damages and loss, but the entire episode caused great disquiet among them as they had believed up until then that their draconian discipline made such a conspiracy impossible. Afterwards they went back to the law, curbing the slaves' movements even further and banning the 'drums' and other African instruments that were used to communicate between the plantations. But nothing could prevent the resurgence of rebellion, and the slaves revolted again in 1683 and 1692.

A couple of months after Fortuna's revelation of the original plot, on 31 August 1675, the most devastating hurricane since the beginning of colonization battered the island. In an age before meteorological reports provided storm warnings and government agencies provided advice and shelters, the arrival of one of these great tempests was a truly apocalyptic event. On that terrible day, the island was enveloped by black clouds and lashed by rain. The wind rose sharply and blustered with such ferocity that it seemed to be coming from all points of the compass. The air, usually so fragrant, stank of sulphur and bitumen produced by the combination of electricity and moisture in the atmosphere. That night the storm grew even more violent and continued to blow till the morning. The Ashby family must have been terrified. When they emerged from their shelter it was to scenes of complete devastation. Over 200 Barbadians were killed, as were many more slaves who did not count in the official numbers. The leeward side of the island was the most affected – only a few buildings there were left standing – while on the windward side many of the houses and sugar works were also obliterated, and the canes uprooted and flattened. The strength of the hurricane winds washed ashore the ships on the coast and all the houses in the bay were blown down, along with most of the churches; and across the island many planters were forced to live in temporary huts. The hurricane induced such terror in the heart of the colonists that for some time no one would invest any capital in land and building, fearing a similar catastrophe.

Not long after this terrible hurricane George Ashby died. We do not know if his passing was directly connected to the tempest, but many islanders did perish during these months, traumatized by the calamity (and perhaps rendered more vulnerable by the other shocks that had preceded it), weakened by injuries, malnourished by lack of food or despairing at the loss of all they had built.

George Ashby's will was entered on 13 July 1676, a few days after his death. It provides such a fascinating insight into the Ashby clan at this time, their social standing, the relationships, and their attitudes towards their property, including slaves, that it is worth quoting in full:

> In the name of God Amen – this third day of October in ye yeare of our Lord god one thousand six hundred seventy and two in ye four and twentieth of ye Reigne of our Sovereigne Lord King Charles the Second – I George Ashby of the Parish of St. Philips and Island of Barbados being very sicke and weak in body but of perfect mind and remembrance praised be to the Lord Almighty therefore doe by God's permission make and declare this my last will and testament in manner and forme following right:

> 1st: – First and principally with all awful reverence and humility I consign my soule unto the hands of Almighty God my maker hoping and assuredly believing

through the merits and bloody passion of my Lord and Saviour Christ Jesus I shall receive a blessed and glorious resurrection to life everlasting. My body I commit to ye earth from whence it was taken to be decently interred at the discretion of my executrix herafter appointed. And as for and concerning such worldly estate whereth it has pleased the Lord in my lifetime of his great mercy and goodnesse to send mee or blesse me with all I doe give Bequeath and dispose of the same in manner forme following, that is to say.

2nd Item: – I doe give and bequeath my loving sone George Ashbey six acres of land part of ye plantation wheron I doe now live . . . to be signed to him and his heirs for ever. Together with ye negro boy called Punch and the dwelling house wherein John Jarman now liveth.

3th Item: – I doe give and bequeath unto my loving son William . . . and his heirs for ever ye quantity of three acres of land or thereabouts together with the dwelling house thereupon standing now in the occupation of Thomas Neale.

4th Item: – I doe give and bequeath unto my daughter Deborah Ashby the quantity of three acres of land and the house theron now in the occupation of Henry Sellman to her and her heirs forever provided that if she the said Deborah my daughter shall or doe happen to to marry with one Edward Joloffe that then my will is and I doe heerby give and bequeath unto her the sum of twelve pence sterling and no more but in case she does not marry the said Edward Joloffe then I doe furthe give unto her my negroe girle named Mame.

5th Item: – I doe give and bequeath unto my dear and loveing wife Deborah Ashby whom I doe herby nominate and appoint to be sole executrix of this last will and testament (my debts and funeral charges being first paid and satisfied.) All and every the rest residue and remainder of my estate whatsoever both real and personal with my dwelling house outhouses and stock of what ever kind or nature so ever during her natural life and afterwards for her to dispose of amongst my children according as she shall think fit. And I doe hereby nominate and appoint and desire my loveing friends Rowland Hutton and John Taylor to be overseers in trust and to be aiding and assisting with my said wife and executrix in the due execution and performance of this my will according to the true intent and meaning thereof to whome and to each for them I doe give and bequeath the sum of twenty shillings sterling a piece and I doe hereby revoke disannull and utterly make voide all former wills gifts legatees and bequests at any time heretofore by me made or given and doe pronounce this to stand and bee for as my last will and testament.

In witness whereof I the said George Ashbey to this my last will and Testament have set my hand and seale the day and year first above written.

The will paints a picture of a humble family that, despite its challenges, had managed not just to secure a decent life but to expand its wealth in trying circumstances, and to maintain strong ties of affection and loyalty.

It also reveals a great deal about George Ashby himself. The devout tone of the will implies that George Ashby had always been or had become a religious man. More specifically there are tantalizing indications that he had become a Quaker. Not only did his will make reference to his 'friends' Rowland Hutton and John Taylor, the term used by the Quakers to describe themselves and their brethren; his wife, Deborah, would later remarry to the aforementioned Hutton, a planter who had also converted to the religion. In Hutton's own will, lodged a few years later, he mentions his wife Deborah Hutton, 'formerly the wife of George Ashby, & her son William Ashbye; poor people called Quakers'. As an inhabitant of St Philip, George was particularly susceptible to the movement, because the parish was an exceptionally active Quaker hub, with two vibrant meeting houses. Indeed, one of their 'large burying places' can still be seen across from St Philip's parish church.

The first Quakers had arrived in Barbados in the middle of the 1650s. Some had arrived willingly, in flight from religious persecution, but a substantial number of this 'malignant source' were forcibly expelled from Britain on the orders of the Crown. Some of these new arrivals planned to settle on the island permanently, but many others came for a few months to promulgate their philosophy, and then left for other colonies in the region. As a result Barbados became the cradle of the Quaker religion in the region. By 1671 there was a flourishing community of Quakers on the island. It was so significant that George Fox, the founder of the sect, visited the island for three months that year to rally his American troops. By 1676 there were more Quakers in Barbados than in any other colony in the English Americas.

The Quakers, otherwise known as the Religious Society of Friends or simply 'the Friends', held doctrines that attracted the colonists, and they gained many converts in the colony. In contrast to the Church of England, Quakers argued that everyone had 'inward light' and that all were assured salvation. But these transgressive ideas, combined with a philosophy that stressed peace, simplicity and equality, were profoundly antithetical to the strife-ridden, materialistic and exploitative society that was early colonial Barbados. As a result the Quakers were in constant conflict with the authorities. So it was unsurprising that George Fox felt compelled to write a letter to the island's governor to contest the 'scandalous lies and slanders that have been put upon us'. The Quaker stand on slavery only heightened the island government's antipathy to the sect; they were first group to include slaves in their religious worship. In 1676 the island's Assembly passed a law that made it illegal for slaves to attend Quaker meetings. Hostility to the sect continued to grow, and in the 1680s there was a mass collective flight of Quakers from the island to settle Pennsylvania on the mainland. (That George Ashby's eldest son, George Jr, also took flight for Pennsylvania during this period is another clue that the family were indeed Quakers.) Certainly my ancestor, George Ashby's second son, William, my grandfather seven times removed, was a fervent Quaker. A mason by trade, William ended up in the stocks, spent a couple of months in jail and was fined 500 pounds of sugar for building a wall in a Quaker burial area on Christmas Day in 1676.

Other revelations provided by the will are concrete ones: it is signed by George Ashby, so he was clearly a literate man. His decision to make his wife his executor was characteristic of many planters on the island, and suggests that he trusted her to carry out his wishes and respected her competence, for together they had carved companionship out of struggle and worked assiduously as a team for the betterment of their family. George Ashby was also typical of many of his contemporaries in other crucial ways. Clearly a loving and concerned parent, his overwhelming priority was the transfer of wealth to his children, and he sought to divide his holdings in a way that would enable them all to survive and thrive on the island.

In other ways George was unusual among his peers, in that he managed to father four children who survived to adulthood.

(His eldest daughter Elizabeth predeceased him, dying at the age of twenty-two.) In Christ Church, the parish with the most complete surviving records, the average was a mere 1.8 children per family. Many of those who peopled the mainland colonies, particularly the New England Puritans, had six or seven offspring, but the islands were different. Barbados fared a little better than its neighbours, but across the English Caribbean islands, the quality of life tended to be lower than in their American counterparts as they lacked the structure provided by Christian principles and strong family units that anchored society back in Europe and on mainland America.

There are hints too of an intriguing family squabble when George Ashby decrees that if his daughter marries 'one Edward Joloffe' she will receive only a paltry twelve pence, instead of the three acres, house and slave that she would otherwise be entitled to. Perhaps George's hostility to Joloffe was because he was a backsliding Quaker or, even worse, an Anglican. Quaker marriages were serious affairs. The Quaker Meeting to which a man or woman belonged decided on whether the marriage was suitable or not, so to reject that choice had repercussions for the whole community. (For the record, Deborah, apparently a pragmatic girl, married a man called Peacock and duly inherited her rightful portion; this is the piece of land that is still planted with cane today.)

The will makes no mention of England, his country of origin, or any family or friends that he may have left behind there. Like many of those who came to 'make' the New World, George seems to have effectively cut off all ties with his old life on his departure. From the moment he took ship, he probably realized that his migration was an irreversible decision; after all, he had risked his money, his reputation, his very life in the undertaking.

In 1680 Barbados held a census, which demonstrated just how comprehensively sugar had reshaped the island. Its sugar planters were now the wealthiest men in English America. Their fortunes dwarfed those of the Chesapeake tobacco planters and those of the New York and Boston merchants, as well as their counterparts in Jamaica and the other Leeward Islands. Indeed, the Barbadians produced more sugar and employed more shipping than the other islands combined. As one historian concluded: 'Almost certainly the exports to England from this small island of less than 100,000 arable acres were more valuable in the 1680s than the total exports to England from all the North American colonies.'

During George Ashby's time on the island, Barbados had been transformed from an anarchic frontier settlement to a rigorously ordered and stratified society, which was completely dominated by the big planters. Despite making up only 6.9 per cent of the population, the planters owned 53.4 per cent of the island's acreage, and had 53.9 per cent of its servants and 54.3 per cent of its slaves. These men dominated the island politically as well as economically, holding key government posts as well as important posts in the militia and the Vestry. As the historian Richard Dunn has said, the island had a distinctive hierarchy:

> Like the terraced cane fields of the island, Barbados society rose level by level from the roughly 40,000 slaves occupying the lowest tier to the 2,300 servants at the next tier, ascending past the 1,200 freemen, the 1,000 small planters, the 400 Bridgetown householders, and the 200 middling planters, to the 175 big planters at the summit who held the best land, sold the most sugar, and monopolized the best offices.

The lifestyle of the elite planters reflected their social status. Not only were there more of these sugar magnates than in the early days, their fortunes were much more noticeable, since they competed with one another to display their wealth. As Father Labat noted when he visited the island in 1700:

> The houses on the plantations are much better built than those of the towns, they are large with good fenestration completely glazed; the arrangements of the rooms is commodious and comfort is well understood. Nearly all have fine avenues of tamarinds, or of other large trees ... which give shade and make the houses very attractive. One notices the opulence and good taste of the inhabitants in their magnificent furniture and silver of which they all have considerable quantities, of an order which if the island were captured, this commodity alone would be worth more than the loss of a few galleons.

Labat was not alone in his admiration for the Barbadians. Another contemporary marvelled at these 'splendid Planters, who for Sumptuous Houses, Cloaths and Liberal Entertainment cannot be exceeded by their peers in the Mother Kingdome itself'.

Virtually the entire society had been transformed by sugar. From the rather rustic town that George Ashby encountered when he first arrived, Bridgetown had expanded and flourished. It now had long, straight and well-planned streets and beautiful houses that were built in the English style, with glass windows and magnificent furnishings. Its warehouses were filled with goods from all parts of the world and its shopkeepers, including numerous goldsmiths, jewellers and clockmakers, did brisk business. One visitor claimed that 'the largest trade in the New World (*l'Amerique*) is carried on here'. And what was true for the capital was true for the rest of island, which was equally prosperous and well developed.

Its racial make-up had also shifted. A world that had been largely European in origin was now predominantly African. Thousands of whites had fled the country in search of new opportunities, while many more blacks were forcibly transported to the island to cultivate sugar cane. According to K.G. Davies, the chief authority on the seventeenth-century English slave trade, Barbados received between 2,000 and 3,000 negroes per annum between 1676 and 1680 to keep the plantations adequately supplied. The total slave population, according to estimates, rose from 32,473 in 1676 to 46,602 in 1684. This huge increase occurred despite the slaves' fearful mortality rate.

The topography of the island had also been transformed by the exigencies of sugar. When George Ashby arrived the plantations were largely confined to the western and southern coasts of the island, leaving the interior, where he made his home, virtually untouched. In those days, amenities such as road networks were rudimentary. But nearly forty years later, at the time of George Ashby's death, the landscape was completely altered. Barbados now had a high population density as well as a sophisticated infrastructure. The rampant wilderness that had dominated the island had been completely tamed, and 90 per cent of its surface area was utilized for agriculture. It did not concern the colonists overmuch that hundreds of animal and fauna species had disappeared in the process.

In 1676 Governor Atkins reported gleefully that the whole island looked like a beautifully cultivated green garden: a sentiment that many other observers echoed. Indeed, the metaphor of the garden was one embraced by the colonists. They had overcome the exuberant explosion of tropical vegetation and imposed instead a vista that represented to them progress, order, achievement and prosperity.

Barbados may have been a flourishing society, but it was a deeply unequal one, and despite its wealth, the quality of life in Barbados was poor. The census demonstrates that the Barbadians still had lonelier, less family-centred lives than the colonists who had chosen New England. Their island was overcrowded, had poor sanitation and suffered a perpetual shortage of food. Small men still laboured in the fields to keep food on the table, while the rich retreated to their manorial-style plantations, gorging and drinking themselves to death. The mortality rate was also very high; the island's populace still succumbed to disease, drink and depression at an alarming rate. And if the islander's lifestyles didn't kill them, strange tropical illnesses and natural disasters did. The plight of the planters was eclipsed, of course, by that of the slaves on the island. One of the big Barbados planters, Edward Littleton, who owned 120 Negroes in 1680, argued in an influential pamphlet that the planter with a hundred slaves had to buy six new ones a year in order to maintain his stock. In other words, he could expect to kill off all his original labour force within seventeen years. Littleton complained bitterly at having to pay £20 for each new slave: 'One of the great Burdens of our Lives is going to buy Negroes,' he wrote. 'But we must have them; we cannot be without them, and the best Men in those Countries must in their own Persons submit to the Indignity.'

Most significantly, both planters and slaves lived in a permanent state of mutual fear and resentment, as their relationship grew ever more toxic. 'Thus sunny Barbados,' according to the historian Richard Dunn, 'was a land of paradox in 1680, both parvenu and traditional, both complacent and insecure, the richest and yet in human terms the least successful colony in English America.'

And, for George Ashby, how did his life in Barbados measure up to what he had dreamt of when he set sail from England? The Ashbys' home parish was now one of the more populous on the island, with 407 planters, 115 white servants and 4,702 Negroes living within its boundaries. It had a thriving sugar cane industry that had seduced most of its inhabitants, including my ancestors. The Ashby family had also managed to clamber a step up the economic ladder. Instead of the paltry nine acres that George had initially acquired when he arrived on the island, the family holdings had expanded to twenty-one. And their labour force had expanded from one indentured servant to nine slaves and one white worker. George Ashby's son and primary heir, George Jr, was now worthy of the appellation 'planter' with all the privileges – the right to vote, to stand for election – that this term implied.

But if George Ashby had dreamt of any great social transformation for his family, he must have been disappointed. In England, his class identity was, like that of all of his countrymen, the product of a complex interaction of factors including heritage, education, accent and property. Once that place was assigned, usually by birth, it was a straitjacket that was virtually impossible to escape. (Even those with money were legally proscribed from mimicking the dress and lifestyle of the upper classes in the seventeenth century.) In Barbados things were different, but not profoundly so. Those who had dreams of social mobility were also largely frustrated: the island was almost as hidebound and hierarchical as the homeland they had left behind. Only great wealth allowed a man to escape the taint of humble roots. So George fraternized with men of his 'degree', and this was still the case when his eldest son came to maturity. In a document drawn up towards the end of the century when George the younger was about to take a sea voyage, he gives power of attorney to his wife and dearest friends: a blacksmith, a miller and a carpenter.

George Ashby had been successful in other ways, however. In his quest for profits he had proved to be wily, persistent and adaptable, learning quickly how to raise a variety of crops and market them. He was, in other words, typical of the kind of person who flourished as a planter in Barbados: 'a good capitalist', according to the Barbadian historian Hilary Beckles, forever 'sensitive to changing market requirements'. But George Ashby had done well because he had been willing – like all his fellow planters – to violate certain norms of morality and certain values. He had subscribed to an ideology that dehumanized his fellow human beings; that allowed him, on the sole basis of their skin colour, to exploit their labour and abuse their well-being. He and his descendants were slave owners, with all the moral and spiritual compromises that implies. But this was unlikely to have concerned the Ashbys any more than it did the rest of the white population of the island. George, like his contemporaries, had migrated to the New World with dreams of financially enhancing his family's fortunes, and against all the odds he had succeeded. Though he hadn't found untold riches, he had – thanks to sugar – established a stake in the island's bounty. It would be another three generations, however, before the Ashby family truly found their El Dorado.

Part Two
THE PLANTOCRAT

9

I pity them greatly but I must be mum,
For how could we do without sugar and rum?

William Cowper

If the prospect of immense wealth that had attracted George Ashby to the colonies continued to elude his descendants, the Ashby family would over the coming decades nonetheless thrive. With the dogged perseverance demonstrated by their founding father they would extend their holdings, acre by acre, slave by slave. Meanwhile George Ashby's surviving children would continue to beat the odds and produce thriving families of their own. Their offspring grew up and were wed in turn, and more babies were born, their parents continuing to use and reuse a handful of names – George and William, Edward and Robert, Deborah and Susannah, Mary and Pamela – assembling and reassembling them in each generation like fragments in a kaleidoscope. Whatever Quaker affiliations my branch of the Ashbys had once held had withered, just as the sect on the island had, and the family were absorbed into the wider Church of England community, which had won the battle for the islanders' hearts and minds.

Some of George Ashby's successors would migrate abroad, like William Ashby, who departed Barbados in the 1710s to try his luck in mainland America, where he joined many others with that surname settled there. But most remained on the island. In the middle of the eighteenth century my branch of the Ashby family relocated from St Philip to the neighbouring parish of Christ Church, when my great-great-great-great-grandfather Robert Ashby and his wife, Mary, purchased part of a sugar estate called Kingsland. This property, which had been cultivating cane for over one hundred years, had once been owned by the prominent English planter family the Applethwaites, and had passed by inheritance to their relatives the Freres. They in turn sold off parts of the estate in order to provide legacies for family members. Thus chunks of Kingsland ended up in the hands of people like the Ashbys, modest planters who were eager to move to bigger holdings.

Most of George Ashby's descendants became entrenched in the same industry that had ensnared him so many years earlier. Their entire world, like his, was built upon an edifice of sugar: it put food on the table and clothes on their backs; it would dictate the rhythms of their days, months and years, as well as shaping their attitudes and beliefs. Had the technology existed to take photographs of subsequent generations of Ashbys in the eighteenth century, the images would have varied very little: skirts a little longer or shorter, hair arranged slightly differently, the jacket a marginally different cut; while in the background, beyond their homesteads, were the same vistas of green cane, the same black bodies labouring in the fields.

If the source of their livelihood did not change much over the years, the way that the Ashbys thought and conducted themselves did. Over the decades, the family's behaviour was transformed by tropical conditions, proximity to an alien culture and the peculiarities of colonial society. So visitors from Britain noted that the local whites were somewhat of a 'foreign character'. And certainly a life lived alongside black slaves had changed everything about them. The Ashbys now danced to different music, ate different food, had a different body language. They even spoke differently: one visitor noted in his diary what he considered to be the 'Africanisms' adopted by Barbadian whites, while another visitor, George Pinckard, felt that the Barbadians pronounced their words with 'a tedious langour'. Their indulgent upbringing frequently made them 'indolent' and 'lacking in ambition'. The benevolence of the climate, the beauty of the island, and the relaxed pace of life encouraged a languorous lifestyle and an attachment to pleasure.

On a collective level, the Barbadian identity too had transformed. The fiery, violent temperament of the first-generation pioneers had mellowed significantly and the islanders were now known for their easy-going and friendly attitudes. And where their sugar-generated prosperity had initially encouraged a tendency towards ostentation, this had dissipated somewhat and was now primarily expressed in their tradition of lavish hospitality. This process of adjustment which migrants made to a new environment and the new cultural ethos they created became known as creolization; and according to the historian Karl Watson, the eighteenth century saw the formation of a distinct 'Barbadian character'.

Earlier distinctions based on the colonists' country of origin, be it England, Scotland or Ireland, which had been so important when George arrived, were long forgotten. So if George Ashby had regarded himself as 'an Englishman transplanted', his descendants were Barbadians through and through. Like many of the white islanders, the Ashbys were Barbadian born, and could trace their ancestry back to the period 1627–60. The island was all they knew. Their relationship with this place had all the intensity of a love affair. Their ancestors had died to conquer and clear it, while subsequent generations had battled and bled to keep it. This dynamic of struggle and subjugation only cemented the islanders' passionate attachment to their land: Barbados was home.

Over the decades the status of their island too had shifted.

Barbados was no longer the economic star of the anglophone Caribbean: that position had been relinquished to Jamaica, more than thirty times the size and with the ability to harvest much greater quantities of sugar. But 'little England' had repositioned itself cleverly; it was 'the civilized isle' which took on the role of 'elder statesman' of the region, guiding Britain's Caribbean interests with a considered and moderate hand. It was also one of the most heavily cultivated spots in the region, with a population of around 85,000 people, four-fifths of whom were slaves. Haunted by the consciousness of how outnumbered they were, how vulnerable they were to the possibility of violent revenge, the islanders ratcheted up their control of, and distance from, the people they enslaved, imposing a system of savage discipline. But it was a terrible paradox: the more they isolated and victimized their slaves, the more fearful they became of rebellion.

The island's productivity was dazzling to visitors: the hills that rimmed Bridgetown were dotted with dozens of circulating windmills powering the processing of the sugar crop and creating an impression of an island in perpetual motion. The tropical wilderness that George Ashby and his contemporaries had conquered was long forgotten: Barbados was now, according to an observer, one giant cane plantation, divided by the exigencies of sugar production into grids and squares as neat and orderly as a chessboard.

A singular portrait of Barbados in the middle of the eighteenth century was provided by the man who was to become America's first president, George Washington, who visited the island as a nineteen-year-old when accompanying his ailing brother there to recover his health. On arrival in 1751 the young man declared himself 'perfectly ravished' by the beauty of the island. He was particularly awed by the capital, Bridgetown, where his ship anchored. One of the busiest ports in the Americas, with an estimated 1,200 buildings, it was the largest city that he had ever seen.

During his four-month stay, Washington was quickly taken up by the island's gentry and introduced to their vibrant social life, and entertained by a round of balls, card parties and invitations to drink tea. He dined at the 'Beefsteak and Tripe Club', where the island's leading gentlemen met to discuss colonial affairs. And it was in Barbados that he experienced his first visit to the theatre, prompting a lifelong interest in the stage.

Slavery in Barbados differed from the model Washington was accustomed to on the American mainland, but he had little to say about these dissimilarities since the institution was as natural as birdsong to him, and probably taken as much for granted. He was, however, impressed by the island's natural fertility, in particular its soil. 'The Earth in parts is extremely rich,' the young surveyor wrote, and as 'black as our richest Marsh Mould'. The Barbadians' sophisticated farming methods, designed to wring out the maximum benefit from their overworked soil, also had a profound impact on Washington, who became one of the most innovative farmers in the US and a prominent advocate for scientific crop rotation and other cultivation techniques. Washington's visit to Barbados was the only trip he ever made outside America, and it left an indelible imprint on him because of the island's urbane social scene and its advanced approach to agricultural science.

By the middle of the eighteenth century the Caribbean sugar islands were more than valuable to their colonial masters: they were priceless. According to one contemporary observer, the French writer Abbé Raynal, their riches 'were the principal cause of the rapid movement which stirs the universe'. In 1763, negotiating a treaty with the British, the French were forced to choose between holding on to Canada (dismissed by Voltaire as 'a few acres of snow') or the sugar islands. They chose the latter. It was no wonder that this cluster of small islands had become a magnet for fortune hunters; or that their capacity to generate obscene profits led many to describe them as 'the best of the west'. Sugar was the commodity that drove the geopolitics of the era, just as oil does today.

In the years since the Ashby family had first become involved in the industry, sugar consumption had grown exponentially, filtering down from the upper classes to those below. The middle classes used sugar in a vast range of foodstuffs: cakes and candies, jams and jellies, pastries and petits fours, trifles and tansies. As production grew to meet this new demand, so the commodity dropped in price, which allowed the British proletariat to purchase it, thereby creating a further explosion in demand. They used it to sweeten other colonial imports such as coffee and cocoa, but primarily tea. Sugared tea assuaged hunger, provided a vital shot of energy in arduous working days, and added variety to a bland and starchy diet. Sugar was also an aspirational product: an affordable treat that allowed the poor access to a foodstuff that was still associated with their 'betters'.

And their appetite for it was insatiable. In 1700, Britain imported 10,000 tons of sugar; by 1800, consumption had increased to 150,000 tons – a rise of 1,500 per cent. In this period the saying 'as wealthy as a West Indian' became proverbial. Hence the tale of George III, who was driving one day outside London when he encountered a Jamaican planter whose carriage and liveried outriders were even more astounding than his own, and is said to have exclaimed: 'Sugar, sugar, eh! . . . All that sugar!'

The member of the Ashby clan who would really transform the family's fortunes was born in 1776. Robert Cooper Ashby was part of the fifth generation of the family to be born on the island, and was George Ashby's great-great-great-grandson. He was the son of the recently relocated Robert Moore Ashby and Mary Arthur, and was born two years into their union. Robert Cooper's earliest years would coincide with a watershed period in the evolution of the West Indian colonies when a backdrop of persistent turmoil, dubbed by historians 'The Age of Revolution', caused the fate of the sugar islands to darken.

The first of these clashes, the American War of Independence (1775–83), began the year before Robert Cooper was born. It had been brewing for some time. The Americans, like many of the other British colonies in the region, had long resented the controls imposed on them by the mother country. And in that year the Thirteen States explicitly rejected the British Parliament's right to govern them without representation. The following year they claimed sovereignty over their own affairs and declared themselves a new nation with the name of the United States of America. The British government inevitably rejected this development and a state of war was declared. France, which had been supplying arms and ammunition to the rebels surreptitiously since the beginning of the conflict, eventually declared war on Britain, and was swiftly joined by Spain and the Dutch Republic.

The timing couldn't have been worse. The West Indians were already jittery. In the years immediately preceding the conflict, slave revolts had ignited across the region like fireworks: in 1768 there was one in Montserrat, in Tobago there were three between 1771 and 1774, while in 1776 there were eruptions in Jamaica, Nevis and Montserrat. Now they had to contend with a war on the American mainland, with all the disruption, bloodshed and anxiety that entailed. What they feared most was the impact that the American rebellion and the rebels' rhetoric of freedom would have on their already unsettled slaves, especially when the British began in 1775 and 1776 to aggressively recruit enslaved Americans to fight on the side of the Crown. Enticed by promises of liberty and land, tens of thousands fled the plantations; even George Washington's own slave, Henry, crossed over to British lines. The initiative, courage and judgement shown by these black warriors dismayed the Caribbean planters, who felt that they might inspire their own captives to take up arms.

The American struggle put the islanders in an awkward position in other ways. On the one hand, Britain was the mother country to which the Barbadians still felt strong ties of loyalty. More pragmatically, they did not feel confident in their ability to stand alone, either economically or militarily. On the other hand, the Barbadians were not without sympathy for the 'Americans': they too had chafed under Britain's heavy hand. Indeed, the American rebels' slogan, 'No taxation without representation', evoked more than a bit of sympathy among the Barbadians. In addition, the North American states were important trading partners for the island: not only would millions of pounds' worth of trade be endangered, the island would be deprived of essential goods.

So the Barbadians attempted to tack an uneasy path in these churning waters, torn between both sides. And soon they found themselves cut off from crucial supplies, both foodstuffs and material for the sugar industry, which traditionally came from the American colonies. The situation was exacerbated by the reappearance of pirates in the region, a reminder that war could break out at any time. By the middle of 1776, the year that Robert Cooper was born, the island was in severe distress. Food shortages were so acute that contemporaries referred to the poor, both black and white, 'dropping down in the streets, or silently pining and expiring in their cottages'. The pervasive deprivation heightened the colonists' perennial fear of slave revolt, and by the latter part of 1777 the Barbadians had no choice but to approach Britain for assistance. But the response was slow; large consignments of flour, beans, peas and fish arrived only in early 1778. By this time the colonists, wrote one observer, 'seemed to be much in a desponding way', and the overall state of the island was 'decayed and impoverished'.

Meanwhile, the military conflict rolled on. Even before the official American Declaration of Independence, the French had made their sympathies with the rebels clear. Animated by the romance of the American cause and longing to avenge the humiliation they had suffered in the Seven Years War against Britain, French nobles like the Comte de Rochambeau, the hero of Saratoga, and the Marquis de Lafayette, who would achieve a generalship in Washington's army, rallied to the cause. France's enthusiasm for America's ambitions was soon evident in their colonies, and Martinique, Barbados's neighbour, was drawn into the conflict when it became an illegal hideout for American corsairs in between their maritime forays against the British troops. Thus in 1777 the governor of Barbados was forced to warn his Martinican counterpart not to harbour 'the rebels, pirates or others who engaged themselves in the conflict'. But it was too late: nothing could turn back the tide of hostilities.

And so, early in 1778, confidential instructions were sent to the British governors in the region directing them to prepare 'in every way possible for the defence of their colonies'. The official entry of France into the war on the side of the Americans, and the outbreak of hostilities between Spain and England the following year, only made the situation worse. Many of the Caribbean islands fell into enemy hands, including St Vincent, Grenada and Tobago, while Britain took the island of St Lucia in December 1778. Barbados inevitably became one of the centres of operation for British forces in the region, and a garrison was established there early in February 1780. Its neighbour Martinique took on the same role for the French and was garrisoned with an extra 2,000 troops. America's War of Independence was the genesis of major change across the globe; indeed, the historian Simon Schama wrote that 'without any question, the [French] Revolution began in America'.

And, just as in George Ashby's time, Barbados was also at the mercy of nature. On 10 October 1780, the most violent hurricane of the eighteenth century devastated the island. There was little indication on the night before that anything was amiss, except for an unusually red and fiery sky and a heavy shower of rain. But by ten o'clock the next morning the wind and rain had worsened and all the ships docked in Bridgetown's harbour fled out to sea, hoping to escape the ferocity of the storm. By six o'clock that evening the velocity of the winds had increased so much that trees were uprooted and blown away. It was becoming clear that the colony was about to be battered by a truly appalling tempest.

Across the island, householders like the Ashbys took what precautions they could to guard against the force of the storm, barricading doors and windows, or fleeing to the sturdiest buildings on their lands. But there was no safety to be found. Even the most robust constructions, such as Government House, with its three-foot-thick walls, were overwhelmed. The morning brought little respite to the exhausted and bleary-eyed populace, and the storm continued, virtually uninterrupted, for nearly forty-eight hours. At its most powerful the strength of the gale was such that it carried a twelve-pound cannon a distance of 140 yards and levelled almost all of the island's public buildings as well as its fortifications. It was difficult initially to make any accurate calculation about how many people had perished in the catastrophe, but it was clear that the numbers were considerable. Many were buried in the ruins of their own homes and a large number were washed away by the sea. The British troops stationed on the island were also hard hit, with both the barracks and the hospital blown down early in the storm. The number of dead bodies that lay interred or washed up from the sea prompted public health concerns. The British Parliament immediately dispatched £80,000 to help the islanders, but it was just a drop in the ocean. This single hurricane was eventually estimated to have cost the region 22,000 souls, and killed at least 211 horses and 6,606 cattle.

Two British army officers stationed on the island left their record of the storm. Major General Vaughan wrote in a dispatch: 'The strongest colours could not paint to your Lordship the miseries of the inhabitants; on the one hand the ground is covered with the mangled bodies of their friends and relations, and on the other, reputable families, wandering through the ruins, seeking for food and shelter; in short, imagination can form but a faint idea of the horrors of this dreadful scene.' Admiral Rodney was also stupefied by the extent of the destruction: 'The whole face of the country appears an entire ruin, and the most beautiful island in the world, has the appearance of a country laid waste by fire, and sword and appears to the imagination more dreadful than it is possible for me to find words to express.'

After the shock had subsided, the entire island was mobilized to clear debris, replant crops and bury the dead. The injury to the Ashbys' property is unknown but it would have been un-avoidable: one official report noted that 'no one house in the island is exempt from damage'. The family therefore would have had to put up with makeshift arrangements for some time, and their finances must have been devastated by the destruction that the hurricane had wrought. They would have found that even if they could raise the money for repairs, lumber and other materials were so scarce and expensive that rebuilding could only take place slowly. To make matters worse, the colony was simultaneously ravaged by outbreaks of yellow fever and small-pox, and by ruinous new duties imposed by Britain. By the end of the American War of Independence in 1783, 'the economic position of Barbados was still poor, and a number of planters left the island rather than undertake to repair the damage done by the hurricane'.

Robert Cooper at the age of four was probably only vaguely conscious of these problems: his world extended little further than his house, his parents and his three younger siblings. Noth-ing remains of his childhood homestead but an inscription on an eighteenth-century map. It reads simply 'Ashby', and marked beside it is a drawing of a single windmill, signifying the estate's limited ability to process sugar. But it was most likely typical of the majority of middling sugar plantations at that time. The nucleus of the property, the 'great house', would have been modest: a single-storey wooden construction perched on large square stones with the ubiquitous veranda around the sides and front; while the neatly kept garden would have been dominated by tropical trees like frangipani, tamarind and cedar. The planter's house was traditionally guarded by a hedge of flowering shrubs like hibiscus, which marked it out as separate from the rest of the plantation and indicated its privileged position on the property. Beyond the compound the land was divided into cane fields, pastures for the plantation's livestock and plots of land the slaves cultivated for their own sustenance. Dotted across this landscape was a higgledy-piggledy collection of livestock, outbuildings and slave quarters.

Here Robert Cooper and his siblings applied themselves to the job of being young. Despite some material deprivation it was a cosseted upbringing, since even relatively small plantations had a glut of domestic servants to cater to the family's needs. Robert Cooper, who was addressed as 'Massa Robert' from his earliest infancy, would have enjoyed the attentions of his own nanny, whose efforts were supplemented by other helpers who bathed and dressed, walked and coddled him. Even the slave children he played with would yield to his every whim. This indulged upbringing, argued one contemporary, explained the creole's volatility and lack of self-control:

> Children, in these West-India islands are, from their Infancy, waited upon by Numbers of Slaves, who . . . are obliged to pay them unlimited Obedience; and . . . when they have thus their favourite Passions nourished with such indulgent Care, it is no Wonder that by Degrees

they acquire . . . an overfond and self-sufficient Opinion
of their own Abilities, and so became impatient as well
as regardless of the Advice of others.

The Ashby children lived almost entirely outdoors, where there
were trees to climb, lizards to chase and horses to ride. On the
plantation there were peaceful places: ponds shaded by trees
where Robert and his companions could lie and read or chat
and dream. There were thrilling places: ravines and dark, vine-
draped pockets of tropical forest, which they could explore with
all the attendant dangers – and excitements – of snakes, scorpions
and huge hairy-limbed spiders. There were mysterious places
in which to hide: nooks and crannies created by fallen trees
or mudslides. Robert Cooper's youth was above all a sensual
experience dominated by intense sensations: the warmth of sun-
baked skin, the feeling of being free and unencumbered, and
above all, that incomparable quality of light.

This childhood idyll was punctuated by the rhythms of sugar
cultivation. Robert Cooper would learn to sleep through
the sound of the bell that summoned the slaves to the fields
just before sun-up, and he took for granted the sight of slave
gangs working in the cane fields. The emblematic image of the
colonies – women carrying bundles of cane upon their heads –
was mundane to him. And like all locals, he was able to ignore
the crack of the whip and the strangled cries of the slaves: a
selective deafness that would amaze newcomers to the island.

Meanwhile, another storm was brewing across the Atlantic that
would have a profound impact on Robert Cooper's future.
This was the emergence of the abolitionist movement, which
had been kick-started by Granville Sharp, an ordnance clerk at
the Tower of London. Sharp's involvement in the struggle had
begun when he intervened on behalf of a runaway slave living in
London, whose master had recaptured him, beaten him bloody

and sold him to a Jamaican planter. Outraged by this incident Sharp committed himself to rescuing blacks from slavery. His reputation as the saviour of the capital's desperate slaves meant that in 1772 he was informed of the plight of another unfortunate called James Somerset. Originally from Virginia, Somerset had been brought to England by his owner and had then escaped, only to be recaptured and put on a slave ship destined for the Americas. Hoping to prove that the actions of Somerset's owner were illegal, Sharp went to court. The case eventually ended up before Lord Chief Justice Mansfield in a trial that one historian described as 'high theatre'. At last, the ugly question of slavery, which was something most Britons saw as taking place on the other side of the world, was brought to their doorstep. The court was filled to overflowing when judgement was given in favour of Somerset.

The burgeoning anti-slavery movement was jubilant; Mansfield's decision was interpreted as meaning that slavery was illegal on English soil. This was not the Lord Chief Justice's intention: he strove only to prove that it was unlawful for the slave to be transported abroad. But whatever the legal subtleties, blacks and abolitionists exulted, and at least fifteen English slaves were freed by judges who cited Somerset as their precedent. As the poet William Cowper declared triumphantly in his poem 'The Task':

> Slaves cannot breathe in England, if their lungs
> Receive our air, that moment they are free;
> They touch our country, and their shackles fall.

The West Indian planters were dismayed and one of their number, the Jamaican planter Edward Long, predicted that hordes of slaves would escape to England, where, with 'the lower class of women . . . who are remarkably fond of blacks, for reasons too brutal to mention . . . they would mongrelize the English who would soon resemble the darker skinned and degraded Portuguese'.

In 1783 another sensational case brought the issue of slavery to the British public's attention. It involved the captain of a slave ship, the *Zong*, who decided to throw the sickest of his cargo overboard, and put in a claim to his insurance company for the drowned captives. The insurers disputed the claim; they regarded it as an act of fraud. But against all expectations the jurors decided in favour of the ship's captain and ordered the insurers to pay £30 per slave. The entirely pecuniary nature of the case, that was willing to overlook mass murder, led Sharp to describe it as 'a villainous act that would provoke divine wrath'. The *Zong* case was just the boost that the anti-slavery movement needed; its astounding barbarity rallied thousands to the cause.

In 1787, the year Robert Cooper turned eleven, the British Society for the Abolition of the Slave Trade was officially formed. Granville Sharp was among its leaders, along with the ex-slaver John Newton, who penned the hymn 'Amazing Grace', and the ex-Anglican priest James Ramsay, who had ministered to slaves in St Kitts. They were joined by Cambridge scholar Thomas Clarkson, who would persuade the politician and philanthropist William Wilberforce to join the movement. Their numbers were further swelled by the founder of the Methodist movement, John Wesley, and the great Quaker potter Josiah Wedgwood, who created the symbol of the movement: a plaque which depicted a kneeling slave in chains, arms raised towards heaven, pleading 'Am I Not a Man and a Brother?'

At last the gauntlet had been thrown down and the battle for abolition was truly on. It would be a long and passionate drama, replete with innumerable setbacks and victories, not least because the forces ranged against the abolitionists were truly formidable. From its earliest days, for example, the slave trade (as distinct from the slave plantations), whose eradication would become the first target of the abolitionists, attracted a large number of investors, many of whom were extremely illustrious. In 1663, the English Company of Royal Adventurers boasted at the head of its shareholder list the king himself. When that company ran into debt and was replaced by the Royal Africa Company in 1672, John Locke, the English philosopher of liberty, joined its shareholders, investing £600 in the first three years. Their enthusiasm for this sort of speculation was easily understandable: the trade in 'black ivory', as the historian James Walvin dubbed it, was almost as profitable as sugar. Indeed, on some occasions was even more so: it was not unheard of for some voyages to make profits as high as 100 per cent. But even with average returns at only 9.5 per cent, the slave trade was a more attractive option than real estate, which at that time yielded on average 4–5 per cent, government bonds, which yielded 3.5–4 per cent, or even Caribbean sugar estates, which yielded at best 6–9 per cent. According to the historian Robin Blackburn, gross receipts from voyages entailing the sale of 1,428,701 Africans by the British during the period 1670–1780 totalled £60 million – the equivalent of over £8 billion in contemporary terms.

By the middle of the eighteenth century, the British, partly as a result of their maritime supremacy, had established themselves as the most profitable operators of the slave trade. And all sorts of people were investing, from little old ladies in Brighton and august reverends in Hampshire, to a tavern keeper in the capital, or a housekeeper in Devon, all of them willing to gamble their small savings on 'a voyage'. There were prominent investors too: Humphrey Morice, for example, a Member of Parliament and governor of the Bank of England, owned a fleet of slave ships which he named after his wife and daughters. His business partner was Jamaica's foremost sugar planter, Peter Beckford, whose son, William Beckford, was both a Member of Parliament and an influential businessman who was twice elected Mayor of the City of London and was a close friend of the Prime Minister William Pitt the Elder.

In the port of Liverpool, the story was the same. Sir Thomas Johnson was both the city's mayor and Member of Parliament, and had a 50 per cent stake in the *Blessing*, one of the city's largest slavers, while Foster Cunliffe, three times mayor of the city, made a huge fortune from the slave trade during the 1730s, coordinating his business activities on the thriving commercial street known as 'Negro Row'. Many of these rich and powerful men would become pillars of the Society of West India Planters and Merchants, the organization that was founded in 1780 to fight the abolitionists.

The abolitionists employed many strategies to counter their enemies, some of the most powerful of which were religious, reflecting the fact that many of the abolitionists' intellectual ideas were underpinned by profound spiritual convictions. Their vigorous mobilization of Christian ethics to justify the abolitionist cause was a complete departure from the past, when the Bible, in particular the story of Ham, had been exploited to support the cause of enslavement and the church had expressed very little concern about the institution of slavery. In Barbados, for example, the Anglican church saw no contradiction between its religious ethics and slave ownership, particularly when it was left two lucrative estates in the will of the planter Christopher Codrington. The church ran these plantations, which had over 700 slaves, for several decades. They branded their charges with their own custom-designed mark, and treated them with no greater compassion than many other slave owners. Most of the early missionaries preached that slavery was ordained by God, and even the island's Quakers frequently owned slaves, justifying their slave ownership with the argument that it provided black pagans with exposure to Christianity's civilizing influence.

Now, however, Granville Sharp remarked, 'Thou shalt love thy neighbour as thy self . . . this is the sum and essence of the whole law of God.' A new breed of missionaries emerged, whose ethos was ably summed up by John Wesley, whose *Thoughts on Slavery* were published in 1774:

> I absolutely deny all slave-holding to be consistent with any degree of natural justice . . . It were better that all those islands should remain uncultivated forever; yea, it were more desirable that they were altogether sunk in the depth of the sea, than that they should be cultivated at so high a price as the violation of justice, mercy and truth; and it would be better that none should labour there, that the work should be left undone, than that myriads of innocent men should be murdered, and myriads more dragged into the basest slavery.

The movement attracted a diverse range of followers across Britain. There were blacks – both slaves and free – philosophers and artists, Quakers and missionaries, the white working class, women, even free-traders. With such a varied membership, the British Society for the Abolition of the Slave Trade found it difficult to define its priorities or secure support for a cohesive strategy. Some felt the Society should play a long game, lobbying genteelly for gradual change; others were eager for immediate transformation. Should they focus on the amelioration of slave conditions, or on raising funds to transport slaves to a new life in Africa? In the end they decided that their first goal should be the abolition of the trade in slaves, which would at least eliminate the horrors of the Middle Passage. They also wondered how best to present the slaves to the public so as to elicit the most support. They chose to downplay the slaves' own efforts to gain their freedom and instead presented them as long-suffering victims in need of rescue. After prolonged debate, they evolved a strategy of such sophistication that it would provide the model for citizens' rights movements even up to the present day.

When it came to making the most compelling case, the abolitionists carried out widespread research into the iniquities of the trade. They collected now-famous images, such as that of the slave ship *Brookes* with the captives crammed like cod beneath deck, and the sketch of a ship's captain whipping a naked female slave, suspended upside down, while three black women wept abjectly in the background. To persuade the uncommitted, Clarkson travelled the country with a grisly collection of slave paraphernalia, including handcuffs, shackles and iron masks designed to prevent starving slaves from eating cane. The movement also produced an endless stream of advertisements, articles and pamphlets; indeed the pamphleteers were the bloggers of their day and their writings most accurately reflect the intellectual passions of the era.

Another potent weapon was slave testimonials. The most famous of these, *The Interesting Narrative of the Life of Olaudah Equiano, or Gustavus Vassa, the African*, was published in 1789. The story of Equiano's capture as a child in Africa and subsequent travails as a slave captured the public's imagination. The erstwhile slave promoted his seven-shilling pamphlet with such panache that the historian Adam Hochschild has described it as 'the first great political book tour'. The abolitionist movement quickly began to gather momentum and in 1792 alone, 519 petitions on slavery were handed in to the House of Commons.

Inevitably, the Society of West India Planters and Merchants fought back, mobilizing their considerable economic power to wangle seats in the English Parliament. They also discharged their own salvos in the propaganda war. One pro-slavery tract, composed by a Barbadian curate, was published in 1788 in the hope of dispelling 'the prejudices which had been hastily taken up' against the West Indians. He felt that outsiders were 'totally unacquainted with the customs and manners of these distant colonies' and argued that slave labour was essential to their economic survival. It offered a relentlessly sunny representation of slavery, and suggested that those in England had no understanding of 'the real and actual condition of the black race . . . who are as happy as circumstances can possibly admit'. He claimed slaves were 'Well fed and clothed' and that their daily work 'was not so laborious as hath been represented'. Typically, he argued that Barbadian slaves were better off than European peasants because when they were unable to work they were taken care of by their owners. Slavery also provided an opportunity to Christianize the heathen slaves. Indeed, he concluded the slaves in the West Indies 'may be said to enjoy more of the sweets of life than many of the whites themselves'.

But the times were against him, and within a few years the abolitionists were ready to make their assault on Parliament. William Pitt's speech on the Proposed Abolition of the Slave Trade 1792, in which the ailing parliamentarian spoke late into the night, was a turning point in the fortunes of the abolitionist movement. Warming to his theme, Pitt thundered: 'Why ought the slave trade be abolished? Because it is an incurable injustice!' He could not imagine any evil greater

> than the tearing of 80,000 persons annually from their native land . . . How could the British nation live with a trade that rendered Africa a scene of bloodshed and misery? Do you think nothing of their families which are left behind? Or the connections which are broken? Of the friendships, attachments and relationships that are burst asunder? Do you think nothing of the miseries . . . that are felt from generation to generation . . .? There is something in the horror of it, that surpasses all the bounds of imagination.

Pitt's views on what to do about 'the barbarous traffic in slaves' were unequivocal: any outcome except its abolition would be a disaster. 'I trust we are now likely to be delivered from the greatest practical evil that has every afflicted the human race, from the severest and most extensive calamity recorded in the history of the world.'

While debate raged and public sympathies shifted in Britain, visiting merchants and other travellers brought reports of the abolitionist campaigns to the Caribbean, and this news naturally filtered down to the slave community. The excited slaves pieced together the fragments of information they gleaned from dock-side conversations and careless table talk, and surreptitiously read newspapers and discussed them feverishly. It was no surprise if they sometimes put together this mosaic inaccurately, or that they believed that emancipation would take place sooner than it really did. But whatever the facts, they were nonetheless emboldened and optimistic. For the first time in centuries, there appeared to be a chink in the armour of the mighty slave system and a tiny ember of hope began to glow in their collective hearts. By the early 1790s colonial whites had begun complaining that Caribbean blacks exhibited a 'new temper and ideas', or were 'no longer the same people'.

And so it proved: the greatest coup of the abolition movement was the one carried out by the slaves themselves. Unfolding over twelve years, the revolution in the French Caribbean colony Saint-Domingue would be a roller-coaster ride of blood and tears, glory and desolation. At one time or another all three of the great powers that dominated the region – France, Spain and England – would become embroiled in the conflict. And it would produce not just one but a whole series of leaders, some now forgotten, others immortalized, who would defy the ideas promulgated by the racist societies of the Atlantic world, and would display a bravery, intelligence and military brilliance that would surprise and captivate the world.

The catalyst was the French Revolution, which began in 1789. As one historian noted: 'In few other societies can the ideals of liberty, equality and fraternity have seemed as dangerous as in these plantation systems founded on bondage, inequality and prejudice.' Not only were slaves stirred by its ideals, but the revolution, which generated widespread conflict, also weakened the white establishment militarily and economically in Europe and throughout the colonies. As a result, the number of slave revolts and conspiracies rose sharply in the Greater Caribbean, reaching at least two per year between 1789 and 1815. In many of these rebellions the leaders had mobilized the population by manufacturing rumours of emancipation – and they were believed.

Saint-Domingue was the western part of the island of Hispaniola, which Christopher Columbus had claimed for Spain way back in 1492. It came into French hands in 1697 under the Treaty of Ryswick, when Spain ceded it to France. Despite its late entry into the sugar industry, Saint-Domingue's rate of growth was phenomenal. Where not a single sugar plantation existed in 1689, within fifteen years there were 120. The island eventually became known as 'the Pearl of the Antilles' and, at its most productive, it exported 60 per cent of the coffee and 40 per cent of the sugar consumed in Europe: more than all the British West Indian colonies combined. Its produce gave life to great cities back in France like Marseilles, Bordeaux and Nantes, where many hundreds of French ships and thousands of seamen were engaged exclusively in handling the trade from its shores.

But as Saint-Domingue's production rose, so too did the demand for slaves. Between the moment of French colonization in 1697 and the eve of the French Revolution in the late 1780s, slave numbers increased by over 100 per cent to around half a million, dwarfing the free coloured and white population, which each equalled around 30,000. The slave population on the island – and in certain circumstances the free coloureds – were treated appallingly. For many years the life expectancy of a slave in the colony was a paltry twenty-one years. One slave, recollecting their sufferings, declared:

> Have they not hung men with heads down-ward, drowned them in sacks, crucified them on planks, buried them alive, crushed in mortars . . . Have they not forced them to eat excrement? Have they not thrown them into boiling cauldrons of cane syrup? Have they not put men and women inside barrels studded with spikes and rolled them down mountainsides into the abyss?

In this violent and uneasy society, in which each of the groups – whites, browns and blacks – had such contesting, even conflicting interests, the guiding principles of 'liberty, equality and fraternity' struck a deep chord. The white planter elite dreamt of independence from the mother country, which would give them the freedom to manage local affairs and to avoid the mercantile controls France placed on their economy. The free coloured population, which owned a third of the country's plantations and a quarter of its slaves, dreamt of receiving the full civil and political rights that their colour still denied them. And the slaves dreamt of freedom and some opportunity to live an independent and comfortable life. The very sight of visitors to the island sporting the tricolour cockade thrilled them. 'The white slaves in France,' they were reported as saying, 'had licked their masters and, now free, were governing themselves and taking over the land.'

On 28 March 1790, the French National Assembly decreed that the right to vote and hold office was to be granted to all property owners of twenty-five years or older. However, when it came to applying this law to the colonies, they left the definition of who was a 'person' to the whites, who predictably chose not to extend these rights beyond their own circles. Furious, a faction of free coloureds petitioned for what they saw as their rights, and this movement quickly escalated into armed rebellion. Outnumbered and outgunned, the rebels were defeated, and their leaders, Vincent Ogé and Jean-Baptiste Chavannes, were brutally punished. The former had his legs and ribs crushed by hammer blows before being tied to a wheel and left under the brutal sun until he died. The severed heads of Ogé and his accomplices were displayed on spikes as a warning to the populace.

The treatment of Ogé and Chavannes provoked an outcry in revolutionary France. Maximilien Robespierre declared it was better the colonies perish than the revolution's ideals be compromised, and concluded that the 'free men of colour shall enjoy all the rights of active citizens'. But the National Assembly, frightened of any change that might jeopardize the colony's contribution to national prosperity, settled for a compromise. Rather than extend rights to the island's entire mixed-race population, only those who were born of 'legally free parents', a tiny minority, would be given their freedom. The law was passed, but the blacks and coloureds, whose expectations had been raised, were not appeased. Nor were they placated when modifications were made to the Code Noir, which claimed to limit the brutality of slave punishments and allowed slaves to give testimony in court.

These new rights were promptly tested in the case of Nicolas Lejeune, a coffee planter from the north of the island who put to death four of his slaves because he suspected them of poisoning. He then tortured two others females whom he believed to have withheld information, first putting them in spiked iron collars, then pulling their arms and legs from their sockets, before burning their feet with torches, injuring them so terribly that they died soon after. Encouraged by the new legislation, a group of Lejeune's slaves brought the case to court. In light of the planter's despicable behaviour, and his flagrant violation of the new laws, the slaves believed that he could not avoid conviction. But they were wrong. Despite the incontrovertible evidence against him, Lejeune, who potentially faced the death penalty, was cleared. The planter class had once again come together to protect one of their own and their absolute rights over their 'property'.

Realizing that they still could not rely on the protection of the law, the slaves began to organize. In early August 1791 a secret meeting of drivers, coachmen and other members of the slave elite was held at a plantation in the Plaine du Nord parish. (They believed wrongly that the French king had decreed that they should receive three days a week of freedom, and that the planters were refusing to carry out this royal decree, which heightened their sense of outrage.) Not long after, on a hot and humid night in mid-August, the slaves, who had eluded the authorities in their thousands, gathered in the Bois Caman, an enormous forest full of sacred trees, for a great voodoo ceremony. It was presided over by a slave originally from Jamaica, a giant of a man called Boukman. Here, amidst the drumming and the chanting, the slaves danced in the glow of the torches while Boukman declaimed: 'The God who creates the sun which gives us light, who rouses the waves and rules the storm, though hidden in the clouds, he watches us. He will arm and aid us . . . Throw down the pictures of the White God, who thirsts for our tears, and hear the sound of liberty in all our hearts.'

His cry for revolt was heeded on 22 August in the dark hours before dawn, when 100,000 slaves, emboldened by the sprits, descended on the plantations of the Plaine du Nord. Invisible at first among the cane fields, the warriors emerged almost naked, smeared in soot and armed with machetes, knives, cudgels and chains. Their collective scream was as shrill as the sound of a thousand banshees. Their goals were straightforward: to devastate the plantations on which they had suffered so terribly. And 'Vengeance! Vengeance!' was their war cry.

At first they fired the cane, and when the conflagration was at its height the rebels descended on the great houses, breaking down doors, clambering through windows and gutting the beautifully decorated rooms. Soon the bells usually used to call the slaves to work rang piercingly, guns were fired off in the distance to warn of rebellion and panic spread across the plantations. The slaves crucified one militiaman on the gate of a plantation; elsewhere, they tied a carpenter between two planks and sawed him in half. Planters and their families, some still in their nightclothes, fled to the safety of Cap François. One witness recounted: 'Imagine all the space that the eye can see . . . from which continually arose thick coils of smoke whose hugeness and blackness could only be likened to frightful clouds laden with thunderstorms. They parted only to give way to equally huge flames, alive and flashing to the very sky.'

Within a few days much of this verdant and undulating island was a charred wasteland; its beautiful coffee copses that looked like sea foam when they were in flower, and became a blanket of purple when the berries emerged, had been destroyed. Such was the quantity of smoke and cane ash that for three weeks it was impossible to distinguish day from night. Soon more outbreaks were occurring in the west and south of the country, and the slaves won a number of convincing battles against the *maréchaussée* (the colonial militia). By the time the authorities finally gained some control over the slave population, 180 plantations had been reduced to ash and 2,000 whites had been killed. Unsurprisingly the reprisals were swift and terrible. Over 10,000 blacks were hanged from trees along the entire length of the road leading to Cap François, where their dangling black bodies were left to rot under the torrid sun, generating a stench that could be detected many miles away. And this was just the opening act.

★

When news of the popular uprising of August 1791 first arrived in France, the most common reaction was disbelief. The stereotypes so carefully nurtured by the planters simply did not allow for such a development. Surely it was impossible for a gang of ignorant and unruly negroes to organize a campaign such as this? And how were they able to act so effectively in concert? Rather than give the slaves any credit, they chose to believe that the blame must lie with outside agitators and miscalculations by the planters. But on the other Caribbean islands, where the news arrived first, the responses were altogether more complex. They too did not want to believe that this sort of thing could happen, but everyone knew someone who had seen the smoke and the flames or talked to a survivor. And they knew that their own slaves had the intelligence – and the motivation – to launch such an attack themselves. And so they fretted, fearful that the dissent would spread and inspire their own slaves to rebellion.

Boukman, who had led the first phase of the slaves' struggle, had been killed shortly after the first skirmishes, but a number of other agitators soon emerged to take his place, not least a forty-five-year-old slave called François Dominique Toussaint Bréda, who had served as a livestock steward on the De Libertas plantation. After protecting his master and mistress from the rebels and dispatching them to the safety of the capital, he joined the rebel slave forces.

As a young man, able to read and write, Toussaint had been particularly inspired by the words written by Abbé Raynal in relation to the slaves of the West Indies: 'Where is he, that great man whom Nature owes to her vexed oppressed and tormented children? Where is he? He will appear, doubt it not, he will come forward and raise the sacred standard of liberty.' Determined to be that man, Toussaint had continued to read widely, honed his body by swimming and became such a fine rider that even at the age of sixty he regularly rode 125 miles a day, earning himself the nickname 'the Centaur of the Savannah'. By the time he joined the rebels his extraordinary intellectual and physical abilities, as well as his strategic genius, made his rise through the rebel ranks inevitable. These qualities were exceeded only by his charisma, for this small, ugly man was an inspired speaker, moving his fighters into battle with the cry, 'We have come here to win or to die!' Over time he became known as Toussaint L'Ouverture (The Opener) and was described by the Caribbean historian C.L.R. James as the most remarkable figure of his era, with the possible exception of his nemesis Napoleon Bonaparte.

The slaves' ambitions in Saint-Domingue were aided by wider developments. In the April of 1792 the French General Assembly had issued a decree enfranchising free blacks and mulattoes but not black slaves, which drew more of them to the cause. All the while, the island's whites and the freed coloureds were still locked in conflict. By early 1793 revolutionary France was at war with both Britain and Spain, and factions of the rebellious slaves on the island were formalizing alliances with the latter. The French government, fearing that it would lose control of the colony altogether and, worse still, that it might fall into the hands of their enemies, decided to abolish slavery on the island on 29 August 1793. By the following February, France extended this policy to all its colonies.

The success of the black revolt in Saint-Domingue caused aftershocks throughout the Atlantic world. It went on to inspire a failed rebellion in the neighbouring island of Grenada the following year in which a coalition of freed coloureds and black slaves had turned against the island's whites, and Barbadians were aware of a new insolence among their own slaves too. For planters across the region the Saint-Domingue slaves' revolution was an apocalyptic development that threatened to wipe out their entire way of life.

Although not caught up in these developments directly, Robert Cooper's early life and education were informed by the ideology that underwrote the sugar industry and its investment in slavery. The wealthiest of the island's planters sent their children off to England to be taught at the best schools, where they gained a reputation for squandering their parents' sugar fortunes 'in drinking, gaming and wenching'. This was not an option for less affluent families like the Ashbys, so Robert Cooper would have been educated at one of the island's local schools, which at that time all catered exclusively for the white male population. The teaching was often indifferent, mainly supplied by 'half-educated adventurers' eager to jump on the sugar train. For those families with greater cultural pretensions, the island's capital had a goodly selection of dancing masters, music teachers and painting instructors. It is unlikely that the Ashbys could afford these opportunities to supplement their children's education, but Robert Cooper certainly received some tutoring; his correspondence was fluent and grammatically correct and he penned an elegant hand.

Education in the Caribbean was not just about giving planters' children the three Rs: it was also about inculcating their society's values. In neighbouring Martinique, for example, the founder of one school, Father Charles François, described his institution's raison d'être as being a way to counter the 'indolence' and 'depravity' inspired by too much proximity to black people and to prepare his pupils to become the masters and mistresses of plantations.

By this time the crude racism of the early years of slavery had been overlaid with competing pseudo-scientific theories about race and the nature of the 'Negro'. Two years before Robert Cooper's birth, the virulently racist planter Edward Long published his *History of Jamaica*, in which he used the concept of the Great Chain of Being to justify his racial views. A popular hypothesis of the time, this idea posited the existence of a hierarchy 'through the most simple forms of life, through to the most intelligent animals including man, and continued further upward to the myriad ranks of celestial creatures until, finally it reached its summit in God'. The white man was in the middle of this hierarchy. (Angels, of course, were above them.) But blacks were not just lower down the chain, 'they were a separate species all together'. To Long, they were a distinct species of human most analogous to the monkey and related genera, with whom, he claimed, 'some races of black men are intimate'; African slavery was therefore natural and acceptable, the product of a divinely ordained pecking order.

Unlike Long, the French naturalist the Comte de Buffon believed that blacks were part of the same species as whites (the monogenist argument), but he argued that they were situated at 'the bottom of the human hierarchy'. In 1775, the year after Long's book was published, the term 'Caucasian race' was coined by the zoologist Johann Friedrich Blumenbach. He believed that the Caucasus was the cradle of human civilization and that all intelligence and beauty originated there. To prove his thesis, he collected a selection of 245 skulls which he duly examined and measured. After this analysis, he created a theory of a five-storey racial pyramid with whites at the top. On the next three levels were Australian Aborigines, American Indians, and 'yellow-skinned' Asians. At the bottom were blacks originating in Africa. Against all scientific reason the term 'Caucasian' remains in use to this day, synonymous with the white minority that Blumenbach claimed sat at the summit of humanity's hierarchy.

Surrounded by such ideas, the young scions of the planter caste who had once played, albeit unequally, with their slaves, now despised them, dismissing them as 'niggers' and chastising them if they addressed them unprompted or looked them directly in the eye. Racism was the factor that underpinned the entire social system of the colonies. It was not just about maintaining a rigid distinction between black and white, but about making sure that white society found some coherence. 'In fact,' wrote the historian Karl Watson, 'the only issue which seemed to have a unifying effect on Barbadian whites was that of race.' Barbados was after all a tiny, densely populated island in which a paranoid white minority lived cheek by jowl with a black majority they perceived as threatening and volatile. But in reality this small group of whites – divided by class, political allegiance and life experience – had little in common, so in times of crisis, they had only one thing to pull them together: their shared skin colour.

This way of thinking was most seamlessly absorbed by those who grew up on the islands, but it was also quickly adopted by outsiders. The whites who went to the Caribbean often started off being hostile to the slave system but, after going through what the twentieth-century writer and historian Edward Brathwaite (also known as Kamau Brathwaite) called 'cultural action' or 'social processing', they often changed their minds. Lieutenant Thomas Howard, who served in the region at the end of the 1790s, was typical:

> When I first came into this Country, I had the most horrid idea of the treatment the Slaves received from their Masters that could possibly be formed; every time I heard the Lash sound over the Back of a Negro my very Blood boiled and I was ready to take away the whip and the Lash of the Master. Since that time . . . I am persuaded my heart is not grown harder . . . yet I see the Business in a very different Light.

10

No man puts a chain about the ankle of his fellow man without at last finding the other end fastened about his own neck.

Frederick Douglass

At the age of eighteen, Robert Cooper's life took a fateful and fortuitous turn when he was propelled by marriage into the upper echelons of Barbadian society. His union with Mary Burke in 1794 was a remarkable social coup for the Ashbys. The bride's family had been well established on the island since the early part of the eighteenth century. They had originally generated their wealth as merchants before making the move into sugar production. Their success as sugar cultivators meant that by the latter part of the eighteenth century they had secured a place in the island's plantocracy. Mary's uncle, Colonel John Burke, was both a leading light in the local militia and Parliamentary Representative for the parish of Christ Church for seventeen consecutive years between 1771 and 1788. As the Ashbys moved within the small social circle of white planters in the Oistins area, they would inevitably have been acquainted with this prestigious clan, albeit from a respectful distance. When they attended the parish church, the colonel and his family would be seated in their specially designated pew and the Ashbys could only dream that one day they would move in the Burkes' orbit as equals.

Given the social discrepancy between the two families, it is interesting to speculate as to why the Burke family agreed to the match. It may simply have been island demographics: by the 1790s, Barbados was one of the few colonial territories in which women slightly outnumbered men, particularly among the white population. The gender balance had been completely upturned since George Ashby's time: as a result of the islanders' eager desire to embrace family life, Barbados now had the most stable family structure of any of the British West Indian islands, hence the growth in the number of women who were born there. Another issue might have been Mary's age. At twenty-four, she was not only a few years older than her husband, but – in terms of the island's planter caste – dangerously close to being on the shelf.

The most likely reason, however, was probably the most prosaic one: she found him attractive. Robert Cooper Ashby was a good-looking man. A portrait of him painted two decades later at the height of his success depicts a type that was regarded as particularly handsome during the period. Impeccably groomed chestnut hair frames an imperious face, and he has green eyes, a long Roman nose, a luxurious moustache – carefully waxed and twirled at the ends – and an exquisitely barbered goatee. In an age that so romanticized the military, it did not hurt that Robert Cooper was painted in his militia uniform. Indeed, one historian noted that military commissions were valued largely because of the prestige they gave the holders with Creole beauties. Sad experience, the writer noted, had taught these girls' parents 'to guard their daughters against dapper braids wearers'.

Courtship among the respectable colonial classes was a rather superficial affair. Once the possibility of the match was mooted, the women of their circle would have seen to it that the pair was brought together in the intimacy of people's homes. Here each exchange was scrutinized by a squadron of matronly ladies who noted the pair's every move. At these soirées Robert

Cooper and Mary Burke could talk for a bit, even flirt a little. He would have courted her with compliments and gallantries; she would have responded appropriately, smiling and demurring at the appropriate moments. As things progressed the pair would be encouraged to attend the occasional ball, which gave them the opportunity to hold hands, even coil their arms around the other's waist. But respectability demanded that they were rarely left alone together.

Since these candlelit meetings were so carefully chaperoned, Robert Cooper's dashing appearance and masterful aura were probably all that Mary Burke got to know about him before the marriage was arranged. And it was probably enough; Creole girls, 'stuffed to the gills with romantic nonsense', tended to be unsophisticated and unrealistic about what marriage would entail. Whatever her fantasies and misconceptions, the reality was that the options for a well-born Creole woman were extremely limited. Only men had agency in this society and at this time in history; only they were able to vote, hold public office, or exert any formal power. A job would have represented an unthinkable social demotion for a well-born woman like Mary Burke, and spinsterhood held little appeal. For a respectable woman, marriage was the gateway to everything: it opened the door to the role of being a wife, the status of being married and the opportunity to become a mother.

The choice of husband was of course crucial, but it was also something of a gamble. At that time, as in England, the accepted maxim was that husband and wife were one person in law. And that 'person' was the man. Thus if a woman chose poorly by marrying someone who was cruel or profligate or a womanizer, she could be trapped in a situation from which it was virtually impossible to escape. In addition, since the entirety of a woman's assets were transferred to her husband on marriage, a woman like Mary Burke who was richer than her husband had a great deal to lose. With the signature of a wedding contract, her wealth, independence and power were swept away. While for Robert Cooper, that final flourish of a pen was almost entirely positive: he gained not only his wife's fortune, but took several steps up the social ladder, acquiring some of her family's considerable cultural cachet along the way.

A child arrived with gratifying swiftness. Their only son, John Burke, named after the Burke family's patriarch, was born in 1796. As was the custom, the birth of the firstborn and male heir was celebrated in style. Robert Cooper would have declared a feast day and even allowed his slaves a day off work. A hog and a cow were butchered and barbecued to feed the visitors and the air was scented with the smell of roasted meat. The slave cooks supplemented this with an array of local delicacies such as candied sweet potatoes, pickled breadfruit and corn seasoned with chilli butter. Rum was distributed among the workers, in preparation for the toast to the new baby's arrival. Then the infant, dressed in impeccably laundered and ornately worked clothes, was wrenched from the breast of his wet nurse and held aloft as visitors and slaves alike roared their approval.

The young family settled on Burkes plantation, which was situated at the southernmost point of the southernmost parish, Christ Church. The property had a history almost as old as the colony itself. There had been a plantation on this site ever since the early days of settlement. In 1663 James Oistine (otherwise spelt Austin or Oistin), 'a wild, mad, drunken fellow whose lewd and extravagant carriage made him infamous in the island', had sold part of the land, which eventually found its way into the hands of the Burke family. In 1796, John Burke the elder died and bequeathed the plantation to his nephew, who in turn died unexpectedly. When his will was proved it became clear he had left this sixty-two-acre plantation to his sister Mary Burke, who had recently married Robert Cooper Ashby. The property was substantially extended by a joint purchase the couple made in 1802, when they acquired 150 acres of land adjacent to their property. No doubt this sizeable acquisition was funded primarily by Mary's inheritance, since it is unlikely that the Ashby clan could have raised anything like the necessary £1,200. The ameliorated Burkes estate now abutted the boundaries of planters such as Henry Chase, Thomas Cryall, William Segall and the Honorable John Ince, who would become the Ashbys' nearest neighbours and, in some cases, closest friends.

Set high on a bluff, caressed by south-east trade winds and bordered on one side by steep escarpments overgrown with cacti and sea grapes which led down to foam-crested turquoise waters, Burkes had a glorious location. The land here is good and boasts the kind of beauty that has drawn people to it over thousands of years. Its soil is naturally fertile and the sea that constitutes its southernmost border is teeming with fish and other sea life. But this place also has a curious feeling of confinement that must have been particularly disturbing to its slave inhabitants; as the waves crash in beneath you, there is a sense of being on the edge of things, as if there is nowhere else to go.

Today, all that remains of the estate is Burkes Mill, a sturdy tower made of coral stone that dates back to around 1800. Its original windows survive, but it has lost the bell that would have been used to summon the slaves to their daily labour. It is now the studio of a well-known local artist, and she and her husband have built their fashionable home beside it. The land that once comprised Burkes, meanwhile, is today dominated by the only metal lighthouse in the Caribbean. Built in 1805, it still fulfils its original function, warning seafarers about the dangers of its coast. The rest of Burkes acreage is now largely residential: a desirable location for the affluent Barbadian middle class. In the wild sea that once acted as the property's border, windsurfers twist and twirl, riding their sails on the waves.

Though few of the original buildings remain, it is possible to reconstruct something of the appearance of Burkes in its heyday through old plans, inventories and an understanding of local convention. As was the tradition, the plantation was built on a slight eminence so that the planter could keep a watchful eye on his investment. But in contrast to the modest property on which Robert Cooper was raised, the great house at Burkes was an altogether more exalted affair; one guest of the estate described this exhibition of wealth, power and vanity as 'a mansion'.

The nineteenth-century visitor, arriving on horseback or by carriage, approached Burkes by a long drive lined by stately trees. At the end of this Arcadian grove was the house itself: an impressive two-storey building surrounded by an impeccably maintained and shady garden dominated by large tamarind, mango and frangipani trees. These orderly grounds with their colourful and luxuriant plants required a devoted cadre of slaves to defend them against the voracity of the island's fast-growing vegetation. Some planters preferred to grow hedges of lime trees around their homes as a safety precaution; not only did the plants yield the limes which were an essential ingredient in the island's famous rum punch, their prickles served also as fortification against any attempt to encroach on the property.

Once visitors had climbed the steep stone steps that led to the entrance of this tropical palace, they were ushered into the house by one of the legion of domestics who served the family, through a handsome reception usually panelled in dark glossy wood. Upstairs were the bedrooms, their heavy mahogany beds shrouded with netting to protect the sleeper from insects. Most of the rooms in Barbadian plantations were also equipped with Venetian blinds, which simultaneously allowed the air to circulate and blocked out some of the blazing sunlight.

On the ground floor was a drawing room furnished with local furniture as well as a few pieces imported from North America and England, including fashionable items like grandfather clocks, lacquered screens and ornate oil lamps. On the walls were the ubiquitous prints of local scenery and maps of the island that the colonials of the period found so captivating. The dining room was dominated by a huge table with matching chairs and a sideboard that contained china plates, silver cutlery, crystal glasses and decanters and ornate candelabras: enough to serve scores of guests. Next door was the study where Robert Cooper kept his records and ledgers.

The entire house was encircled by a wide wrap-around balcony with slatted railings. On this veranda the family could sit and enjoy the breeze. Here the Ashbys collected to entertain their guests and chat, sip cool drinks and play cards. Most planters also had a spyglass, strategically positioned, so that they could survey their domain. With this, Robert Cooper could watch the distant ships sail across the horizon, scrutinize his workers in the fields and monitor the approach of any visitors as they rode towards his property.

It is not hard to imagine the Ashby family in these rooms, slumbering on canopied beds piled lushly with cushions and covered with embroidered sheets, as the ubiquitous bats soared and dipped against the starlit night and the plantation dogs barked their messages to their neighbours; or gorging on lavish plantation meals; or sitting on the balcony's wicker furniture enjoying their lime water; or playing backgammon on the patio; or strolling in the garden against a backdrop of green pastures and a vivid sky, while the sounds of the slaves cutting cane wafted over to them from the far-off fields. Their lives were perpetually perfumed by the unique smells of plantation life – a heady combination of tropical flowers and horse manure, heat and the cloying smell of sugar cane – which drifted in through the doors and windows. All the while, they were served by an army of ever-present slaves, who slipped around the house as unremarked upon as ghosts.

At its most expansive, the Burkes property comprised 350 acres and over 200 slaves. To those who lived there, it must have felt sometimes as if it was the entire world. Like most plantations it was a self-sufficient community, as self-contained and independent as any small town. In addition to the plantation house and slave huts it included scores of buildings, including windmills to power the sugar works and boiling and curing houses with their smoking chimneys, as well as barns for livestock and storage sheds for cane and plantation supplies; it even had its own hospital and jail. It was sustained largely by what was grown on the property, including sweet potatoes, plantains and okra that the slaves cultivated alongside guavas, oranges and bananas. There were pigs, cows and poultry in its fields, and fish in its waters. While the cane crop provided the backbone of the plantation's economy, Burkes also sold small amounts of other produce like cotton, vegetables and eggs.

Surrounding all of this were the lands of the plantation itself. Some parts were devoted to grazing fields for cattle, others to the cultivation of foodstuffs, with the odd gully abandoned to nature, covered in draping vines and choked with foliage. All the rest was a sea of sugar cane, extending so wide and deep that it seemed to touch the horizon. The cane had as many moods as an ocean: on a still day it absorbed the heat of the sun and sent it back into the sky in shimmers, at other times when it was breezy, the cane waved ceaselessly, creating what the historian C.L.R. James called 'the song that never ceased'.

These early years at Burkes were a period of transition for Robert Cooper Ashby. It was one thing to be brought up on a plantation, but quite another to run one. Though he would have been familiar with many of the processes involved in 'civilizing sugar' and would have an instinctive understanding of how to recognize a diseased cane plant or when it was time to harvest, he had never before been responsible for making sure this complex operation ran smoothly and profitably. But it was probably a challenge he relished. Robert Cooper was an ambitious man, and Burkes was an altogether grander canvas on which to paint his dreams than the modest farm on which he grew up.

Robert Cooper's first task when he took over control of the plantation in 1795 was to familiarize himself with the property, so he spent many hours on horseback riding up and down the cane breaks, inspecting Burkes' buildings and boundaries, meeting employees and going through the slave ledgers and accounts. He needed to know where this operation was solid and where it was vulnerable. Was the estate yielding as much sugar as it could? Did the factory need repairing or extending? Was the overseer getting the best out of his slaves? Was the bookkeeper embezzling the family's profits, taking advantage of the death of its previous owner? Perhaps he needed to get a loan to carry out his plans? Only then, when he had a clear idea of how best to proceed, would Robert Cooper roll up his sleeves and get to work.

Later on, the priority was to increase his human 'stock'. Though his wife had inherited the property with its existing slave population, once Burkes had been extended Robert Cooper needed more hands to farm the estate. Therefore he spent some of his time in these early years going backwards and forwards to the slave market in Bridgetown. It was one of the busiest in the region, with slaves on sale every day but Sunday, and it attracted buyers from all over the Americas. One nineteenth-century traveller to the island recollected such an occasion:

> I went one day to a sale of Negroes. Here an elderly Negro woman and her four children, all born in the island, were exposed to sale. Two of the boys were purchased by a mulatto woman who had the countenance of a perfect Virago. And she examined the boys with all possible indelicacy. I pitied them greatly; they were to be separated from their mother and sent to Demerara. The

other two children were females and bought by a decent looking white man to take with him to Berbice, and the mother was sold to a planter of St Lucia.

The biggest challenge for Robert Cooper would have been learning how to govern such a large and recalcitrant workforce. Luckily, advice was readily available. Just as cattle farmers had evolved many theories for raising a healthy herd, so the West Indian planters had written manuals – the product of over a hundred years of practical experience – about how to manage their slaves. For example, in 1786 a group of prominent Barbadian slave owners published a pamphlet in London entitled 'Instructions . . . offered to the Consideration of Proprietors and Managers of Plantations in Barbados'. It outlined a number of factors that the estate manager should consider in his daily manipulation of the black workforce in order to achieve high levels of productivity and social stability.

The West Indian proprietors had evolved an organizational structure that was extremely hierarchical and it was this system that Robert Cooper inevitably implemented at Burkes. At its summit was the planter, Robert Cooper, who ruled like an absolute monarch, and his wife and child, who enjoyed the privileges of any royal family. Here he was master of a large community of slaves over whom he literally had the power of life and death, since for most of his time as a planter the murder of a slave was punishable only by a fine of £15. So when Robert Cooper rode across Burkes in his planter's uniform of jodhpurs and white frock coat with shiny buttons, wielding his whip or gold-topped cane, the work rate would have quickened while every eye surreptitiously followed him, fearing to draw his attention or displease him.

His role as head of the plantation was crucial, for just as one could not run a country without a head of state, so it was inadvisable to run a plantation without someone who did not have its long-term interests at heart. On islands such as Jamaica, where the percentage of absentee planters was high, individual plantations tended to be more unruly and less profitable in the long run, and the island itself was more violent and unstable. Indeed, Jamaica had more rebellions than the rest of the British islands put together. As the Gothic novel writer turned Jamaican planter Matthew Lewis noted, the declaration 'You belong no massa' was one of the most contemptuous remarks that one slave could throw at another. Lewis mistakenly put this down to the slaves' desire to be ruled, rather than a recognition of how dangerous it was to live on a plantation without an ultimate authority figure. There was virtually no protection for its black inhabitants under the law, which meant that workers' well-being was utterly dependent on the nature and values of those in charge of them.

Beneath Robert Cooper were a handful of white men, including clerks, attorneys and bookkeepers, who tended to be a transient, disgruntled community. They frequently found the work lonely and dispiriting and quibbled ceaselessly about wages and conditions. The most important of them were the overseers, who were responsible for slave performance; they spent most of their time directly supervising slaves in the cane fields or in the boiling house. As de facto deputies, these men were also in charge of the plantation when Robert Cooper went away.

Overseers were often second sons who had no other way of making a living, or poor boys from Britain who hoped to make their fortune in the colonies. But their wages were not usually sufficient to fulfil their dreams of establishing their own plantations. These men were frequently a source of aggravation to planters because so few of them were reliable or efficient. Poorly educated and frequently pickled with drink, they were usually unmarried – planters felt that wives were a distraction – but virtually never celibate. Indeed, they were notorious for their rapacious attentions to their female slaves, whom they assaulted in the cane fields or co-opted as their mistresses. Some were too interested in fornicating to keep their minds on the job, while others were either too lenient or too harsh to get the best out of the workers, though excesses were rarely curtailed unless it affected production.

One such case occurred in 1824, when the Martinican planter Pierre Desalles noted in his diary that his slaves had been lobbying for many months against a vicious overseer. They told him: 'Your negroes are giving in to despair . . . nothing amuses them, they no longer get dressed, and when they think of M. Chignac, the hospital fills up, and they let themselves die.' In the end the planter gave in and fired the man, admitting: 'All our misfortunes were caused by the slaves' hatred for him.' Desalles understood, as Robert Cooper eventually would, that a good planter had to be responsive to the subtle shifts in the interpersonal dynamics on his plantation in order to neutralize potential conflict.

Just below overseers in the pyramid, and almost as valued, was a group of slaves known as rangers or drivers. Notable for their physical strength and vigour, these men were chosen to help the overseer impose discipline in the fields. Armed with whips and sometimes even knives and guns, they were allowed to administer ad hoc punishment to field slaves who were not working fast or hard enough. With a punch in the face or a well-aimed kick, they urged the exhausted slaves onwards. They even had permission to apply whippings – usually a preset number sanctioned by the overseer – to slaves they believed had misbehaved. Their power extended beyond the canes; at night they rampaged through the slave settlement like pirates, stealing food and possessions or grabbing a woman or girl.

At the top of this group was the head driver or ranger, who traditionally was an unusually strong and impressive figure. He had authority from the overseer to direct all the slaves in each gang, and to instruct them in the tasks that he believed to be necessary. He was also the conduit between the slaves and the white managers, a role that demanded that he be an excellent negotiator and possess the ability to inspire both fear and respect in the slaves. This position was so important that a bad or indifferent head driver could seriously compromise the success of the plantation.

The 1786 manual also stressed the importance of carefully handling slaves of special ability, partly because of their potential contribution to plantation life but also because they were the biggest challenge to an estate's equilibrium and could easily turn their energies towards subversion. The canny planter provided such slaves with privileges and authority, selecting them for management roles: alongside the driver and rangers were artisans like carpenters, masons and blacksmiths and specialists who worked in the sugar factory such as boiler men. Women too were sometimes elevated to more privileged positions, as skilled domestic labourers, such as cooks, nurses and launderers, as well as midwives or healers.

At the base of this pyramid, and supporting the entire edifice, was an army of Africans who did the work of planting, harvesting and transporting of the cane. They were organized into a gang system. The first gang was for the strongest slaves, both male and female, who undertook the most strenuous jobs on the plantation such as the sowing and harvesting. One planter described them as 'the flower of all field battalions, drafted and recruited from all the other gangs as they come of age to endure severe labour. They were drilled to become veterans of the most arduous field undertakings . . . They are the very essence of an estate, its support in all weathers and necessities.' The spectacle of these slaves at work awed outsiders. One visitor to the islands wrote in 1812: 'It has often occurred to me that a gang of Negroes in the act of holing for canes, when hard driven, appeared to be as formidable as a phalanx of infantry by the rapid movement of their hoes . . . while I have been astonished how such habits could enable beings to persevere, so many hours in such violent effort.'

The second gang was responsible for the weeding and clearing; it included mothers of suckling children, youths aged between twelve and eighteen, and elderly people who were still strong enough for field work. They cleaned up the fields and cleared the floor of crushed cane and trash in the factory. The third gang was comprised of the most vulnerable people on the plantation: the very young and the old, the frail and recuperating. They did the light work of clearing weeds and rocks, as well as taking care of the other gangs and the animals, hence the sight of youngsters running up and down the canes carrying buckets of water, or feeding the cattle hay.

The plantation system provided a strong blueprint, but each estate had its own history, set of relationships and mix of characters, so no single strategy could ever be successful. An effective plantation was one where all the levels of this hierarchy worked in functional harmony. While this could and did accommodate a high degree of brutality and discord, there was a tipping point beyond which productivity was impaired.

The daily life of the plantation had a distinct rhythm in which the slaves played their part and the planter his. Plantation dwellers tended to be early risers, but Robert Cooper was woken by his body slave, who, after rousing him, padded around the room opening the jalousied windows that overlooked the manicured grounds of the great house. Then the slave ferried vat after vat of boiling water upstairs from the kitchen fire to fill a bath, where he washed Robert Cooper's hair and soaped his back. He dried him meticulously, helped him dress and finally arranged his hair.

Breakfast followed. This was usually a prodigious affair, particularly if guests were staying. One such visitor declared that it was 'as if they had never eaten before'. And no wonder, as the meal that she was treated to comprised 'a dish of tea, another of coffee, a bumper of claret, another large one of hock negus; then Madeira, sangaree, hot and cold meat, stews and fries, hot and cold fish, pickled and plain, peppers, ginger sweetmeats, acid fruit, sweet jellies – in short it was all as astounding as it was disgusting'.

The majority of Robert Cooper's black charges had an altogether more rude entry to the day. Woken before sun-up by the clamorous sound of the bell atop the mill, the first gang hauled themselves off the floors of their fetid huts and quickly splashed their faces with cold water, before being led to the cane fields by the overseer. When they arrived a register was called and the absentees were noted, to be punished later. Then the slaves, armed with their hoes and machetes, fork and baskets, were set to work until nine o'clock, when they were allowed half an hour to consume their starchy breakfast of food such as boiled yams and plantains; a diet which had not changed much since the time of George Ashby.

After breakfast, the slaves returned to the fields until midday, when they were allowed a two-hour break for lunch, which was yet another starchy meal enlivened with salt fish or pig's tail, which they received as part of their weekly rations. Desperate to up productivity, some planters gave their charges less time to recuperate, but this was almost always counterproductive as exhausted slaves worked less effectively or fell ill. Then the slaves returned to work under the blazing sun, tormented by rats, snakes and scorpions. Meanwhile Robert Cooper, after his daily tour around the plantation to check on his assets, retired to his study to pore over his ledgers. Then there was usually a substantial cooked lunch and perhaps a rejuvenating post-prandial nap.

Arising refreshed, Robert Cooper returned to study while his slaves toiled until sunset, when they were dismissed by the sound of the bell, having worked for a minimum of ten hours. The slaves returned to their quarters often worn to distraction, but knowing that their day was not over: there were children to attend to, homes to be cleaned, allotments to be tended and food to be cooked.

It was a point of honour in plantation society that no menial activity was undertaken by anyone but a slave, so Robert Cooper and his contemporaries would do as little for themselves as was humanly possible. Slaves were called to swat flies and lift balls of wool that had fallen to the ground. This 'learned helplessness' provoked frequent comment from visitors to the island. One army officer related this tale:

> I was one evening . . . witness to the lazy pride of a creole lady, an opposite neighbour. She was seated at her window, in the true style of Barbadian indolence, and I walking in our gallery. When she was wanted some tamarind water, which stood at the farther end of the room, she called out 'Judy', 'Judy', then 'Mary', 'Mary'; again in a louder tone, 'Here somebody.' Thus she continued until she got a fit of coughing and I laughed heartily . . . These lazy creoles if they drop a pin, will not stoop to pick it up.

After a generous dinner and a couple of hours either with his family or in the solitude of his study, Robert Cooper climbed the stairs to his room, where his body servant pulled off his boots, helped him out of his clothes, and held the chamber pot for him to piss in. As he clambered into bed, the slave extinguished the oil lamps and said good night. Then the slave slipped out of the room and returned to the slave quarters, or lay down on his pallet on the bedroom floor, hoping that his master would not need him in the night.

★

Despite his power at the head of this vast organization, Robert Cooper himself served a hard master: sugar. The demands of that crop shaped his hours, days and months, as it did everyone's at Burkes. In Barbados the climate was sympathetic enough to allow the canes to be planted at almost any season, but a pattern emerged around the harvest, which began roughly at the end of January and continued to the end of July. Since the sugar was simultaneously harvested and processed during these months, this was easily the busiest period, during which the overseer shouted louder, the slave-drivers pushed the workers harder, the drivers resorted to the whip more frequently, and the slaves worked their fingers to the bone, while the master fretted himself to the point of sleeplessness. Frequently the field hands worked all through the night cutting cane in order to get it to the mill on time. If the harvest went well it would finance Burkes for another year; if it went badly the whole plantation might be in jeopardy.

The day before cutting, the fields were burned to destroy vermin and the top leaves that slowed down the reapers. These conflagrations were astonishing visual spectacles but also made conditions on the plantation uncomfortable for everyone: the sound of the roaring flames was hellish, and the heat made such a furnace out of the fields that it was like breathing in steam, while the ashes that floated down on the crop irritated the skin and the sickly scent of burnt sugar hovered in the air. Then the harvest began in earnest. It was a two-stage process: first the reaping of the cane and then the complex factory process which transformed its syrup into those delectable brown or white crystals that had titillated the taste buds of the world. Robert Cooper would have overseen both these activities, riding up and down the cane breaks surveying his 'shock troops' as they worked and liaising anxiously with the overseer about their progress.

Despite the West Indian planters' rather euphemistic

representation of cane cutting as an ancient art – as exotic as pearl diving in Japan or grape picking in Italy – harvesting sugar is both arduous and dangerous. Historian Adam Hochschild claimed that:

> Caribbean slavery was, by every measure, far more deadly than slavery in the American South. This was not because Southern masters were the kind and gentle ones of *Gone With the Wind*, but because cultivating sugar cane by hand was – and still is – one of the hardest ways of life on earth. Almost everywhere in the Americas where slaves were working other than on sugar plantations they lived longer.

Cane cutting has its own technique: the cutter steps forward, wraps his arms around a bundle of stalks and raises the blade up over the shoulder, bringing it down vigorously at the base, then he shaves the leaves off with a quick flick of the machete and piles the canes neatly. The discomfort of this motion means that the field hand has to learn quickly how to swing his blade with the least resistance. Cane cutters, both male and female, tend to have a unique physique, taut-muscled and broad-shouldered like a dancer or professional athlete. The sheer physical exertion associated with the task is such that an otherwise fit person is reduced to a standstill within twenty minutes, bent double and soaked with sweat. For those fuelled by an inadequate diet, as so many slaves were, the work was unimaginably exhausting.

But the physical dangers of cane cutting do not end with fatigue. There is also the ever-present danger of the wrenched back, the twisted ankle, rat and insect bites, pierced eardrums or the eye stabbed by a sharp cane leaf. But most gory of all is the slip of the blade, which is so common that cane cutters across the globe were – and still are – identifiable by the terrible scars on their lower legs. The monotony of the work is also debilitating, and the labourers must find that delicate balance between being attentive lest they injure themselves, and allowing their mind to drift away lest they go mad with boredom. Trapped within a prison of green and brown stalks, where sound is distorted and distances are impossible to calculate, the slaves must sometimes have been overwhelmed by claustrophobia, which could only be escaped if they kept on cutting.

The only work harder than cane cutting was cane holing. This task, which was usually undertaken in the August heat, first required the slaves to prepare the land for planting by slashing and burning grass, shrubs and old cane; and then, working in pairs and equipped with hoes, they dug holes around eight inches deep and three feet long at very tight intervals. Cane tops were then inserted into the holes and packed with manure. In the French Antilles workers were expected to plant twenty-eight holes per hour, otherwise they were flogged. The work was so arduous that many planters, like Matthew Lewis in Jamaica, hired in jobbing slave gangs rather than use their own people. These slaves usually had a working life expectancy of only seven years before dying, according to one observer, like 'overwrought or over-driven horses'.

The cane was transported from the fields to the factory either by mule or on the heads of the labourers. Then slaves fed the lengths of cane through the vertical rollers of the mills, while others cleared away the desiccated trash. Meanwhile, the sweet greyish liquid poured through the gutters straight into the boiling house. In this humid inferno the cane juice was crystallized by evaporation. After being allowed to stand in several large receivers, the juice was initially heated in shallow pans called clarifiers where it was tempered with lime. The calcium carbonate acted as a catalyst, prompting the sediment to sink to the bottom and the impurities to rise to the surface. Slaves continuously skimmed this 'crust' off the liquid until it was tempered. Then the juice was boiled in a series of progressively smaller 'coppers' until it was ready to enter the 'tache' in which it was finally crystallized or 'struck'.

The 'striking' of the sugar was a delicate and crucial task which was left to one of the most valuable workers on the plantation: the boiler man. It was his job to test the bubbling brown liquid between thumb and forefinger until it could form a strand of a certain length. If his judgement was wrong an entire batch of sugar could be ruined, so a good boiler man was worth his weight in gold. Once this critical moment arrived, the sugar was ready to granulate, and was transferred to 'coolers', pans around which water was constantly pumped. Then the raw sugar was 'potted': that is, ladled into 1,800-pound hogsheads. These were placed on stone troughs in the curing house for two days, and then they were tapped and left to drain and mature for several weeks before being weighed, transported and shipped. Meanwhile the dark molasses that was drained from the hogsheads burbled further down into the distillery or 'still house', where it was either siphoned into containers and exported raw, or processed into rum. (This was another extremely lucrative by-product of cane, since every man in Britain's navy was guaranteed a ration of rum each day.)

More than one observer compared the scenes in the sugar mills to Dante's inferno. Here near-naked slaves laboured in the glow of the flames and the roaring noise and the ferocious heat of the boiler room. Since cane juice ferments swiftly after it is pressed from the canes, this entire process of 'civilizing sugar' is a brisk and brutal one. Slaves worked up to eighteen hours a day during the harvest, first to cut and transport the canes and then to extract the juice and manufacture the raw sugar. Inevitably they were exhausted and accidents were commonplace; and so an axe was kept handy to severe the limbs that got trapped in the machinery. The range of potential perils for workers in the factory was intimidating: as one contemporary noted, 'If a stiller slips into a rum cistern, it is sudden death: for it stiffes in a moment. If a mill-feeder be catch'd by the finger, his whole body is drawn in, and he is squeezed to pieces. If a boyler get any part into the scalding sugar, it sticks like glue or birdlime, and 'tis hard to save either limb or life.' The danger of this work explains the oft-repeated tale of two Barbadian female mill feeders. Chained together as a punishment, when one caught her arm in the roller, despite the fact that 'every effort was used to stop the mill', wrote Joseph Senhouse, the other 'female negro, was dragged so close to those cylinders, that her head was severed from her body'.

Settling the sugar islands took one kind of man; exploiting them took another. Frontiersmen like George Ashby had stolen most of the dramatic roles: taming a wilderness, battling indigenous populations, resisting pirates. The work left to planters like Robert Cooper was altogether more quotidian. His goal was to maintain the plantation and increase its turnover, which required him to be a farmer, a factory manager and an accountant, all rolled into one. He also had to be a good businessman, adroit at negotiating the best price for his sugar and constantly mindful of the bottom line. Most importantly, he had to know how to inspire and intimidate his charges so that he got the best out of them. As Trevor Burnard concluded: 'Managing a sugar estate was hard work and required a hard man.'

For most of the year, Robert Cooper would have spent more time in his study than in the fields. He was responsible for ordering all the essentials for the estate, right down to the smallest detail. A sugar planter had to order at least five different kinds of ropes, including one for the mill, one for the cattle, another for the trees. For the great house, there were candles, furniture and food; for the field there were cutlasses, hoes and spades; whips, shackles and chains. For the factory, there were ladles and skimmers as well as harnesses for the cattle that transported the cane. The carpenters on the property needed a constant supply of nails, boards and hammers; the masons needed bricks and stones; the shoemakers needed leather and blades; the blacksmith needed bellows and irons. There were horses to be purchased, vegetable gardens to be restocked and poultry to be replaced.

Juggling the finances of a plantation was a truly onerous business and many planters were perpetually in debt. In part this was because a sugar estate required a substantial initial investment before they could even get up and running; then if anything went wrong, such as a hurricane or a war or a poor crop, the estate owner was forced to hand his property back to his financiers. Indeed, this was how the Burke family had got into the sugar business in the first place. The solution for Robert Cooper was to be careful with his expenditure, curb his debts, and aggressively pursue money owed to him. It seems that he excelled at this diligent administrative work; he had a reputation as a prudent and skilful manager and he ended his career a great dealer richer than when he started.

At its most productive, Burkes' annual crop yielded eighty large hogsheads and around 100,000 pounds of sugar. But the plantation also produced vats of molasses, rum, vegetables and butter. The most valuable asset that a slave owner had, however, was his human stock, and Robert Cooper's record keeping on them was meticulous. His ledger included the name, sex and date of birth of all the plantation's slaves, and documented whether the individual was born on the plantation or purchased elsewhere. It listed how much the slave cost and when he or she was purchased; whether the slave worked in a domestic or field capacity; and it specified the slave's occupation. If any slaves were sold, the register showed their price, the date of the transaction and the name of the purchaser. For the contemporary observer, these slave ledgers are some of the most disturbing reminders of the slave system: human lives and suffering reduced to notations in an account book like objects or livestock.

Yet many planters argued that their relationship to their workforce was that of a father to his family, that they acted *in loco parentis* to their enslaved 'children', protecting their welfare and teaching them good habits, in particular 'submission to the state, in which it pleased God to place them'. In the American South, for example, some masters insisted on being addressed as 'father' or 'Big Pappy', and described their slaves as 'sons and daughters'. The Caribbean planters in turn frequently referred to 'their people', with all the attendant associations of possessiveness and care.

And indeed, planters were theoretically responsible for their slaves from cradle to grave. On any given day at Burkes, Robert Cooper was besieged by a seemingly endless series of requests and duties in his official capacity as head of the plantation. There were babies to be named, for example. But even well-meaning planters often did not think to consult the parents in such matters. Matthew Lewis, for example, decreed that a child on his plantation should be named Wellington, 'after the greatest Captain that the world could produce', supremely unconcerned that the bemused parents probably had no idea who this 'hero' was.

Robert Cooper presided over any ritual designed to welcome the newborn. Formal baptisms were not sanctioned by most planters, since many slaves mistakenly believed that it was a step to freedom, but more informal blessings were common. One planter described such an occasion: 'The ceremony was performed with perfect gravity and propriety by all parties . . . I read a couple of prayers, marked the forehead of the children with the sign of the cross and instead of the concluding prayer, I substituted a wish that God would bless them and make them live to be as good servants to me as I prayed to make me a kind massa to them.'

The slaves' material needs were also supposed to be met by

Corvette.

Brigantin.

Barque.

WEST INDIA VESSELS OF THE CLOSE OF THE SEVENTEENTH CENTURY.*

(A) 17th-century ships of the kind that George Ashby might have travelled on across the Atlantic and later on business trips around the islands.

(B) Richard Ligon's map of Barbados, 1657.

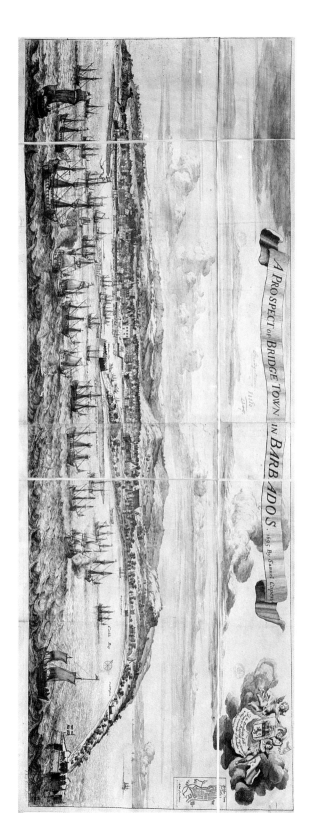

(C) 'A Prospect of Bridge Town in Barbados', 1695.

(D) Sugar cane.

(E) Sir Henry Morgan, the 'Emperor of Buccaneers', in Portobello.

Engraved for the Universal Magazine according to Act of Parliament 1749 for J. Hinton at ye Kings Arms in St Pauls Church Yard London

(F) The art of making sugar, 1749.

(G) *Barbadoes Mulatto Girl*, Agostino Brunias, 1765.

(H) Portrait assumed to be of
Robert Cooper Ashby.

A

DIALOGUE,

CONCERNING THE

SLAVERY

OF THE

AFRICANS;

Shewing it to be the *Duty* and *Interest* of the *American* Colonies to emancipate all their *African* Slaves:

WITH AN

ADDRESS to the Owners of such Slaves.

DEDICATED TO THE HONORABLE THE

Continental Congress.

Open thy mouth, judge righteously, and plead the cause of the poor and needy   PROV. XXXI. 9.
And as ye would that men should do to you, do ye also to them likewise.   LUKE VI 31.

NORWICH:
Printed and sold by JUDAH P. SPOONER. 1776.

(I) An abolitionist pamphlet, 1776

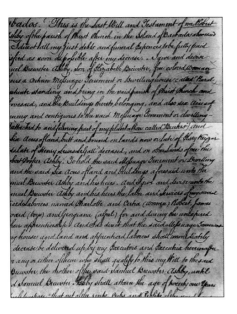

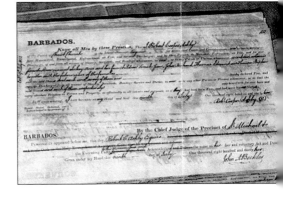

(J–Left) Robert Cooper Ashby's last
will and testament, 1839.

(K–Above) Sukey Ann's
document of manumission, 1832.

(L) The great house Drax Hall, a product of the region's first great sugar fortune.

(M) Edward Everton Barnes Ashby, aka Vere, my maternal grandfather.

(N) Muriel Haynes Skinner, my maternal grandmother.

(O) Barbara Cecille Ashby, my mother.

(P) Kenneth Lamonte Stuart, my father.

their owner. The law required Robert Cooper to dispense an annual quota of clothing, which came in the form of a length of linen to make into work clothes as well a cap and jacket for every man, and a bonnet and a petticoat for each woman. He was also responsible for ordering essential condiments like salt, and rations of guinea corn, salt fish and dried peas which supplemented what the slaves grew in their allotments. He occasionally dispensed rum to warm them up on rainy and cool days, as a way to keep them going in the long days during harvest and as a reward on official holidays and feast days. Historians estimated that the annual costs for each slave varied from £1 to £4. But their rations were often cut and, for large periods over the history of slavery, the enslaved population suffered extreme malnutrition.

Robert Cooper organized the slaves' timetables, scheduling their daily work in the fields and factory as well as their free time, which was usually every Sunday and every other Saturday, when they were expected to care for their allotments. He would also decide whether to grant permission for them to indulge in their few leisure activities, such as holding a dance. The slaves also needed Robert Cooper's authorization to leave the plantation or to carry out other extracurricular activities like the buying and selling of vegetables, livestock and trinkets, which was one of the only ways they had of generating the funds they might use to free themselves.

The planter was also responsible for his slaves' health. Every Monday morning, Robert Cooper (or Mary, since some planters delegated this task to their wives) walked over to the hospital (or 'sickhouse' as the slaves preferred to call it), where they surveyed a line of men and women claiming to be suffering from numerous complaints. It was his duty to examine them and decide who was genuinely ill and who was simply malingering. The planters' behaviour towards their slaves' bodies was often shockingly intrusive. Some would examine their slaves' private parts and note their peculiarities, personally applying poultices as well as removing their tapeworms.

Robert Cooper employed a doctor to visit the hospital weekly and treat ill slaves. If the physician was required to do any unusual or extra work – for example, performing an amputation – he expected to be paid extra. He also charged more for treating white patients, since he gave them more careful attention. But there was no way to check a physician's qualifications once they had arrived in the colonies, and many of them were quacks whose remedies – purges, poultices, blood-letting and enemas – were more dangerous than efficacious. Kenneth Kiple, a leading authority on West Indian medical history, wrote that 'the slaves would probably have been better off with their own practitioners, for white medicine in the West Indies was, to put it charitably, of low quality'.

As Robert Cooper was expected to be there at the beginning of the slaves' lives, so he was expected to be there at the end. As slaves aged beyond their capacity to work, the planter was expected to feed, clothe and maintain them until their death, and then ensure a proper burial.

But all these obligations were, in reality, optional. While planters endlessly lamented the burden of having to care for their slaves, the truth was that many of them consistently failed to live up to that 'sacred obligation'. For example, they were often less than scrupulous in caring for young babies. In the early years of slavery, before there was any interest in maintaining slave numbers through natural increase, many planters saw children as a nuisance and were known to dash their heads against walls lest their mothers become distracted from work. In direct response to the abolitionist pressure and the anticipated end of the slave trade, the Barbadian planters had by the 1790s adopted amelioration measures or pro-natalist policies to increase childbirth on the plantations. But planters often neglected the maintenance of the slave quarters and failed to provide the slaves with clothing; hence the frequent observations of visitors to the islands of 'half naked slaves dressed only in rags'. In times of scarcity the first group to suffer was the slaves, whose limited rations were cut to the bone in order that the planter's table remain as lavish as ever.

Many also reneged on that final and most sombre duty: the care of the elderly and the dying. Some planters simply threw ageing slaves off the plantation, leaving them to spend their last days begging on the streets in the capital. One Jamaican planter flouted this convention in particularly brutal style. 'It was his constant practice,' wrote a neighbour:

> whenever a sick negro was pronounced incurable, to order the poor wretch to be carried to a solitary vale upon his estate, called the Gulley, where he was thrown down, and abandoned to his fate; which was to be half devoured by john-crows, before death had put an end to his sufferings. By this proceeding the avaricious owner avoided the expense of maintaining the slave during his last illness; and in order that he be as little a loser as possible, he always enjoined the negro bearer of the dying man, to strip him before leaving the Gulley, and not to forget to bring back his frock coat and the board on which he had been carried down.

A British army officer stationed in Barbados reported a similar case:

> Two of our sergeants came and informed me that some time ago they had brought in a poor sick Negro whose master had turned him out thinking him passed recovery. However, by their care and attention, the Negro recovered and the moment the unfeeling master heard of it he claimed the man as his property, finding

he was able to work again, without so much as thanking those sergeants.

When Robert Cooper wasn't working there were relatively few distractions. The literature then available in the colonies tended to be of poor quality. Bookshops were rare and their stock tended to be potboilers with racy plots and limited literary merit. Though the island was well served for newspapers, they were often rather thin affairs, printed on coarse paper and designed to impart practical information rather than fulfil any intellectual considerations. The foreign news was lifted directly from the English papers, while the other editorial content focused primarily on the misdeeds of local politicians, described in lurid and vitriolic terms. The rest of the pages were dominated by advertisements selling horses or bolts of cloth and, of course, slaves: 'To be sold a mulatto man, a compleat taylor and sadler, understands a butler's place very well, is a capital groom and can drive a carriage; also two healthy young girls, all the same property and sold for no fault whatever.'

Plantation life also tended to be isolated and insular. The indifferent quality of the roads of that era meant that travel was nowhere near as quick and easy as it is today. Time too passed at a different pace. The fastest of all expeditions took place at a gallop and most were taken at the stately trot of a phaeton or buggy, so any journey, even on such a small island, was a serious undertaking. Like most planters, therefore, Robert Cooper lived in relative seclusion, passing the days alone with his family, a handful of white employees and his slaves. The 'loneliness of plantation life' was a recognized syndrome throughout the sugar islands, as a letter written by one depressed planter to his brother in France demonstrates: 'nowhere does the time pass more slowly or with so much suffering.'

What cultural events that did occur – plays, recitals and dance performances – were concentrated in the capital, Bridgetown, or in bigger towns like Oistins or Speightstown. But for Creoles like Robert Cooper their popularity was eclipsed by the decadent and debauched distractions available in these urban centres. As in George Ashby's day, Bridgetown was one of the Caribbean's most lively locations. Soldiers, sailors and sundry other visitors flocked to its bars, brothels and taverns, where hundreds of ravishing black and mulatto women were dedicated to the art of giving pleasure to the visitors. Alongside the prostitution and drunkenness, they brawled and sometimes duelled. Gambling was widespread and they bet on everything: cock-fights and dogs and especially cards, and there were legendary tales of daughters sold into marriage or entire plantations changing hands during a single night at the tables.

Otherwise, Robert Cooper devoted his leisure time to pursuits that were also typical of his caste. He became a member of the Christ Church Vestry, the organization that controlled local affairs. Since it was an elected position chosen by local grandees, his inclusion was a mark of his growing visibility among the local planter community. Robert Cooper also became passionately involved with the local militia. Founded in the 1630s, this region-wide organization was designed to protect the colonies against both slave revolts and external invasion. Every free man between the ages of sixteen and sixty was expected to serve; only clergymen were exempt. But its role was more than martial. Becoming a member of the militia was a rite of passage for the island's young men, and one's ability to rise up through its ranks was a badge of social status. Favouritism was rife and strings were aggressively pulled to advance militia careers. Robert Cooper, who had joined the Christ Church branch of the organization in his youth, tenaciously climbed the ranks until he reached the top echelons of its hierarchy alongside the island's most prominent planters. At their regular monthly meetings, where they drilled and practised their marksmanship, Robert Cooper made some of his closest friendships and his most important contacts.

Occasionally, too, the Ashbys hosted or were invited to lunches, picnics, suppers or trips to the races. There were balls at Government House where guests danced to the accompaniment of a slave orchestra or strolled over torch-lit lawns, taking refreshments and watching fireworks. If these entertainments were inevitably sumptuously catered and set in beautiful tropical surroundings, they were also boring. For the Creole community was not famous for its interest in cultural or intellectual affairs. Indeed the 'Creole repugnance for learning' was legendary and the phrase 'as ignorant as a Creole' was widely repeated during this era. One visitor who was subjected to a planter's monologue on sugar – the boilers and bagasse (the fibrous matter left after the juice has been pressed out of the cane), the state of the market and the impact of the weather – feared she would faint with boredom. Despite its pretensions, Barbados was like all the Caribbean colonies, a male-dominated laager whose crude manners and paucity of conversation led one traveller to conclude: 'It is a sad society that of the Creoles.'

These negative characterizations inevitably annoyed the local whites greatly. While planters like Robert Cooper saw themselves as businessmen attempting to make a living in dangerous and precarious circumstances, at the same time they realized that visitors observed their society with a mixture of morbid curiosity and revulsion; and that these hostile perceptions would be seized upon by the abolitionists. They also knew that these scornful outsiders would return to 'civilization', ready to bemoan the white islanders' lack of refinement and the corruption brought on by their proximity to heathens. Over time, therefore, the Creoles turned in on themselves, protecting their traditions and growing ever more clannish. Feeling profoundly misunderstood by outsiders, the community became fiercely independent, pugnacious, even a bit paranoid. And indeed, their way of life would prove to be unsustainable, for the times were irrevocably changing.

11

The history of liberty is a history of resistance.
Woodrow Wilson

While the islanders strove to further consolidate their sugar empire, the outside world was once again nipping at their heels. As a result of the three successive wars that would be fought between Britain and France, the constant threat of invasion that had hung over the island for the last quarter of the eighteenth century would also persist for the next twenty-five years. There were also difficulties closer to home, as the second act of the Haitian saga began.

Under the guise of restoring order, the British, always covetous of this lucrative colony, landed troops on the island in 1793. They assumed an easy ride, but were to be profoundly mistaken. The recently freed slaves realized that if they wished to maintain their freedom, they would have to fight for it. Their ferocious bravery and determination intimidated the British armed forces, just as Toussaint L'Ouverture's sophisticated guerrilla tactics had wrong-footed their generals. The slave armies were used to fighting in the torrid, mountainous conditions of Haiti, whereas the British in their flannel underwear and red wool coats were completely unprepared. Overwhelmed by the sheer number of slaves willing to die for their liberty, the British forces were eventually demoralized. Describing the fate of the British troops, one observer remarked that they were 'like a vessel traversing the ocean – the waves yielded for the moment, but united again as the vessel passed'. The invading forces also had to cope with tropical diseases like malaria and yellow fever, while the transfer of soldiers to other conflicts in the region depleted their numbers further. By 1798 it was clear that the British army could not maintain its position and in October of that year the Union Jack was lowered and Toussaint, the 'black Spartacus', rode into the capital, Port-au-Prince, as the liberator.

In 1800, Toussaint L'Ouverture became governor of the island. Hearing of his victory, slaves in the nearby island of Jamaica sang gleefully: 'Black, white, brown, all de same!' Over the next couple of years Toussaint proved himself to be not just a formidable warrior but also a thoughtful statesman. Working with his multiracial team that included black army officers, mulatto administrators and white advisers, including Age, his white chief of staff, he managed to stimulate trade, boost agriculture and construct roads and schools. But it was the constitution promulgated in 1801 that was most extraordinary. It declared: 'There cannot exist slavery in this territory, servitude is then forever abolished. All men are born, live and die free and French.' Not only had Haiti become the first slave nation in the New World to liberate itself, Toussaint had created a blueprint for a society in which freedom reigned, and access to education combined with the willingness to work hard meant that equal opportunities were open to all. It was no wonder that the slave world exulted or that the planters of the region continued to watch the events there with profound concern.

But the struggle on Haiti was not over. In 1802 Napoleon Bonaparte stepped onto the stage. His interest in the island was, according to some historians, highly personal. Apparently the family of his adored Creole wife, the 'incomparable' Josephine, had a plantation on the island, and the recent events had deprived them of crucial funds. But Napoleon had reasons of his own, millions of them, to rue the loss of revenue from Saint-Domingue, since this was the number of francs that the island's independence represented to the French national purse. Napoleon had only refrained from entering the fray earlier because he had been preoccupied by waging war against Britain, so as soon as the Peace of Amiens was made in 1802 he turned his attention to bringing the rebellious ex-colony to heel. First he attempted to reimpose slavery in Haiti, and when that proved unenforceable, he dispatched his brother-in-law General Leclerc to subdue the island.

Supremely confident of success, Leclerc's ship and the flotilla of vessels that followed him departed full of exquisite furniture and art, as well as Toussaint's sons, whom Napoleon had detained in France as a bargaining tool. Napoleon's plan, which still survives in Parisian archives, was to initially appear conciliatory, threatening action only against those who revolted. But his real intention was to round up and transport the rebel leaders to France for trial and execution. Toussaint had his own spies and was warned in advance of the fleet's arrival, though he had no idea of the size of the forces being dispatched against him. So when, positioned on a hilltop, he saw the huge fleet for the first time, he is reputed to have cried out in alarm: 'All France has come against us!'

But Toussaint, with his typical energy and strategic foresight, rallied. He bought some time by delaying a planned meeting with Leclerc, meanwhile giving certain instructions to his followers. When the French commander approached Cap François two days later, he realized that he had been completely outmanoeuvred. The city he had planned to enter so triumphantly was a pile of ash and a wall of fire was devouring the surrounding hills. There followed many months of protracted fighting which punished Napoleon's forces as they had never been punished in Europe. What made matters worse was the outbreak of yellow fever. At its end, Napoleon's

Caribbean campaign was a bloody failure. Sixty thousand Frenchmen had died, among them Leclerc, claimed by yellow fever; and 150,000 slaves had been drowned, hanged or burned alive. The brave Toussaint, inveigled into a meeting with his French counterpart General Brunet, was kidnapped and transported to the castle Joux in France, where he died of abuse and neglect within a year.

In the following months one of his pronouncements would prove prophetic: 'In overthrowing me, you have done no more than cut down the tree of black liberty in [Haiti] – it will spring back from the roots, for they are numerous and deep.' When it was finally over in 1804, after twelve years of civil war and bitter battles against the invading Napoleonic forces, a free, black state existed in the heart of the Caribbean. Renamed Haiti – an ancient Amerindian word, resurrected from the indigenous history of the region – the island was the proverbial beacon of hope for the slave population in the colonies and across the region, and a source of profound dismay for white planter families like the Ashbys. And the world was confronted with the fact that an army of barefoot black slaves had defeated both the great British Empire and the glorious French Republic.

In subsequent years Haiti would be punished terribly for its audacity. The island's freedom represented a challenge to the entire slave system, so the European powers and the United States forgot their differences and drew together to act against the renegade nation. They refused to accept Haitian independence unless it was first recognized by France, and France would only do so if they were compensated for their loss of property during the revolution. For twenty-one years, the Haitians refused to comply, but under consistent international pressure they finally submitted in 1825. The payment of the compensation of 150 million gold francs would bleed its national treasury dry and contribute to the poverty that has continued to dog the nation up till the present day. What was just as terrible was that the bravery of the Haitian people, their resourcefulness and tenacity have been virtually written out of history; and many have little idea of how this indomitable people struggled and died to become the first free colony of the New World.

The ripples caused by Haiti's revolution spread throughout the colonies. From Brazil to Cuba, the slave population was energized. As the only rebellion in the Americas that had succeeded in permanently abolishing slavery, the Haitian uprising was their beacon of hope. For the planters, the colony's descent into violence and its phoenix-like rise to independence were horrifying. In Barbados, the events on the island that had once been their greatest competitor felt perilously close.

As epic and extraordinary as the events in Haiti were, they were in many ways a magnified version of the struggle that was waged on every plantation, in every slave territory. For as John Locke, the great sage of the American Revolution, wrote, any person who 'attempts to get another Man into his Absolute Power, does thereby put himself into a State of War with him'. Thus the plantation system was built upon two factions in perpetual conflict. On one side, the master desperately tried to ensure his profits by controlling his workers with an unprecedented regime of violence and intimidation; on the other, his captives each day, in every possible way, attempted to disrupt the success of his operation and escape the bonds of slavery.

The situation at Burkes was no exception. Some of the slaves' acts of sabotage were small: throwing away cutlery, sewing garments incorrectly, planting crops in shallow soil, breaking their tools, poisoning food. At other times they let livestock loose in the fields, committed arson or, provoked beyond endurance, attacked their tormentors. They also sometimes maimed livestock. These gestures of defiance could not undermine the wider slave system, but they were a real nuisance to the planters who had to spend time and money identifying the culprits, bringing them to justice and remedying the problems.

Understanding their own value as property, slaves also some-times harmed themselves, irritating sores and wounds, eating dirt, and performing any number of other actions that meant they could not work. Others pretended to be ill: one planter claimed that of the forty slaves in his hospital only four were genuinely unwell. Some simply refused to labour. As one of Matthew Lewis's slaves declared, despite enduring innumerable punishments, 'he did not mean to work, and nobody could make him'.

In order to save their children from a life of slavery and to deprive their hated owners of valuable property, some slave women aborted their children. Pierre Desalles was told by a senior slave on the plantation that

> every year we had eight, ten, twelve, and fourteen preg-nancies, but that the negresses got rid of their fruits and that it was known throughout the work gang that Marie-Jeanne had very recently destroyed her child. And indeed, she was believed to be pregnant; she had an enormous belly, which one morning was gone, to everyone's great astonishment.

(However, terminations were often a convenient excuse for spontaneous abortions brought on by poor nutrition or abuse.) One of Robert Cooper's biggest frustrations was when slaves ran away; it challenged his authority, reduced his workforce and inspired other slaves to do the same. These flights ranged from unauthorized absences to permanent escape. Despite the island's topography – flat and small – slaves had gone missing from the earliest days of colonization. The large areas of untamed land that existed then meant that slaves could disappear with impunity, hiding for long periods in uncleared gullies and forested areas.

Later the planters passed legislation to ensure that slaves moving about the island had to carry a pass showing that he or she was on his master's 'necessary or lawful business'. And by the early eighteenth century, it was difficult to remain concealed, as one English official stationed on the island remarked: 'Barbados contains fewer hiding places for marronage [i.e. permanent escape] than any other West Indian colony.' The best hope of lasting liberty for slaves was to find a boat to take them off the island.

The planters also employed the services of professional 'Negro-hunters' or 'slave-catchers', individuals who made their living tracking down runaways. Once recaptured, the slave was often confined in the stocks or put into the slave prison in Bridgetown known as the 'cage', which was a small, low, dirty-looking building with grated doors and windows. The penalty for absenteeism was harsh, ranging from branding or whipping even to public execution for repeat offenders; but despite the severity of these sanctions, the problem persisted, as the frequent newspaper advertisements attest. The *Barbados Mercury* posted these notices in early 1816: 'Lydia Ann, aged 13 or 14 was suspected to be harboured about Baxters Road for in that neighbourhood she has a mother named Kate Harper . . . and her father . . . Harry Evans belonging to Mrs. Thorne'. Another read: 'Frank was likely to be harboured by his father . . . at St. Ann's.'

All too often, however, the most potent form of disruption was taking their own lives. Many planters saw a slave's suicide as the ultimate act of sabotage. It was a deed that simultaneously lightened their workforce and represented a substantial financial loss. In his time as a planter, Pierre Desalles lost slave after slave this way. At one point two Africans hanged themselves. He claimed to be bemused: 'nobody had done anything to them; they were having a perfectly jolly and amiable time'. On another occasion Desalles, who simply did not have the imagination to appreciate why his slaves might become despondent, noted: 'Twelve have died since January and several of them are threatening to die.' And when a slave called Toussaint, who had repeatedly self-harmed, finally died, Desalles was livid:

> These are things that the abolitionists would not understand. They would not fail to say that the despair at being a slave drove this negro to destroy himself. Laziness and dread of work, these are the motives that cause him to let himself die . . . The criminal! He is the fourth member of his family to do this to his owner!

As in the early days of the settlement, some planters responded to their slaves' defiant or desperate acts with further barbarity, and displayed the severed heads of persistent runaways or suicides on poles by the roadside: a sinister reminder to other slaves contemplating the same action that their fate would have repercussions in the next world too. As one planter explained to a visitor: 'They are fully persuaded they will return to Guinea after their decease, they imagine they would cut but a sorry figure to appear there without a Head.'

A miasma of fear hung over the plantations, as the planters' casual cruelty extended from the fields to the great house. One visitor was shocked when his genial host punched in the face the young maid who was serving them because she had inadvertently slopped some tea into the saucer. Another traveller to the French slave islands was horrified to discover that just prior to dinner his charming hostess had had her cook thrown alive into the oven and watched impassively as he burned to death. His crime? He had burned a cake.

The career of the Jamaican planter Thomas Thistlewood, who arrived in Jamaica in 1750 hoping to make his fortune in the sugar industry, is an enduring testament to the fact that violence lubricated the entire slave system. As the historian James Walvin wrote:

> In his very first days on the island, he had learned what was required to keep slaves in their place. He had seen a runaway slave savagely whipped, the wounds then marinated in salt, pepper and lime juice. The body of another runaway slave had been burned, but not before the head had been cut off and displayed on a pole. Thus he was instructed in the basics of Jamaican life . . . Later, Thistlewood witnessed the trial of a slave who had drawn a knife on a white man. Found guilty, the wretched man was immediately hanged from the nearest tree, the offending hand cut off and the body left to rot . . . There could have been no doubt in Thistlewood's mind that capricious whippings, legalised executions and dismembering all formed the everyday ingredients of a culture of violence and fear which kept the plantation system in place.

The plantation was a space where the incarcerated population was controlled by a regime of surveillance and punishment and manipulated by what one historian described as 'the psychology of terror'.

After exposure to the sadistic mores of slave society Thistlewood, who had previously displayed no predilection for violence, was soon carrying out the vilest acts. In order to punish a slave who persistently stole food in a time of famine, he developed his own unique form of punishment. His diary entry for 26 May 1756 notes that Derby had once again offended: 'Had him well flogged and pickled, then made Hector [another slave] shit in his mouth.' This unfortunate slave would give his name to this uniquely depraved form of castigation, and 'to derby-dose' someone became a widely used term. A couple of months later another slave was similarly chastised. 'Gave him a moderate whipping, pickled him well, made Hector shit in his mouth, immediately put in a gag whilst his mouth was full & made him wear it 4 or 5 hours.' Thistlewood dreamt up other imaginative atrocities. Recording his treatment of a runaway, he wrote: 'gagged him: locked his hands together; rubbed him with molasses & exposed him naked to the flies all day, and to the mosquitoes all night, without fire'. As extreme as Thistlewood's behaviour seems to modern eyes, tellingly he was not notorious among his peers for the ill treatment of his slaves. Indeed, his behaviour only came to light because he chose to record it; which suggests that many other planters could have been treating their slaves just as viciously.

Beatings, brandings and being burned alive were accepted punishments for a sliding scale of offences. The slaves were thrashed whether they were sick or well; whether they worked too slowly or too hastily. Many of these chastisements were dispensed in an ad hoc fashion; it was only those punishments that could permanently damage a planters 'stock' (like amputation) for which they had to get approval from higher up the chain. And there were few, if any, legal constraints on the more bizarre cruelties that had evolved in the plantation zone. Slaves were covered in honey and staked out on anthills to be stung to death; gunpowder was inserted into the offender's orifices and then ignited; others were made to eat their own amputated limbs. They cropped their slaves' ears, slit their nostrils and branded their cheeks. Indeed torture and the mangling of slaves' bodies was such an intrinsic part of labour organization that planters, overseers and drivers felt free to abuse, wound and ill-treat their charges.

The most common retribution for serious infractions was flogging. This was necessarily a public punishment, since it was designed to inculcate fear in the entire slave population. At the appointed time the overseer stopped work and summoned the workers, along with an impassive owner, to watch. Meanwhile the terrified accused was escorted to the place of punishment where he (or she) was disrobed, had his hands bound and was suspended from the high branch of a sturdy tree. The choice of the whip depended on the severity of the misdemeanour; the most excoriating was the bull-whip, which could cut human skin open with a single stroke. While the slave struggled against the rope and screamed out, the prescribed number of strokes – ten, twenty, even thirty were common – was administered. The slave was then cut down, falling into the dirt and staining the ground with his blood. Sometimes salt, lime or pepper was rubbed into the wound to worsen the pain.

The colonists believed fervently that violence was intrinsic to maintaining the safety of their society. So new planters arriving on the island were instructed with the maxim: 'At all times they must fear you, they simply must.' Hardly a day passed on any plantation when some sort of violence did not take place. One observer estimated that many larger plantations had sixty or so chastisements a day. Every estate dweller recognized the terrible, desperate screams evoked by such punishments. They were so loud that they rang throughout the estate from the field to boiling house. Visitors to the islands were shocked that whites there didn't appear to hear these noises and would carry on eating or chatting as if nothing had happened. It was part of the soundtrack of their lives, as familiar as the rustling of the cane and the bell summoning slaves to the field. As the French abolitionist Victor Schoelcher concluded:

> The whip is the soul of the colonies . . . It is the clock
> of the plantation; it announced the moment of waking
> up and of going to bed; it marked the hour of work; it
> also marked the hour of rest . . . the day of his death is

the only one in which the negro is allowed to forget the wake-up call of the whip.

The psychological impact of living in a world in which violence was endemic was powerfully recorded by the American ex-slave turned abolitionist Frederick Douglass. He describes how one overseer's prolonged campaign of abuse, which included sleep deprivation, violent punishments and lack of food, affected him:

> I was broken in body soul and spirit. My natural elasticity was crushed; my intellect languished; the disposition to read departed; the cheerful spark that lingered abut my eye died; the dark night of slavery closed in upon me; and behold a man transformed into a brute.

Mary Prince, the author of the only female Caribbean slave narrative, didn't find her gender any protection from the 'horrors of slavery'. She endured a succession of violent owners, passing, as she put it, from 'butcher to butcher':

> I lay down at night and rose up in the morning in fear and sorrow; and often wished that . . . I could escape from this cruel bondage and be at rest in the grave . . . It was then, however, my heavy lot to weep, weep, weep and that for years; to pass from one misery to another, and from one cruel master to a worse.

Those who did attempt to model a kinder, more gentle slavery inevitably attracted the derision and ire of their fellow planters. This Matthew Lewis found out when a group of his neighbours, outraged at his lenient treatment of his workers, attempted to persuade the grand jury in the nearest town to prosecute him. With amazement he noted in his own journal: 'for over-indulgence to my own negroes!'

Another idealistic planter was the Englishman Joshua Steele, who arrived in Barbados in 1780 to take personal control of his plantations. Influenced by Enlightenment and abolitionist principles, he was determined to encourage a new style of im-proved plantation management that, he hoped, would eventually culminate in the end of slavery. But his success was very limited; the local planters were almost universally hostile to his vision and determined to see it fail. In their view, Steele's philosophy undermined the central tenet of their society, white supremacy; it also eroded the power of their paternalism, and encouraged slaves to become more demanding, which they felt would make everyone discontented. His attempt to bequeath his fortune to his enslaved partner and two children in order to guarantee their lifestyle and education was a failure because slaves could not inherit property. (The gesture also proved to his fellow planters how beyond the pale Steele actually was.)

It would be nice to credit Robert Cooper with being a benign, liberal slave owner. But there is no evidence to suggest that was the case. Had he pioneered some progressive scheme to eliminate exploitation from plantation life, it would certainly have been recorded in the accounts of the period, since such behaviour was so rare. Indeed, Robert Cooper had a reputation for being a canny planter who made sure he extracted the maximum profits from his property, be it land or slaves. So it is almost inevitable that the crop at Burkes was harvested at the usual cost of beatings and brutality and that Robert Cooper resorted to the full panoply of intimidatory violence that most planters employed.

Some contemporary commentators speculated on why the atmosphere of the colonies was capable of reducing civilized Europeans to brutes. The abolitionist James Stephen, for example, wondered why men who were 'conspicuously liberal and humane' changed their 'moral character' when they settled in the West Indies. His explanation was straightforward: they were corrupted by the system they were forced to become part of:

> Annoyed and irritated by those vices which slavery very rarely fails to produce in its degraded subjects, they have recourse to the established modes of correction: at first they do so with reluctance, and sparingly; but are soon persuaded that severer discipline is necessary; and every successive infliction of punishment, rubs off something of that humane sensibility with which they at first set out; till at length they acquire the common apathy, and the common aversion, towards that unfortunate class.

Typical of this change of heart was Governor Fenlon, who wrote in 1764: 'I arrived in Martinique with all the prejudices of Europe against the harshness with which the Negroes are treated,' but after a short stay he declared that 'the safety of the whites requires that the Negroes be treated like animals'.

As Fenlon's words suggest, at the root of it all was fear. Colonial whites worried that those mighty arms, which could chop with one stroke straight through a bundle of canes, might one day put the blade to their throats; that the hands that prepared their food might one mealtime sprinkle it with poison; that their domestic slaves might one night rise up and murder them in their beds.

Guilt, suppressed and unacknowledged, also played a part, but the moral transformation displayed by so many colonists was also due to something else altogether: the soul-corroding effect that such absolute power over their fellow human beings had on them. In the colonies a white man could do things that he could do virtually nowhere else. If he had a sadistic streak he could indulge it here with impunity; if he wished to rape or beat or sodomize a black man, woman or child there was little anyone could or would do to stop him. The colonies became Joseph Conrad's 'heart of darkness', some of the few places in the world where individuals were entirely free to indulge their ugliest impulses without the normal social constraints. This total power corrupted locals and newcomers alike, distorting their personalities and turning them into beasts.

As Frederick Douglass eloquently put it:

> The slaveholder, as well as the slave, is the victim of the slave system. A man's character greatly takes its hue and shape from the form and colour of things about him. Under the whole heavens there is no relation more unfavourable to the development of honourable character, than that sustained by the slaveholders to the slave. Reason is imprisoned here, and passions run wild.

12

Slavery is terrible for men but it is far more terrible for women. Super added to the burden common to all, they have wrongs, and sufferings and mortifications peculiarly their own.

Harriet Jacobs, Amerian slave

Slavery did not exist just on Robert Cooper's land; it permeated the intimacy of his home, his family and his bed. The great house was the hub of the plantation, and more than 10 per cent of the enslaved population at Burkes worked there as domestics. The atmosphere in the great house was like that of a royal court, with people coming and going in search of favours and carrying out errands. So Burkes was constantly busy, alive with intrigue and suspicion, gossiping and bickering. In an attempt to obviate their powerlessness, the slaves acted like courtiers, collecting information, lobbying for position and status, attempting to shore up their position and further their interests. Meanwhile the Ashbys behaved like any royals, believing that they had the inalienable right to know all the details of their subjects' existence, dispensing rewards and punishment, even meddling in their slaves' personal affairs, with the justification that every child that was born and survived on the plantation added to their wealth. Thus the slaves who worked at Burkes' great house were inextricably entangled in every aspect of the Ashby family's daily – and nightly – life.

This lack of privacy surprised and exasperated newcomers to plantation life, as Matthew Lewis commented:

> The greatest drawback upon one's comfort in a Jamaica existence seems to me to be being obliged to live perpetually in public . . . The houses are absolutely transparent; the walls are nothing but windows – and all the doors stand wide open. No servants are in waiting to announce arrivals visitors, negroes, dogs, cats, poultry, all walk in and out and up and down your living-rooms, without the slightest ceremony.

He added on another occasion: 'Certainly, if a man was desirous of leading a life of vice here, he must have set himself totally above shame, for he may depend upon everything done being seen and known.' According to the historian Karl Watson, this intimacy was particularly marked in Barbados: 'Both blacks and whites knew each other well. The point is clearly illustrated by the advertisements issued for runaway slaves, in which precise details of physical features, residential location and social relationships are stated.'

Living in such close proximity, sexual encounters between the owners and the owned were almost inevitable, and this was a feature of life at Burkes as it was on most plantations. The result was a complicated extended family, with Robert Cooper at its nucleus, which was a product of his relationships with numerous female slaves ranging from the casually exploitative to the passionate and long term. By the time the entire web had been spun it included at least five women and seventeen children. These relationships were not necessary sequential; many of them overlapped with one another, so at any one time Robert Cooper would have been juggling a number of concubines alongside his legitimate relationship with his wife, Mary Ashby.

The sexual exploitation of slave women was so omnipresent in Atlantic slavery that few visitors to the region failed to mention it in their reports. While many observers found the practice 'disgraceful and iniquitous', it was nonetheless evident from the earliest days of slavery. The historian Hilary Beckles notes that one of the major problems the enslaved black woman faced was 'getting the slave master off her back in the day time and off her belly in the night time'. White men often had their first sexual experience with a woman of colour and continued to assume rights of access thereafter. Thus if a female slave tried to resist she was quite likely to be met with cruel beatings or other punishments. Unsurprisingly, some women chose simply to submit and used these relationships to further their own economic and social goals.

One of the most revealing accounts of a planter's sexual relationships with his slaves was provided by the plantation manager Thomas Thistlewood, who as well as recording the obscene punishments he inflicted on his slaves in his diary also kept a detailed account, written in an elaborate code, of his sex life on the various Jamaican plantations where he worked. With the exception of a handful of sexual encounters with white prostitutes, all of his partners were women who worked for him. Whether they were young or old, sick or well, none was safe from his sexual marauding. He molested women on the way to the fields, in the kitchens, in their cabins as they rested. Not even venereal disease hindered his sexual exploits. These assaults began almost as soon as he arrived on the island. In the first few weeks he recorded sex with Franke under a cotton tree and with Mirtilla in a slave cabin and in a field by the riverside. After that the attacks would carry on almost unbroken for the rest of his time in Jamaica.

For Thistlewood, sex with his slaves, whether consensual or not, was one of the perks of plantation life. He made no effort to hide any of these encounters. And why should he? These women were in his complete power – as were any witnesses – and there was no one to whom they could complain or from whom they could obtain redress. In an average year he had sex 108 times with around fourteen different partners. The only evidence of any guilt was the trinkets or coins he would sometimes stuff into his victims' hands after the deed was done. By his own account, after a total of thirty-seven years on the island, Thistlewood had had intercourse on 3,852 occasions.

Thistlewood also pandered his slaves to his friends. When visitors came to the estate they only had to indicate an interest in a particular female and she would be summarily dispatched to their room. Even those visitors who expressed no such inclination would often be sent some poor girl anyway. They were a demonstration of his hospitality, like copious food and ever-flowing rum. Alongside his philandering, Thistlewood also had more committed relationships, in particular one with Phibbah, who worked as housekeeper at the first plantation where he was employed. Their relationship lasted almost all the years he spent in Jamaica. They quarrelled and made up like any ordinary couple; presents were exchanged, and this enterprising woman would even lend him money she had earned through her sideline of buying and selling produce. Phibbah bore him a son in 1760, whom Thistlewood referred to as 'Mulatto John'.

The sheer number of Thistlewood's sexual encounters is shocking, but perhaps not untypical of that time and place. One Barbadian planter, for example, famously claimed to have fathered seventy-four illegitimate children with his slaves. Another Martinican planter boasted that at least a third of the children on his plantation were 'the product of his loins'. Again, Thistlewood's own behaviour did not come to light because his neighbours regarded his sexual conduct as scandalous, but because he was meticulous enough to record it. In this context, Robert Cooper's network of liaisons was unremarkable. He probably assumed these relationships were his right as planter, and he would not have been overburdened with embarrassment or remorse.

The effect on the slave community of such casual sexual marauding would have been immense. Beyond the damage done to the women themselves, their mothers, fathers, lovers and brothers were forced to continue serving their abusers, powerless to protect or avenge them. In this way, the planters' sexual liberty intimidated slaves across the plantation. Robert Cooper's ability to take any woman on the estate was a mark of his complete control over his slaves' bodies and lives. And random rapacious attacks were part of the system of violence that maintained order at plantations like Burkes and across the wider slave system.

There was often something of a pattern to these liaisons. Those in the early days of a planter's marriage tended to be more short-lived and tentative than many of those which followed. The first transgressions often felt dangerous and were carried out anxiously and furtively, lest their wives or friends object. But as time passed, men's confidence grew. They realized that their wives would not – or more significantly could not – leave them. They also knew that their neighbours and contemporaries were often doing exactly the same thing, that their whole community would turn a blind eye – often with a nudge and a wink. The law was also on their side. For most of the duration of slavery in Barbados a man could not be accused of 'raping' his slave because the slave was property and therefore had no legal rights. As time went on and 'concubinage' (the keeping of black mistresses) became an integral part of island life, the legislature wisely decided to stay out of it. As the Jamaican planter Edward Long remarked: 'He who should presume to show any displeasure against such a thing as simple fornication, would for his pains be accounted a simple blockhead; since not one in twenty can be persuaded, that there is either sin; or shame in cohabiting with his slave.' (The taboos against white women having sex with black men grew stronger as white men's permission to take black women increased.) Realizing that they could get away with these affairs, Robert Cooper and his contemporaries became emboldened and increasingly little effort was invested in being discreet.

In 1809, for example, Robert Cooper began a relationship with Susannah, more commonly known as Sukey Ann, a young slave girl who was about his son's age. Born around 1795, Susannah was listed as a 'stock-keeper' and was fourteen years old when she was baptized. This probably marked the start of her relationship with Robert Cooper, since some planters baptized their slave mistresses before becoming too embroiled with them. Their reasoning showed up some of the nonsensical attitudes of slave society. Men like Robert Cooper were quite happy to seduce a girl barely out of childhood but were not willing to have sex with a heathen. The relationship with Sukey Ann would continue for a number of years, and would produce four children: Sarah Jane, John Richard, Thomas Edmund and Thomas Stephen.

The memoirs of the American slave Harriet Jacobs have left us a moving portrait of the vulnerability of young female slaves like Sukey Ann:

> The slave girl is reared in an atmosphere of licentiousness and fear. The lash and the foul talk of her master and his sons are her teachers. When she is fourteen or fifteen, her owner, or his sons, or the overseer, or perhaps all of them, begin to bribe her with presents. If these fail to

accomplish their purpose, she is whipped or starved into submission to their will.

The reasons that slave girls resisted were myriad:

> She may have had religious principles . . . she may have a lover, whose good opinion and peace of mind are dear to her heart; or the profligate men who have power over her may be exceedingly odious to her. But resistance is hopeless.

The enslaved woman was in a particularly vulnerable situation if she was pretty: 'That which commands admiration in the white woman only hastens the degradation of the female slave.'

Jacobs's own trials began when she entered her fifteenth year, 'a sad epoch in the life of a slave girl', when her master, Dr Flint, forty years her senior, 'began to whisper foul words' in her ear. 'Young as I was, I could not remain ignorant of their import.' His pursuit of her was relentless. Sometimes he was gentle and charming; at other times 'stormy' and 'terrifying'. He reminded her constantly that she was his property; 'that I must be subject to his will in all things'. His wife, meanwhile, was so overcome with jealousy that she refused to protect her young charge.

Dr Flint was unusual in that he wanted Jacobs to submit to him without rape, but nonetheless she was appalled. She trembled at the sound of his footsteps and shuddered when she saw him approaching. She was acutely aware of her legal vulnerability: 'there is no shadow of law to protect her from insult, from violence, or even from death; all these are inflicted by fiends who bear the shape of men'. The psychological impact of the situation was profound: 'I know that some are too much brutalized by slavery to feel the humiliation of their position; but it is hard to tell how much I suffered in the presence of these wrongs, nor how I am still pained in retrospect.' Jacobs only escaped her owner's sexual attentions when she took up with a younger and equally powerful white man.

Even after the woman had succumbed, her vulnerability continued. The planter Hugh Perry Keane, whose estate was situated on the island of St Vincent, kept a diary that detailed his tumultuous five-year affair with his 'sable Venus' Betty Keane. It was serious enough for him to purchase her from his father in 1791, and Keane Senior was happy to facilitate their liaison since he had his own 'Betty' on the plantation. Though he was a single man, Keane was too conventional to make their relationship public as some planters did. So to the outside world he was a handsome single dandy pursuing eligible Vincentian ladies, while in private he was in a ménage with his black slave. It was a passionate relationship. His diary begins with the words: 'I wrote a few lines to Miss B.' And when she was away from the plantation for a few weeks he could not sleep there and pined for her horribly. Their union was marked by much drama, jealous rages on both sides, and unfounded accusations of infidelity; on numerous occasions she pouted and he locked her out of the house.

Their liaison did not mean that Betty escaped the whip; she was beaten when Keane felt jealous or frustrated. But her role was more than just sexual: she was his lover, confidante and helpmate. In lieu of a lawful spouse, she was his 'plantation wife', delegating work to the domestic staff, ordering essentials for the great house and generally overseeing his household. She also provided a vital link between him and his slaves; her greater understanding of plantation dynamics meant that she was able to give him invaluable advice on managing his charges. Their relationship eventually ended after a night out in the capital when Betty was raped by a sailor while Keane was collapsed in a drunken stupor. Instead of sympathizing, he blamed her for the incident and labelled her 'a Jezebel'. Despite her pleas,

Keane refused to take her back and Betty was left to fend for herself. Their respective fates reflect the injustice of history: Hugh Keane went on to marry an English heiress, while Betty disappeared into obscurity. Despite visiting his plantations in St Vincent many times subsequently, he never mentioned her again.

Whether Robert Cooper and Sukey Ann's relationship was as tumultuous as Keane and Betty's is unknown, but it is evident that he had some affection for the woman, or at least some sense of obligation to her, otherwise he would not have manumitted her and her children. What this relationship meant for Sukey Ann remains a mystery. Can we even speak of commitment or choice or desire in such an unequal situation? Was it the living hell of repeated rape? Or was she willing to trade sex for the opportunity to gain the greater comfort and security that black concubines enjoyed amidst the dangers and the deprivations of plantation life? Is it possible, despite the profoundly unequal, even tragic circumstances of their relationship, that these two could have somehow loved each other? One imagines that several of these things might simultaneously have been true. The historian Barbara Bush stresses that not all interracial relationships were predicated on violence and abuse. Indeed, she argues that it is possible that the sensational accounts of sexual exploitation of women of colour by white men have overshadowed the fact that there may have been healthy and loving sexual relationships between these two groups during slavery. Contemporary accounts support this, as John Waller wrote: 'I have observed many instances of [white men] being perfectly captivated by their mulatto mistresses, who thus obtain their freedom and that of their children from the master who cohabits with them.'

The most significant of Robert Cooper's illicit relationships was with a mulatto woman called Mary Anne. She was his wife

Mary Ashby's body servant: the person who woke her in the morning, drew her bath, cared for her clothes and styled her hair. The relationship between a mistress and a personal servant was one of the most intimate on the plantation. The work took most of the hours of Mary Anne's day, and it is possible that she often slept in Mary Ashby's bedroom. The two women would have spent more time in each other's company than Mary Ashby would have spent with her husband. She was the person most knowledgeable about Mary Ashby's habits and who learned how to anticipate and meet her needs. The role of body servant was so important that Mary Anne was a significant figure on the plantation; but Mary Anne was a mulatto and a slave and Mary Ashby was white and free, so an unspoken but yawning gulf existed between them.

When Robert Cooper became interested in Mary Anne, it was a scenario worthy of the most steamy plantation novel. Unquestionably the close daily intimacy they shared – even with his wife present – made it easier and more likely for them to develop a relationship. But this proximity must also have lent their clandestine relationship a very tense and claustrophobic quality. And since this particular plot turned on sexual rivalry and complex power struggles, the *ménage à trois* was no doubt the talk of Burkes. The principal players were locked into a complex power struggle that went way beyond mere jealousy. The central protagonist, Robert Cooper, had the luxury of being largely in control of the situation. We don't know if he enjoyed the illicit nature of this liaison, or whether he felt guilty or worried. After all, even in slave society, conducting an affair with someone so close to one's wife was potentially disastrous.

Mary Ashby could not have been unaware of her husband's relationships with his female slaves, but I wonder what she felt about these women. Many planters' wives regarded their husband's relationships with slave women as inevitable, but this didn't mean that it didn't upset them. Traveller after traveller noted the open resentment that white women displayed towards their female slaves. Edward Thompson, who visited Barbados in 1756, remarked that Barbadian white women frequently swore at their slaves 'in a vulgar corrupt dialect'. He blamed their behaviour on Barbadian men 'who carry on amours with the ladies' slaves'. Many wives may even have feared these lovers, since there were stories in circulation about slave-mistresses who poisoned their rivals in order to get the 'top job'. Being perpetually in her company must have been excruciating as she imagined (or noticed) her husband and maid exchanging surreptitious glances over her head. But perhaps Mary Ashby believed, as so many in her position did, that she should simply put up with things, playing the part of the mistress of the plantation in public and never revealing her chagrin.

The situation was exacerbated by the fact that Mary Ashby had little else to distract her. There were so many servants bustling around Burkes' great house that were was scarcely any domestic work left for her to do; and it is safe to assume that Mary Ashby did not roam the house making the beds, or emptying the chamber pots. She may, like many plantation wives, have had a few specialities such as cake baking or jam making, but the role of mistress was essentially supervisory: she stood at the ends of beds berating slaves on the way they tidied rooms, or read out the recipes as their slaves stirred the batter. Therefore women like Mary Ashby had a lot of time for thinking, brooding, and 'persecuting their slaves'.

Then there were the children: a living reminder of her husband's infidelities, and of her rejection, impotence and shame. We cannot know for sure how Mary Ashby coped with her husband's bastards running around the plantation, whether she even knew which children he had fathered or whether she was reduced to scrutinizing the young faces she encountered, wondering whether they were his. According to one American slave, many women regarded these illegitimate children as a constant offence:

> She hates its very presence, and when a slave holding woman hates, she wants not means to give that hate telling effect. Women – white women, I mean – are Idols in the south, not wives, for the slave women are preferred in many instances; and if these idols but nod or lift a finger woe to the poor victim: kicks, cuts and stripes are sure to follow. Masters are frequently compelled to sell this class of their slaves, out of deference to the feelings of their white wives; and shocking and scandalous as it may seem for a man to sell his own blood to the traffickers in human flesh, it is often an act of humanity toward the slave-child to be thus removed from his merciless tormentors.

While the situation was less taboo in the West Indies, some wives did agitate for the sale of their rival's children. They often conspired with their own families, and even his, to make sure that these women wouldn't be included in wills or receive other benefits. Other wives chose to keep their dignity intact and ignore the adultery that was taking place within their own home. A wife was, after all, socially and financially at the mercy of her husband; as was his mistress.

What of Mary Anne, the maid? Her story was in many ways typical of the experience of many female house servants. It was largely in the domestic sphere that women were able to gain promotion to the level of skilled workers, and certainly this was preferable in many ways to the brutal outdoor work of cane cultivation. But so great was the assumption that these women were sexually available to the men of the house that many were employed merely because their masters found them attractive. Indeed, the sale price of domestics was often inflated in advertisements and at the slave market to reflect the expectation that they would be fulfilling two jobs: as concubine and maid.

In such an unequal society, some women would have regarded a relationship with their owners as an opportunity. Many mulatto women avoided having relationships with slave men. They were either in long-term relationships with white men on the plantation, or they married other mixed-race servants from other properties. This is upsetting from a contemporary perspective, where people of colour are encouraged to value solidarity in the face of oppression, but with the limited choices available to them, these women sometimes embraced the chance to safeguard themselves and their children from the worst vicissitudes of a racist society.

In deciding to become his mistress, Mary Anne had to weigh the potential advantages against the possible dangers. In most of these situations, the relationship between the wife and the mistress was permanently soured, and so Mary Anne risked endless slights or even violence. She would also have realized that Robert Cooper's long-term attentions were by no means guaranteed and that she could be discarded as easily as she had been taken up.

It appears that Robert Cooper and Mary Anne did come to care for each other profoundly. They would, after all, have ten children together. The eldest was Robert Henry Ashby. He was followed in quick succession by Alice Christian Ashby, Elizabeth Mary Ashby, Margaret Ann Ashby, Caroline Kezar Ashby, Alexander Lindsay Ashby, John George Ashby, Thomas Cooper Ashby, Arabella Ann Ashby, and William Armstrong Ashby. Theirs was clearly a stable and domesticated relationship, which grew even more so after the death of Mary Ashby. But I cannot help but wonder how many years it took, and how many children were born, before she stopped calling him 'Massa' and was allowed the privilege of calling him 'Robert'.

13

'Tisn't he who has stood and looked on, that can tell you what slavery is — 'tis he who has endured.

John Little, fugitive slave

Numbered among Robert Cooper's impressive seraglio was my great-great-great-great-grandmother. What can we know for sure about this woman? Regrettably, very little, as Frederick Douglass declared: 'Genealogical trees do not flourish amongst slaves.' Deprived of the time, information and education to record their own lives, slaves had no way to keep track of their families; indeed, most didn't even know their own date of birth. So even if I could ask her, she might not have been able to solve the puzzle. Had she been one of Robert Cooper's favourites she might have appeared in the manumission records, if he had chosen to set her free; or in wills or deeds, if he had provided her with goods or property. But this was not the case. So it is most likely that she was just another casual sexual conquest.

She was probably born on the plantation, since most of Burkes' slaves had enduring roots on the property. It was extremely unlikely that she was a 'saltwater' slave — that is, someone born in Africa — because by the end of the eighteenth century most Barbadian slaves were born on the island. She was probably young, as Robert Cooper seemed to prefer his women that way. West Indian planters frequently joked that girls, like fruit, ripened more quickly in the tropics.

We know of this woman's existence only because she bore Robert Cooper a son: John Stephen Ashby, my first identifiable slave forebear. He was born in 1803 and probably delivered by a slave midwife at Burkes. His mother could not have helped being apprehensive during her pregnancy. Giving birth in the early nineteenth century, whether you were black or white, enslaved or free, was a perilous business. But John Stephen's mother was lucky. Had she lived a few generations earlier, her experience of pregnancy and childbirth would have been very different.

In the earliest days of slavery, when the Barbadian planters had no interest in increasing the slave population, newborns were regarded as a nuisance, a distraction that kept women from work. New mothers were expected to return to the fields almost immediately after giving birth and were allowed to nurse their children only if they kept on working. Shocked at the sight of these women in the cane fields with their babies strapped to them, Richard Ligon remarked: 'For they carry burdens on their backs and yet work too.' His perspective was, of course, very different from that of the slave women themselves; for them the work was the burden, not the child. Unsurprisingly, the island shared the terrible infant mortality rates that bedevilled all the sugar isles.

By the late eighteenth century, however, the Barbadian planters had decided it was more economical to 'breed rather than buy' and had shifted to pro-natalist policies in the hope of increasing the birth rate among the slave population. This meant that pregnant women were often withdrawn from the first gang, which did the most strenuous work, and put in slightly less demanding positions until they delivered.

In these newly enlightened times then, John Stephen's mother was probably encouraged to bear her child safely. But she certainly would not be supported in raising him. As one slave noted:

> The slave mother can be spared long enough from the field to endure all the bitterness of a mother's anguish when it adds another name to a master's ledger, but not long enough to receive the joyous reward afforded by the intelligent smiles of her child. I never think of this terrible interference of slavery with infantile affections, and its diverting them from their natural course, without feelings to which I can give no adequate expression.

So not long after John Stephen's birth, his mother was forced to return to work and consign her child to the care of other women, those in their fifties and sixties who could no longer manage the rigours of field work. Frederick Douglass wrote that 'The practice of separating children from their mothers . . . is a marked feature of the cruelty and barbarity of the slave system.' He noted that the custom had a terrible impact on slave women, who had 'children but no family!' But he was even more grieved on his own behalf, because he felt that he had been denied the natural connection a child should have with his mother. Today we use the term 'attachment disorder' to describe the profound impact on children's emotional and psychological development of being denied a consistent and intimate relationship with a trusted caregiver. We can only guess at how John Stephen and millions like him were affected by being denied the core human experience of a parent–child relationship.

Just as it is impossible to name John Stephen's mother, so it is difficult to definitively verify that Robert Cooper was his father, since planters virtually never declared themselves as parents of slaves on plantation records. The social rules and the law functioned both to facilitate white men's sexual exploitation of black women, and also to protect the men themselves from the consequences of their actions. As one American slave who was also the child of a white estate owner noted: 'Men do not love those who remind them of their sins – unless they have a mind to repent – and the mulatto child's face is a standing accusation against him who is master and father to the child.' But the situation was somewhat different in the Caribbean, where interracial liaisons were more openly tolerated, and, though not publically claimed, paternity was often acknowledged in more subtle ways. In the case of John Stephen, the evidence pointing towards Robert Cooper being his father is convincing: apart from island lore, there was the lighter skin that marked his father out as white, as well as the physical resemblance to the Ashbys. There is a hint in his name too. Robert Cooper had a penchant for giving his illegitimate children traditional English two-handed names like his own. Thus his mixed-race children, including John Stephen, Robert Henry and Alice Christian, stand out among the rather more traditional slave names that dominate his ledgers. These small distinctions and offerings are often the clearest clue to a slave's parentage. As the historian James Walvin noted: 'Few planters accepted their slave children as legitimate offspring, but they often bestowed on them and their mothers a string of material benefits and privileges generally denied to other slaves.' According to local historian Robert Morris, it is doubtful that Robert Cooper would have allowed John Stephen to marry using his surname unless he had given him explicit permission to do so, and it is reasonable to assume that this was because he accepted John Stephen was his son.

Whether or not this tacit paternity extended to a formal relationship between father and son, John Stephen's mixed-race identity was one of the most formative facts of his life. By the time that John Stephen was born, miscegenation or 'race mixing' was a source of great anxiety in the region. But this had not always been the case. In the first days of settlement, when island society was still fluid and unformed, and when indentured servitude was still the dominant form of labour, there were marriages recorded between white and black people. During these years, before the ideology of racism had taken root, the English authorities suggested that the offspring of these couples should be free. But with the emergence of slavery, attitudes had hardened. As early as 1644, the island of Antigua passed a law that prohibited the 'carnal copulation between Christian and heathen'. Miscegenation could, it was now argued, undermine the entire system: 'Interracial sex was said to be a violation of both natural and divine law,' noted the American writer Edward Ball, 'as it produced a "mixed" race of people previously not seen on earth and also unsanctioned by God.'

Although unwilling to curb the sexual freedoms of white men, the Barbadian authorities were equally concerned that interracial dalliances would undermine white supremacy. Mixed-race people disrupted the binary opposition between black and white, a polarization that depended on a perception of skin colour as immutable and species-specific. As the structure of the Atlantic slave system hinged on matters of race, categorizing the children of black-white liaisons was an obsession across the Americas. Hence the notorious 'one drop rule' adopted in the American South, which eliminated anyone who was not 'pure' white from assuming the privileges associated with the planter caste. In Saint-Domingue the islanders divided the offspring of white and black people into an astounding 128 categories. In Barbados these classifications were more simple: the non-white population was divided into 'black' or 'negro' (referring to those who were dark-skinned people of African origin or descent) and 'coloured' or 'mulatto' (which were used interchangeably to refer to the product of black and white parents).

The term 'mulatto', which was widely used from the middle of the seventeenth century, is commonly thought to have originated from the Portuguese word for mule (*mulo*). It was considered a derogatory label, since the mulatto person – like its zoological counterpart – was assumed to be sterile. This idea was of course swiftly abandoned when the fecundity of mixed-race people proved to be equal to that of any other group. On the American mainland, for reasons both religious and demographic, the taboos around interracial sex were more intense, and so the rejection of the resultant children was more extreme. But in the sugar islands, the mixed-race population continued to increase. The community grew so large that Janet Schaw, a Scotswoman who visited the Caribbean in the 1770s, complained about 'the crowds of Mullatoes, which you meet in the streets, houses and indeed everywhere' and regarded them as the visible signs of 'licentious and unnatural . . . liaisons between white masters and black slave women'. And indeed, John Stephen, along with this illegitimate siblings and half-siblings, was the product of a dynasty that would eventually dwarf Robert Cooper's legitimate family.

John Stephen's early years were very different from those of his father or his legitimate half-brother, despite their parentage and their shared experience of a plantation childhood, John Burke Jr. He was not raised in the comfort and elegance of the great house, but in the squalor of the slave quarters. He did not enjoy a cosseted childhood, but a rather neglected and knockabout one. Even so, as a young boy, Burkes must have seemed like an adventure playground. He must have explored every corner of this place: its cliffs and gullies, its recesses and caves. It is not hard to imagine him, even now: a barefoot, brown-skinned boy scampering along the dry stony paths that connected the slave quarters to the great house, cane fields and factory. Every face that he passed was familiar to him, just as his darting figure was to them. He would peer out across the ocean, his hand shielding his eyes, while the sea birds whirled and danced above his head. Burkes was his home and his prison. Everything he knew, loved and loathed existed within its boundaries, and he would live in this little community without interruption for more than half his life.

The plantation records show that John Stephen's childhood contemporaries were slaves like Ben and Goridon and Elrick. He would have played with them and probably also with the white children on the estate, though this was not necessarily a pleasant experience. As one contemporary explained:

> The rage of a creole is most violent when once excited – owing to the manner in which they are brought up. Often I have seen children, of five and six years of age, knocking the poor Negroes about the cheeks with all the passion and the cruelty possible; and these little imps' treatment to dumb animals is truly horrible. They are never checked by their parents, and, of course, these propensities increased with their age and which the poor slaves feel the effects of.

He would almost certainly have come into contact with his legitimate half-brother too. Since there were no secrets on a sugar estate, John Burke Jr probably knew that John Stephen was also Robert Cooper's child. On some plantations this fact would have gone unremarked and unacknowledged; children like John Stephen were just 'slave brats' and were treated as such. But on other plantations, particularly where the master's wife resented her husband's dalliances, these illegitimate offspring became scapegoats, bullied by the legitimate children in order to avenge their wronged mother. Any resentment John Stephen felt towards John Burke Jr was of course carefully repressed. This was 'Massa John', who must be treated with deference at all times, masking any hostility or envy.

John Stephen had a number of other half-brothers and half-sisters. But it is unlikely that they considered themselves a family. The very concept of family had been so fractured and debased by plantation culture that one slave noted: 'Brothers and sisters we were by blood; but slavery had made us strangers. I heard the words brother and sisters, and knew they must mean something; but slavery had robbed these terms of their true meaning.' Many slaves found it hard to generate any positive feelings for their siblings and fell instead into bickering and open competition. As the same slave concluded: 'There is not, beneath the sky, an enemy to filial affections so destructive as slavery. It had made my brothers and sisters strangers to me; it converted the mother that bore me into a myth; it shrouded my father in mystery, and left me without an intelligible beginning in the world.'

Life was hard for enslaved children, but nowhere near as hard as it would become, so many recalled their youth with fondness. Mary Prince wrote: 'This was the happiest period of my life; I was too young to understand rightly my condition as a slave, and too thoughtless and full of spirits to look forward to the days of toil and sorrow.'

The days of 'toil and sorrow' began pretty quickly, since the planters made sure that children were put to work early in order to accustom them to what would be a life of incessant labour. Even as a toddler, therefore, John Stephen would have been given a miniature basket and hoe and encouraged to collect rocks, pull up weeds or collect eggs. He would already be beginning to develop his own understanding of what it meant to be black and what it meant to be white. By six, he was eligible for the Third Gang, which was primarily made up of the very young and the very old. Here he was instructed on how to perform simple tasks such as carrying the grass to the cattle and bringing food and refreshments to the adults labouring in the fields.

Frederick Douglass began to think seriously about being

a slave when he was seven or eight; and the realization that he was merchandise, and that he had been 'born for another's benefit', came to him forcefully around twelve, when he found that he could not live his life as he wished. About that epiphany he wrote: 'I was a slave – born a slave – and though the fact was incomprehensible to me, it conveyed to me a sense of entire dependence on the will of somebody I had never seen.' 'The ever-gnawing and soul devouring thought' of his enslavement made Douglass both mentally and physically 'wretched'.

Despite the inherent hardship of daily life, John Stephen's early years took place against a backdrop of great optimism for the slave population. Not only was the epic drama of Haiti sill unfolding but the abolition movement was once more building up steam. It had gone dormant at the turn of the century as a result of a threefold fear of Jacobinism, the French Revolution, and the violence in Haiti. But in 1804, the Abolition Committee was re-formed. Alongside old faithfuls such as Thomas Clarkson was a dynamic set of new members including James Stephen, a barrister who had been radicalized by a traumatic visit to Barbados and who was also married to Wilberforce's sister. Then there was Zachary Macaulay, who had served as governor of Sierra Leone and had links to the Colonial Office; and Henry Brougham, a rising young lawyer with Whig connections.

Rather than rushing into a new popular campaign, they focused primarily on lobbying important legislators and senior civil servants. Their rhetoric was frequently as much anti-French as pro-black. In one of Stephen's pamphlets, he declared: 'What are [Bonaparte] and his ruffians to stab and drown all the poor labourers of [Haiti] because they chuse to work as men for wages, and not like horses under the driver's lash.' Indeed, they argued that the Haitian revolution pointed to the inherent fragility of the slave system and the need to make changes. A few also noted how important African-born slaves had been to the rebels, and thus how dangerous these 'saltwater slaves' were to the peace of the region. They proposed that abolition of the slave trade would provoke a speedy growth of the natural black population and that this, in the end, would enhance British West Indian interests.

The Abolition Committee's first attempt in 1804 to make the legislature rethink the issue met with defeat; as did a new Abolition Bill in 1805, even though Pitt had personally endorsed it. But despite these setbacks, support was growing among both the people and the oligarchy, who realized that abolition of the slave trade might actually be in the mother country's interest. As the historian Robin Blackburn explained:

> In 1805 the slave population of the French-controlled Caribbean stood at 175,000, the slave population of Spanish Cuba about the same, while that of the British-controlled Caribbean stood at 715,000. A mutual agreement to end the slave trade would only perpetuate British preponderance.

The agitation of the abolitionists soon gave rise to legal and social change in the West Indies. In 1805, for example, 'An Act for the Better Protection of the Slaves of this Island' was presented in the Barbados House of Assembly. This legislation proposed that the ludicrously lenient punishment for the murder of a slave, which had been merely a fine of £15, be repealed. And the imperial government, pressured by pro-abolitionist sentiments at home, intervened to push it through. Now the murder of a slave was a felony, and the following year a man called John Welch was the first person to be indicted. Nobody was surprised that he was not convicted, but slaves and abolitionists were nonetheless content: the most iniquitous of the old statutes had fallen and slave murder was now a capital offence. The impact of this legislation was profound. John Beckles, Speaker of the

Barbadian House of Assembly in 1805, claimed that slaves might exploit this situation by provoking whites into killing them, so that they would be tried and executed. This remarkable argument illustrates the extraordinary lengths to which the planters believed slaves would go to be revenged on their hated masters.

On 10 June 1806, the House of Commons passed a resolution by a margin of ninety-five to fifteen declaring that the slave trade was founded 'on principles contrary to justice, humanity and sound policy' and demanding the government institute measures for its total abolition. By a much slimmer majority, the House of Lords supported the motion of the lower house and it was presented to the king, 'praying his majesty to negotiate with foreign powers for their cooperation towards effecting a total abolition of the trade to Africa for slaves'. It was a huge victory for the campaigners and a mortal blow for the slave trade.

Emboldened, the abolitionists stepped up their attacks on the West India lobby. In early 1807 Thomas Clarkson published 'Three Letters to Slave Merchants on Compensation', pleading with the West Indians to treat their slaves better:

> Let all the Negroes have sufficient provisions. Let them work in moderation . . . Give them more time to themselves. Curtail the power of their drivers. Lessen the frequency and the severity of their punishments . . . You will also be happier yourselves . . . in as much as you will have the pleasure, which . . . results from the discharge of the office of doing good.

'An Act for the Abolition of the Slave Trade' finally became law on 25 March 1807. The Barbadians were the only sugar islanders who could remain relatively sanguine about its passing, since their 'it is cheaper to breed rather buy' philosophy meant they had been ameliorating slave conditions for several generations. In fact the passing of the law was something of an opportunity for the Barbadians, who realized that they could now sell their surplus slaves to plantation owners from neighbouring islands at a premium in this newly constricted market. But even though Barbados was somewhat less affected than the other British colonies, the planters still saw the legislation as a cause for grave concern. The Act that had abolished the slave trade said nothing about freeing the slaves, but it was the first major victory for the abolitionists, and as such was simultaneously a slap in the face for the planters and a great boost to the aspirations of the region's enslaved people. They rightly saw it as an important nail in the coffin of Atlantic slavery and a giant step towards their ultimate goal of emancipation.

14

The soul that is within me no man can degrade.

Frederick Douglass

Much to the slaves' chagrin, these momentous developments did not lead to an immediate transformation of their condition. Indeed, the realities of the plantation remained much the same and John Stephen's early life followed its predestined course. He was enslaved and, for the first three decades or so of his existence – every hour of his day and night – his life was determined by this fact. The only change in John Stephen's fortunes came about not as a result of wider political change, but through the chance benevolence of his unacknowledged father. At the age of around thirteen, when other slaves were being promoted to the Second Gang, on their way to the terrible pressure of the First Gang, John Stephen was lucky enough to bypass the rigours of field work and was apprenticed to a carpenter on the plantation. Bestowing such a privileged position on a by-blow was a common gesture for a planter who wanted to enhance the future prospects of an illegitimate child he did not plan to openly acknowledge. At this point, John Stephen was categorized in the slave registers as a 'Boy Carpenter Learning' and consigned to the custody of the plantation's head carpenter. Here, in Burkes' carpentry workshop, the young John Stephen was taught how to use hammers and augers, adzes and axes, and when to use a jackplane or a joiner plane. As he gained experience he learned how to make simple benches, tables and stools, as well as boxes and coffins, and later he learned to construct storehouses, a new fowl coop and a pigsty.

Other than his vocational training, the educational opportunities available to John Stephen were extremely limited. Though a few planters in the French islands paid to educate their illegitimate children, most believed that it was imperative that slaves 'be kept in the profoundest ignorance', arguing, 'If they are not instructed in any arts or skills other than those required for un-paid labour, they are less likely to contemplate alternatives and so resist their masters.' As a result, there were for many years virtually no educational institutions that catered for the black people of Barbados. The only exceptions were the Sunday schools provided by the hard-pressed Moravian and Methodist missionaries, where some slave children were able to gain a very rudimentary schooling, based largely on Christian teachings.

More than becoming literate or numerate, the most important lesson for the slaves to learn concerned their place in society. Just as planters' children were taught to view themselves as different from and superior to their slaves, so their slaves were socialized to recognize that they were what the Barbadian novelist George Lamming called an 'instrument of production'. To the planters of the Atlantic system this was the real 'education' that needed to be inculcated in their charges so that they could endure the ceaseless, punishing and dull work to which their race had sentenced them, and in order that they would come to believe in their own inferiority. This was the justification for feeding them a diet of humiliation and abuse, for the insults that assailed them as they served round the table, for the whippings and the rapes.

Parents and plantation elders would also pass on advice about how to cope with the perils of being owned by their fellow man. A lot of this wisdom was encoded in the folk tales that emerged in slave societies across the New World: the Anansi stories in which a wily spider triumphs against the odds; and Brer Rabbit, whose endless battles with Brer Wolf proved that a powerful and ruthless opponent could be overcome with cunning and a good heart. Whites saw these tales as the fanciful product of an ignorant and superstitious people. But for the slaves, these stories provided valuable lessons for living in a harsh and arbitrary world: they were an allegory of their own lives.

A central message of these folk tales was to appreciate that whites, even the apparently kindly ones, were potentially hazardous figures. John Stephen and his little friends were taught to be cautious, remain silent or act dumb when being questioned by white people. They were reminded never to hold their gaze for too long or to speak to them unless they were spoken to first. Above all they were taught to stick together, to protect other slaves' interests. If a slave did something wrong, like steal food or break equipment, his fellows usually drew together and concealed their knowledge of the transgression. Those who broke ranks suffered the wrath of the rest.

Young slaves learned early the advantage of silence and of obeying orders with a blank expression, giving no sign of understanding what was going on around them. They learned to slip into a posture of cowering deference when in the presence of almost any white person, and to use the language of subservience and the submissive bobbing and bowing and entreaties of 'Yassuh Massa', 'Nossuh Massa!' to hide their real feelings. With such a need to dissemble, it was no wonder that many planters believed that slaves were inherently untrustworthy and unknowable. As one American slave owner wrote:

> Persons live and die in the midst of Negroes and know
> comparatively little of their real character . . . The

Negroes are a distinct class in community, and keep themselves very much to themselves. They are one thing before the whites, and another before their own colour. Deception towards the former is characteristic of them, whether bond or free.

After five years' apprenticeship, John Stephen was classified as an 'Ordinary Carpenter' in the slave books. As such he was heir to an established tradition of slave carpentry that had existed for over two centuries, combining the skills of their African ancestors with the best aspects of the European tradition. John Stephen was now involved with all the important areas of the plantation work: he repaired the great house banisters, window frames and guttering, as well as doing the highly skilled jobs of mending the factory coolers or the wooden parts of the mills. And though most of the great house's furniture was imported, he was also trained to do the fine work, fashioning louvred windows, beautiful tables and chairs, bookcases and cupboards.

As he grew in experience he was expected to oversee others: the young apprentices that he was training, and the slaves who were cutting and hauling large logs across the plantation to make shingles for the great house. Sometimes he would work with the sawyers who cut the timber or fix lathes for the masons to plaster. By the time he approached twenty, John Stephen's status on the plantation had risen substantially; and there was still the possibility that he would rise even higher, to the position of head carpenter. By virtue of his trade, John Stephen was valuable and he knew it. Indeed in the slave economy, the ordinary carpenter was thought to be worth more than a head driver, and a head carpenter was valued at as much as £300 – the price of four healthy field slaves.

Robert Cooper's gift of a trade considerably improved John Stephen's life of servitude. His superior status was recognized by everyone on the plantation, black and white. He was also allowed to hire himself out, paying a certain percentage of his fees to his owner, Robert Cooper, and keeping the rest for himself. This gave him a way of earning additional money that he could spend as he wished or save up to buy himself out of slavery, but it also meant that he had more mobility than his fellow slaves. As a jobbing carpenter, he was allowed to travel around the island virtually unsupervised as he moved to and from appointments.

This freedom of movement was one of most valuable perks of his job. He was able to visit the local area of Oistins regularly and even went as far as Bridgetown, the bustling capital, where he would have encountered raucous street musicians and foreign sailors and traders from every corner of the globe. Some of the most colourful figures in the capital were the female hucksters or vendors. These were the slaves who came into town from country plantations like Burkes to sell the produce that they grew in their provision grounds. They were formidable women who often carried their vast trays of produce – corn, tomatoes, okra – on their heads. Their poise amazed visitors to the islands. One Barbadian higgler was seen balancing an entire brood of chickens, with the nest, coop and all. Their entrepreneurship and aggressive hawking caused the authorities profound consternation, since their success often undermined the sales of conventional merchants. As a result the higglers were accused of monopolizing the marketplace, pushing up prices and setting a dangerous example to the other slaves. But the authorities were also nervous about banning them altogether, because early attempts to do so had caused intense unrest among the slave population.

One aspect of the capital that would have impressed John Stephen was the lifestyle of the slaves there, which was very different from what he had known on the plantation. Rather than living in relative isolation, the blacks and whites of the city interacted not just with one another but with a wide variety of visitors to the islands, so the slaves tended to be more worldly: they often knew how to read and write and had greater access to wider news.

But it was the exposure to free people of colour that probably had the most profound impact on John Stephen, because he would undoubtedly have wished to join their ranks. A large percentage of them were mulattoes like him who had been freed by their fathers-cum-owners. These people lived curious lives. They had a status that any slave would envy: they were legally British subjects and could theoretically lay claim to some of the legal rights held by white freemen; they also shared obligations of citizenship such as paying taxes and serving in the militia. But in reality they found themselves confined to a subordinate social position with restricted civil rights and social privileges. They could not become church ministers or take communion at the same time as whites, and they were segregated at church. They were also excluded from parish schools, though they supported them through their taxes. They couldn't join libraries, hold any commissions or become magistrates. And in the social arena they were still expected to maintain a respectful deference to whites.

Inevitably these restrictions provoked resentment, and in the 1790s the free coloureds had begun their struggle for civil rights. By the time John Stephen was an adult, they were a force to be reckoned with. They used a variety of methods to improve their lot, from serious political agitation and raising petitions, to making addresses to the governor and legislative lobbying – all of which the planters resisted furiously. Freedmen of colour represented something dangerous in a slave society; despite the limits on their rights, they were an important inspiration for many slaves, proving that their enslaved status was neither inevitable nor permanent.

So John Stephen was part of a community that was

simultaneously sanctioned and rejected, accepted and reviled. His brown skin gave him greater privileges and economic opportunities than the darker-skinned population, and better life chances. In a society where both blacks and whites had internalized poisonous ideas about racial hierarchies, and where skin colour was a largely reliable indicator of social place, the mixed-race population was often treated with greater respect than the majority of slaves; and in some islands they were addressed as 'Miss' or 'Mr' to indicate their special status. But these privileges came at a price, and many mulattoes found themselves caught between blacks and whites – different from either, and distrusted by both.

As a mixed-race or 'coloured' person John Stephen was sometimes regarded with suspicion by other blacks, who feared that he might throw his lot in with the planters if he felt it would increase his rights and opportunities. If a coloured person had also been freed, his allegiances were even more suspect. As two visitors to the island noted, the free coloured population tended to see themselves as superior to mere slaves: 'They have no fellow feeling with the slaves. In fact they had prejudices against the Negroes no less bitter than those that the whites have exercised towards them. There are honourable exceptions to this . . . but such, we are convinced, is the general fact.'

Whites were also wary of mixed-race people, whom they saw as a potential Trojan horse that could infiltrate white society and then turn against them at any moment. They were the offspring of black women, after all, and their roots were in the slave population. It was feared that people like John Stephen could use his advantages, particularly if he had received an education, to inform his slave brethren about current events and even inspire them to insurgency, as had happened in Haiti.

Unsurprisingly, mixed-race people evolved their own social world where they could get together without hostility. One late-eighteenth-century visitor to the island was intrigued by the events they held, which neither whites nor blacks were encouraged to attend: 'In the evening, I went to a grand mulatto ball, commonly called a Dignity Ball, at Susy Austen's. The ladies were all splendidly dressed and they danced uncommonly well. The ballroom was brilliantly lighted and highly perfumed.' John Stephen would have been aware of these gatherings, and probably attended more than a few.

More than his racial identity, it was John Stephen's status as a slave that most profoundly shaped his individual experience. He was a man born into slavery who had thus far had no experience of a free life. The ubiquitous brutality of plantation life was all that he knew, and the perpetual petty insults of a slave's life were something that he was all too familiar with. What he probably couldn't be aware of was how pernicious an influence the slave system could have on his inner life. In a slave society, the only relationship that counted was the one the slave had with his master, and the authorities refused to recognize any other, whether between enslaved men and women or between enslaved parents and their children. This meant that however ardently these ties were felt, they would never be deemed legitimate or binding. Thus a slave could not prevent the master or overseer from taking his woman; nor could he prevent his family from being sold away. He could not even carry out the normal duties of a parent: to remain with his children and keep them from harm.

In this way, the system of slavery effectively abolished families, which had a particularly alienating effect on males like John Stephen. They were encouraged to have sexual relations to increase a planter's stock and were discouraged from taking a role in raising their offspring, who would in any case not take their father's name, but the one bestowed upon them by their owner, and they would be known as 'the slave of Mister So-and-so', or 'So-and-so's boy'. Without the possibility of establishing these crucial ties and assuming their responsibilities, the male slave's own development was permanently stunted, as the American Frederick Douglass lamented: 'I could grow, though I could not become a man, but must remain all my life a minor – a mere boy.'

This disfiguring psychological process was supported by the power structure of the entire slave system, enshrined in law, and enforced by that society's traditions and its military might. On a day-to-day basis, it was sustained by a consistent campaign of violence and brutality, random whippings, mutilation and brandings, mobilized to remind the slave of who he was: merely and simply 'a slave' – someone with virtually no rights or protection; and who had but one obligation: to satisfy his owner. A slave's life therefore was defined by his extreme powerlessness, over his person and the persons of his loved ones. This lack of autonomy engendered a sense of humiliation and dishonour. And this was the most pernicious heritage of slavery: that the slaves frequently internalized the master's denigration and abuse and turned it into self-loathing, creating the mental slavery that imprisoned the slaves as surely as their shackles; what the Caribbean historian and poet Edward Brathwaite dubbed the 'inner plantation'.

However, no matter how all-powerful and all-pervasive the slave system tried to be, it could not entirely control or mould the slave's reality. This was due to pragmatics if nothing else. Although it is impossible to speak of freedom in relation to a system that so resolutely desecrated its subjects' human rights, the regime on each plantation evolved out of the interaction between the individual owner and his slaves. So at Burkes, as at other estates, there had to be a degree of compromise to allow daily tasks to be carried out despite the master's anxiety and the slaves' unquenchable desire for freedom. So there were moments in the routine when the tight controls loosened a little, and there were circumstances in which transgressive behaviour was allowed to pass unpunished.

There was even a tiny minority of slaves who managed to bend the rules of the plantation system to their will. This was demonstrated by a clan of slaves at Newton estate, near Burkes, in the late eighteenth century. A protracted exchange of letters between its slaves, owners and managers revealed how one slave family, headed by a black female house slave called Old Doll, was able to exploit familial connections and clever negotiation skills to manipulate their owners until they had 'a kind of right to be idle'. Ultimately, they would even negotiate freedom for many of their number. This degree of influence was extremely unusual, since most slaves had neither the opportunity nor the education to pull off such a feat, but even within the most repressive environments, the slaves nonetheless carved out for themselves some small spaces of respite, as well as lacunas of power, of pleasure, of care. Each day, some slave, somewhere, found stolen moments in which the yoke of slavery didn't feel so heavy: a joke shared, a flirtatious exchange, a secret embrace.

The ability to squeeze joy from a stone depended, in part, on the slaves themselves, for John Stephen and his contemporaries all had their own personalities and idiosyncrasies that could not be obliterated by their enslavement. And there is always a danger when documenting their stories of turning them into mere symbols of what this terrible system could do to people. (As Orlando Patterson has argued, it 'is impossible to generalize about the inner psychology of any group'.) To do so would dehumanize them just as surely as slavery tried to do. So we can only hope to understand the enormity of the system that they were resisting and exercise compassion when we judge the strategies they used to endure it. If defeating the slave system was impossible for any individual, that some survived without losing entirely their ability for love and laughter was in itself a victory.

★

When he was not working, most of John Stephen's time was spent in the quarters where the slaves lived. Although they were set in the wider world of Burkes, they had their own social structure, their own leaders and followers, their own manners and habits, and their own traditions and history. Because their days were not their own, the social world of the slaves at Burkes largely sprang to life at night and weekends. So every evening after work, the slaves, preferring to be outdoors rather than in their poky cabins, would gather on the piece of open land around which the huts were loosely organized. This was the place where they could relax and let their guard down, so they laughed and flirted, told stories of their ancestors, sang songs, admonished their offspring and shared secrets and gossip: jokes about the unreasonable behaviour of their masters or mistresses, and rumours of rebellions and the progress of the abolitionists.

I sometimes picture John Stephen here, after a hard day's work, finally allowing the mask of obedient slavehood to slip, his shoulders relaxing, his accent becoming more broad and his behaviour less inhibited. Here he is a different man: a person of authority, treated with respect. He is squatting on the ground, chatting to friends, eating dinner. For him and the other slaves, these hours in the quarters are virtually the only times when the authorities on the plantation are not actively checking up on them and harassing them. It is their brief hiatus of peace and they make the most of it.

The quarters were also alive with music; it was the wind that blew away fatigue, grief and fear. For just as slaves accompanied their work in the fields and mills with song, so music leavened their leisure hours. But this singing was not, as many planters claimed, an indication of their well-being. As Frederick Douglass wrote:

> I have often sung to drown my sorrow, but seldom to express my happiness. Crying for joy, and singing for

joy were alike uncommon to me while in the jaws of slavery. The singing of a man cast away upon a desolate island might as appropriately be considered as evidence of contentment and happiness, as the singing of a slave; the songs of the one and the other are prompted by the same emotion.

So at night, Burkes was haunted with the sounds of melodious voices and a variety of instruments such as fiddles and pipes. Virtually alone of all the islands, Barbadian slaves were for many years deprived of the consolations of the drums which had such importance in the aural lexicons of their forefathers, because the slave laws of 1688 proscribed the keeping of loud instruments 'which may call together, or give sign or notice to one another of their wicked designs and purposes' by slaves. Nonetheless the slaves in the Caribbean, like those in mainland America, developed their own unique musical styles, a fusion of African and European traditions that became the genesis of many popular musical forms, from blues to jazz, from reggae to hip hop.

This new musical style took pride of place at the events that were most important in the slaves' lives, such as births, marriages and funerals. It was the soundtrack of the impromptu gatherings, informal dances and grand balls that were held to celebrate special occasions like Christmas and 'crop over'. On these nights, slaves travelled to neighbouring plantations, with the grudging permission of their owners, who did not approve of these amusements but did not as a rule obstruct them, aware that these orgies of dancing and forgetting were a safety valve that helped slaves cope with the rigours of servitude.

Many things were different in the shadow world of the slave settlements, including their medicine. Despite the regular visits of the white doctor employed by Robert Cooper, most slaves relied on black healers on the plantation, whose practice drew on both traditions brought from Africa and skills learned on the island, particularly those inherited from the Amerindian people of the region, some of whom had been transported to Barbados in the early days of slavery. Local leaves and herbs were mixed with various roots and tree barks to make teas and tonics. These healing practices were associated with African traditions of magic and a faith in the supernatural known as 'obeah'. Obeah men and women were akin to conjurors in parts of mainland America, and were not only engaged in healing, but also claimed to be able to ward off evil, bring good fortune or make people fall in love.

Most larger plantations like Burkes had their own obeah practitioners who were notable for their paraphenalia: dried herbs, beads, knotted cords, cats' teeth. They promised believers a life (often back in Africa) after death, where they would coexist with a world of spirits. Root doctors and obeah men and women were regarded with awe and deference across the island. Whites were, of course, aware of this world of healers and obeah – indeed, their preparations were so effective that the whites often used them as well. But they didn't fully understand the tradition, and frequently used these beliefs to justify their view of slaves as unsophisticated, superstitious heathens. The planters also feared these heterodox healers because they had such a huge influence on the slave population and often played a prominent role in rebellions and subversion. As one American lamented, 'They avail themselves of the passions and prejudices of the poor people and thus fit them for their own purposes.' They were also aware of their skills as poisoners, and were unnerved by their mysterious physical powers: one obeah man, burned slowly alive, displayed no pain and declared that 'It was not in the power of the White people to kill him.'

There was another group tussling with the obeah men for control of the slaves' souls. This was the church. In the early days of settlement the Church of England was largely uninterested in ministering to black slaves, lest it provoke aspirations for freedom, but later on this changed and religion began to be used to subdue the black population and justify their enslavement. The Anglican ministers, funded by the planter-controlled Vestry, encouraged slaves to come to terms with 'the place that God in his wisdom had chosen to put them'. As the Jamaican plantocrat Peter Beckford concluded: 'Let him [the slave] be taught to revere God; and then his duty to his master; may he be made efficient – his labour easy, his life comfortable and his mind resigned.'

But it was the nonconformist missionaries, rather than the Anglican church, that captured the loyalty of the enslaved population. And what emerged from their encounter with this unorthodox branch of Christianity was a group of charismatic black preachers who travelled around, spreading the word of God and the consolations of Christianity. They preached in secluded places or ramshackle 'churches', no more than wooden huts, where the congregation filled the rooms with song. The planters regarded these churches as ill-disciplined, loud and primitive, but put up with them provided they did not openly preach resistance to the slave system. As time passed, this hybrid form of worship began to undermine the influence of the older beliefs like obeah, but could never fully supplant it. So for many years, the slaves went to church and bought their charms and powders at the same time.

Thus from the earliest days of settlement, the enslaved Africans who found themselves uprooted and transplanted had evolved a hybrid culture, transforming the rituals and tastes of the world they had left behind to fit their new environment. They forged a new language out of the languages that they had once used and the English tongue that had been imposed upon them. They melded old recipes with new ingredients to create an entirely different cuisine. And they integrated traditional instruments with western melodic traditions to create an innovative form of music. These new ways of thinking and being created a way of life which would guide and shape their descendants' experience in this New World and also shape important aspects of the wider culture that still resonate today.

Whatever whites felt about such practices, beliefs and behaviours, they were part of the interior landscape of slaves like John Stephen. At Burkes, as at other plantations in the region, this alternative Afro-Caribbean culture had its own worldview and coherence, one that resisted and challenged the hegemony of white European culture. By its very existence it said that Robert Cooper's world of great white houses and neatly etched sugar fields was not the only way of being, and that there were other ways of thinking that included the possibility of a life free from slavery.

The reality was that, on almost every level, slaves and their owners saw things across an unbridgeable divide. The imbalance of power between the two groups meant that their understanding and interpretation of each other's motivations were often vastly different. So, while an owner might see a slave's suicide as a form of revenge, the slave saw it as an honourable way of escaping unendurable suffering. Abortion and infanticide were not murder but a gesture of mercy, a way of sparing a beloved child from the horrors to come. Running away was also seen through a very different lens. Thus when 'Jack, a light-skinned carpenter' absconded, his master assumed he was trying to 'pass as a white man'. The planters perceived such escapes as a challenge to their authority and characterized the runaways as outlaws and rebels. But for the slaves, escapes such as Jack's were not so much political as deeply personal: they often reflected a simple desire to avoid the immediate and specific circumstances of enslavement, and the runaways were seen as daring, inspirational heroes. Whether they were tales of a man absconding to enjoy a weekend with a sweetheart or visit a family member, or a more permanent bid for freedom, their stories travelled from plantation to plantation, were whispered about in local towns and settlements like Oistins and Bridgetown, and were talked about openly and gleefully in the quarters and at places of worship. It did not matter that so few of these tales ended happily, or that many runaways' efforts were rewarded with painful punishments or even death. Their tales of courage shaped the imagination of the slaves and provided them with the hope for another life that could be attained if they were brave and bold enough.

This visceral desire to escape a shackled existence was shared by all slaves and united all enslaved communities. Hence a piece of slave lore that recurs across the Americas, from Brazil to Barbados, from Cuba to Maryland: whether it is told in the Spanish-, French- or English-speaking territories, the story is essentially the same. One day in the cane or cotton fields, after a wretched loss or before a brutal punishment, a slave, troubled and tormented, simply rises up and, hovering for a time just out of the reach of his abusers, flies away. It is a piece of mythology that says everything about the enslaved person's desire for transcendence and sums up all of the slave's terrible longing and desperation to elude his terrible fate.

Such differences in perspective between owners and slaves shaped every aspect of life on the plantation, even down to the way the two groups responded to the land. Thus if the manicured driveway that led up to Burkes, as well as the imposing great house itself, embodied Robert Cooper's position as patriarch, ruler of an orderly, well-managed universe, so the plantation's anarchic little pathways and ramshackle quarters represented the alternative lives of the slaves. The island as a whole was contested ground. The planters were reassured by the order that farming had imposed upon its original unruliness. Barbados was now dominated by seven hundred or so grand sugar estates that were served by roads easily policed by the militia. But for the slaves the very symmetry and uniformity were a constant reminder of the all-encompassing power of the planter elite and the brutal circumscription of their own lives.

At night, as Robert Cooper and his family sat on the Burkes veranda, he could look out across his vast estate with an easy sense of achievement. Year after year, he had the satisfaction of seeing the working plantation over which he ruled increase his wealth and prestige. For John Stephen and his fellow slaves, gathered around the fire in their quarters, Burkes represented something far more complicated. By the nineteenth century, when John Stephen was growing up, most sugar estates in Barbados had been owned by the same family for a hundred years, so that on a plantation like Burkes, several generations of slaves had been born, raised and died in the same villages. And, in spite of the shifting political landscape, the slaves at Burkes, like most of those on the island, had a fierce attachment to their plantation. Unable to quite believe in the possibility of freedom, they knew they would only leave Burkes if they were sold, which would have been regarded by them as a terrible fate. As a group of Barbadian slaves questioned by one visitor to the island explained: 'Here we are born, and here are the graves of our fathers. Can we say to their bones, arise and go with us into a foreign land?'

So Burkes for them was home, just as it was for the Ashbys. And just like the dwellers in the great house, the slaves could appreciate the beauty of the plantation and of their island. They too enjoyed the sunrises that ushered in the day with such abruptness, and the glorious molten sunsets that signalled its end. They could watch the turquoise sea in all its varying humours, and enjoy the lulling sound of the waves as they crashed against the cliffs. They were accustomed to the ubiquitous noises of plantation life: the songs and groans of the slaves at their toil, the clangs and rumbles of the factory's machinery, the perpetual song of the wind whistling through the canes. And at night, they too were lulled to sleep by the melody of the Caribbean night: that wondrous chorus of tree frogs, cicadas and other insects. Yet they could never forget that alongside the beauty, there was the ugly reality of their enslavement. Burkes was also a place of humiliating squalor, onerous toil, terrible restriction and unpredictable violence; it was both familiar and threatening, a home and a prison.

By the second decade of the nineteenth century, when John Stephen grew into manhood, the tensions between these two communities had grown even more acute, as the slaves' dreams of freedom inched ever closer to becoming reality. The abolitionist movement had profoundly altered the opinions of people across the colonies. For the first time since the inception of Atlantic slavery, the West Indian proprietors had to justify both their ideas about race and their treatment of their charges. To their slaves' delight, the planters were now on the defensive. When the campaigner William Wilberforce was scheduled to visit a plantation, one absentee planter pleaded with his overseers 'not to let a slave be corrected in his presence', in the hope that Wilberforce would leave the island 'possessed with favourable impressions'. Elsewhere, an estate manager noted that the abolitionist movement had 'led the slaves to assume an air of self-importance not known or expressed among them in former times'.

Even though the planters were far away from the machinations of the abolitionists in Britain, they were aware of the progress of their campaign. Friends in the West India lobby reported back from the metropolis, while news of the abolitionists' latest actions were minutely recorded in the local papers. They were aware that the figure of the West Indian planter was now widely criticized and ridiculed. Cartoonists like James Gillray had earlier satirized them as bloated, red-faced drunkards who tortured their slaves. The islanders felt that they were being disavowed and dismissed by the populace of Great Britain, who were increasingly aligning themselves with the values of compassion and decency that were claimed by the abolitionists. The planters of course passionately rejected the idea that they were somehow a different sort of white person than those in England, but the charge stuck. It was felt particularly acutely in Barbados because its white citizens had long been seen and had portrayed themselves as the empire's most loyal subjects, as evidenced by the self-description of the island as 'Little England', which gained currency in this period.

I can have no doubt about the position of my ancestor, Robert Cooper Ashby. In an interview many years later, he admitted that for most of his life he regarded William Wilberforce as 'the devil'. So it is almost inevitable that, like many of his contemporaries, Robert Cooper fervently wished that the abolitionists would be eradicated from the face of the earth and things could return to 'normal'. No doubt he would have agreed with the Martinican planter Pierre Desalles, who believed the abolitionists' entire agenda was pernicious: 'To make the negro think about all these ideas for improvement is to expose the colonies to the most baneful disorders.' He added that 'to touch the internal system designed to regulate the work and discipline of individual plantations is to promote revolt and compromise the livelihood of the whites'. To improve conditions on one plantation but not on another, he continued, 'will say to the negroes of the latter, "Go and obtain by force what your masters will not give us voluntarily."'

After the abolition of the slave trade in 1807 the disquiet among the slave population only intensified. Their hostility to their masters manifested itself in numerous ways, from insolence and escape to open rebellion. During a House of Assembly debate on 10 December 1810, it was noted that 'the abolitionist activities of Mr Wilberforce' had provoked 'the increase of arrogance and vice among the slaves'. This refractory mood prompted the government into serious discussions about the state of the internal defence system and the effects that it produced among the slaves. Robert Haynes, a planter-assemblyman, warned that there was 'something brewing up in their minds', and it was decided to tighten police control on the island.

The slaves had two options when it came to pursuing their freedom. They could press for further ameliorative measures or they could organize armed revolt. The more moderate choice was quashed in 1811–12 when the Barbadian planters once again rejected requests by the free people of colour for further civil rights. In the face of such intransigence, many slaves felt the only option was to take direct action. This feeling was exacerbated by the Slave Registration bill that had recently been proposed, which was designed to prevent illegal slave trading by keeping track of every slave on each individual plantation. The planters believed that it would diminish the value of their property and destabilize the region. When the bill was passed, John Pinney wrote: 'I consider my property reduced in value upwards of 50,000 pounds, and all this by Wilberforce!' The jubilant slaves saw the passing of the bill as a prelude to complete emancipation and became ever more restless and unmanageable. As the historian Hilary Beckles concluded: 'Ideologically, the colony was in deepening crisis, and it was within this context of diminishing planter hegemony that slaves organized for their overthrow by violent means.'

15

To the attack, grenadier
Who gets killed, that's his affair
Forget your ma,
Forget your pa,
To the attack grenadier,
Who gets killed that's his affair.

Haitian rebels' marching song

The tinderbox that was Barbadian slave society exploded on 14 April 1816, when half the island went up in flames. Curiously, it had been a prosperous year. The Barbadian House of Assembly later commented that it 'was remarkable for having yielded the most abundant returns with which Providence had ever rewarded the labours of the Inhabitants of this Island'. This was particularly true of the parish of St Philip, which was the flashpoint of the revolt, where a plentiful harvest meant that bellies were full. The slaves therefore rebelled not because they were in material distress but because they desired a different social order.

The rebellion that one army officer evocatively described as 'a hell-broth' was led by a slave known as Bussa. Today a statue widely believed to be a model of him is sited on one of the island's most prominent roundabouts. Positioned like a triumphant boxer, the figure stands cast in bronze, his face turned to the skies, clenched fist raised at right angles to his head, with broken shackles dangling from his wrists.

In 1816, Bussa was chief ranger on the Bayleys plantation in St Philip. Later to be dubbed 'General' by his followers, he was probably somewhere between thirty and forty years old and was an African-born slave. This was significant, since 'saltwater' slaves, with their memories of a free life, were traditionally regarded as the most refractory and prone to revolt. It is likely that he was a member of the Bussa nation (hence his nickname), a faction of the powerful Mande people, who had spread over much of West Africa during the fourteenth and fifteenth centuries as conquerors and traders in gold and kola nuts. Their commercial and political prominence emerged particularly in the context of their dealings with the Portuguese at Elmina, the infamous slave fort. If Bussa was by inclination rebellious, he also had more prosaic reasons to resist his enslavement. The plantation on which he laboured had recently changed hands and its relaxed, liberal owner Joseph Bayley had been replaced by a new manager, Mr Thomas, a hard man who had a reputation as a 'severe disciplinarian'.

Bussa had been plotting the uprising for over a year, along with a number of co-conspirators, who were also elite slaves. Among them was Jackey, a head driver at Simmons plantation; Johnny the Cooper, who also worked at Bayleys, and a free coloured man called Joseph Franklyn. One of the most radical of the plotters was a woman called Nanny Grigg, who called for armed struggle long before her male counterparts were ready to take that extreme step. As skilled slaves, their privileged positions meant that while they had less material need to rebel, they were the kind of people who found the indignities of enslavement most difficult to bear. As John Vaughan, a manager of the Codrington plantation, acknowledged long before the rebellion: '[It] is those slaves who are our chiefest favourites and such that we put most confidence in that are generally the first and greatest conspirators.'

Their special status meant that this coterie of slaves was allowed to travel and thus plot unnoticed, while their superior standing in the slave community gave their opinions great credence. In a sophisticated propaganda campaign that fed on the hopes that had been raised by the abolitionist movement in England, they spread the idea that the British government had actually granted slaves their freedom and that local planters were resisting this development. It was the slaves' patriotic duty, they argued, to rebel and implement the will of His Majesty's Parliament. As the island's House of Assembly concluded later, the 'insurrection was entirely owing to these hopes, so originating and so fostered, and that the slaves were led to attempt by force that which they mainly expected as an original gift from England'.

The conspirators' overall objective was to overthrow the planter class and free all black Barbadians from slavery. The plan was to unfold over successive days. The first evening would begin with a surprise attack when rebels would emerge from the thick vegetation and set fire to the canes and plantations. That night the whites, watching their investment burn, were to cry 'Water!' The next night armed combat would begin and the planters were to cry 'Blood!' Each of the plantations involved had its own leader, who had worked out battle plans with those above them. They used a series of messengers to communicate with the high command as and when they needed advice on how to proceed. The final evening of planning took place under the cover of a dance at River plantation on Good Friday, 12 April. It was decided that if victory were achieved, Joseph Franklyn would be appointed as governor of the island.

The timing of the rebellion was carefully chosen. The rebels hoped that the Easter celebrations would distract the white community and make them more vulnerable to assault. It was also the height of the harvest, so the mature sugar canes would provide good cover for both their ambushes and their flight, while the burning of the canes would mean that the planters would lose their most valuable asset. Finally the choice of Easter had great symbolic value for the slaves: according to their understanding of Christianity, it was the start of a 'new life', so it seemed an unusually auspicious time to launch their final emancipation. All in all it was not a bad plan. But the slaves had an Achilles heel: their inability to get access to arms. It was to be their downfall.

The outbreak of arson that precipitated the rebellion began in St Philip at around 8.30 p.m. on 14 April. From there it spread throughout the adjacent parishes, including Christ Church, where Burkes plantation was situated. Robert Cooper and his slaves would have watched as fire swept across the cane fields in the distance, section by section. All around them was the noise of the crackling and burning cane, the sound swelling and growing as the conflagration spread from the produce fields to the pastures. As the flames moved nearer to Burkes the sky began to rain cane ash and the night air was ripe with the cloying smell of scorched sugar.

The rumours spread as swiftly as the flames. Was this just an accident, a 'burn' that had got out of hand, or a real rebellion, the first on the island for over a hundred years? At first the colonists were reluctant to believe anything was wrong: there were whispers of revolts all the time but none in living memory had ever come to anything. And it seemed barely credible that the slaves could hope to resist the combination of local militia and the British troops stationed on the island. But the gravity of the situation became clear when a rider galloped up to the plantation to fetch Robert Cooper for militia duty: a revolt was indeed occurring. In an interview many years later Robert Cooper recalled that night. Forced to leave the plantation hurriedly, he realized en route that the plantation's 'float' – worth about US $5,000 – had been left unguarded. The only thing he could do was to send the slave who had accompanied him back to the plantation to take care of it. It was the dilemma that confronted virtually every Caribbean planter: his slaves may have been his enemies but they were also often the only people on whom he could rely.

Burkes' slave community was also in an invidious position. It is likely that many of them were sympathetic to the rebels but the reality was that in over two centuries of Atlantic slavery only one rebellion – that in Haiti – had been unequivocally successful. Thus to become actively involved, or even to be known to passively support the conspirators, was in effect a death sentence. The slaves feared for their own lives but also for family and friends. Most of them also had some material investment in the slave system, be it a small stash of money, a plot of land or even just a change of clothes, that they wished to protect and retain. They knew that if they got involved in the revolution they would almost inevitably lose everything. Slaves like John Stephen who were the offspring of white men felt particularly vulnerable: if the insurgency was successful would they be penalized for their parentage?

As Robert Cooper rode off into the haunted Caribbean night dressed in his braided officer's uniform, his mind must have been swirling. He too would have worried about his wife and heir. They were either barricaded on the plantation or part of the white flight to the capital, desperate to avoid being butchered in their beds. He was probably concerned too about his other family, that multi-hued network of women and children he had spawned on the plantation. Would they suffer as a result of their connection to him? Or were they, his flesh and blood, part of this conspiracy? And what of his beloved Burkes? His mind must have raced with images of rebels breaking down the doors and climbing though its windows, burning his furniture and destroying his valuables, leaving everything he had worked for and built nothing but a pile of smoking wood and ash.

After Robert Cooper met up with his troops, similarly armed

with their shining swords and their brown muskets, all was action. The night was alive with torches, the whinnying of horses and the barking of dogs. The officers considered reports from the field; news circulated of nearby skirmishes and armed rebels who attacked and melted into the darkness after it was over. Strategies were considered and plans made. The sense of urgency only increased when news arrived at headquarters that the insurrection had spread to other parts of the island. One of Robert Cooper's fellow officers recollected the first battle: 'It was about twelve o'clock that we met a large body of the insurgent slaves in the yard of Lowthers plantation, several of whom were armed with muskets, who displayed the colours of the St Philip Battalion which they had stolen and who, upon seeing the division cheered, and cried out to us, "Come on!"' Among their banners exhorting other slaves to join them, one provocateur was carrying an eye-catching red flag that depicted a white woman and a black man making love, the ultimate taboo in plantation society.

The sight of the insurgents roaring abuse, shrouded in a haze of smoke against the backdrop of leaping flames and collapsing buildings, inevitably terrified the white colonists. But the slaves were poorly equipped, armed only with machetes and billhooks, cudgels and axes, that they had looted from a hardware store. Therefore they 'were quickly dispersed, upon being fired upon'. Under Colonel John Rycroft Best's command the militia regrouped. 'We pursued and killed some; their rapid flight however saved numbers. We had to march from estate to estate to quell the insurgents for they were all set to plunder and destroy the dwelling houses. We killed about 30 men!' There was only one militia casualty, who was slightly wounded by a pistol shot. 'The villain was shot down immediately.'

The victory at Lowthers was greatly facilitated, according to Best, by the 'intrepid courage' of the free coloured men who belonged to the militia, who dashed 'singly into a house full of rebels without looking behind for support and dug out the fellows'. Their behaviour must have dismayed the slaves, who might have hoped that they would make common cause with them as had happened in Haiti; but the free coloureds had other ideas. They had been struggling to ameliorate their situation for a long time through constitutional lobbying, and saw this as an opportunity to prove their loyalty. They were rewarded the following year, when they were given the right to give testimony in court against whites, a much-longed-for objective in their fight for civil rights.

After the success at Lowthers, the militia engaged in a mopping-up expedition in which they killed another ten blacks. In retaliation, the slaves resorted to widespread arson. Best reported:

> Large quantities of canes were burnt and I think more on the second night than the first, which proved that although the rebels were subdued by arms, they were nevertheless determined to do all possible mischief. Houses were gutted and the very floors taken up. The destruction is dreadful, the plundering beyond anything you can conceive could be effected in so short a time.

This early defeat was a terrible disappointment for the rebels, who had been counting on victory to pursue their full strategy. Their fortunes continued to decline when the British troops on the island tardily joined the conflict. Cannily, however, the commander of the garrison included among his force 150 black men from the West India Regiment, who were to fight alongside 250 other soldiers.

The black troops of the West India Regiment arrived outside Bayleys plantation on Monday evening at sunset. The battle started at dawn. On spotting the black soldiers, some of the slaves were disorientated. As one officer wrote: 'The insurgents did not think our men would fight against black men, but thank

God they were deceived . . . The conduct of our Bourbons Blacks, particularly the light Company under Captain Smith, has been the admiration of everybody and deservedly.' But these men had their own agenda, too. The army had given them special privileges, they had never been part of the general slave population and they had no allegiance to the rebels. Put on the back foot by the soldiers, the slaves hesitated, and in the firefight that followed, forty rebels were killed and seventy taken prisoner. A large group fled north and reassembled at Golden Grove plantation just under a mile away, where they took over the great house.

Despite their successes, the planters could not yet relax. Other groups of rebels were causing havoc in St John and Bridgetown. Various contingents were dispatched to deal with these problems and by Tuesday night, according to Colonel Codd, 'conflagrations had ceased and the dismay and alarm which had seized the colonists in a great degree subsided'. By midday on Wednesday the 18th, the revolt was all but contained, the arson had stopped and so had the fighting. At least 150 blacks had been slaughtered and 400 had been arrested. Bussa had been killed in the battle at Bayleys and many of the other ringleaders were dead.

After four days of pandemonium, the most 'momentous crisis in the annals of the country was finally over'. Robert Cooper returned to Burkes in a cloud of heat and dust to discover that his family were safe, his plantation had survived virtually unscathed and the slave he had entrusted with his money had buried it safely under a tree. Whether this was out of loyalty or judicious forethought we will never know. But he was rewarded and Robert Cooper claimed that his faith in his slaves was reaffirmed.

In the chaotic and violent aftermath of the rebellion, Burkes became a friendly outpost for militia contingents, whose horses thundered across the countryside, policing the island's

still-smoking landscape to search for runaway rebels and sympathizers as well as to intimidate the general slave population.
The atmosphere across the island was one of profound paranoia.
The smoke from the fires lingered for weeks alongside the sickly
smell of burnt cane and rotting livestock. Refugees were still
in the capital, reluctant to return to their plantations, while
armed parties of militiamen patrolled ceaselessly. The planters
couldn't understand how the slaves had managed to keep
this conspiracy a secret for so long or to plot so extensively.
After all, Barbados was small and the rewards for informing on
conspiracies lucrative.

In their febrile state the colonists nervously rehashed tales of
suspicious slave conversations, or secret slave ceremonies that
were alleged to have taken place, or recalled obeah tokens
spotted around their plantations such as decapitated roosters,
hatchets impaled in doors or marks painted in blood. Their fear
made them implement even more brutal methods of domination
to control their slaves, and discipline on the plantations became
even more draconian. The slave quarters were searched and re-
searched, while innocent slaves were roused from their daily
routines, questioned and frequently beaten. There were other,
more terrible stories of female slaves being violated and children
being tortured.

Unsurprisingly, retaliations by the military were speedy and
cruel. Even before official judicial measures were put in place,
some British troops were involved in the random executions
of rebellious captives and other unlucky slaves. The rebels who
were taken alive arguably suffered even more: the methods
for extracting information in the sugar islands rivalled those of
the Spanish Inquisition and few victims could withstand their
torturers' efforts. Since a slave society functions on fear, trials
were as public and as brutal as possible, and often took place
at local plantations, where slaves were encouraged or even
compelled to attend.

One of the primary 'contrivers' of the rebellion, Johnny, the cooper from Bayleys plantation, was transported to the parish of St Peter and hanged on Trent's Hill 'for the sake of an example to the blacks in that part of Island'. His swift and public execution would be followed by several others: some slaves were shot, others were hanged, while the unlucky ones were tied to wooden poles and burned by slow fire. These unfortunate souls sometimes took three days to burn with no opportunity to pass out or die quickly. 'By these means the planters hoped to imprint indelibly upon the consciousness of the blacks through out the island, the full reality of the consequences of armed rebellion.'

Over the next couple of months hundreds of captives were tried for insurrection, others for inciting blacks to revolt; a few were acquitted, some were sentenced to transportation, some were flogged or maimed. A large proportion, however, were executed. Soon the island's highways were festooned with the bodies of hanged slaves decomposing in the heat: a feast for the buzzards.

In June 1816 a white Barbadian described the post-rebellion feelings among the blacks and outlined the dangers it posed for colonial society:

> The disposition of the slaves in general is very bad. They are sullen and sulky and seem to cherish feelings of deep revenge. We hold the West Indies by a very precarious tenure – that of military strength only. I would not vie a year's purchase for any island we now have.

Long after martial law was lifted on 12 July, the planters were still not convinced that the rebels were fully rooted out. Inevitably some innocent slaves were convicted, and though a number of their masters interceded on their behalf, it was usually to no avail. In the fervid and pitiless atmosphere that prevailed immediately after the revolt, justice was a mere detail.

In September a small group of blacks was arrested for planning another insurrection. 'Murder was to have been the order of the day,' declared Colonel Best, who acted as judge in their trial. 'As on the former occasion, the drivers, rangers, carpenters, and watchmen were chiefly concerned and a few field labourers . . . I am under no apprehension as to the consequences . . . It is no longer delusion amongst the slaves . . . They convinced themselves to be sufficiently numerous to become the masters . . . of the island.' The desperate rebels had lost the battle, but they did not accept that the war was over. The struggle against slavery continued though at a less organized level.

In fact, although it failed in its immediate aim, the uprising was the beginning of the end of Barbados slave society. The Barbadian colonists realized that no one on the island, white or black, was free from fear. But even though they could never truly feel secure while slavery existed, they couldn't imagine a world without it.

16

One pays a high price for fortune if it brings distress to the soul.

Pierre Desalles

Bussa's rebellion was a profound shock to both the Barbadians and the British. The oldest and apparently most settled of the sugar colonies had suffered a major revolt. If the Barbadian slaves, inhabitants of the cradle of the Empire's sugar production and prosperity, could erupt into violence, what hope was there for the rest of the region? And yet, for the enslaved population of the island, the aftermath of Bussa's rebellion was a profoundly depressing time. Not only were they still slaves, but their hopes and dreams for a better life seemed further away than ever. Ironically, this was in part because of their rebellion. When sensationalized accounts of the uprising had crossed the Atlantic, the British oligarchy was so shaken that even the man whom the slaves believed was their 'champion', William Wilberforce, was forced to back away from the abolitionist cause. The extent of his volte-face was made clear when he sponsored a Parliamentary Address which formally declared that 'there existed no plan for introducing emancipation into the West Indies'.

Locally too, the picture for the slaves seemed bleak. The planters stepped up efforts to consolidate their power, developing better surveillance and more sophisticated political networks to maintain their supremacy. It was no surprise then that Robert Cooper reached the zenith of his career as a planter during this period, expanding his holdings and increasing his wealth, and becoming in the process both socially and politically influential across the colony. Now firmly established as part of the planter elite, he was Robert Cooper Esquire in all his official dealings, but more widely referred to as 'the Colonel' because of his exalted position in the island's militia.

Throughout the 1810s and 1820s, my ancestor proved himself a gleeful capitalist, throwing himself into the pastime that so captivated his Creole contemporaries: the buying and selling of land and slaves. Of the documents that Robert Cooper left behind, the vast majority concerned contracts for sale or purchase. Slaves passed between family and friends with impressive regularity, as did equipment, property and horses. His speculations were further enabled by a legacy from his father, who had died in 1811, leaving him the bulk of his fortune. He was so successful that he managed to generate the funds to acquire another estate entirely: a 100-acre property called Brittons. Situated in the parish of St Michael, this plantation had been in existence since at least 1766. It proved a good investment. When his estate was sold in 1844 to the Drayton family, the down payment amounted to £2,000.

The scope of Robert Cooper's ambition can be most clearly demonstrated by the changes he made to Burkes. Originally only sixty-two acres, Burkes had first been extended by a further 150 acres in 1803. Over the subsequent years, Robert Cooper bought up parcel after parcel of adjacent land until he had extended Burkes by another 100 acres. Alongside this, his slave holdings also grew considerably as he required more and more souls to farm his extended property. This burgeoning slave population was achieved largely through natural increase, supplemented by the odd purchase from the regional market of slaves which still thrived after the abolition of the slave trade.

A detailed picture of Robert Cooper's expanding empire is revealed by the yearly slave returns that planters were forced to submit after 1816. These accounts, which the abolitionists demanded in order to keep track of slaves' movements and prevent illegal trading, provide a detailed picture of life at Burkes plantation in the decades before emancipation.

The yearly returns 'of Robert Cooper Ashby of Slaves, his own property', as submitted to the authorities of the parish of Christ Church, divide the information into seven columns. The first, entitled 'Causes of Increase or Decrease', is clearly optional as Robert Cooper did not bother to fill it in, preferring to note deaths, births and manumissions at the end of each return. The following column is 'Sex', then 'Name', 'Age', 'Colour', 'Country' (whether the slave was born in Africa or Barbados) and finally 'Employment', which notes whether the slave worked as a domestic or a labourer. The names on the returns include the double-barrelled, traditionally English designations that Robert Cooper preferred for his own offspring such as 'Robert Henry' or 'William Thomas', as well as whimsical ones such as 'Juddy Christmas' or 'Mimba Rose'. The register also reflects the fashions of the day: the classical craze that resulted in 'Scipio' or 'Roman'; and names that commemorated English culture and history such as 'Hamlet', 'Prince William' or 'Nelson'.

It was here on the 1817 return, three-quarters of the way down its opening page, that I found the first mention of my great-great-great-grandfather, John Stephen. The first sight of his name took my breath away: 'John Stephen', aged '14', 'coloured', 'Barbadian'-born, 'Labourer'. With each successive year I watched his age climb, wondering how he was faring and trying to imagine how he felt. I know that the group of people listed on this return alongside him represented his closest community, and that some of the names must denote his best friends and worst enemies. These returns were one of the only ways to track my ancestor, a typical fate for a man who was a slave for the first half of his life: it was almost impossible to find a trace of him that didn't list him as a piece of property.

Burkes was at its most extensive sixteen years later, when John Stephen was thirty years of age. The returns for that year provide a fascinating snapshot of life on a plantation, its social make-up and its day-to-day running. By this time, its land comprised 330 acres and its slave population had swollen to 223. Around a quarter of its slave population was either too young (below the age of twelve) or too old (sixty and above) to do intensive labour. Of the working population, of around 163 slaves, around twenty-three were domestics. (This represented around 14 per cent, which is a relatively modest percentage in comparison with many plantation households.) Only three of these domestics were male, so the great house was a very feminine environment – and, considering what we know of Robert Cooper's sexual peccadilloes, this probably made for a somewhat charged atmosphere.

Nine babies had been born that year, and two slaves had died. Women outnumbered men slightly on the plantation, many of them working in the fields. Only seven slaves were African-born, which represents around 3 per cent of the plantation's population; so the vast majority of Burkes' enslaved population were born and bred on the island and would have described themselves patriotically as neither African nor Creole but 'true Barbadian'. They were also 'true Burkeans' too, as many of them had spent all their lives on Robert Cooper's plantation.

Twenty-two of the slaves at Burkes were described as 'coloured', which represents just under 10 per cent of its total slave population. Of these, more than half are linked to Robert Cooper Ashby directly, either as mistresses or offspring. The rest, we can assume, are the children of other white men working on the plantation, such as overseers and bookkeepers.

★

Given the size of Robert Cooper's holdings, the Ashbys were now one of only 120 families who dominated the island's political, financial and military institutions. Reflecting this social and economic prominence, Robert Cooper had also been appointed a colonial magistrate. This local official, often referred to as a justice of the peace or simply 'judge', was not a professional lawmaker but usually a religious, social or political leader who had a good reputation in the parish. He dealt mostly with petty cases that arose in the local area, covering local, criminal, civil, domestic and juvenile matters. He was empowered, without consulting either a jury or lawyers, to sentence those he convicted of robbery, vandalism or breaches of the peace, to fines, flogging or imprisonment. The longer terms were usually served in the 'cage', that infamous building in the centre of Bridgetown through whose slatted bars passers-by could observe the prisoners in their squalor and suffering.

But Robert Cooper's role extended beyond the strictly legal. Like other successful planters in the slave colonies, he was expected to be one of the arbiters of local stability and order – that is, to ensure that the conventions and customs of slave society were respected and enforced. Slaves from other plantations could come to him if they had problems with their masters: for example, if a slave had run away, they might approach Robert Cooper and ask him to beg for leniency on their behalf. He would also be expected to intervene between other landowners who, in this materialist and touchy society, were perpetually in conflict over property, slaves and politics.

During these years Robert Cooper was most frequently in the news as a result of his military activities. In *The Barbadian* newspaper in March 1827 a notice was placed that read: 'A court martial to be held at Town Hall on 14 inst. At 8 o'clock for trial of prisoners.' Presiding over the event were 'Colonel Thomas Pierrepont of Life Guards, President; Lt. Col. William Oxley of Royal Regt.; Lt. Robert Cooper Ashby of Christ Church

Battalion'. A few years later, in a list of the militia published on 8 March 1831, he had progressed further up the ranks and 'Colonel Robert C. Ashby' is listed as the most senior member of the Christ Church militia, in command of twenty-seven men, including a lieutenant colonel, a major, and numerous captains, as well as a surgeon and a quartermaster. In his capacity as one of the most senior members of the parish militia he had numerous official duties, from military matters to the opening of new buildings.

Robert Cooper's dominance of the Vestry, the organization that controlled local affairs, made him one of the most powerful men in the parish. For much of the first half of the nineteenth century, his elegant autograph is at the top of the list of signatures that ratified its documents. It was an elected appointment voted for by existing members, and he would hold it almost continuously for around thirty years. At its regular meeting the Vestry handled matters as varied as repairing the highways and regulating local hucksters, as well as dispensing funds for the burial of indigents. It levied funds from the local planters, who had to contribute 20 pence per acre for 'fees for the relief of the poor and other parish charges'. In addition to these more routine matters, the Vestry also responded to local emergencies such as hurricanes, earthquakes and war. One of Robert Cooper's most significant achievements as a vestryman was his involvement in launching Foundation School. Established in 1809 for the poor children of the parish, the school had been financed at least in part by subscription, that is, from funds raised by wealthy local contributors.

It had taken five generations, but the Ashby family had finally managed to elevate themselves from the bottom of this society to near the top. As a result of good luck, hard graft and more than a splash of ruthlessness, Robert Cooper Ashby was now firmly ensconced in the island's plantocracy. Appropriately, it was during these years that he commissioned the single surviving portrait of himself. It was a common if extravagant gesture among the island's social elite: a way to capture themselves at the peak of their wealth and prestige. His decision to pose in his colonel's uniform was unusual. It is a good indication of how important his military status was to his self-image, and reveals how he wished others to view him.

Looking at his portrait, I see a man of immense authority, discipline and self-assurance; but I am also struck by his cold, rather flinty eyes and the uncompromising quality of his stare. If one can draw any conclusions about what kind of man he was from this picture, it seems reasonable to conclude that Robert Cooper had been hardened by his many years as a planter. Although he probably would not have realized it, the most corrupting aspect of his life was the twenty-something years he had spent at Burkes holding sway over his slaves. Worse than the demise of his father and brothers, worse even than revolution and the perpetual alarums of living in this period, was the soul-corroding effect of absolute power. This despotic position, with its terrible temptations and its inevitable spiritual degradation, as well as the loneliness that this power carried with it, had made Robert Cooper the man he was.

His role as planter allowed – demanded – that he deny the humanity of the black people around him, that he participate in a culture of breathtaking cruelty, that he abuse women and children and justify that abuse as the will of God and his privilege as a gentleman. It endorsed rape, torture and the separation of mothers from children.

Of course, Robert Cooper did not think of himself as a bad man. He believed that he was doing what was necessary to keep order in his society and maintain the social order designed by God. In a clear illustration of the banality of evil, he played his part as willing helper to one of history's great genocides in complacent denial that he was doing anything other than his duty or exercising his rights.

★

While Robert Cooper was consolidating his fortunes, however, dangerous doctrines were growing in influence. As was so often the way, when the official abolitionist movement was dormant, the grass-roots anti-slavery movement continued to flourish. And the Haitian torch continued to light a series of new fires, this time in Spanish America.

Just before the Bussa Rebellion in 1816, the Venezuelan military and political commander Simón Bolívar had approached the president of the Republic of Haiti, Alexandre Pétion, for help in his struggle to free the Spanish territories of South America from the Spanish Empire. Pétion agreed to help Bolívar on condition he freed the slaves in any land he liberated. Bolívar enthusiastically agreed; not only was he profoundly anti-slavery, but the move would provide him with a much larger pool of potential followers and warriors. The force he gathered in Haiti landed in Venezuela in 1817, and he went on to take the city of Angostura and then Venezuela itself. In subsequent years, Bolívar, internationally known as El Libertador (The Liberator), managed to unshackle other Spanish colonies including Colombia, Panama and Ecuador. His escapades as he swept across South America entranced the world, both free and enslaved. And multitudes were attracted to his cause, including thousands of Britons, among them Lord Cochrane, the naval officer and radical politician who had shot to fame during the sea battles against Napoleon.

Though Bolívar's dream of establishing an American-style federation of these newly independent republics didn't ultimately come to fruition, he was nonetheless successful in achieving independence for them and freeing many slaves in the process. In addition to his military victories, he established and forged political institutions for a new organization for all of Hispanic America. By the time of his premature death from tuberculosis nine years later, the new states of Spanish America, with the curious exception of Paraguay, possessed more advanced anti-slavery legislation than any in the remaining European New World. One contemporary described Bolívar as 'the singular genius of the nineteenth century'.

The success of the South American republics in doing away with the institution of slavery in turn inspired the British abolition movement to get back in the fray. Its resurgence was marked by a meeting at the King's Head public house in London in 1823. But it was a tentative start, as their new name suggested: 'The London Society for Mitigating and Gradually Abolishing the State of Slavery in the British Dominions'. Before long, a much older Thomas Clarkson was back on his horse, traversing the highways and byways of Britain building up support, and within a year there were 230 branches and 777 petitions had been presented to Parliament.

In this reinvigorated movement women were the undisputed leaders. As one prominent male activist later acknowledged:

> Ladies' Associations . . . did everything. They circulated publications: they procured the money to publish; they dunned & talked & coaxed & lectured: they got up public meetings & filled our halls & platforms when the day arrived; they carried round petitions & enforced the duty of signing them . . . In a word they formed the cement of the whole Antislavery building – without their aid we never should have kept standing.

In a slew of pamphlets, articles and lectures these women dismissed 'gradualism', the idea that the conditions of slavery should slowly be ameliorated instead of abolished. Notable among these forgotten heroines was Elizabeth Heyrick, a former schoolteacher and Quaker, who published a bestselling pamphlet entitled 'Immediate Not Gradual Abolition: or, An

Inquiry into the Shortest, Safest, & Most Effectual Means of Getting Rid of West Indian Slavery'. Here she made explicit the links between the sufferings of the slave and the consumption of sugar and called for the nation to once again stop purchasing it. 'By buying sugar we participate in the crime,' she declared. 'The laws of our country may hold the sugar-cane to our lips, steeped in the blood of our fellow creatures; but they cannot compel us to drink the loathsome potion.'

And then in 1823 another rebellion broke out out in the British West Indies. This time it was in the British colony of Demerara, part of what is now called Guyana. The trouble began in the east of the territory, where slaves had been emboldened by rumours that the British Parliament had directed the colonial powers to improve their conditions. When the news reached the governor that they had downed tools, he set out to meet with the protesters accompanied by a regiment of militia. They were confronted by a crowd of slaves armed with pikes, machetes and fowling hooks. When the governor asked them what they wanted they replied succinctly: 'Our rights.' After further discussion they explained that they wanted three days off and an opportunity to go to church on Sunday. The governor refused, and the plantations were soon ablaze. As always, the retaliation was much more terrible than the rebellion. More than a hundred slaves were killed in the conflict and many were brutally flogged or executed immediately after. The Methodist minister whom the authorities believed had inspired the revolution, an Englishman called John Smith, was sentenced to death, but he expired of consumption before the punishment could be carried out. And the bullet-ridden body of one of the ringleaders, a slave called Quamina, was displayed in front of the plantation where the revolt first started. According to one witness, it was a ghastly sight: 'a colony of wasps had actually built a nest in the cavity of his stomach, and were flying in and out of the jaws which hung frightfully open'.

★

As well as all these external problems, these were difficult years personally for Robert Cooper. In 1821 John Burke, his only legitimate child and heir, died. One assumes that this was a source of profound grief for Robert Cooper, even if, as family lore has intimated, John Burke was a sickly young man whose end had been anticipated. It also had practical implications: traditionally Burkes would have gone to his son, but now Robert Cooper would have to rethink his legacy.

Then in 1824, the Ashby family was embroiled in a murderous scandal that captivated the entire island. It was a drama that would prove profoundly revelatory about the nature of a slave society, exposing its illogic and inhumanity and the terrible price that all its members paid – even the white ones – to sustain it. In that year Robert Cooper's cousin, Susanna, was murdered and her husband, Michael D'Egville, was charged with the crime. D'Egville was the son of the ballet master at London's Royal Opera House, and his family had achieved great celebrity in fashionable circles in the metropolis as dance teachers. He had arrived in Barbados in 1794 with the ambition to open an academy of dance on the island. It proved successful and he eventually made enough money to settle down and marry Susanna Ashby.

But it was a stormy union. D'Egville was a drunkard who enjoyed dissolute society and frequently beat and abused his wife. Eventually Susanna decided upon a separation. The relationship between the pair remained relatively amicable, however, and one day he sent her a piece of cheese delivered by a mulatto boy slave. The next morning, Susanna was found dead in her bed, and Mrs Llewellyn, the woman with whom she shared her house, and two or three of the black servants were gravely ill. The post-mortem revealed poisoned cheese in Susanna's stomach and in the vomit recovered from the suffering servants. D'Egville was immediately suspected, since the collapse of his business meant he was desperately in need of funds, and he knew that his estranged wife had bequeathed him £500 in her will. He also had the means. A few days before Susanna's death he had purchased arsenic from a druggist's shop. On being asked if the poison was required to get rid of rats, he was said to have retorted: 'Yes, and I shouldn't much care if they were two-legged ones!'

In his defence, D'Egville's lawyer pointed out that rats were a veritable epidemic in Barbados because of the cane fields, and so virtually all households on the islands had arsenic in their stores for pest control. In addition, his lawyer argued that 'a link in the chain of evidence was wanting'. This was evidence from the little mulatto boy who had delivered the cheese to Susanna's home. But since under Barbadian law slaves were not allowed to give evidence in court, the boy's testimony, which would have supported D'Egville, could not be admitted in the hearing. At the end of the first trial, nine jurors found him not guilty and three found him guilty. But at a retrial a guilty verdict was returned and D'Egville, who had protested his innocence throughout, was hanged in the parish of St Michael.

Some years later, a slave named Christian, who had belonged to Susanna and who, according to her father's will, was due to be freed on her death, confessed to the crime. On his deathbed the slave admitted that he had taken the cheese from the boy and put in the arsenic, all in a desperate bid to be free. To complete the irony of this sensational case, which was written up in 1864 by the American publication *Harper's Weekly*, Susanna's death was for nothing. The wishes expressed in her father's will were ignored and the desperate slave was never freed; while the warped system that disallowed the testimony of slaves meant that an innocent man had been executed.

The D'Egville case had particular impact and resonance because it hinged on an issue that was the subject of heated political debate in the region: a slave's inability to give testimony in court. This law, which was currently under attack by the abolitionists, was the product of one of the fundamental beliefs of slave society, that blacks were stupid, feckless and inherently dishonest and thus could not reliably provide evidence. But recent events were making this proscription more and more insupportable. The freed coloureds had already won the right to give testimony as a result of the part they played in the restoration of order after Bussa's rebellion. And it was becoming clear that the thousands of black soldiers now fighting – and dying – for the British Empire in the New World could not in all justice be excluded from this right. But of course the planters fretted. The issue presented them with an unpleasant dilemma: if the free coloureds and the soldiers were regarded as sensible and intelligent enough to give testimony, surely the right had to be extended to all people of colour in the region? Inevitably, the law was fervently resisted.

In 1826 Robert Cooper's wife, Mary Ashby, died. It is impossible to know exactly what Robert Cooper felt. Despite his other liaisons, their marriage had endured for thirty years, and she had borne him a precious son. Without her, he would never have got his hands on Burkes or developed into the notable planter he had become. Whatever his feelings about her passing, it was undoubtedly the end of an era.

One of the changes precipitated by his wife's death was that Robert Cooper could finally live openly with his mistress Mary Anne and their large brood. It was a new beginning for them. In the past she must have felt sidelined, even hidden away, but now she could be a visible presence at Burkes. We can only wonder at the popular reaction to Robert Cooper when he appeared openly in Oistins with his coloured consort and their children. Marriage was not an option, of course; the legal and social taboos against such an act were still insurmountable. Despite the length and stability of their relationship, she was destined to remain his concubine.

Such long-term relationships between white men and free mixed-race women were so common in the Spanish and French colonies, such as Louisiana, Haiti and New Orleans, that they became standardized. A conventional betrothal was not a possibility in these societies, since matrimony across the colour line was illegal according to the Code Noir, just as it was prohibited in the other sugar colonies. Instead of marriage, there was *plaçage*, which comes from the French word *placer*, meaning 'to place with'. It had emerged in the very earliest days of the colonies, when it was difficult to tempt young European women to follow men to these tropical wildernesses. But it had latterly evolved into an extra-legal system to protect women of colour in their relationships with white men, which were known among the black population as marriages *de la main gauche* or left-hand marriages.

Whereas in the past women in these unions had no protection when the white men who had kept them either got married or found another lover, this system meant that men had certain obligations to their mixed-race lovers, whether or not the relationship endured. The man was expected to provide a house, an annual allowance, and a commitment to educate any offspring they might produce. In return the woman gave him her love and devotion and was expected to be a combination of sensual courtesan, solicitous confidante and warm companion. A man who reneged on his commitments would find it impossible to attract another Creole companion; and his reputation was besmirched, even among the white population. That these rules emerged at all was not just a sign of how ubiquitous these arrangements were, but also an indication of the power of the free coloured communities in these societies, and their growing social and political power to protect their own members.

Though less formalized, such relationships were just as common in the English-speaking islands. So concubinage emerged as a way of describing long-term relationships that existed outside the legal framework. Mary Anne would have understood all this; she knew that marriage and social respectability could never be the end point of her relationship with Robert Cooper. But though they were unable to wed, Mary Anne and Robert Cooper lived a married life in all but name. With Mary Ashby's death, Mary Anne and her children were able to live on a more secure and public footing, and to have greater expectations and hopes for the future.

In that same year, 1826, the legal landscape for the slaves on the island was also shifting. In response to the revival of the abolition movement, the planters had initially been bullish. The Barbadian slave owners, whom the historian Hilary Beckles characterizes as being 'perhaps the most conservative in the region', argued that their own reform measures, which had led to higher life expectancy among their slaves, meant that emancipation was unnecessary. But this did not appease the activists and soon the planters were on the defensive. Now, under pressure from the Colonial Office, the Barbadians finally passed an act 'to con-solidate and improve' the slaves' position, granting them the right 'to own property' and offering 'a reduction in manumission fees'. They were also extended the privilege 'of giving evidence in court in all cases', which was just twelve months too late to save D'Egville's life. To the planters, this seemed an enormous concession, but since the bill still upheld the slave owners' rights in many areas – including the crucial entitlement to be able to put to death any slave who threatened the life of a white person, a law that had excused any number of unjustified slave deaths – it was seen by the abolitionists as too little, too late.

The movement's official policy of 'gradualism' clearly was not working. And during this period the grass roots were growing increasingly fractious, as Clarkson noted in his diary:

'Everywhere people are asking me about immediate abolition, and whether that would not be best . . . and whether they should not leave off West India sugar.' Unable to mediate these differences, there was another lull in the movement, until they built up a new head of steam. Meanwhile John Clarkson, the younger brother of Thomas Clarkson, died, and radicalized many more ordinary people with his famous last words. Lying in bed listening to yet another account about the terrible conditions in the West Indies, he is reported to have lamented: 'It is dreadful to think after my brother and his friends have been labouring for forty years, that such things should still be.'

The gulf between the leaders of the movement and the mass of supporters became clear at a meeting of the abolitionist movement in May of 1830, at the Freemason's Hall in London. Beneath the chandeliers more than two thousand people gathered, with hundreds more clamouring outside. It was to be a stormy encounter. After a couple of cautious speeches by the old guard implying that the slaves were not yet ready for freedom, the younger more radical element, frustrated by what James Stephen's son George described as 'the demon of procrastination that seemed to have possessed our leaders', shouted them down. Then, much to the elders' surprise, a string of resolutions was swiftly passed and the majority moved in support of a motion 'That from and after the 1st of January 1830, every slave born within the King's dominion shall be free'.

But the more staid elements of the abolitionist movement were still dragging their feet. And so the following year, George Stephen formed a new subcommittee that would become known as the Agency Anti-slavery Committee. He also managed to raise the necessary funds, mainly from a pair of wealthy Quaker businessmen, to hire six full-time 'lecturers', who were paid £200 annually to travel around the country stirring up public opinion. These men worked tirelessly alongside the dogged

Ladies' Societies, and soon the number of anti-slavery groups around the country soared to more than 1,200. The news of the revitalized movement gave heart to the West Indian slaves, who increasingly resisted their enslavement by hatching more conspiracies and running away more frequently.

Getting rid of slavery was proving a more difficult task than getting rid of the slave trade. A lot of this had to do with class. Those involved in the trade tended to be from lower down the social scale, 'roughnecks' who wouldn't be welcome in the more salubrious drawing rooms of the metropolis. The planters, on the other hand, were from the same caste as many of the country's legislators, and indeed many had close friendships with top-ranking abolitionists such as William Wilberforce. The power of the West India lobby had also grown even stronger. The historian Robin Blackburn notes that in the House of Commons in the years 1828–32, the number of West Indian Members of Parliament was as high as fifty-six; and there were even more in the House of Lords. So although the countdown to abolition was under way, it was still being resisted at every point.

Once again the most dramatic moments in the political life of the region coincided with a natural disaster, when another terrible hurricane devastated Barbados in August 1831. Known as 'The Great Barbados Hurricane', it was what would today be classified as a category four storm, almost as terrible as the one that hit the island in Robert Cooper's youth. Winds of up to 130 miles per hour slammed into the island, levelling the capital and causing widespread damage. The dead, who totalled 1,500, perished because they were either crushed beneath collapsed buildings or swept away in the seventeen-foot waves. As the hurricane moved on during 11, 12 and 13 August, the populace noticed a strange and amazing visual disturbance in the atmosphere. They claimed that 'the sun took on a decidedly blue appearance, giving off an eerie blue light when it shone into rooms and other enclosed places'. The hurricane, which raged for six days, swept through the Caribbean, laying waste to Cuba and Puerto Rico before crossing over to the American mainland, lashing Louisiana and Florida among other states.

The damage wrought by this horrendous hurricane compelled the British government to authorize a loan of £500,000 for its colonies in the region. In Barbados, Robert Cooper was actively involved in rebuilding Foundation School, which had been completely destroyed by the storm. At a meeting led by Cooper on 22 August 1831, the Christ Church Vestry addressed the need to find 'the best and most economical means of preparing a place in which Divine service might be regularly performed'. This was a problem across the island since, in the eleven parishes, seven churches were totally destroyed and four others were damaged to some extent. The committee moved to find an alternative place of worship and to start raising funds for the repair of the parish church. They also agreed to provide the church warden, the Reverend Dr Orderson, himself a vestryman, with alternative living arrangements, and to assist those who had been injured or made homeless as a result of the 'late awful hurricane'.

Just as the islanders were recovering from the impact of the storm, news came of a revolt in Jamaica. It was incited in part by a period of unusual sickness and distress brought on by poor rainfall and reduced crops. But it was also a result of the widespread belief that they would soon get their 'freedom papers' from England. When the governor denied this rumour and told the slaves that they would not get an extra day's holiday despite the fact that Christmas that year fell on a Sunday, the enslaved population was enraged. The result was the 'Christmas Rebellion', otherwise known as the Baptist War or the Great Jamaican Slave Revolt of 1831–2. It was led by a charismatic slave called Samuel Sharpe, also known variously as 'Daddy' or 'Schoolmaster', who as well as being literate and a great orator was also a deacon of the Baptist church. One missionary described him as 'the most intelligent and remarkable slave I had ever met with'.

Originally planned as a peaceful sit-in, the revolt soon took on a life of its own and became the greatest slave rebellion the British Caribbean had ever witnessed. The fighters were so disciplined that they had their own uniforms (blue jackets and black cross-belts). It began a couple of days after Christmas at the Kensington great house in St James in the north of the island. The unrest soon spread to the neighbouring parish, and as many as 40,000 of Jamaica's 300,000 slaves were swept up in the conflict. One onlooker noted that the rebels seemed to be animated with a rare passion. One female slave converted to the cause declared, just before she was shot: 'I know I shall die for it but my children shall be free!' Soon the sounds of the horns, shells and drums reverberated across the island and the great houses, boiling houses and warehouses were in flames.

It took more than a month to subdue the rebels, and at its end 200 slaves and fourteen whites had died. At least another 400 slaves were killed in reprisals afterwards. In Montego Bay the Methodist missionary Henry Bleby described the executions:

> Generally four, seldom less than three, were hung at once. The bodies remained stiffening in the breeze . . . Other victims would then be brought out and strung up in their place, and cut down in their turn to make room for more; the whole heap of bodies remaining just as they fell, until the workhouse negroes came in the evening and took them away to cast them into a pit dug for the purpose, a little distance out of the town.

The casualties included the rebellion's leader, Samuel Sharpe. His composure as he was taken to the gallows profoundly impressed the spectators, just as his oft-repeated last words were used to recruit more people to the abolitionists' cause: 'I would rather die upon yonder gallows than live in slavery.'

It was in this strained context of revolt and change that, in 1832, Robert Cooper decided to grant freedom to one of his slave families: Sukey Ann and her four children. This was an interesting decision on his part, since full emancipation was now likely and there was a certain cachet in becoming a freed person before the official date for liberation: Sukey Ann and her children would be classified as free coloureds, rather than just being part of the mass of liberated slaves. But it was still an intrepid move for a planter, since across the Americas the manumission of slaves had been discouraged by the authorities, who feared that if too many slaves were liberated they might destabilize the social order. For many years, freeing a slave had been an expensive gesture that the planter had to justify before a magistrate, usually on the basis that the slave had provided exceptional service.

Robert Cooper's decision to manumit Sukey Ann and her children implies a real sentimental attachment, but there might have been other motives: perhaps he felt guilty about replacing her with other women? Pragmatically, it was also now a much more affordable gift. The cost of manumission, which had soared from £300 for females and £200 for males, was now, after the Bussa Rebellion, down to £50 plus a £4 annuity fee for both sexes. In fact, the liberation of female slaves with whom planters had relationships was common. Women made up 60 per cent of those manumitted in Barbados, and the most common reason was as a present to a black concubine by a white planter, which one described as 'the only adequate reward for such an endearing service'.

The document recording Sukey Ann's freedom reads:

> Know all Men by these Presents, That I Robert
> Cooper Ashby of the Parish of Christ Church in the
> island abovesaid, Esquire for divers good Causes and
> Considerations – me hereunto moving have Manumitted,
> Emancipated, Enfranchised, Set Free and forever
> Discharge . . . from all manner of Slavery, Servitude, and
> Bondage whatsoever, to me or to any Person or Persons
> whomsoever, a certain coloured female slave named
> Sukey Ann and her four children, Sarah Jane, John
> Richard, Thomas Edmund, Thomas Stephen together
> with the future issue of the females and the said Slaves and
> each of them are entirely discharged from all manner of
> Slavery, Servitude, Bondage, Service and duties to me or
> any other Person or Persons whomsoever, so as that the
> said slaves and each of them respectively may henceforth
> ever have and enjoy absolute Freedom in Person and
> Property as effectually to all intent and purpose as if they
> had been born free and had never been slaves.
>
> In Witness whereof I have hereunto set my hand and
> Seal the ninth day of July One Thousand Eight Hundred
> and Thirty Two.

After the Christmas Rebellion, the march towards emancipation
had become unstoppable: the worst revolt in the history of the
English sugar isles had reinforced the abolitionist arguments that
slavery was an institution Britain could not afford to maintain.
In 1833, a petition signed by 187,157 abolitionist women was
presented to Parliament. They focused particularly on the
plight of female slaves, reminding the nation's monarch, Queen
Victoria, that women and fellow mothers were being raped,
brutalized and sometimes beaten to death. (Though the new
queen said very little directly about slavery, she was assumed

to be supportive of the abolitionists because of her willingness to entertain blacks and anti-slavery personalities like Harriet Beecher Stowe. And certainly the belief that she was sympathetic to the abolitionist cause did nothing to diminish Victoria's well-nurtured image as matriarch of the nation.) To bring the point home, the abolitionists produced a new Wedgwood cameo that depicted a kneeling woman and was captioned: 'Am I Not a Woman and a Sister?'

Their pro-female stance had been buoyed by the fame of *The History of Mary Prince* (1831), the only memoir of a British West Indian slave woman to be published in that era. Born in 1788, Prince had worked as a household slave in Bermuda and Antigua and in the salt mines on Turk's Island, where she suffered relentless abuse. She was taken as a slave to London by yet another family in 1828, before escaping to live at a mission house. There she went to work for someone from the anti-slavery league who arranged for the publication of her story. John Wood, the owner who had transported her to London, sued to have her reinstated as his property; but mercifully he lost. Mary, whose back was severally disfigured by an intricate lattice of scars, the product of innumerable whippings, became a living indictment of the evils of slavery, and her book was a powerful plea for the sympathy of the English public: 'I feel great sorrow when I hear some people in this country say, that the slaves do not need better usage and do not want to be free . . . I say, Not so. How can slaves be happy when they have the halter round their neck and the whip upon their back.'

In the end, the abolition of slavery came about through a combination of events, and the pressure of popular opposition to the practice, whether from slaves themselves or from the abolitionist movement, was only part of it. One major factor was economic, for the financial significance of the colonies that relied upon slavery was beginning to wane. As the historian

Robin Blackburn noted, the value of West Indian imports from the mother country was falling, while exports to Asia were rising; so they were no longer such a vital market for English goods. And though the British colonies still produced most of the sugar consumed in the mother country, it was so heavily subsidized that many argued that the British public was propping up the West Indian proprietors. There was also greater competition from cheaper sugar from places like Cuba. Domestic politics played a role, too. In a Britain beset by internal unrest brought about by the changing conditions of the industrial revolution, throwing the public a bone in the form of the abolition of slavery was a clever way of avoiding greater losses, at a point when the whole colonial system was in decline.

In 1833, a new governor was dispatched to the island to sell emancipation to the Barbadians. The islanders knew that the battle to maintain slavery was lost and had already shifted their attention to the matter of compensation. In July the Barbadian Assembly sent a strongly worded missive to Parliament. 'As England is avowedly the author and was for a long time the chief gainer [of slavery] . . . let her bear her share of the penalty of expiation . . . Let a fair and just indemnity be first secured to the owner of the property which is to be put at risk.' It ended with the warning that without 'the cooperation and instrumentality of the resident Colonists', the hope for a peaceful emancipation process was doomed, and could only be attained 'through rapine violence and bloodshed, destroying all the elements of civilisation and ending in anarchy'.

The mood in Barbados was predictably gloomy. The slaves were impatient for change. Most of the West Indian planters felt paranoid and misunderstood. They resisted the spirit of the times and took whatever measures they could to maintain 'the distinctions they deemed necessary to their safety', including the harassment of the missionaries, whom they felt were stirring up the black population. In the end, it was a relief when compensation was finally agreed on and Britain granted the West Indian proprietors the sum of £20 million in lieu of the 'loss of their lawful property'.

Critics of compensation who feared that it would be a drain on the Crown's reserves proved to be misguided: in fact it was a long-term money spinner since much of the sum went to the great sugar planters of the region, and then found its way back to England, invested in the city or real estate. A few years later an editorial in *The Barbadian* complained about this pernicious trend. 'We should like to know,' enquired the editorialist,

> the number of proprietors of extensive landed interests and wealth who are living in England or luxuriating in the soft delicate climes of France and Italy spending their handsome income amongst strangers and leaving it to a few of inferior fortunes to carry out the business of their native country and to battle the watch on the numerous opponents of decency and order.

In August 1833, the Emancipation Bill that had been introduced in the House of Commons by the Secretary of State for the Colonies three months earlier was finally passed. The Act became effective on 1 August 1834. Despite the anxiety of the planters, the day passed peacefully and the Bishop of Barbados was able to report favourably to the Society for the Propagation of the Gospel: '800,000 human beings lay down last night as slaves and rose in the morning as free as ourselves. It might have been expected that on such an occasion there would have been some outburst of public feeling. I was present but there was no gathering that affected the public peace.' Indeed, the most raucous aspect of the slaves' festivities was the folk song 'Lick and Lock Up' with which they celebrated their freedom.

God bless de Queen fuh set we free
Hurrah for Jin-Jin [Queen Victoria]
Now lick and lock up done wid
Hurrah for Jin-Jin.

17

Every emancipation has in it the seeds of a new slavery,
and every truth easily becomes a lie.

I.F. Stone

It was in this celebratory atmosphere that John Stephen decided to marry a seamstress called Mary Fitzpatrick. It is likely that the couple met on one of his professional trips to her owner's plantation. They had a lot in common: both were the mixed-race progeny of esteemed white planters who had provided them with solid professions and secured them a place at the top of the slave hierarchy. Mary's father, James Fitzpatrick, was an elderly planter who, like Robert Cooper, had taken a coloured mistress called Nanny Hill after the death of his wife. He owned a number of plantations, including the modest property Hopewell, which he sold to the planter John Archer, who had become notorious for the murder of one of his slaves. Mary had a number of brothers and sisters also carrying the Fitzpatrick surname. One of them, James Fitzpatrick, became the long-standing headmaster of Foundation School, which Robert Cooper had built on Ashby land and which would go on to play a prominent role in the elevation of this branch of the Ashby family.

John Stephen would have had to make strenuous efforts to see his lover, visiting her whenever he was in the vicinity. Like most other slaves in love with women on other plantations, or whose partners and children had been sold away, he probably slipped away from Burkes on some evenings so he could see her. These 'nocturnal perambulations' were so common that most planters overlooked them, provided the absence did not interfere with work or last too long.

On 12 January 1835, John Stephen was baptized in the parish of Christ Church. This was probably a prelude to his marriage, since many slaves who had recently converted to Christianity and wished to marry in church got baptized before they organized their nuptials. The baptism record describes him as an 'Adult, owned by Robert Cooper Ashby'. On 14 February 1835, the marriage records show that 'John Stephen Ashby, apprentice labourer of Burkes estate, married Mary Christian, apprentice labourer of Mr James Evelyn.' Witnesses to the occasion were James Osborne and Edward Thomas Fitzpatrick. The marriage was a triumph for them both. For Mary Christian, John Stephen represented the security of an older husband who, as a skilled carpenter, was one of the most respected members of the non-white community. His work for nearby planters and householders meant that he had been able to build up what was – for a slave – a considerable nest egg with which to begin family life. For John Stephen, Mary Christian brought with her the privileges associated with her planter parent: her lighter skin and enhanced social status, as well as the skills she had and the money she could earn as a seamstress. He might also have been considered lucky, as many mulatto women preferred liaisons with white partners because of the financial and social advantages that came with them.

During this period, Robert Cooper, too, had found new love with a freed coloured woman called Elizabeth Brewster. His relationship with her ran alongside his more established one with Mary Anne. A young and comely widow, Elizabeth had been manumitted some time before emancipation and was therefore part of the freed coloured community that had been battling so intensely for their rights for most of the nineteenth century. She was also a slaveholder. The ownership of slaves by formerly enslaved persons seems shocking, even incomprehensible, to modern sensibilities, but it was a feature of virtually all slave societies despite the attempts of some lawmakers to hinder the practice. The reason was simple: slaves were a valuable form of investment, no different from land or livestock, and freed slaves purchased them as part of their accrual of wealth. (Manumitted persons would often in turn save up to purchase other family members out of slavery.)

Since slaves traditionally did all the menial tasks in slave societies, many affluent freed coloureds were as used to being served by slaves as the white population, and considered them an intrinsic part of their lifestyle. As one declared: 'Many of our children who are now grown almost to the years of maturity have from their earliest infancy been accustomed to be attended by slaves.' No doubt also some freed coloureds saw owning slaves as a status symbol: an affirmation of their distance from their lowly past as slaves themselves, and a mark of their aspiration to equality with the white slave-owning class.

By all indications Robert Cooper's relationship with Elizabeth was a serious one. He would provide her with her own bit of land, six acres carved out of one of the borders of Burkes. The property was called 'Rural Felicity' and had its own dwelling place and provision grounds. Their son, Samuel Brewster Ashby, would in adulthood become a notable campaigner for coloured rights.

The new dawn that many of Robert Cooper's children had dreamt about did not arrive immediately. Emancipation was a bitter disappointment. The terms of the Act meant that only those under the age of six received their freedom straight away.

Everyone else had to undertake a mandatory six-year apprenticeship before they could be free. The justification for this
was that the slaves needed time to get used to their liberty. The
planters' fear that emancipation would bring 'to a dramatic close
the golden era of Caribbean history' proved premature. The
resentful planters approached apprenticeship not as a transition
but as an opportunity to extend the status quo. Indeed, many
became more severe and capricious during this period. Requests
from the slaves to work the provision grounds were arbitrarily
denied; spouses on different plantations were refused permission
to visit one another; punishments became harsher; and the
predatory behaviour towards female slaves continued as before.

In 1837 James Thome and Horace Kimball, two North American emissaries of the American anti-slavery movement, hoping to convince their countrymen of the advantages of free
labour, toured the West Indies for six months. During their
stay in Barbados, they interviewed my great-great-great-great-
grandfather, Robert Cooper Ashby. Their account begins: 'We
were kindly invited to spend a day at the mansion of Colonel
Ashby, an aged and experienced planter, who is the proprietor
of the estate on which he resides.' Taking the 'easy and pleasant,
nine mile drive from Bridgetown', they arrived at Burkes,
where, after the predictable exchange of pleasantries, the pair
discovered something of Robert Cooper's backstory. In keeping
with their wider anti-slavery agenda, Thome and Kimball also
quizzed him about the inequities of life under slavery, and he
happily confirmed their views: 'Colonel A. remarked to us,
that he had witnessed many cruelties and enormities under "the
reign of terror".' He told them that the abolition of slavery had
been an incalculable blessing, but added that he had not always
entertained the same views respecting emancipation. Before it
took place, he was a violent opponent of any measure tending
to abolition. He regarded the English abolitionists and the

anti-slavery members in Parliament with unmitigated hatred. He had often cursed Wilberforce most bitterly, and thought that no doom, either in this life or in the life to come, was too bad for him. "'But," he exclaimed, "how mistaken I was about that man − I am convinced of it now − O he was a Good man − a noble philanthropist − if there is a chair in heaven, Wilberforce is in it!'"

Colonel Ashby went on to confirm reassuringly 'that he found no trouble in managing his apprentices', stating that 'the negroes were not disposed to leave their employment, unless the master was intolerably passionate, and hard with them; as for himself, he did not fear losing a single labourer after 1810'. He was also very emphatic about the idea that the slaves were deserving of their freedom. Whether this was a genuinely held opinion or whether he was simply telling them what they wanted to hear is impossible to ascertain, but they certainly found him very convincing:

> He dwelt much on the trustiness and strong attachment of the negroes, where they are well treated. There were no people in the world that he would trust his property or life with sooner than negroes . . . provided he had the previous management of them long enough to secure their confidence . . . Colonel A. said that it was impossible for him to mistrust the negroes as a body. He spoke in terms of praise also of the conjugal attachment of the negroes. His son, a merchant, recounted a story that supported this view. The wife of a negro man whom he knew, became afflicted with that loathsome disease the leprosy. The man continued to live with her, not withstanding the disease was universally considered contagious, and was peculiarly dreaded by the negroes. The man, on being asked why he lived with his wife under such circumstances, said, that he had lived with

her when she was well, and he could not bear to forsake
her when she was in distress.

As one would expect from any genial host aware of the views
of his interlocutors, my ancestor made numerous inquiries
respecting slavery in America.

He said there would certainly be insurrections in the
slave-holding states unless slavery was abolished. Nothing
but abolition could put an end to insurrections. Mr
Thomas, a neighbouring planter, dined with us. He had
not carried a complaint for several months. He remarked
particularly that 'emancipation had been a great blessing
to the master; it brought freedom to him as well as to the
slave'.

With such sympathetic answers it was no wonder that Thome
and Kimball left Barbados believing that the 'star of hope was
rising on the black and brown community'.

Robert Cooper had every reason to be sanguine about
emancipation. In reality, very little in his world had changed.
He was still the master of Burkes and his slaves, latterly called
'apprentices', were still effectively his property. They had
largely stayed put; not out of enthusiasm for cane cutting but
because there was nowhere else to go. Unlike Jamaica and
many of the other sugar territories, Barbados was so densely
cultivated that there was little opportunity for them to claim
their own land. Emancipation had also made Robert Cooper
Ashby a very wealthy man, as he was awarded £4,293 12s 5d in
compensation, worth around £400,000 in today's money.

Unsurprisingly apprenticeship, which proved to be slavery by
another name, became the new target for the abolitionists, and it
was repealed two years early. Thus the real end of slavery came

on 1 August 1838. Throughout the West Indies, slaves were delirious. In Jamaica, a vast crowd of the newly free surrounded a coffin, inscribed 'Colonial slavery, died July 31st, 1838, aged 276 years'. On the stroke of midnight the abolitionist missionary William Knibb cried: 'The monster is dead! The negro is free! Three cheers for the queen!' Then the coffin, a chain, handcuffs and an iron collar were buried and, in the soil above them, a tree of liberty was planted.

The initial impact of true emancipation would be felt by oppressor and oppressed alike. For the planters, the thought of living without the institution that was the source of their wealth, power and authority generated profound fear and melancholy, while the newly freed people of Barbados struggled too, despite their exhilaration. For them bondage and oppression were all they had ever known, but now the old ways were dying and new ways were not yet fully born. They were suddenly responsible for organizing their own lives and contemplating the chance of a different destiny for their children as schools for black and coloured children were being planned. And the ex-slaves were now being told that they could look to the authorities, who had so long been their most implacable oppressors, to support them in their goals. The scale of the transition was almost unimaginable and the epic journey from slavery to freedom was only just beginning.

The following year, on 23 October 1839, *The Barbadian* newspaper published a death notice. It read: 'Died on 18th [of this month] at Burke's Christchurch in his 65th year, Robert Cooper Ashby an old vestryman and many years Colonel of Christ Church Regiment of Militia'. According to family lore, Robert Cooper passed away on a wooden lounge chair on the veranda of the plantation. That evening the family would have gathered for his last night above ground. Robert Henry, the eldest of his children with Mary Anne, would have been in charge: allowing the visitors to say goodbye to the body, and explaining to the younger ones what had happened. Among the friends and family were some ex-slaves who must have felt profoundly ambivalent about the passing of the man who had dictated their lives for so many years.

Robert Cooper's funeral was a grand event. As had been the custom since the early days of slavery, dozens of his ex-slaves, all dressed in black, walked before the coffin; it was followed by a long cavalcade of at least three dozen carriages carrying his militia comrades, relatives and fellow planters. On arrival at Christ Church parish church, the mourners organized themselves without prompting according to their status: the 'widow' Mary Anne and acknowledged family at the very front, then local dignitaries, vestrymen and planters. In the first of the coloured pews were people like John Stephen and his wife, whom all present recognized had a special relationship with the deceased, as well as other skilled or favoured workers. Behind them sat the scores of black and brown labourers who had sown and harvested his sugar cane, maintained his house and cooked his food.

Before the service, the mourners paid their last respects and the lid was closed. It is possible that John Stephen, as one of the plantation's carpenters, might have made the coffin. But whoever constructed it, it was undoubtedly a handsome casket made of the most precious wood and finished with beautifully crafted fixtures and carefully detailed decorations. The pallbearers, dominated by Robert Cooper's sons, loaded his body onto the horse-drawn carriage and transported it to the cemetery. There Robert Cooper's body was interred in a large, white – but unnamed – tomb that adjoins the church on its eastern side. His descendants still squabble about who has the right to be buried there alongside him.

In death, as in life, Robert Cooper's timing was good. He was a product of the licentious Georgian era, who died just as the puritanical Victorian age was establishing itself. His was a milieu that was running out of time. The heyday of sugar had passed, although the plantations and the particular lifestyle associated with them would endure well into the twentieth century. The dominance of West Indian cane was already being threatened by the production of that commodity in other territories in the east. The reign of 'King Sugar' would soon be over, conquered by the ascent of sugar beet.

Whether white or black, ex-slave or always free, those who attended his funeral were witness to a critical moment in their own lives and that of the plantation. With 'the Colonel' gone, the past was silenced, and now the seductive calls of the future could be heard more unmistakably and more vehemently.

Documented on seven pages of yellowing oilskin paper, Robert Cooper Ashby's last will and testament is still available to view in the Barbados Archives. Though the sense of what Robert Cooper is trying to convey is strangled somewhat by the repetitive legalese typical of such official documents, it none-theless provides a vivid picture of his emotional priorities at the time it was written. After the traditional direction that his funeral expenses be 'fully paid and satisfied', Robert Cooper immediately turned his attention to settling the future of his youngest child, Samuel Ashby, the offspring of his most recent liaison with Elizabeth Brewster, bequeathing the baby the house 'Rural Felicity' and the surrounding six acres of land on which they already lived. In addition, he left to the child six apprentice labourers, Charlotte, Greta, Robert, James, Edward and Georgiana, 'for and during the unexpired term of their apprenticeships'. Their labour and the yield from the land were to be put towards maintaining young Samuel until his majority. In the event of his premature decease, however, the property was to be transferred to his mother, Elizabeth Brewster, and 'her heirs forever'.

Only after safeguarding the vulnerable pair does Robert Cooper turn his attention to his more established family. He bequeaths to Mary Anne and her children the 'remainder or balance of my said plantation', Burkes. For the first five years the plantation was to be kept intact and the funds, 'Crops, Produce and Profits', were to be devoted primarily towards 'the maintenance and support of his youngest children', Elizabeth Mary Ashby, Arabella Ann Ashby, William Armstrong Ashby, Caroline Kezar Ashby, Alexander Lindsay Ashby and John George Ashby, until they reached the age of twenty-one, with a slightly smaller proportion of the plantation's yields going to supporting his partner Mary Anne and their eldest children, Robert Henry and Alice Christian. Five years after his death, the property was to be sold and, profits divided and passed on to Mary Anne and her children. In a codicil to the will, he instructs his executors to sell and dispose of his plantation Brittons 'for the benefit of the above children'.

It was an extraordinary document. Without ever stating explicitly the nature of his relationship to either of the women currently in his life, or declaring unequivocally that their children were also his, Robert Cooper Ashby nonetheless made clear his priorities and commitments. His decision to make Mary Anne and her eldest son, Robert Henry, his executors is also informative: it is a tacit acknowledgement of her standing as his common–law wife and her eldest son's status as his most senior heir.

What is omitted from Robert Cooper's will is also fascinating. The exclusion of his first wife, Mary Ashby, and his son, John Burke Jr, is no surprise since they had both died years before. But numerous members of his extended slave family also go unmentioned. Sukey Ann and her four children, for example, are not mentioned; perhaps he felt that their manumission a few years previously had been gift enough. John Stephen also had no share in the bounty. This was probably because he had never been treated as well as those half-siblings whose mothers Robert Cooper had eventually become attached to. And perhaps Robert Cooper felt that John Stephen's future was already secured: he was an adult, had a lucrative trade, and was married now with children of his own.

Robert Cooper's decision to leave his wealth to his slave children was uncommon but not unique. A few years earlier Jacob Hinds, a planter from St Andrew, had also made a will that left everything to his extended mulatto clan. Jacob Hinds had seven separate family arrangements with black or coloured women living on his plantation that resulted in eighteen children. Where Hinds differed from Robert Cooper is that he explicitly acknowledged these children as his progeny. Unsurprisingly, his will is one of the longest on deposit in the Barbados Archives. Aware of the intense vulnerability of these slave children, Hinds wrote an emotional letter to his executor, begging him to enforce the stipulations of his will. It begins, 'The first wish of my heart and request of you is that I commit your friendship to my poor unfortunate distressed children,' and it concludes, 'If you have any love or regard for me never neglect them or turn your back on them . . . for the love of heaven don't let them be distressed or inconvenienced.'

For both Robert Cooper and Jacob Hinds, the decision to acknowledge their alternative family transgressed the traditional behaviour of the planter class, who had for many years taken care to ensure their wealth remained in the hands of the white ruling caste (as was evident in the furore that erupted when Joshua Steele attempted to leave his estate to his enslaved offspring). Robert Cooper's will was an unconventional act by an otherwise conventional man, so it is therefore interesting to speculate about what motivated him. Perhaps the years of living openly with Mary Anne and her brood, and his subsequent affection for Elizabeth Brewster and their young son, had changed him. Or perhaps it was about timing. The

Barbados that he knew was over, slavery had been abolished and black and brown people were openly working to expand their opportunities. Perhaps in this context, his actions did not feel quite so transgressive after all.

The various fates of Robert Cooper Ashby's illegitimate children mirrored those of many people of colour emerging from nineteenth-century slavery. Some of them had become free before emancipation and acquired the privileges associated with their freed coloured status, while others had not. Some, encountering the enormity of racial prejudice, would reject their black ancestry; others would continue to claim it. Those children who were embraced within the will were given the opportunity for an education and a share in 'the Colonel's' personal wealth. But they also had other advantages. Mary Anne's children, who were only one-quarter black, had moved even further away from their African roots towards the white community of the man whose surname they bore. With three white grandparents and one black grandparent, these children were still racially classified as mulattoes, but in reality had greater opportunities than their darker-skinned siblings. Virtually all of them forged marriages with prominent families with either land holdings or merchant businesses. Elizabeth Mary Ashby married Joseph Keeling Valverde, of mixed coloured and Jewish ancestry, while Arabella Ann Ashby married John Thomas Bentham, coloured son of a prominent doctor and plantation owner.

These astute matrimonial choices may have augured well for the progress of this branch of the family, but the members of this branch still endured the complex realities of a society in which racism stained all social relationships. In appearance they were white, and they enjoyed real privileges because of their 'brighter' skin colour, but their mixed-race heritage, which would have been widely known across the island, still connected them to the recently enslaved population.

Their financial situation was also not as secure as their father would have hoped. Robert Cooper's decision that the property should be sold five years after his death, with the proceeds going to Mary Anne's eleven children, was undoubtedly born of good motives: he wanted to make sure that they benefited equally. But the result was disastrous economically, since the wealth embodied in Burkes estate was spread perilously thin. It is difficult to create a detailed picture of the estate's fate after Robert Cooper's death, but it is clear that his decision to sell and divide the estate caused financial problems. By 1850 the estate was in receivership and a legal case had been lodged against it, with numerous parties making claims. The case was only settled in 1870, after which Burkes was purchased by the Clark family, who owned a number of similar properties. By the end of the nineteenth century, very few of those who were chosen as Robert Cooper's heirs were prominent in the economics and politics of Christ Church and Oistins.

John Stephen's story is less glamorous than that of some of Robert Cooper's children, but it is more typical. Like the majority of enslaved coloured offspring, he was neither freed by his father nor bestowed with an inheritance, and he would not find a place among the elite freed coloured community that developed before abolition. The benefits he received from his father were limited to a brown skin and a profitable trade. But the value of the former bequest, one that he shared with all of Robert Cooper's descendants, should not be underestimated. According to the local historian Robert Morris, 'They all carried the badge of colour, a plantation source of origin, and the link to a prominent father, all possible sources of success in the society of the day.' John Stephen's marriage would produce six children, and though his will has never been found, that of his wife, Mary Christian, which was proved on 13 January 1891, demonstrated that their union had generated enough wealth to leave substantial legacies for her children, the generation for whom real change finally took place.

I am the descendant of John Stephen and Mary Christian's third child, Benjamin Ashby, who was part of the first generation of black Ashbys to be born free. It was likely that Benjamin received at least an elementary education, since schools that admitted black and coloured children were being pioneered around this time. In his teens Benjamin was apprenticed to a shoemaker in the area of Providence. When the time came for marriage he would, like his father, become engaged to a woman who was the mixed-race descendant of a powerful white family. Her name was Elizabeth Armstrong and their wedding took place in 1862. Benjamin and his new wife then settled in Lodge Road in Oistins, where he became a shopkeeper.

Even before emancipation, the coloured population had displayed a strong pull towards urban centres, and now people like Benjamin Ashby started to abandon the plantations and settle in towns like Bridgetown, Speightstown and Oistins to restart their lives. Once there, they tended to work as artisans, tradesmen and merchants, hoteliers and hostel keepers – all professions that allowed them to generate wealth outside the purview of the all-powerful plantocracy. Perhaps because of family influence, Benjamin was awarded the contract to supply Foundation School with groceries and its boarders with shoes. He also forged strong ties with the Vestry, which that had absorbed so much of his grandfather's time.

The considerable wealth he amassed is revealed by his wife's will and later his own. Elizabeth Armstrong Ashby's will, entered in 1910, revealed that she owned land in her own right which she left to her children. The relatives mentioned as beneficiaries included her husband, Benjamin, her son Benjamin Jr, and other children: John Clifford Ashby, Jeanette Armstrong Ashby, Helena and Eloise Ashby. Witnesses to the will were George

Elphinstone Deane and Charles Frederick Ashby. By the time Benjamin himself died in 1925, he was well known in Oistins as a prominent village shopkeeper with easy access to the Vestry, and the owner of significant properties in Lodge Road and Maxwell. His heirs included his sons Benjamin Jr, Walter Fitz-Thomas, Charles Frederick, Edward Albert and Reginald Thomas Ashby.

As well as financial security, Benjamin had ensured that his sons received a proper education at a time when few could afford to do so, and some attended Foundation School, which their planter ancestor had been so influential in creating. All would go on to marry into members of the Barbados middle class. Charles Frederick wed Henrietta Nurse, the daughter of a schoolteacher, while Benjamin Jr married Hester Frances Gall of a landowning family of Shot Hall. My great-grandfather Edward Albert married Edith Barnes, the child of a white family. Between the 1920s and the abolition of the Vestry system in the 1950s, the Ashby name was continually represented on this powerful local government body.

The fate of this generation of Ashbys and those who followed reflects the way that life evolved for the entire caste of coloured families descended from planter class origins. Indeed, as one local historian has noted:

> One of the most important legacies of the plantation culture was the creation of a class of leaders poised between the Caucasians who dominated all aspects of the society and the slaves, later the teeming masses of the population. This intermediate group of free coloureds, or coloureds, not always free, mainly derived from the relationship between a rich white male, and a coloured or black woman with whom he established sexual relationships.

A similar caste emerged across much of the Atlantic slave world. In the United States, for example, the white patriarchs of these coloured clans included not just a legion of anonymous planters but also men as famous as the eighteenth-century president, Thomas Jefferson. Their biracial descendants would take up the same social place in their cultures as John Stephen and his contemporaries did in the sugar islands. This relatively privileged group enjoyed the benefit of financial legacies and access to education that eventually enabled them to become leaders in black society, what the writer Edward Ball has called 'the home class of ministers, politicians and business people'.

Even after his death, Robert Cooper Ashby cast a long shadow. His memory lingers to this day, and his descendants still make reference to the exploits of 'the Colonel' and pass his possessions from generation to generation in their wills. Thanks to his canny exploitation of sugar and slaves, he provided genuine financial and educational advantages to many of his mixed-race progeny; and he bequeathed to them not just their lighter skin but social confidence. The Ashby family therefore went into the future with certain distinct advantages that would shelter them somewhat from the vicissitudes of life in post-emancipation Barbados and the momentous challenges they would encounter in the twentieth century.

Part Three
THE LEGACY

18

We are never as steeped in history as when we pretend not to be.

Michel-Rolph Trouillot

By the time my grandfather Edward Everton Ashby was born in 1899, Barbados had become a place to leave. The heyday of cane sugar had passed, eclipsed in popularity by the highly subsidized sugar beet produced in Europe. And Barbados, 'the most esteemed and ancient of the British colonies', was in a desperate state. Across the island, living standards had deteriorated: wages had plummeted and jobs had disappeared. Food shortages meant that prices rose, malnourishment was pervasive and infant mortality soared. The situation was only exacerbated by a hurricane in 1898 that destroyed the homes of thousands of workers and prompted outbreaks of typhoid, dysentery and later smallpox. By 1902, Barbados seemed on the point of economic and social collapse and its citizens were departing in droves, eager to try their luck elsewhere.

Migration was an instinctive solution for the population of a region where restlessness and movement had been a way of life for centuries. Most of these migrants were desperate to escape what the historian Sidney Mintz described as the 'iron grip' of sugar, and the economic and social limitations it had created in their society. They left in the first instance largely for other

Caribbean colonies like Jamaica, Trinidad and British Guiana, which were bigger and offered more opportunities. Hopefuls would often take on short contracts and return home with their pockets heavy. After 1880, the epic construction project that was the Panama Canal attracted tens of thousands of Barbadians and Jamaicans whose livelihood had been affected by the dip in sugar prices. Many of these workers, who moved backwards and forwards between Panama and their home territories, eventually returned to the sugar islands, boosting the economies there with their earnings. But a goodly number moved towards the land of opportunity: America. These 'dusky destiny seekers', whose number peaked at the end of the 1910s and the early 1920s, settled primarily in Harlem and Brooklyn and soon carved out prominent roles for themselves in the intellectual, political and economic leadership of the communities they established there.

By the second decade of the twentieth century, virtually every black family in the Caribbean had lost someone to the dream of migration: field workers who had been turned off the land; tradesmen who fantasized about expanding their horizons; middle-class people frustrated by the lack of change; all of them determined to find a way out of a system that was as unyielding as cement. Some left on a whim, others planned meticulously; some left fearfully, others in a fever of optimism. So many people were leaving that locals referred to it as 'the Exodus'.

In 1923, the *Barbados Weekly Herald* wrote:

> We are sensitive in Barbados over this question of immigration. It is perhaps regrettable that with the West Indies and British Guiana full of undeveloped resources it should be necessary for nationals to seek employment elsewhere. But people must eat . . . Who is to blame the ambitious, near destitute, who goes forth to find what he is not likely to find at home? We yield to no one in our understanding and appreciation of the excellencies of the

British flag but we cannot shut our eyes to the fact that
in the present state of affairs emigration to America is
indispensably necessary to the West Indies.

My grandfather Edward Everton, known as 'Vere', was amongst this group of eager émigrés. Born in 1899, he was the second son of Edward Albert Ashby and his wife, a white woman (or 'near white', since most of the people in the Caribbean who identify as Caucasian are really of mixed-race origin) called Edith Barnes. Their rather stormy marriage nonetheless managed to produce four children: my grandfather, my great-aunt Una, my great-aunt Reba, who migrated early to America and lost touch with the family, and my great-uncle Ross, a dashing, handsome man, who became a merchant marine and was killed during the Second World War.

Vere's father, Edward Albert, had, like other descendants of Robert Cooper, benefited from the social and financial advantages associated with his background. Known as 'the Colonel' like his illustrious ancestor, he owned a number of shops as well as several valuable properties in the Oistins area. Edward Albert's brothers, Reginald and Charles Frederick, had also taken advantage of their good fortune and were successful merchants in Bridgetown. Indeed the latter's various emporiums on Swan Street, which sold everything from jewellery to hardware and bicycles, marked him out as one of the pioneering coloured merchants of the era, opening the doors for other members of his caste to succeed as entrepreneurs. The Ashby family would also be associated with the founding of the Barbados Progressive Bank, which had ambitions to break the stranglehold that whites held on the business community.

At the age of twenty-five my grandfather Vere Ashby married Muriel Haynes Skinner, who was six years his junior. For him it was love at first sight. He was besotted, he claimed, as soon as he saw her 'plump yellow thighs' ascending a flight of stairs. She was probably quite impressed with him, too. As a youth my grandfather was a good-looking, rather foppish young man, who sported immaculately tailored clothes and had round, soulful, puppy-dog eyes. But marriages among the mixed-race middle classes of this era were more than a romantic liaison. A certain amount of social engineering was encouraged. The status of families like the Ashbys was still precarious. The 'wrong marriage' to someone darker or poorer could easily precipitate a slide back into that world of powerlessness and discrimination to which the majority of those of African descent were consigned. But marriage to a person of equal or lighter skin colour and some material worth would maintain or even boost the privileges of the next generation. It was unsurprising, therefore, that his bride-to-be also came from a successful mixed-race family; and that her father was also a merchant, who had a number of shops in Speightstown on the west coast of the island.

Almost immediately after the wedding, the couple decamped for Harlem in New York, where my grandfather had spent a number of his teenage years and early manhood and had many relatives. Initially they stayed with my grandmother's family, the Barneses, who had migrated there after the turn of the century. Later they took an apartment in central Harlem and my grandmother gave piano lessons to the offspring of the more affluent black migrants who had moved there from the South. My grandfather took a job as a bellhop at a large Manhattan hotel that was, according to my mother, 'a desirable occupation for a coloured man at that time'. Of course, this was true only in an American context; back in Barbados my grandfather would never have dreamt of taking a job in the service industries, as he would have considered it far beneath him. This downward mobility was typical of the lot of many migrants who took positions they considered inferior to get a foothold in the American job market.

My grandfather was not alone in his enthusiasm for Harlem. Black migration there had begun before the wars, when Caribbean immigrants joined the droves of African-Americans from the South who were migrating north in search of new beginnings. These groups had many parallel experiences. Americans from below the Mason–Dixon line (the cultural boundary that separated the northern United States from the South) had fled from racial persecution – the spectre of lynching and those 'strange fruit' hanging from Southern trees; or men in white sheets, burning crosses on lawns; or black women who were too well dressed arrested for 'acting white'; or separate entrances and second-class carriages – and the West Indians too had their own stories of racial violence, denigration and segregation. (As late as the 1940s one of Barbados's foremost political leaders could drop his white wife off at the island's Yacht Club but could not go in.)

It was no wonder therefore that these migrants' numbers were so prodigious. According to the historian Irma Watkins-Owens, 'Between 1900 and 1930 some 40,000 immigrants of African descent, most of them from the British held colonies of the Caribbean, settled in Harlem as it was emerging as a black community in New York City.' So during the first few decades of the century, for an adventurous and aspirational person of colour like my grandfather, all roads led to Harlem: New York's Jazz Age Mecca, which had been an exciting place since the late nineteenth century but had become even more so at the end of the First World War.

Post-war Harlem was also a magnet for white people. The atmosphere of social experiment and licentiousness that had emerged there in these years meant that black Harlem in the middle of white America had become the most glamorous destination of all. Indeed, Harlem in the 1910s and 1920s had become a commodity, an aphrodisiac, where whites, emboldened by bootlegged alcohol, acted out their enchantment with the primal and exotic. They flocked to venues like the legendary Cotton Club and the Plantation Club, or to the more seedy, dingy speakeasies like the Clam Bake, to be scandalized by the double entendres of singers like Bessie Smith, to watch sex shows and to take marijuana. Part of the whites' penchant for 'slumming uptown' was based on the stereotypes they held about black people being hypersexual and musical, but the black Harlemites – enriched by these tourists – often colluded in these fantasies. Harlem became a 'city within a city', a place that encouraged its reputation for 'anything goes', becoming one of the few areas in America that was tolerant towards homosexuality, for example. Whatever the real thoughts of its local residents, it was a place where people could take 'shore leave' from accepted morality; where they could do what they dared not do anywhere else.

Though undoubtedly a playground for whites, Harlem was also a hub for ambitious black people in the post-war period. It was the height of the 'Harlem Renaissance' and black musicians, writers and performers flocked there. Here they could at last taste the glamorous urban life of the North, as immortalized in the black popular songs of they day. Harlem was awash with music: blues, spirituals, jazz. In venues as varied as the Hot Cha and the Apollo Theater, black musicians like Duke Ellington and Jelly Roll Morton and singers like Ma Rainey and Bessie Smith articulated the pains and possibilities of modern life for those blacks who had fled to urban centres eager to reinvent themselves after emancipation.

The Harlem Renaissance was more than Josephine Baker and jazz. It was also a literary and political movement in which Caribbean-born Americans would achieve genuine prominence and distinction. Alongside luminaries such as Zora Neale Hurston and Langston Hughes were writers of Caribbean origin like the Jamaican-born Claude Mckay, whose bestseller *Home to Harlem* was published in 1928, and Eric Walrond, whose background was rooted in both British Guiana and Barbados. What characterized their work was the idea of the 'New Negro', whose art, music and literature challenged the pernicious racial stereotypes that were propagated all around them. It is often forgotten how seminal the West Indian presence was in the Harlem of 1920s.

Many West Indians also found a prominent place in the radical movements of Harlem's political scene. Most significant was the emergence of the Jamaican-born Marcus Garvey, founder of the Universal Negro Improvement Association which enjoyed its heyday in the years between 1917 and 1922. Garvey, whom W.E.B. DuBois described as 'a little fat, black man, ugly but with intelligent eyes', began his career as one of those infamous stepladder orators who roared their speeches at passers-by traversing the streets of Harlem. He promoted a radical message that eschewed the conciliatory goals of social integration in favour of the desirability of a return to Africa, declaiming passionately: 'Black men, you were once great, you shall be great again.' His was a vision that was particularly beguiling for many disillusioned black Americans and Afro-Caribbeans, and remained influential even after 1923, when Garvey was 'got out of the way' on trumped-up charges of mail fraud. Indeed, I can still remember my uncle Lionel Yard, the husband of yet another Barbadian aunt who had migrated to New York, declaring many years later that he was 'the greatest man who ever lived'. (Lionel Yard would go on to write the definitive biography of Garvey's wife, Amy.)

There were many others, too: men like Colin Powell, Shirley Chisholm, Sidney Poitier and Harry Belafonte, as well as radicals like Stokely Carmichael and Malcolm X. Over the years, these Caribbean migrants would not only enrich their adopted country materially but also become some of its most notable citizens of African descent. As early as the 1920s, W.A. Domingo in his book *Gift of the Black Tropics* noted that 'it is probably not realized . . . to what extent West Indian Negroes have contributed to the wealth and power of the United States'.

The legacy of the Harlem Renaissance was profound. It changed how black Americans were viewed, not just by other Americans but across the world. It provided black people with a new racial consciousness and gave them an appreciation of their own culture and a spirit of self-determination. Indeed, many argue that the Harlem Renaissance laid the foundation for the post-war Civil Rights movement.

Among the other members of the Ashby clan who migrated to America during the same period as my grandfather was the family of my Brooklyn-based cousin Andrea Ramsey, who is a descendant of Robert Cooper and his slave Sukey Ann. Their American chronicle began when two of Andrea's great-grandfather's sisters, Anne and Sarah Nurse, migrated to the United States just after the turn of the nineteenth century, eager 'to expand their options'. Several years later, in 1909, they were followed by their brother, William Edmund Thomas Sinclair Nurse, a headmaster. His wife, Charlotte Ashby Nurse, followed the next year, but though the couple never divorced, they never lived together after her arrival. The marriage had been doomed virtually from the start, as the family members recalled: 'He wouldn't give and she wouldn't give!' Instead Charlotte settled on the Upper West Side and worked as a laundress for private families. Like my grandparents, these Ashbys had to adjust their expectations and take the work they were offered.

Indeed, many of these new migrants quickly found their exhilaration at being in America tempered by frustration, once they had had a chance to settle in. While the status of black people was better than it had been and there were now high-profile advocates for change, things were by no means equal: the segregation laws were still very much in place in the South and discrimination was still a feature of their everyday life. As a result there were sporadic outbreaks of rioting and racial violence, and employment opportunities were extremely limited.

The novelist Eric Walrond wrote:

> On coming to the United States the West Indian often finds himself out of patience with the attitude he meets there respecting the position of white and Negroes. He is bewildered . . . at being shoved down certain blocks and alleys 'among his own people'. He is angry and amazed at the futility of seeking out certain types of employment for which he may be specially adapted. And about the cruellest injury that could be inflicted upon him is to ask him to submit to the notion that because he is black it is useless for him to aspire to be more than a tap drummer at Small's, a red cap at Pennsylvania Station or a clerk in the Bowling Green Post Office.

These limitations had a profound impact on Andrea Ramsey's great-grandparents. Despite letters of reference, her great-grandfather William was never able to find a teaching job and instead worked in the Brooklyn Navy Yard as a policeman. Many new immigrants like my grandmother and father accepted this downward social mobility as the sacrifice they would have to make to step onto the employment ladder and to ensure their descendants had greater opportunities in the future, but some voiced their frustrations. According to family lore, William had a reputation as a perfectionist and was difficult to deal with. Despite being 'so light skinned, that he was often mistaken for white', he was 'very outspoken about being a Negro and lived his entire life in New York in the heart of the black Harlem community'. Like many Caribbean migrants, he was militant in not allowing any injustice to pass uncontested. As Andrea recalls: 'They tried to fire him or lay him off three times, but each time he appealed the decision to multiple political, government and

Naval officials and got his job back. His civilian personnel file weighed over 3lbs!'

For this generation, then, the experience of migration to America was distinctly mixed. William was impressed that in America he could exercise his rights to fight for his job, but he never found a position that was commensurate with the one he left behind in Barbados. His sisters, Sarah and Anne, found it impossible to adapt to this new place – to the alienating hubbub of a large city with its restless, anonymous mass of people, its inclement weather and inexplicable ways of doing things – and eventually returned to the island.

As well as the tensions between the black and white communities, encounters between Caribbean blacks and African-Americans were often deeply ambivalent. Both the Caribbean and mainland America had been shaped by the Atlantic slave system in which blacks toiled in order to create vast wealth for whites. Across the region, people of African origin were the descendants of slaves, and their cultural experiences had been determined by the racial theories, social hierarchies and justifications that such a system brought about. The two groups also had a shared imagery of the past: the well-upholstered planter and the ragged slave; the 'Big House' with its endless luxury and the meanness of the slave quarters; the cane and cotton fields, ministered to by black backs bent beneath an unforgiving sun.

But there were also important differences. It seems hard to imagine now, bearing in mind what we know of the horror of Southern slavery, but the Caribbean slave system was appreciably harsher than that of mainland America. In part this was because cutting cane in the torrid conditions of the Caribbean was one of the most terrible occupations in the world. It can also be traced back to the West Indian planters' initial decision that it made economic sense to work their slaves to death rather than sustain them from generation to generation. As a result, the region had an obscene death rate, and a steady stream of new Africans who brought with them fresh energy and newly minted resentment. Thus there had been a long tradition of violent revolt across the region and many felt that this made the West Indians more aggressive in response to injustices they encountered in America, more willing to take on the system.

Yet the Caribbean blacks' experience of life in the years following emancipation had probably been easier than for their Southern counterparts. By the time slavery was abolished, the black population formed a huge majority in the Caribbean, but only a minority in the United States. The West Indians, therefore, were raised in a society in which political changes had widespread impact: their children would eventually become accustomed to seeing other blacks in a wide range of occupations – teacher, doctor or political leader. These role models gave them ambition and confidence, and perhaps a greater degree of impatience, when they came to America.

There was also a very different attitude to the mixed-race population in the two territories. In the Caribbean, miscegenation was implicitly accepted and the products of interracial liaisons, like my ancestor John Stephen, frequently received some sort of recognition from their planter fathers. The plantocracy of the Caribbean were also aware that they were vastly outnumbered by the slave population, so they extended privileges to their brown descendants in order that this group could then act as a buffer between them and the mass of black slaves. But the United States, with its 'one drop rule', had a more rigid and hostile attitude to this community, so this group had less support to develop and enrich itself.

These variations in experience and expectations sometimes led to hostility between the two communities. African-Americans frequently denigrated Caribbean migrants' small-island origins and referred to them derisorily as 'monkey chasers'. Eric

Walrond noted that African-Americans not only discriminated against them in the workplace but also burlesqued their accent on stage and street corner, and dismissed their pride in their British heritage as putting on 'airs'. West Indians, in their turn, felt that African-Americans were 'too touchy' about white people and were frustrated that they were so passive and dispirited in their acceptance of the status quo. As Claude Mckay explained, he felt more confident than 'Aframericans who, long deracinated, were still rootless among phantoms and pale shadows and enfeebled by self-effacement before condescending patronage, social negativism and miscegenation'. These tensions lingered for a generations. As a little girl growing up in the Bronx, Andrea Ramsey told me: 'I remember my grandmother being called "a monkey chaser". When I visited Barbados and saw the green monkeys, I just had to laugh.'

Whereas my grandfather loved the excitement of New York – the escape it offered from the insularity, rigid hierarchies and stultifying preconceptions of island life – my grandmother did not. To her, as to my cousin's great-aunts, Harlem was a strange world indeed. The rigours of a North American winter made her miserable, and the omnipresent prejudice of American life at the height of segregation demoralized her. She was not the sort of person to be apologetic about her race and she bitterly resented the limitations imposed on her life because of it. She yearned for Barbados, where she was known in her community and where her fair complexion and straight hair, as well as her middle-class background, marked her out as part of a social elite. According to my mother, 'She missed her father, and the way of life she was used to – sheltered, well connected, affluent – with domestic staff, a comfortable home.' To a proud woman who believed fervently that she was just as good as anybody else, and a great deal better than some, America was a rude awakening. Her sojourn in Harlem was probably the first time that she had ever been reduced solely to a phenotype: that is simply and merely 'black'.

Perhaps Vere was also enjoying New York a bit too much. He was a convivial man who often found himself 'falling among thieves', his way of describing his impromptu and extended sessions of drinking and carousing that so exasperated his wife. And nowhere provided as much temptation as his new neighbourhood. Harlem was so replete with dives and taverns that one African-American Baptist minister called it 'little less than a corner of hell'. So hazardous was Harlem to righteous living that the minister concluded: 'Fathers and mothers away down south or far off in the West Indies, little know of the shame and degradation that have overtaken many of their sons and daughters who have come to this city to improve their condition and perhaps aid their parents, but have been lost to them and the world.' Whatever the reason, or combination of reasons, my grandmother's antipathy to their new life continued, and within a year, they were back in Barbados in time for the birth of their first child, my grandfather's dream of relocating to America well and truly over.

19

The architecture of our future is not only unfinished, the scaffolding has hardly gone up.

George Lamming

My grandparents returned to an island that was still in the doldrums. The Barbadian economy had enjoyed a brief return to prosperity around the time of the First World War, when the production of sugar beet was disrupted by the hostilities and demand for cane sugar soared. But when beet cultivation restarted, the island's economy was once again in trouble. The situation was worsened by the epic cloud of the Great Depression, which descended over the entire international economy. Socially, too, Barbados remained a depressed and depressing place. In many ways, it had not changed since the days of Robert Cooper Ashby. The island remained rigidly hierarchical, with a small white elite at the top, a slightly larger coloured middle class beneath them and at the bottom, only inches away from absolute poverty, the mass of black workers.

Initially the couple and their baby son Edward (named after his father and grandfather) settled in Bridgetown, presumably because my grandfather, who was fond of urban distractions, wanted to live there. He set up a small business in the capital while his wife stayed in Speightstown to manage the smaller of her father's businesses. 'She was good at it,' my mother remembers, 'while my father seems to have been poor at it and, I rather think, hated it.' Vere would come home to his family at the weekend, but he felt unsettled. It was a difficult period for them both, made more so by the death of the infant Edward. But the marriage somehow survived. They had two more children during this time – my aunt Muriel and my mother, Barbara – and soon the entire family moved to a house in the Garrison (once the military headquarters for the Imperial forces) with my grandfather's sister's family, the Donovans.

It was only later, after the failure of a number of commercial ventures, that Vere was finally forced to consider Plumgrove, the sugar estate he had inherited from his now dead father, which had been abandoned and was daily growing more derelict. When they moved there, my grandmother was delighted. She had happy memories of her father's plantation, Checker Hall in the parish of St Lucy. But Vere was desperate. Not only was he forced to live in Barbados, he had to become a planter – a role he had no desire to assume.

It is interesting to speculate on why both my great-grandfathers would want, so to speak, to return the scene of the crime by purchasing sugar plantations. On one level, the explanation is rather mundane: the acquisition of a piece of land was the aspiration of every islander, and was the most common way to cement a family's middle-class status. But why a sugar estate? Again, the answer comes down at least partly to economics: despite the plummeting prices, sugar was still the biggest game in town, and no one could quite envisage what would take its place. It was a route to power, too, since for the first half of the twentieth century the planters still had a monopoly on the political machinery of the Caribbean islands: a sugar estate represented both wealth and social superiority.

But the idealization of plantation life was not just about

privilege. It also sprang from an intense nostalgia for the certainties and security of the past. Despite the dark realities of plantation life, the image propogated by planters was of a world of leisure and luxury, ease and elegance, and it remained a potent romantic symbol for some. Maybe there was also some wistfulness for what was seen as the planter's role: being one's own boss and not being beholden to anyone. Conceivably, my great-grandfather, Edward Albert, also shared with planters that passionate attachment to place, and the synthesis offered by estate life of where one lived and how one lived. But on another, more profound level, perhaps it was a psychological attempt to reclaim the past. In a curious variation of the Caribbean historian Edward Brathwaite's idea of 'the inner plantation', in which the enslaved individual internalizes the pernicious values of the plantation and oppresses himself and his fellows, the slave now gains the opportunity to recast himself as master, thus finally escaping his enslaved status.

So the past continued to shape the aspirations of the post-emancipation generation and, like many newly affluent, mixed-race descendants of planters, my great-grandfather had pursued the plantation dream. He was one of only a handful who would realize these aspirations, however. Indeed, Edward Albert was the only descendant of 'the Colonel' through the line of John Stephen who would also become a planter. And although Vere only took up his inheritance reluctantly, Plumgrove became the heartland of the modern Ashby family. For the generations who followed it would be the place from which they would journey and to which they would return, as well as where they would live and love, sin and repent. The intensity of the relationship that its inhabitants had with this land is proof that we are made by the places we love, just as we make them.

Plumgrove was situated about ten miles from Bridgetown. It was accessible either by the coast road via Oistins, where their ancestor Benjamin had had his shop and where Robert Cooper had gone boldly about with his vast illegitimate brood; or through the back roads, cutting across Kingsland, the property from which Robert Cooper's father had carved out his little fiefdom. The estate had its origins in a much larger plantation called Waterland Hall which, like so many plantations, had been broken up and sold off during the difficult times of the early twentieth century.

The estate was divided informally into zones, each fulfilling a different function. At the front of the property, where the land was rocky and infertile, was the tenantry which housed the labourers and their families. This community was a jumble of small wooden houses, perched jauntily on blocks of limestone and painted in the candy-box colours the islanders are so fond of. Behind them, separated by a strip of scrub and grass, were acres and acres of whistling cane. Nestled in the middle, and accessible by a rocky marl track known as 'The Gap', was the great house, set in its own lush and beautiful grounds. As was the tradition, this large stone monolith, built in a variation of the Palladian style, was visible from any point on the land. The Ashby family and their tenants could therefore catch sight of one another through the trees as they went about their daily lives, always aware of the gulf of status and life experience that separated them.

Life at Plumgrove was not dissimilar to that at Burkes so many years before. As in the days before emancipation, the Ashby family was very much the ruling family at Plumgrove, around whom all plantation life revolved. My mother and her brothers and sisters took it for granted that, even as children, they were addressed as 'Miss Barbara' or 'Master John', just as their parents were addressed as 'Master' and 'Missus'. The great house was as busy as a railway station, with cooks, cleaners and maids going in and out along with other workers and tenants. The family members were approached with requests for favours, guidance or financial assistance, while they blithely meddled in the affairs of their tenants, dispensing (often unwanted) advice, admonishments and opinions. In this environment, where the violence of plantation life had been almost entirely eliminated (despite the presence of my grandfather's ubiquitous shotgun), the pleasure of this incestuous, villagey world was easier to understand and my mother recalls her plantation childhood with affection, warmth and humour.

Like their nineteenth-century forebears, the twentieth-century Ashbys found that their life was punctuated by the rhythms of sugar production. The 'burns' that signalled the beginning of the harvest affected them just as they had previous generations: their skin was irritated by the cane ash and their noses were assailed by the cloying scent of burnt sugar. And even as children, my mother and her siblings were aware of the tensions during crop time, when everything felt more urgent, and my grandfather and his hands worked more intensely. Indeed, the harvest looms large in my mother's recollection of her plantation childhood. One of her first memories is of being put along with her siblings on a blanket that was placed adjacent to the fields, and being given 'fingers' of newly cut cane to suck.

For all its local specificity, however, family life among the Caribbean middle classes still aspired to a notion of Englishness. Indoctrinated to be ashamed of their African roots, this generation rushed to leave behind any evidence of this heritage as they climbed the social ladder. Of course, their Caribbean customs weren't banished completely – it was there in the food they ate, the way they moved and the exuberance with which they lived – but in many other ways they modelled themselves on their counterparts in the 'mother country', valuing conventionality and a conspicuous respectability. So the Ashby family's façade was not that different from that of much of the English middle class of that era. It featured an avuncular patriarch and a suitably submissive matriarch, and children who were appropriately laundered and pressed. Regular church attendance was mandatory and, like every affluent home, they had antimacassars on the furniture and a piano in the lounge that my grandmother played beautifully.

As was common in those days, Vere was rather a semi-detached figure within his own family; it was his wife, Muriel, who acted as the nucleus. She was a force to be reckoned with: the eldest of her siblings and her father's favourite, she was beautiful, talented and had a wicked sense of humour. She was also well educated, so she was the one the children consulted when they needed help with homework. She had inherited her father's business acumen and never lost it, continuing to assist with the rents and accounts at Plumgrove till her death. 'She was so glamorous,' my mother once told me. 'Watching our mother dress for a dance was like going to a movie. We'd sit on the bed and watch her going through all the stages of beautification – she would choose in advance her accessories and shoes. It was a creative process that was truly fascinating and the results were often stunning.'

Glamorous moments aside, my grandmother's role as mistress of the house was not unlike that of Mary Ashby so many years before. She too was expected to oversee the household and servants, making sure that everything ran smoothly, and providing the sweetness that made everyone content and get along peacefully. But since Plumgrove was neither as large nor as productive a plantation as Burkes, money was always a worry and my grandmother had to work much harder than Mary ever did.

My grandfather's role was also very similar to that of his fore-father: there were workers to oversee, rents to be collected, repairs to be initiated and books to be balanced. His relationship with the tenants had echoes of his planter ancestor, too: he often regarded them as lazy and unreliable, and adopted a posture towards them that was by turns paternal and exasperated, bullying and indulgent; while they no doubt sometimes regarded him as overbearing and arbitrary, or mean and uncaring. But there were also some profound differences between my grandfather and his hallowed ancestor. Vere would not have chosen the life of a planter: he was not the sort of man who enjoyed the pedantry of listing expenditures and keeping accounts. In fact, according to my uncle Trevor, he was 'terrible with money' and always in shallow water financially. Intensely sociable, Vere had been much more at home in the dives of Harlem with his polyglot friends and their urban interests, rather than mouldering away in rural Barbados farming sugar.

Though Vere felt obligated to play 'the planter', bluff and loud and straightforward, his own interests were miles away from sugar prices, farming equipment and seeds. He read a lot of Rosicrucian literature, and was a firm believer in homeopathic medicine long before it was popular, as well as a user of health food products including shark oil. He loved experimenting with cooking: at breakfast he would find innumerable ways to serve eggs, and at Christmas he made an excellent sorrel liquor and cured pork leg or ham. He had a share in a fishing boat because he believed, rather far-sightedly, that fish was healthier than meat, and he once tried his hand at goat rearing. So life with Vere was a roller coaster: eternally precarious, both financially and emotionally, as he alternated between intervals of torpor and manic schemes to make money. Vere was never able to reconcile the disparity between the man he thought he should be and the man he really was. My mother has said: 'Quite early, I felt my father's vulnerability. I think he was a weak man but not a vicious one, easily influenced, wanting to be popular but having very little judgement about people or situations.' And one of his contemporaries described him as a complex man, perpetually 'uneasy in his own skin'.

To make life even more frustrating for him, there were the

wider problems associated with an industry in decline. Making any kind of living from sugar during this period was a challenge, so Vere was forced to try a number of other crops – such as corn and cotton – to make a go of things. But the situation didn't improve and he finally had to take another job to shore up the family's finances. Following in the Ashby family tradition, he joined the local Vestry, as one of the Poor Law Inspectors who made periodic inspections of poor relief institutions. It was an important job because of the level of fiscal distress in many parts of the island, but it was also disheartening, since the annual reports he submitted could recommend improvements but not enforce them.

If my grandfather had the status and responsibilities of a planter, he also had the vices. Not only did he manage to gamble away a good portion of his wife's inheritance, he was an epic drinker. His alcohol-induced excesses were legendary: in a drunken frenzy he once took pot shots at the workers on the land, though mercifully his aim was so poor that no one was hurt. But the legacy of plantation life was most evident in the way that my grandfather conducted his illicit private life. Much like Robert Cooper, he had a taste, as my cousin put it, for 'low-bite' women: that is, those from further down the social scale. These liaisons produced a number of illegitimate children, some of whom were born to women who worked on the Plumgrove estate.

His legitimate children often found out about these half-brothers and sisters in rather serendipitous ways. My uncle Trevor, who went to Foundation School, which his planter ancestor had helped to establish, remembers striking up a conversation with a pupil, who then pointed out a other boy in the classroom, and said: 'Do you know who that guy is? He's your half-brother.' My uncle was surprised, but not too surprised. As time passed they became close. And eventually Trevor told his mother about his new friend. Muriel, not a woman to harbour illusions, said she would like to meet the young man. But the boy refused: he felt that my grandmother was too 'great a lady' to be sullied by an encounter with her husband's by-blow. His shame at his illegitimate status illustrated how persistently the internalized values of the slave system lingered on in modern Barbados.

Of my grandparents, it was my glamorous grandmother Muriel who was the more shrewd businessperson, and on the rare occasions when Vere's pride would allow her to manage their affairs, things would begin to improve. But these interludes were short-lived; Vere was very conventional in this regard and insisted that a woman's place was at home. Nonetheless, she stayed married to this flawed and complicated man for almost half a century. In their long and tumultuous marriage, my granny Muriel would bear him seven children, two of whom died soon after birth. In many ways, her life was a harder one than she had been prepared for. As a little girl, I would sit on her capacious lap at the dining table at Plumgrove as she flicked through the glossy fashion magazines that were her favourite escape from reality. I remember her motto, which was one that experience had clearly taught her to live by: 'It's a great life, if you don't weaken.'

20

Success is to be measured not so much by the position
that one has reached in life as by the obstacles which he
has overcome while trying to succeed.

Booker T. Washington

Thanks to my maternal family's prominent involvement in the sugar industry, I have been able to follow their story through the documents and records of several centuries. Tracing my black father's line is more of a challenge. Although my father's family had links with the industry – indeed, in Barbados it was almost impossible not to – they were not themselves planters, so the history I have been able to uncover is far more recent.

My grandfather Egbert Augustus Stuart was born in the late 1800s, and his forerunners had probably laboured as cane cutters on the Springhead plantation in St James on the west of the island. In his twenties, Egbert Stuart married a woman named Louisa Rock, from St Lucy, and the couple settled in an area called Black Rock, which was favoured by the black middle classes after the turn of the century. For much of his career, Egbert Stuart worked as the senior steward at the Bridgetown Club. This exclusive retreat in the heart of the capital was a genuine power hub, preferred by the island's white elite: affluent planters, politicians and professionals who met to discuss local affairs, make deals and forge alliances. (It admitted black people

349

as members only in the 1970s.) Egbert had a rather Victorian perspective on many things and was a stern disciplinarian. He believed devoutly in the maxim 'Spare the rod and spoil the child' and his preferred method of chastisement was the infamous tamarind switch. His marriage to my grandmother was not an easy fit. Granny Louise was in many ways the real 'paterfamilias'. According to my father, she initiated many of the activities that would have been the formal responsibility of a father: choosing the schools the children should attend, saving for a house in a more upmarket locality and the purchase of the family's first car. She was a much more voluble and flamboyant character than her husband, who loved cooking and gossiping with her woman friends and, after their children had left home, the couple would separate. In subsequent years my grandmother would rather melodramatically refer to her failed marriage as 'my tragedy at the altar'.

My father, Kenneth Lamonte Stuart, was born on 16 June 1920 and his childhood was typical of the era. The Bridgetown of his youth had almost as many horse and donkey carts as it did cars, and many of the island's street lamps were lit by gaslight. Across Barbados, people from the various villages gathered under them at night to chat and dissect the day's doings. His little community had a public bath that served both sexes and stank of disinfectant. When not at school he preferred to be by the sea; he was an excellent swimmer, and he spent a lot of time there bathing and splashing with friends, or watching the fisherman pull in their huge nets filled with silvery, twitching flying fish. Tired and hungry, he and his friends would return to Black Rock and with a penny buy a 'cutter', a round salt bread sandwich stuffed with fish, or fragrant coconut cakes, shavings of coconut bound with sugar syrup. The rest of the time he spent running, jumping and climbing with friends. His was the eternal brinkmanship of childhood, searching for adventure without provoking the heavy hand of my grandfather.

★

In a society as stratified as that of Barbados, children like my father from modest black families had just one route to advancement: education. Had he been born two decades earlier he would have had no chance at all. In a 1905 edition of the planter newspaper, the *Barbados Agricultural Report*, an editorial expressed the ruling caste's attitude to the education of those of African descent: 'Some book learning is of course essential, but the mistake of conveying to the child the idea that such education as he acquires at school is calculated to make him eligible for the highest honours in life must be avoided.' So it was no wonder then that for many children of my father's generation the very possibility of an education felt like a tremendous privilege.

My father's formal education began at the age of five, and between the ages of eight to twelve he went to a local school called Wesley Hall. Here little brown- and black-skinned boys experienced a traditional colonial education, one that was a mimicry of that taught to children in the classrooms of England. In neatly pressed uniforms, and seated at their rudimentary desks, they were taught about thrones and empires, about William the Conqueror and the Battle of Hastings. Their own history – Barbados's tempestuous and bloody story of sugar, slavery and colonialism – was the elephant in the room and barely spoken of. The children were also constantly reminded of the island's ties to the 'mother country': the links between Big England and Little England had not been broken since the seventeenth century and the reign of James I.

A British school inspector arrived regularly in an official car with a miniature British flag flying on its bonnet to inspect the facilities and the classes. He also made other visits to mark special occasions such as 'Empire Day' or the monarch's birthday. At these times the school was festooned with Union Jacks; they flew from the mast atop the building, they were looped together in banners that draped the walls, and for good measure oversized versions were pinned to doors. After a lecture in which the boys were reminded of the 'God-ordained' role of the British Empire to bring peace and prosperity to the world, the children were prompted to cheer 'hip-hip-hooray' in perfect unison and pledge allegiance to the monarch:

> God save our gracious king,
> Long live our noble king,
> God save the king.

My mother, Barbara, has similar memories of her school. She had started at Foundation in 1937, at the age of eight. With its long history, it is a school with a strong sense of tradition – indeed, the uniform she wore then was virtually the same as the one that the girls wear today: a yellow dress and navy-blue belt with a striped diagonal tie in yellow and blue, topped with a panama hat held on by an elastic band under the chin. And, as at Wesley Hall, her education was absurdly Anglo-Saxon. On an island where the changes of weather were predicated on notes of hot and dry, wet and humid, my mother recollects being recruited for a play about the seasons. She played autumn, a time of year that she had never experienced, dressed in a costume of paper leaves of rust and yellow. She also recollects the school putting on a play based on Dick Whittington, but since she was brown-skinned she could not play the female lead. 'I played Dick,' she recalled, while 'the little white girls played the pretty-up parts'. In colonial Barbados it took a long time before 'black' was allowed to be 'beautiful'. Her educational opportunities were even more proscribed than my father's, since very few of the scholarships available at either secondary or university level were open to female students.

For my father, Kenneth, his only hope of progressing beyond Wesley Hall was through winning an exhibition scholarship that would give him the opportunity to move on to one of the elite secondary schools. As he was under twelve, this was a verbal examination that demonstrated his articulacy and his knowledge of British history. He passed with distinction and was presented with his award at a school ceremony where he and the other winners were reminded that that 'the future was theirs'. Once again his timing was good: for many decades these scholarships were the sole preserve of the lighter-skinned children of the middle classes, and allegations of bias against darker-skinned applicants were frequent.

His scholarship gave him a place at Harrison College, then the island's premier boys' secondary school and still today one of most prestigious educational institutions in the region. It was founded in 1733 by the Bridgetown merchant Thomas Harrison, who intended it to serve as a 'Public Free School for the poor and indigent boys of the parish', though of course this did not include those of African descent. By 1870 the school's role had shifted to serve the coloured community. Later it became a grammar school, 'for children of the better classes', both white and coloured, and in July 1923 a newspaper quoting the school magazine, the *Harrisonian*, summed up its new raison d'être:

> The school intended to supply a thoroughly sound secondary education, first satisfying all the requirements of pupils intended for commercial pursuits, secondly by preparing for both English Public School and University and for Competitive Examinations through which every department of the Public Service is now accessible.

Once again, Harrison College made no concessions to its Caribbean context; there was no place for colonial history or local perspectives and the entire curriculum was orientated towards inculcating the culture of the colonial power. It was an entirely British affair, with teachers imported from Britain, using British textbooks as dictated by the Cambridge examination syllabus. British hymns were sung and poems by Kipling and Dryden were recited. And so young men like my father graduated with 'a good knowledge of the Greek classics and read North American novelists but showed no knowledge of or interest in Caribbean or African affairs'. By exposing children only to the products of Anglo-Saxon culture and banning any exploration of the island's history or African traditions, the students were encouraged to see black people as ignorant, and their customs as primitive and risible. As one contemporary of my father's explained:

> Colonialism was not just an economic and political system, it was also a cultural system. Loyalty to empire was created through language, as well as through the church and the school. Both of these institutions taught the superiority of Europeans, their beliefs and their culture, and the inferiority of Africans, and, for that matter, of all non-British peoples.

The poet H.A. Vaughan, who has been described as the first Barbadian Black Power poet, wrote in these years:

> Turn sideways now and let them see
> What loveliness escapes the schools,
> Then turn again, and smile, and be
> The perfect answer to those fools
> Who always prate of Greece and Rome,
> 'The face that launched a thousand ships'
> And such like things, but keep tight lips
> For burnished beauty nearer home.

The writer George Lamming also looked back on his education with dismay:

Today I shudder to think how a country so foreign to our instincts could have achieved the miracle of being called Mother . . . Empire was not a very dirty word, and seemed to bear little relation to those forms of domination we now call Imperialist . . . the colonial experience of my generation was almost wholly without violence. No violence, no concentration camp, no mysterious disappearances of hostile natives, no army encamped . . . The Caribbean endured a different kind of subjugation. It was a terror of the mind.

But beyond the classroom, the atmosphere was charged with the possibility of real change. During the 1930s, economic hardship had done more than provoke despair, it had also sparked a spirit of resistance that had not been seen before, as the working classes embraced a form of self-help and organizational independence. These developments were largely inspired by Marcus Garvey's pan-Caribbean and international 'Black Power' movement. As one historian noted: 'Garvey's politics, more than any other single factor, rooted within the consciousness of Barbadian workers the fact that only organised mass political action could deliver in a general way those social and economic objectives that they had pursued through their friendly societies.'

In 1937, the agitation of the workers came to a head, when the black majority attended a rally headlined by the charismatic Trinidadian labour leader Clement Payne. In his hypnotic speech he called the workers to action. Regarded as a dangerous rabble-rouser, he was almost immediately put on trial in July of that year for deceiving the immigration authorities that he had been born in Barbados. His followers were outraged. Determined to demonstrate against the arrest, a crowd gathered outside the governor's house, only to discover that Payne had already been deported.

Incensed, the workers converged on Bridgetown and a riot

ensued. Private and public property was targeted and cars were smashed. The demonstrations were squashed temporarily, but flared up again a few days later on 26 July, when the protesters, armed with bottles, sticks and stones, converged on the commercial area of the city, smashing office fronts and store windows and overturning cars. They besieged the employees of the Barbados Mutual Office in their building, and threatened to burn it down. At first the authorities retaliated with a blank volley of shots. But this failed to deter the demonstrators and by midday on the 27th, when the police had been instructed to use any means necessary to 'restrain or subdue the rebels', they regrouped with fixed bayonets, and shot live rounds at the crowd. Several people were killed; the demonstration broke up and the protesters fled. Meanwhile, outside the capital, workers had been looting planters' stocks and raiding potato fields. In response, the planters raised a force of special constables who killed a number of them. In total fourteen blacks were killed, forty-seven injured and 500 arrested. One hundred years after emancipation, as one historian concluded, the 'open wounds of colonisation in Barbados were there for all to see'.

In response to these events the Barbados Labour Party, led by the up-and-coming politician Grantley Adams, was launched in October 1938. It was a middle-class movement designed 'to provide political expression for the island's law-abiding inhabitants', as distinct from the so-called 'lawless poor' that Payne was associated with. The following year, in 1939, Adams diagnosed the island's problems. Reporting to a Royal Commission appointed to 'investigate social and economic conditions in the West Indies', Adams stated: 'I suggest that the plantation system is basically the cause of our trouble, and I think that the system which has survived in Barbados for three hundred years, of having a small, narrow, wealthy class and a mass of cheap labour on the other side, should be abolished.'

★

For my father, meanwhile, the educational saga continued. As before, his future after secondary school pivoted on a very limited number of variables. His only chance for a first-rate university education was enshrined in the 'Barbados Scholarship', which funded one student each year to go abroad and study at a top university in either England or Canada. It was an intensely competitive situation, since every academically gifted child on the island applied. On his second attempt my father was successful and in 1940 he set off on his intellectual adventure. Traditionally, he would have gone to Oxford or Cambridge, but with the outbreak of the Second World War he was sent to McGill University in Canada, on a slow banana boat, to read the Classics. He was twenty years old and he would not see his island home again for twelve years.

His memories of Montreal are fragmentary – life in a big northern city; the unimaginable cold of a Canadian winter; all those white faces! When he was not studying, he worked to supplement his grant, labouring at the Steel Company of Canada and Ford; it was a far cry from the perpetual sunshine and languorous rhythms of Caribbean life. Determined to study medicine, he applied, despite the ongoing war, to go to Britain to study. It was probably a fortuitous choice, since his opportunities in Canada were still restricted by the endemic racial prejudice there. One white West Indian who applied abroad to study medicine in 1930 was told by an unnamed Canadian university that they could offer him a place only if he was white, 'but if I were coloured they would be unable to admit me as they did not have facilities for coloured men to be examining white women in the Dept. of Obstetrics and Gynaecology'.

In 1942 Kenneth and a handful of other West Indians gathered in Halifax, Nova Scotia, and boarded a ship for England. Although his journey took place three centuries later than George Ashby's, it was just as dangerous. The convoy in which they travelled was on permanent alert as they crossed the war-torn Atlantic, and one of the ships was torpedoed along the way. My father's ship docked in Avonmouth, the port of the city of Bristol. What lingers in his memory of that first night on English soil was the meagre meal he and his companions were served, the product of wartime rationing: white fish on a white plate, accompanied by an unidentifiable green vegetable and three small boiled potatoes.

The following day, the group of students got on a train to London and moved into a hostel for international students near Russell Square. Life in the city was punctuated by the shrill sound of air raid warnings and retreats to shelters in tube stations, where cups of tea were doled out and camaraderie shared. It was a curiously convivial time for my father despite the danger, since so many West Indians he knew had come to the capital to study, work or volunteer for the war effort. These included people like my aunt Margaret Clairmonte, who believed devoutly that it was her duty as a British subject to serve the mother country. Her picture now hangs in the Barbados Museum, a young woman posing in her WAAF (Women's Auxiliary Air Force) uniform, smiling proudly for the camera. Then there was my father's great friend Errol Barrow, who would become one of Barbados's most revered and long-serving prime ministers. He was one of a batch of twelve brave and patriotic Barbadians recruited that year specifically for the Royal Air Force, only half of whom came back.

Despite their contributions to the British war effort, there are virtually no black faces represented in the English accounts of Second World War servicemen. The Americans are there, and the Canadians, as well as Poles and Australians, but not the West Indians. The academic Benedict Anderson has argued that a nation can be defined as an 'imagined community' because it is impossible, in even the smallest states, that an individual can ever know 'most of their fellow-members, meet them or even hear of them', so representation is particularly important. By excluding these West Indians who served and often died for the 'mother country', Britain has not only betrayed their memories; it has created a self-image that is a lie.

In 1943 my father Kenneth left the beleaguered capital for Queen's University Belfast, where he would remain for five years taking his medical degree. Whereas in London there were enough black faces to provoke a degree of hostility, in Belfast blacks were so novel that most people were merely curious. (Of the scores of young men who made up that year's intake only three were not white.) In contrast to the staid formality of the English, he found the Irish closer in character to the West Indians: more relaxed and with an innate joy in listening to and telling stories. After Belfast, he would spend a couple of years in Liverpool and Edinburgh gaining postgraduate degrees, by which time he had been away from Barbados for over a decade.

In the years my father was absent from the island the rate of change accelerated considerably. As a result of the widespread social and political unrest, the British government had sent a commission to the West Indies in 1939 which made wide-ranging recommendations around education, immigration and the island's financial management. Then the voting franchise was extended, which meant that the 1944 general election involved a much bigger electoral population. For the first time the Elector's Association, the planters' party, was under attack. On 4 November 1944, the *Barbados Observer* wrote:

> Throughout the history of this island, it has been dominated by a small and selfish clique and it is indeed remarkable that now this clan senses that it has reached a crisis, it has actually had the shamelessness and temerity to publicly appeal to the people of this island and ask them to help them consolidate their weakening status.

Two weeks later the paper noted:

> Barbados is in revolt against the status quo. Throughout the country thousands of middle class and working class men and women are voicing the most determined protests against poverty and unemployment. These thousands are resolved to put more of the wealth in the colony at the service of the people . . . this spirit may well be called the NEW DEMOCRACY.

In the post-war years, this confidence was palpable across the entire Caribbean region, where the efforts of the commission began to bear fruit. Its effects, the historian C.L.R. James argued, manifested themselves in 'vastly greater opportunities for West Indians in their own country and abroad'. In Barbados, for example, universal suffrage was established in 1950 and new educational reforms soon began to open up opportunities for a wider range of the population. Newly emboldened, excited West Indians across the region also began to look forward to the thought of achieving 'dominion status' and a measure of control over their own affairs.

These aspirations soon became to seem achievable. Financially crippled by the war, England had become eager to offload its expensive colonies, so the only criterion necessary for independence was that the state in question could afford the obligations of this transition. The floodgates had been opened by India, Pakistan and Ceylon (now Sri Lanka) in the period 1947–8. Then, one by one, the African colonies also shed their ties with Britain, including Sudan in 1956, Ghana in 1957, and Nigeria in 1960.

Much of the Caribbean region's restless longings for independence during this period were projected onto one sport: cricket. This arcane game is inexplicable to many parts of the globe, not least because its languorous rhythms, in which matches can last for days, seem so antithetical to the pace of modern life. To many the game, so popular in the erstwhile British colonies, seems like a pastime from an obsolete world, conjuring up images of bygone scenes of rural England, large country houses and young English aristocrats lolling about on grassy knolls. So it may seem strange, even somewhat absurd, today that a game should become the symbolic battleground between the mother country and these newly revitalized colonies. But on closer examination it makes perfect sense. Cricket was intrinsically bound up with the notion of 'Englishness' and the game became a way of inculcating colonial values in colonial subjects and impressing on them the superiority of 'Britishness'. Thus the sport, an obsession at all levels of Barbadian society, which purported to be an agent for social cohesion, also served to enhance the island's rigid social structure and its inflexible social distinctions.

Cricket was particularly close to my family's heart. In the 1940s my mother's eldest sister, Muriel, would court and then marry a young man who would become a cricketing legend. Born on 17 January 1926, Clyde Leopold Walcott came from a background not dissimilar to that of my aunt. His father was a solid member of the middle class, an engineer with the Barbados Advocate, who lived in the comfort of a home built for a plantation manager. A big bruiser of a brown-skinned man, he became one of the 'three Ws', along with Frank Worrell and Everton Weekes, who have been described by one cricket aficionado as 'possibly the greatest array of talent in the middle order of any batting eleven in history'. Clyde Walcott would go on to play his part in the West Indies' historic triumph on English soil in 1950, when he scored 168 not out. This, the West Indies' first longed-for and deliciously sweet victory over their colonial masters, was a turning point in the island's self-esteem. By beating the English literally 'at their own game', the West Indians never felt quite so diminished again. Their conquest not only asserted their equality and independence, it demonstrated their skill, panache and tenacity.

In September 1955 Hurricane Janet ravaged the island. In contrast to the great storms of the past, however, modern-day meteorological science meant the islanders had at least been forewarned. They took the normal precautions: covering glass, boarding up doors, storing water. But everyone believed that Janet would hit the north of the island, and instead it hit the south and east, with Christ Church – where Plumgrove was located – getting a particular battering. The winds began blowing up in the morning and soon built into a category three hurricane. With its two-feet-thick walls, the family plantation was designed to withstand a tempest, so my grandmother and grandfather, my mother and four of her siblings were initially relatively sanguine, and took shelter upstairs in the living room. My mother remembered being mesmerized by the sight of a cup and saucer lifted by the wind and moving several feet from the dresser to the table, before settling together there unbroken.

As the hurricane gathered strength it was clear that sheltering upstairs was ill-advised; the wind had found its way under the roof. So the family fled downstairs to the basement, where they were joined by many of the tenants on the land, who knew that their little wooden chattel houses had no hope of surviving such a storm, as well as a menagerie of animals including sheep and goats. There this ill-assorted group stayed for several hours, occasionally nipping upstairs during lulls in the storm to replenish supplies from the kitchen and check out the damage. My mother remembers the mood being tense: 'People were frightened. They were anxious about their friends and families, and worried that their homes wouldn't be there when it was all over.' They barely spoke and instead watched in amazement as sheet after sheet of galvanized steel, ripped by the wind from people's houses, 'flew through the air like birds'.

By nightfall it was all over; much of the plantation roof had been blown off, but the section over the bedrooms had held. The full extent of the damage became clear with the dawn: trees were flattened, furniture destroyed, debris was everywhere. But the Ashby family and their fellow refugees had been lucky; some of the estate's other tenants had taken shelter in a new church on Lodge Road, assuming that it would be sturdily built, but once the ferocity of the wind got going, the structure collapsed and several were crushed to death inside.

By the time Hurricane Janet had passed over the island, it had killed thirty-eight people and made over 20,000 homeless. That same day Janet slammed the neighbouring island of St Lucia with such ferocity that fifteen- to twenty-foot waves were reported to have engulfed the coast. By the time it hit Mexico and blew through Belize and back through the Grenadines it was a category five hurricane, responsible for millions of pounds' worth of damage and the deaths of over 800 people. In tribute to its terrible power, the name 'Janet' was retired, never to be used for a hurricane again. At a remembrance service held in Barbados fifty-five years later, one speaker stated that while Janet was 'not the worst thing that ever happened to the island, it was the most terrible thing that had occurred in living memory'.

This memorable storm was followed the next year by a memorable meeting, that of my mother and father. He first saw her walking through Bridgetown. When asked today what he thought then, he says jovially: 'Pretty good!' But friends say he was smitten. Ferreting around his social circle, he finally found out who she was and discovered that they had mutual friends, who, pressured by my father, invited the pair to a 'little get-together'. Theirs was primarily an epistolary courtship because my father, Kenneth, was doing medical research on the neighbouring island of St Kitts. As was the tradition in the conservative Barbados of the 1950s, my father also paid assiduous court to my mother's parents. His charm offensive worked on my granny Muriel but was less successful with my grandfather Vere, who referred to him rather dismissively as 'the doctor boy'. No doubt Vere's resistance was in part because my mother was his favourite child and no man would have been good enough for her. But it is also possible that my rather conventional grandfather would have preferred her to marry one of the brown-skinned boys from their own social circle rather than this dark-skinned interloper.

Despite my grandpa's reservations, Kenneth and Barbara married in 1958. It was in many ways a good match for both of them. My father got a bright beauty from an old plantation family; and my mother got one of the 'coming men', that dynamic minority of black Barbadians who had seized newly available educational opportunities to take a prominent place in the professions. The event itself was low-key. Much to the amusement of his friends, my father was green and sweating throughout the wedding ceremony; apparently the clergyman, a real old-style blood and thunder merchant, had taken him aside before the service and given him a stern lecture about the responsibilities and commitments of married life. The couple honeymooned in Barbados, at Sam Lord's Castle, the hotel which had once been the estate of one of the island's most notorious buccaneers. Afterwards, Kenneth returned to work at the university campus in Jamaica and awaited his new bride, as one friend said, 'in a terrible state of nerves'. Several weeks later my mother packed up her existence, boarded a small boat and set off on a week-long sea journey, to start life with a man whom she admits she 'didn't know very well'.

The life of the newly-weds was centred around the Jamaican campus of the University College of the West Indies, the first university in the Caribbean. Before it had been established in 1948, those hoping to do any further academic studies were compelled, as my father had been, to leave their islands. It represented a huge step forward for the Caribbean sense of independence and its importance continued to grow as, one by one, the sugar islands' local governments, including that of Barbados, decided to extend the benefits of free secondary education to all children. These developments had far-reaching repercussions: now colour, poverty or social status was no longer a bar to receiving a higher education. Although social class still was – and remains – a strong factor in educational achievement, it had now become possible for a bright child from humble origins to 'break through'.

In 1952, Kenneth joined the Department of Medicine as a Medical Registrar, and steadily worked his way up through the academic ranks from lecturer to reader to professor and then Dean of the Medical School. He was part of a coterie of academics who were absorbed in this pioneering project of bringing higher education to a region that previously had none. They were an idealistic and heterogeneous group drawn from across the world: our neighbourhood included Indians, Africans, Europeans and Jews, as well as every possible variety of West Indian. There was an unspoken utopianism underpinning the whole enterprise. The 1960s were beckoning and everyone (or almost everyone) hoped that our little united nations was the world of the future.

My mother and father settled into university housing at no. 2 College Common, where, in 1962, I was born, followed by my brother, Steven, eighteenth months later. These early years together were interrupted by two successive research fellowships to Harvard University, when our family moved into an apartment in Cambridge, Massachusetts, and where I first saw snow. On our return to Jamaica, we moved a few doors down to no. 7 College Common, where I spent most of my childhood and where, in 1968, my sister, Lynda, was born. Set in two acres of grounds, no. 7 was a bungalow-style house of a type common in the Caribbean. There was a veranda at the front that led to open-plan living and dining areas. The family's sleeping quarters and my father's study were to the left of this room, and to the right were a kitchen, laundry room and two small rooms, one of which was usually rented out to a student at the university and the other of which was for a live-in maid. Domestic help was ubiquitous in the Caribbean of my childhood, and our family was supported by a regiment of nannies, maids and gardeners, many of whom were in flight from labouring on the land.

The miracle of no. 7 was in the land. The area directly in front of the house was big enough to play a game of rounders or cricket on, while the rest of the grounds were planted with an abundance of exotic fruit trees, which the previous tenant, an agriculturalist, had gathered from across the tropics. There was a Bombay mango tree in the front of the house and a Julie mango tree in the back. There were three types of oranges, and varieties of fruit trees common in the Caribbean: a Jamaican cherry which made a delicious ice; a guinnep tree, whose round green skin covered a sweet slippery interior; and an ackee tree, whose fruit is poisonous unless it is picked at precisely the right time, and which is the main ingredient in Jamaica's signature dish, ackee and salt fish. We even had a cashew nut tree from Africa and an oatahite apple tree, which bore purple pear-shaped fruit with cool white flesh and was indigenous to the South Pacific. The sheer vegetal exuberance of our garden made it a magnet for the neighbourhood's children, who congregated there, climbing the trees and scavenging for fruit. Sheltered from the poverty and exploitation of our forefathers, we were a generation of black children who could blithely enjoy the wonders of a Caribbean childhood.

Every summer we returned to Barbados to spend time with our extended family. As a young girl I was particularly impressed by the austere habits of my paternal grandfather, Egbert. In his later years, he ate one meal a day, went to church every evening, and whenever I saw him, no matter how hot the weather, he was dressed in a sombre grey three-piece suit, with belt, braces and hat. After his divorce, Egbert had remained in the family home, and we used to visit him there, in a hot wooden house perched alongside a main road. It was impeccably clean and somewhat crowded with the conventional bric-a-brac of a Caribbean home of that period: religious iconography, porcelain figurines, crystal vases, chiming clocks.

My paternal grandmother, Louise, meanwhile had become a hotelier, owning and running the Blue Caribbean, an establishment that fronted onto the sea and was situated on the corner of St Lawrence Gap, now one of the busiest tourist strips on the island. Our family stayed there when we visited, and as small children my brother, sister and I would play in the sea and, to her annoyance, trail sand across the balcony where guests would sit to enjoy the view. In her latter years she would share her life with an elderly gay Englishman called Robin, who helped her to run the hotel and while away the evening hours. I remember her as a rather exquisite creature, an ebony-skinned woman who favoured large hooped earrings and colourful kaftans.

We also spent time with my maternal family at Plumgrove, which was still a working plantation farmed by working-class Barbadians. Our father would drive our rental car up the bumpy rocky track known as 'The Gap' past the large standpipe from which water was collected and in which nutmeg-skinned boys bathed naked. At the road's end, past the tenants' chattel houses, was the large two-storey stone house. It was dominated by an imposing central staircase so steep that, long after I could walk, I would climb up it on hands and knees. This led to a gallery area, which in turn led to a living-cum-dining area that stretched almost the entire length of the house, and was decorated with a mixture of local furniture and antiques. My grandfather Vere was gone – he had died a year before my birth

– but my grandmother Muriel was still there holding court, sitting me on her lap while she read magazines or shelled peas. The three bedrooms overlooked the cane fields at the back of the house, while the small rudimentary bathroom and kitchen were sidelined to the east of the house. Downstairs two great double doors opened onto a dark cool space which included a few more bedrooms and vast play and storage areas. It was down here, I remember hearing with awe, that my mother sheltered alongside her family, the field workers and the livestock, as the worst hurricane of the last century raged around them.

Immediately surrounding the house was a meticulously culti-vated garden, dominated by large tamarind and frangipani trees whose flowers and leaves almost obscured the house; these were offset by hibiscus, pines and bougainvillea that added an irresistible scent to the air. To the west there was a small grotto of mysterious origin, with two little arches standing amidst the plants; in front of the house were the exotic trees that provided fruit like custard apples and sour-sops. To the north stood a covered well, the subject of many tales among us children: that if you threw in a penny into it your wish would come true; that it was so deep that you could not hear the stone splash when it finally hit the water; that a slave had once drowned in it and the spirit now haunted the property.

On the east of the house, near the laundry lines, were the remnants of a drip stone, whose provenance was so ancient it dates the property back to the seventeenth century. The drip stone, an invention of the Amerindians who once populated the region, purified water, filtering rainfall through its two-tiered edifice of coral stone and collecting it in an impervious marble bowl at its base. The dripstone continued its work even when I was a child, but the bowl to collect the fresh water had been moved to feed the pigs, so it leaked incessantly, its clear sweet water evaporating in the bright sunshine.

Some days we would venture beyond this magic circle, to the

pond draped in vines adjacent to the house or to the wood with its mahogany and fustic trees, where the ground was covered in a tangle of weeds which grew around their swollen ebony roots. At other times we rampaged through the cane fields, never waiting long before somebody would cut us a 'finger' of cane so that we could suck the sweetness from its fibrous strands, just as my mother had done so many years before. At night we sat around the house, as the cane shivered in the breeze and the ubiquitous cane rats scratched on the roof.

21

*The sigh of History rises over ruins, not over landscapes,
and in the Antilles there are few ruins to sigh over, apart
from the ruins of sugar estates and abandoned forts.*

Derek Walcott

In 1966, when I was four years old, my parents returned to
Barbados to celebrate the island's independence. For many of
the islanders, sovereignty had seemed a very long time coming.
Beyond their shores, they heard the rhetoric of the American
Civil Rights and Black Power movements, and they had
been inspired by the radical politics of Black Panther Stokely
Carmichael and the towering Malcolm X. So when two other
notable British West Indian islands, Jamaica and Trinidad,
declared their own independence in 1963, it seemed the time
had truly come. Two years later, in late 1965, Barbados's
Democratic Labour Party, led by my father's old friend, the war
hero Errol Barrow, was ready to present to Parliament a draft
Constitution calling for independence. This was rubber-stamped
by the British government the following year, and plans for the
celebrations began.

Alongside a flood of other ecstatic Barbadians who believed
that independence was 'the road to destiny', my parents flew
back to the island. On 29 November 1966, a crowd of about
50,000 people gathered at the Garrison Savannah, the vast green

situated on the outskirts of the capital, Bridgetown, where races are held, cricket is played and concerts are enjoyed. At midnight, they watched as the Governor General and the Prime Minister lowered the Union Jack that had flown over Barbados for more than 300 years. Then the new blue and gold flag of an independent Barbados was raised in its place. Afterwards my mother in her black and white sequined dress danced the night away in my father's arms, to the music of Diana Ross and the Supremes.

Perhaps it had been 'the road to destiny' after all, since Barbados was one of the few ex-colonies that fared better after independence than it had done before. This was partly to do with the rise of the tourist industry. The business of entertaining visitors had begun in a gentle way in the early twentieth century, when the island began to attract holidaymakers from Britain and from North and South America. According to the historian F. A. Hoyos, 'Some of these tourists [visited] Barbados during the winter months, staying at the island's hotels which were soon to enter a boom period. Others, notably the South Americans, came from Brazil on the Lamport and Holt ships, which were accustomed to stop at the island for essential supplies like coal and water.' They would stay for a longer periods, renting 'bay houses', chiefly in the district known as Worthing, which had taken its name from the English seaside town.

Barbados quickly learned the art of catering to visitors, and hotels like the Crane and the Marine began appearing along its golden coastline. By 1912, the Colonial Secretary was able to claim that 'the colony owes much of its increasing prosperity to the visitors who stay in the island'. The new wave of tourists was attracted by the idyllic vistas – the panoramic blue skies, the sparkling seas and the pale, sun-warmed sand – that had bewitched the original planters, and had kept luring pirates, dreamers and entrepreneurs for centuries. There was a rapid increase in the development of the tourist industry after the Second World War, particularly with the invention of the jetliner in the 1950s. And by the 1970s, tourism had overtaken sugar as the island's most valuable industry. This transition from agricultural outpost of empire to independent luxury resort would soon begin to alter the lives of the islanders just as comprehensively as the 'white gold' once had.

Barbados for us was a holiday haven, peaceful and safe, in contrast to the island where we had based our lives. For in Jamaica the post-independence dream was decaying. It was a shocking reversal for the English colony that was predicted to be 'most likely to succeed' after emancipation. But by the middle of the 1970s, the traditional star of the anglophone colonies was in chaos, torn apart by political factionalism. On one side was the left-wing People's National Party (PNP), led by the charismatic Michael Manley, on the other the conservative Jamaica Labour Party (JLP), led by Edward Seaga. Both of them were battling it out for political control of the country and the opportunity to exploit its wealth. The intensity of this conflict was exacerbated by Cold War politics. Jamaica was a key player in the region, and so external forces quickly became involved in the island's clashes; and there were allegations that money and guns were being smuggled into the island by the American CIA as well as the Communist regime in nearby Cuba, both groups hoping to sway the island towards their particular ideological position.

Most of the violence was centred around the inner city of Kingston, in places like Trench Town, which had originally been established as a social housing project for workers, but had by the 1970s become a place for the poor and dispossessed. These ghettos were divided into factional terrains, one section claimed for the PNP, the other for the JLP; and politicians from both sides provided their supporters with guns and funds in order to cement votes and loyalties. Here illiterate teenage boys, armed with Kalashnikovs or US-import Glocks, roamed the streets picking off enemies who threatened the integrity of their territory. Inevitably some of the money and weapons went to seed the narcotics business. And thus out of the smouldering ashes of these violent streets emerged the 'Yardies', who became one of the most significant crime cartels in the world. It was a frightening and dangerous time, with violence erupting unpredictably and constantly.

At least some of the country's problems had their roots in Jamaica's brutal slave past. As the richest of the British colonies, it had attracted the most rapacious attention from its colonizers and suffered the most terrible cruelty and abasement of all the English sugar islands. The violent resentment this provoked had simmered for centuries and was now spilling over into all areas of Jamaican society. By the midpoint of the decade the professional middle classes were migrating from the island as quickly as they could, and in 1976 my family also took flight. The country we were destined for was the very one that George Ashby had left behind over three centuries before.

We landed in a country that was a cauldron of bitter rhetoric about migration which left us in no doubt how unwelcome we were. The backstory to this had begun in the post-war period, when Britain had experienced a shortage of labour in key areas of its reconstruction programme, such as transport, catering and the National Health Service. Desperate for new workers, the government launched a widespread advertising campaign in the Caribbean to lure the islanders to Britain. It played on their loyalty to the 'mother country', and stressed their patriotic duty to help with rebuilding the nation. As a result, in the years spanning 1948–73, over half a million Caribbean people migrated to Britain, most of them arriving before 1962. These people became known as the 'Windrush generation', after the first ship of these migrants to dock in Britain. Most were Jamaican; only

25,247 or 8.5 per cent were Barbadians. But by the time we arrived in the 1970s, Britain was in recession and unemployment was rising, and a vociferous minority were demanding that these migrants be sent home. Their most respectable spokesperson was the Conservative MP Enoch Powell. His infamous 'rivers of blood' speech criticizing Commonwealth immigration, delivered at the Conservative Pary conference in 1968, had warned that Britain would disintegrate into open conflict if the repatriation of these people did not take place.

Even as a fourteen-year-old, I could appreciate that this was a debate beset with ironies. The British, who had first colonized the Caribbean and enriched themselves on black backs, now wanted people of Caribbean descent out of Britain because they were 'costing' the country too much. And their unworthiness to stay in England was justified by the very same racist theories that George Ashby and Robert Cooper had used to validate their own misuse of their slaves.

This was a particularly bewildering time for my family (despite the pride we felt at my father's knighthood that year for his services to medicine in the Caribbean and wider Commonwealth). We were socially isolated, as most of my parents' contemporaries had resettled in the United States or Canada. We had little in common with the Caribbean migrants who had arrived here in the post-war years. Our move was not a wager, or an attempt to transform our social position, but instead an astute career move for my father who, having been offered two jobs, one in America and one in Britain, chose the latter. Thus we had few familial links with the Windrush generation, and our life experience was very different. I can remember one of my Caribbean aunts, who came to study law, remarking snobbishly, 'We wouldn't talk to them there, so why should me mix with them here?'

In addition we were the sort of black family that did not then exist in the British imagination: affluent, professional, relatively cultured. So in our leisure time our mother would take us to the opera or ballet or piano recitals at the South Bank. And every day I set off for my exclusive private girls' school, where I was the only pupil of Afro-Caribbean descent, and my brother and sister did the same. In the Caribbean, where nearly everyone was like me, some shade of black, my race was largely irrelevant and I rarely thought of myself in that context. Now, for the first time in my life, I was acutely aware of my colour and all the stereotypes associated with it. Like my Barbadian ancestors – white, black and brown – I was discovering that the colour of my skin was what people noticed first and foremost.

As I grew up, I realized that my perpetual sense of displacement, the fate of most migrants, was something that would never leave me and that I could make a life nonetheless. I understood that migration was a kind of death, in which one's old self must be buried in order for a new self to be born, and that this move has made me who I am today. Inevitably, my feelings about the 'mother country' are rather ambivalent. So much here is now famililar and so much remains completely strange. My colour still enters the room before I do, and in some situations I have to work inordinately hard to make others put it aside. I know that despite the privileges of my upbringing, some people see me just as another inferior, troublesome black face. And I cannot help resenting the notion that while I am, according to some, not good enough to be British, my ancestors were nonetheless good enough to help build Britain, defend it and die for it.

I have settled in a country where the epic forces that created my family are still shaping British life, despite being largely unacknowledged. Sugar surrounds me here. Each year, thousands of locals and tourists visit the grand Tate Galleries without remembering that its collections were funded by the exploitative sugar company Tate & Lyle. And they wander though the grandeur of All Souls College, Oxford, without being aware that it was paid for by the profits generated by the slaves who toiled and died at the Codrington estate in Barbados. Sugar built the magnificent Harewood House in Leeds and many of the lovely mansions in Bristol's majestic Queen Square; while much of the profits that the West Indian proprietors collected in compensation for their 'losses' at emancipation fed back to the City of London, shoring it up and helping make it the dynamic, global business centre it has become.

Just as it is easy to forget that the 'white gold' of sugar paid for the bricks that built many of the grand buildings, homes, museums and collections that make up Britain's cultural heritage and enabled its cities to flourish, so too we ignore the fact that the impact of the trade in 'black ivory' is evident in the many-hued faces that throng their streets. Most of us do not understand the forces that brought our ancestors together from opposite ends of the world. Nor do we fully acknowledge that these forces continue to shape our communities and our life chances to this day. Over 150 years after slavery was abolished, Africans and the descendants of Africans remain markedly disadvantaged compared to the descendants of those who promoted the trade against them. The pernicious racial thinking that evolved to feed our insatiable hunger for sugar, and was used to justify our trangression of the laws of humanity, continues to influence us all.

In the Caribbean, the legacy of the sugar boom and the slave trade is not so easily ignored or forgotten. Although sugar is no longer the vibrant industry it once was, it is still cultivated, and the vista of endless fields of cane is still emblematic of the region, as is the sweet syrupy smell of the fields as they are fired and raised. Sugar has transformed the landscape and changed the region's ecosystem. It has shaped our economies, traditions and national identities. Indeed, by pulling together the unique racial mix of the islands – black, white, Amerindian, East Indian, Syrian, Chinese – it is written across our very faces.

The continuing politics of colour – the association of lighter complexions with status and influence, and darker skins with poverty and powerlessness – is still palplably alive, particularly among older people who remember the plantations with both horror and nostalgia. Many families like my own are mixed-race on both sides, blending the histories of both oppressor and oppressed.

Epilogue

We have come over a way that with tears has been watered,
We have come treading our past through the blood of the
slaughtered.
James Weldon Johnson

The great seventeenth-century wave of migration which saw hundreds of thousands of people leave England in search of a better life is so deeply embedded in global history that most of us do not give it conscious thought. But its reverberations continue to be felt. George Ashby and his continental counterparts would enrich Europe beyond its wildest imaginings and extend that subcontinent's influence and ideologies across the globe. They also transformed two continents, North and South America, as well as the glittering archipelago of islands that circle their waist. They populated these vast tracts of land, instigating seismic change in their landscape and social geography. And they introduced new species of animal and plant life into the places they settled, and made extinct many more. They also precipitated dramatic cataclysms among indigenous populations, not just through military action but also by exposing them to new diseases. And they instigated the arrival of millions of unwilling Africans, killing many a multitude in the process. (There are now over 100 million people of African descent in the New World.)

Mass emigration shaped the England that George Ashby left behind, as well. A nation that had never before tasted a potato or a tomato or smoked tobacco now embraced these new sensations with alacrity. England was flooded with exotic tropical foodstuffs, such as cocoa and sugar, that would transform its people's tastes and diets. These commodities would enrich the mother country exponentially, creating new industries and generating tens of thousands of new jobs. Through the traffic between the colonies and the various trading centres of the mother country, like Bristol and Liverpool, they encountered races they had never met before: Africans, Indians, Chinese. (By the eighteenth century the black population of London alone numbered around 20,000.) These encounters with new civilizations influenced the art, music and dress of Britain, just as the debates around the rights and wrongs of slavery stimulated an entirely new type of discussion about human rights, race and religion.

With all that grew out of this epic movement of people, did this act of mass resettlement achieve the goals of those who chose to participate in it? Were the exploitation and loss of life that resulted worth what they gained by coming to the New World? Certainly, in immediate terms, George Ashby had made the right decision: he and his children were undoubtedly better off than they would have been if they had stayed put. But whether their migration was a good thing overall is debatable. Lord Rosebery, the Liberal British statesman and towering figure of British politics at the end of the 1800s, called the British Empire 'the greatest secular agency for good that the world has seen'. But the economist J.A. Hobson, in his magnum opus *Imperialism*, published in 1902, argued that far from being a 'force for good', imperialism was merely a search for new markets and investment opportunities that had a deleterious effect not just on the majority of overseas subjects but also on those left behind in Britain.

Whatever its rights and wrongs, it is impossible not to be in awe of the daring of the migrants who found the strength in themselves to leave behind the limitations imposed on them in their home country, in the hope of finding something better elsewhere. Somehow they managed to push past the natural inertia that binds most of us to the familiar, and despite the fear of perishing in a strange land, they went anyway. Once there, the success of people like George Ashby was largely a result of how well he adjusted to the New World and how successfully he came to terms with the loss of the Old. After settling in Barbados, George Ashby, like many others, never looked back. But if he had abandoned his birthplace, he would discover to his chagrin that the turmoil of the mother country would still be felt in his new island home.

However, just as we admire these migrants' courage, we cannot help but lament the effect they had and profoundly question their judgement. In Barbados, the island on which George Ashby took his gamble, he and his eager contemporaries converted its topography from a primeval forest into a land as neat as a patchwork quilt, and transformed an uninhabited island into a European enclave and then a predominantly black one. What they brought together in the crucible of the New World was undoubtedly terrible. The sugar industry that they founded was an insatiable maw that swallowed millions of lives and spewed out a racist ideology that has blighted the lives of many to this day. In the process, a prelapsarian paradise became a moral quagmire, where black people were brutally and relentlessly exploited for others' financial enrichment.

But, to paraphrase the poet Sheena Pugh, 'sometimes things do not always go from bad to worse'. And modern-day Barbados has been something of a good-news story. Though only a tiny dot on the map, the island is buoyant. A stable economy, a well-developed infrastructure and an excellent education system have made it one of the most attractive places to live in the entire Caribbean. Thus the nation described in the mid-1960s as having 'a fairly homogeneous level of under-development' had, by

1992, climbed up the United Nations Development Programme Index to 'the highest placed country in the developing world', with almost 100 per cent literacy, an impressive human rights record, and one of the longest life expectancies of any country in the world.

Socially, too, it has evolved. With independence, the coloured elite, who had previously tended to ally themselves with the colonial authorities and the white plantocracy, realized that the realities of life in a functioning democracy demanded a new perspective, and that they could only maintain political power by collaborating with the black masses who made up the majority of voters. So the old colonial values were gradually thrown off and new national symbols were created. There was a resurgence of interest in the nation's African roots and an emergence of a new racial consciousness that gave pride to the majority of the island's inhabitants. Of course, some colonial fallout remains: there is a curious diffidence among islanders, and Barbados is still, as my father puts it, 'a colour-coded society', in which outside the workplace some white Barbadians tend to avoid socializing with their black counterparts.

Despite this, ties with Britain remain strong and survive in the army and in its legal and parliamentary systems. But Britain's influence on the island is waning, replaced by that of America, whose proximity to the island and status as a world superpower mean that it has – for now – more sway. But even American dominance in the region is being threatened by that rising star, China, which is working hard to secure influence in the Caribbean basin.

By the end of the twentieth century, Barbados had a greater claim than Jamaica to be considered the success story of the anglophone Caribbean. But how did an island so much smaller and poorer in natural resources emerge in front of its more naturally blessed neighbour? The Barbadian economist Courtney Blackman attributed the Barbadian economical miracle to several sources, including its lack of an indigenous population and its geographical position, which meant that it enjoyed a relatively peaceful early colonial career, especially in comparison to many other islands which changed hands numerous times or were forced to fight prolonged internal wars. The failure of the Bussa Rebellion too proved a historical gift to the island when set alongside the terrible price Haiti paid for its successful revolution. At the time, Haiti bucked the might of the European world, but it is now the most impoverished state in the region. Barbados also has the advantage of a long unbroken tradition of democratic government, whose leaders proved willing to invest in education, infrastructure and welfare programmes, rather than pocket the island's wealth for themselves. A strong commitment to the rule of law and religious tolerance also played their part. All of these factors, along with a goodly dose of luck, help to explain the island's unlikely triumph.

Tourism continues to play a major role. It drives the island's economy, but not without cost. Where once Barbados was dominated by plantations, now its most prestigious sites are occupied by resorts. Tourism has transformed Barbados from an agricultural economy to a service one; and it has changed the human and geographical face of the island. Just as the shift to sugar brought the first wave of English settlers, so tourism has introduced a second wave of British expatriates, as well as Americans and Canadians. In recent years the annual number of foreign visitors has at times exceeded one million people, almost five times the island's population. Tourism has sculpted the landscape just as definitively as 'King Sugar' once did: mangrove swamps have been dredged to create marinas; streams have been diverted or have dried up; and the glorious sight of the Caribbean coastline with its brilliant blue waters and sugar-fine white sand is increasingly hard to discern, obscured by high-rise condos and huge hotels.

As the exclusive glittering coastline has become more

economically important than the farm-friendly interior, the relationship of the citizens to the island they live on has shifted and the pattern of land ownership has changed. When my parents were young, the parish of St James was not especially popular with locals; it was overgrown and swampy, with only a few homes perched on the edge of the sea. Indeed, driving along that coast at night was positively spooky, with the large trees creating a dark canopy across the road, which buzzed with a cloud of mosquitoes. Now St James is dubbed 'the platinum coast', and the cost of property has been so inflated by the wealthy visitors who have built their holiday homes there that locals can only dream of living within its boundaries. In some places too their island has been reduced to a theme park in which the real has been superseded by the fake. Six Men's Village, one of the last places on the island where fishing boats are made, is destined to become a marina; and Port St Charles, a new tourist development, sits on a beach created with sand imported from Miami.

If today Barbados is the playground of the rich and famous, the legacy of sugar, slavery and settlement is becoming less visible with time. The fields of sugar cane are still a common sight across the island but the landscape is littered with the skeletons of the windmills that once powered the sugar factories. And virtually no slave dwellings remain standing. These fragile structures, cheaply built of wattle and daub, have long since succumbed to storms and the passage of time. The plantation great houses, designed to last, have of course fared much better. A few of these are still occupied by well-to-do families, while others have been converted into 'boutique' hotels. Still others have been co-opted by the 'heritage industry', converted into tourist attractions where visitors are taken on tours through their gracious rooms and beautiful grounds. Here, as in the American South, the old days have been commercially buffed and burnished, so that every trace of the blood and brutality of slavery has disappeared. Plantation life is sanitized into an era of gracious comfort, with the assumption that the visitor would identify with the slave owner and not the slave.

Meanwhile, beyond Barbados, sugar continued to leave a toxic trail of bloodshed, corruption and abuse wherever it moved. For much of the nineteenth century it was produced at considerable human cost in Cuba and Louisiana. In subsequent decades sugar continued to propel people across the globe. Chinese, Japanese, Korean and Filipino workers were transported to Hawaii to cultivate cane. In Australia, indentured Melanesians were imported to do the same. In the West Indies, the demands of sugar attracted a whole new population of workers: hundreds and thousands of Indian and Chinese labourers were transported to the Caribbean to endure a 'new system of slavery'. Just like the white indentured servants who were originally enticed over to settle the Americas, these new migrants were often deceived about the terms of their indenture and the conditions they would endure on arrival.

In the twentieth century, sugar has also been implicated in a number of violent struggles. In the 1930s it was the catalyst for the murder of tens of thousands of migrant Haitian workers by the Dominican dictator Trujillo. It also played a role in the Bay of Pigs fiasco in 1961, since it was Fidel Castro's appropriation of 70,000 acres of US-held sugar territory on Cuba that, in part, prompted American military action. And despite legal strictures to eliminate it, as the sugar historian Elizabeth Abbott explains, child labour continues to thrive in the sugar world, particularly in El Salvador, Dominica and parts of Brazil. In mainland America, the connection between sugar and forced labour did not end with emancipation. Throughout the first half of the last century, workers in the American sugar industry were exploited shamelessly. In 1942 the abuse of local workers was so egregious that the federal government indicted the United States Sugar

Corporation for 'peonage' or involuntary servitude, arguing that it transgressed the Third Amendment. So today, in Florida, American workers have been replaced by a steady stream of temporary Caribbean labourers, who are manipulated through their fear of deportation. Paid at rates that would be illegal for American workers, these temporary migrants are forced to subsist on poor food, have to live in ghastly barrack-style accommodation and are bullied mercilessly by abusive crew bosses. These terrible conditions have been maintained by the 'Big Sugar' lobby, which is as busy as ever supporting a system of protectionism, grants and quota levies which effectively pushes foreign-grown sugar out of the United States. Sugar and corruption still seem to go hand in hand.

The environmental impact of sugar remains appalling. Just as in Barbados, where the crop destroyed a complete natural ecosystem, in Florida too its legacy is disastrous: it bleeds water from the Everglades and pollutes its run-offs. In India, sugar mill waste has contaminated streams and coastal waters, killing off marine life. Its impact on global health has also been devastating. It is the key ingredient in ubiquitous products like Coca-Cola, ice cream and candy. It is also the hidden persuader in the most unlikely range of products from soup to ketchup and bread. As a result it is a significant contributor to obesity and diabetes, which is colloquially known as having 'sugar in the blood'. And, as in the past, it is the poor and the disadvantaged who suffer most from the dietary dangers associated with sugar. Indeed, the only upside in what Elizabeth Abbott calls sugar's 'relentlessly sad and bad story' is its potential to create ethanol, a cane-based, ecologically friendly fuel that might one day replace oil.

For the Ashby family specifically, the picture is largely positive. George Ashby spawned a succession of descendants who were raised in a place that he could never even have conceived of before he arrived. The world that became their home was a land of sunlight and warmth where they became accustomed to different foods, traditions and beliefs. They mutated from a traditional English family to a multi-hued one with white, brown and black faces. Of George Ashby's descendants who migrated in their turn, their fates have been as varied and complex. Many of them suffered extreme hardship, while others achieved great success and happiness. The pattern of their movement – to other islands in the Caribbean, to the US and UK, to Canada and as far away as Australia – has mirrored that of their fellow islanders. Those who remained in Barbados have done well, but perhaps suffered more from the complex psychological pressures that evolved from slavery, since it is still a country deeply influenced by the interactions of colour and class. My mother's two sisters found out for themselves how slowly social change comes about. One fell for a dark-skinned Barbadian; but even in the 1970s, the familial pressure was such that she felt she could not marry him. The other, meanwhile, fell in love with a married white man. He loved her in return but would not leave his wife for a brown-skinned woman.

In a material sense, at least in Barbados, the Ashbys' impact cannot be denied. Their handprint is firmly impressed on the local area, where they have made a lasting contribution to the nation George Ashby helped found. You can see it in the new development at Plumgrove, with the old mansion still at its centre; and on Lodge Road, where signs point to Ashby Land, and where Robert Cooper's descendants still live; and in Benjamin Ashby's store, which is now a Jehovah's Witness church. It's there if you go to the top of Oistins Hill, where Ashby-owned property was sold in the nineteenth century to build Foundation School, or down into Oistins, where a broad swath of land from Cashel to Welches belonged to the family. Everywhere, there are reminders of the powerful station this family held in its heyday.

★

So today, I return to Plumgrove, the focus of some of my earliest, most vivid memories: being enfolded in my grandmother's warm and perfumed arms, eating roast pork and plantain round the large wooden dining table, and at night looking out of the windows at the rustling cane, which swayed like an army of stick-like shadows against the starlit night. Some of the wider changes that have occurred across the island are mirrored in the land around me. There is no trace of Waterland Hall, the great sugar plantation from which Plumgrove was carved. Because real estate is now more valuable than cane land, its endless fields of sugar cane have largely been replaced by residential districts. The plantation, too, is a different place. Within the span of a few decades, most of its acreage has been converted from the cultivation of sugar to a modern housing development built for middle-income Barbadians; the little wooden houses that once perched so precariously on their coral blocks have now been replaced by sturdy stone dwellings.

Instead of a sleepy backwater, the modern Plumgrove is never silent. Indeed, no property in contemporary Barbados could ever be. The land hums with incessant activity: engines starting, tractors rolling, nails hitting plywood as houses are being constructed. This perpetual babble almost overwhelms the perennial soundtrack of the plantation: the strangely soothing and sad noise of the cane. Sitting here now – with cane behind me and the development in front of me, the main road and its busy stream of cars just out of sight – Plumgrove's great house still provides the perfect vantage point to feel both the rural isolation of the plantation and the busyness of modern Barbadian life. The plantation house is fated to be converted to condominiums, but perhaps, however sad, its demolition is fitting: a way of finally laying the ghost of the plantation system to rest.

Yet I can never simply regard Plumgrove casually. For me, this land is haunted. It is a haven for restless souls for whom not even death has provided any respite. These spectres disturb the air, waiting for me to face and name them, as all our ghosts do. Every time I visit it, Plumgrove catches my heart so intensely that I'm left dizzy by the force of emotion. The house and the land that surrounds it are peopled with memories that are so clear that they disturb my sense of reality. I am immediately carried back to my childhood self: jumping from hot paving stones onto cool green grass, chasing my brother and sister around the garden, or hiding behind gigantic tamarind trees, trying to catch fireflies in the starlit Caribbean night.

Plumgrove has been for me a place of refuge and a place of profound sadness. It has always been central to the mythology of my maternal family, the Ashbys; but it is also, I now see, a place of loss and death and endings. As a child this place was a strange and wonderful playground; as an adult, I can almost taste the aura of unhappiness that surrounds it. I can sense the spirits of my ancestors here – George Ashby, Robert Cooper, Mary Anne, John Stephen, and all the names I will never know – who strived and suffered on this island. So the plantation house our family still owns stands as a monument to things lost: not just my youth, my sense of belonging, my Caribbean self, but also my predecessors, their hopes, dreams, and despair. When I visit Plumgrove I am assailed by existential questions. Where do I belong? Who am I? And I realize that the sights and sounds and smells of this place have permeated my thoughts and shaped my personality in ways that will last a lifetime – just as my ancestors' plantation experiences did theirs.

If George Ashby's story began with a journey, it would end with the eternal enigma that is arrival. Every migration – voluntary or forced – is a dangerous gamble, initiating a series of events that cannot be anticipated or even fully understood. When he embarked for the New World in the seventeenth century, no one, least of all George Ashby himself, could have anticipated how his descendants would mutate and multiply, spreading virtually across the globe. In an era when we are undergoing our own great migration, with millions of people on the move in search of opportunity, perhaps we can learn something from the past. Somewhere in all of our family stories is a 'George Ashby', and we are all the descendants of migrants – those resilient souls making the best of history's terrible backhanders, like slavery or the Holocaust; or those brave opportunists taking a chance on the future and striking out to forge a life for themselves in a new world.

Notes

B. Arch.   Barbados Archives, Black Rock, Bridgetown, Barbados
BDA   Barbados Archives
JBHMS   *Journal of the Barbados Museum and Historical Society*
PRO   Public Record Office, Kew, London

Chapter 1

7   *the late 1630s*   There is no record of George Ashby's outward
      journey, so this is an approximate date only, calculated on the
      basis of land sale patterns.

8   *a will-o'-the-wisp*   Bridenbaugh and Bridenbaugh 1972: 18.

11   *so momentous a development*   Arciniegas 2004: 3.

–   *wedded to their native Soile*   Bridenbaugh 1968: 396.

–   *non-separating puritans*   Bridenbaugh 1968: 401.

12   *the typical Sunday service*   Bridenbaugh 1968: 402.

–   *Get thee out of the country*   Genesis 12:1–2, quoted in
      Bridenbaugh 1968: 402

–   *If hee have any graine*   Smith 2006: vol. 2, 125.

13   *Thus was the king's coffers*   Hill 1972: 29.

14   *probably amongst the most terrible years*   Peter Bowden, quoted in
      Thirske 1967: 621.

–   *last scene of my life*   Ligon 1657: i.

15   *pearls and other such riches*   This and the following extracts from
      Richard Eden are quoted in Sale 1992: 254.

16   *a succulent maiden*   Sale 1992: 258.

–   *Licence my roving hands*   Donne, Elegie XIX 'To His Mistress

390

Going to Bed', quoted in Sale 1992: 258.

17 *He wondered that your lordship*   Shakespeare, *Two Gentlemen of Verona*, I.ii.4–9, quoted in Davis 1887: 20.

–   *the Wild West*   Dunn 1972: 9.

–   *provinces of El Dorado*   Naipaul 1970: 93.

–   *to educate the English public*   Bridenbaugh 1968: 400.

18 *Bee not too much in love with that countrie*   Richard Eburne, quoted in Bridenbaugh 1968: 401.

–   *varnishing their owne actions*   Bridenbaugh 1968: 403.

20 *The West Indian Colonist of the Seventeenth Century*   Jaeffreson 1878: 35.

21 *Before you come be careful to be strongly instructed*   Anderson 1991: 53.

22 *having tasted much of God's mercy*   Bridenbaugh 1968: 6.

Chapter 2

24 *in a very small room*   Coad, quoted in Bridenbaugh and Bridenbaugh 1972: 113.

25 *operation and the several faces that watery Element puts on*   Ligon 1657: 1.

–   *a prosperous gale*   Colt, quoted in Harlow 1925: 50.

26 *the living fed upon the dead*   Bridenbaugh 1968: 8.

–   *Our ship was so pestered*   Bridenbaugh 1968: 8.

27 *had well nigh putt an end to this my Journall*   Colt, quoted in Harlow 1925: 78.

–   *Death is better*   Colt, quoted in Harlow 1925: 79.

28 *a long sleeved shirt*   Colt, quoted in Harlow 1925: 99.

29 *a competency*   Anderson 1991: 123.

–   *sometimes rough with mighty mountains*   Richard Mather, quoted in Anderson 1991: 80.

–   *our greatest bullocks*   Colt, quoted in Harlow 1925: 107.

30 *One might almost believe that the puny sun*   W.B.W. 1789: 131.

–   *Surely the Journey is as great*   Colt, quoted in Harlow 1925: 62.

31 *There is no place so void and empty*   Ligon 1657: 28.

–   *sixpence throwne down*   Colt, quoted in Harlow 1925: 63.

–   *the woman with childe*   Colt, quoted in Harlow 1925: 64.

–   *more healthful than any of hir neighbours*   Colt, quoted in Harlow 1924: 43.

33 *The nearer we came*   Ligon 1657: 30.

35   *Their main oversight*   Ligon 1657: 37.
36   *Sir William Tufton had Severe Measure*   Davis 1887: 53.

Chapter 3

38   *growne over with trees*   Father Andrew White, quoted in Gragg 2003: 14.
41   *the woods were so thick*   Ligon 1657: 37.
42   *It was as if the whole Atlantic ocean*   W.B.W. 1789: 132.
–   *Richard Ligon was beguiled by the plants* Ligon 1657: 107.
43   *the Prince of all fruits*   Gragg 2003: 20.
44   *find you sleeping*   Ligon 1657: 62.
–   *a scorching island*   Gragg 2003: 16.
45   *as ordinary as taverns and tippling houses*   Gately 2001: 48.
–   *all these spectacles*   Paul Hentzner, quoted in Gately 2001: 47.
–   *In our time the use of tobacco*   Francis Bacon, quoted in Gately 2001: 50.
46   *very ill-conditioned*   John Winthrop, quoted in Beckles 1990: 44.
47   *Anyone who has seen them bent double*   Davies 1666: 180.
–   *When a shipload of Frenchmen*   Pares 1960: 18.
49   *a plantation in this place is worth nothing*   Beckles 1996: 574.
50   *21 lashes on the bare back*   Beckles 1990: 41.
–   *great damage to their master*   Beckles 1990: 44.
51   *sell their servants to one another*   Ligon 1657: 59.
–   *the urge to try something noble*   This and the following extracts come from von Uchteritz 1969: 91–4.
53   *Truly I have seen such cruelty*   Ligon 1657: 51.
–   *The masters are obliged to support them*   Biet, quoted in Handler 1967: 66.
54   *there hardly passes a year but they make one or two irruptions*   Charles de Rochefort, quoted in Bridenbaugh and Bridenbaugh 1972: 172.
55   *agreeable, and not repugnant unto reason*   Phillips 1990: 423.
–   *the twentieth part of all profits*   Phillips 1990: 423.
–   *a drunken, vindictive tyrant*   Gragg 1996–7: 4.
56   *such great drunkards*   Thomas Verney, quoted in Gragg 2003: 71.
–   *They settle their differences by fist fighting*   Biet, quoted in Handler 1967: 68.

57   *tough guys*   Pares 1960: 15.

–   *This Island is the Dunghill*   Henry Whistler, quoted in Firth 1900: 146.

58   *it is enough to believe that there is a God*   Captain Holdip, quoted in Gragg 2003: 80.

–   *who live in pride, drunkenesse*   Rous 1656: 1–8.

–   *The hard labour and want of victuals*   Ligon 1657: 60.

59   *new men, for few or none of them that first set foot there*   Ligon 1657: 54.

–   *girls for sale*   Pares 1960: 6.

60   *the soldiers of the London garrison visited various brothels*   Gragg 2003: 167.

61   *a Baud brought ouer puts on a demur comportment*   Whistler 1900: 146.

–   *roofs so low, as for the most part*   Ligon 1657: 59.

62   *ill dyet they keep, and drinking*   Ligon 1657: 31.

63   *We have felt his heavy hand in wrath*   Richard Vines, quoted in Puckrein 1984: 192.

–   *Their sufferings being grown to a great height*   Ligon 1657: 66.

Chapter 4

68   *the production of sugar is immense in this province*   Marco Polo, quoted in Aykroyd 1967: 11.

69   *they died like fish in a bucket*   Aykroyd 1967: 20.

70   *People the colour of the very night*   Schwartz 2004: 37.

71   *At the time we landed on this island*   This and the following extract from Ligon 1657: 119–20.

74   *tyrant and murderer; and a public and implacable enemy*   This and the following extracts from historylearningsite.co.uk/Charles I_execution.htm.

75   *with cries of 'God and the Cause!'*   Davis 1887: 113.

–   *They did not see why they should not repair their fortunes*   Davis 1887: 150.

76   *that devout Zealot of the deeds of the devil*   Davis 1887: 147.

77   *the profits of the said Estates to be disposed of by his Lordship*   Davis 1887: 150.

–   *There must have been mounting in hot haste*   Davis 1887: 209.

78   *those Loose and scandalous papers with much Industry*   Davis 1887: 147.

Chapter 8

83   *wee shall be soe thinned of Christian people*   Parker 2011: 147.

84   *If any Africans were carried away*   Aykroyd 1967: 18.

86   *the men are very well timbered*   This and the next extract from Ligon 1657: 73.

87   *intrinsically treacherous*   These extracts from Ligon 1657: 75.

–   *go onto the next life without its head*   Ligon 1657: 73.

88   *a new scale and intensity*   Eltis, quoted in Beckles 2002: 13.

89   *the most magnificent drama*   DuBois, quoted in Rediker 1997: 5.

91   *In the meanwhile, a burning Iron*   William Bosman, quoted in Hartman 2007: 80.

92   *hold anything good in store for them*   Paul Isert, quoted in Hartman 2007: 114.

93   *instruments of woe*   Rediker 1997: 154.

94   *all the while oppressed and weighed down by grief*   This and the following extracts from Equiano 1797: 53–4.

95   *carried to these white people's country*   Equiano 1797: 57.

Chapter 6

98   *the most important surviving piece of legislation*   Dunn 1972: 239.

99   *a heathenish, brutish, uncertain and dangerous*   Marshall 2009.

–   *liberal Code*   Franklin Knight, quoted in Beckles 2002: 64.

100 *Whereas the Plantations and Estates of this Island*   Phillips 1990: 427.

101 *many enormities were committed*   Marshall 2009.

104 *straight from the ship like horses at a market*   Ligon 1657: 68.

–   *moment of rupture*   Rediker 1997: 153.

105 *One dreadful shriek assaults*   James Field Stanfield, quoted in Rediker 1997: 153.

–   *I can assure you*   John Pinney, quoted in Pares 1950: 121.

106 *It is unnecessary I flatter myself*   John Pinney, quoted in Pares 1950: 121.

108 *Slaves differed from other human beings*   Patterson 1982: 5.

110 *were cannibals who were capturing them*   Equiano 1791: 54.

–   *apt to die out of pure grief*   This and the following extract from Davies 1666: 20.

111 *The English take very little care of their slaves*   Labat 1957: 168.

Chapter 7

115 *was accompanied to his ship*   Handler 1967: 69.

– *seasoned with sweet Herbs finely minc'd*   Ligon 1657: 56.

116 *the richest and most splendid of all early West Indian Grandees*
Craton 1991: 330.

118 *excellent Juice is of much more importance*   Tryon 2009: 94.

120 *the more inconsiderable of the Inhabitants*   Davies 1666: 198.

121 *the nursery for planting other places*   Bridenbaugh 1968: 101.

– *They are a perfect medley or hotch potch*   Quoted in Watson
1997: 91.

122 *Carolina opened possibilities*   Dunn 1972: 114.

123 *Barbados played a unique role*   Hottens 1982: iv.

Chapter 8

124 *a notably lethal crossroads*   D. Phillip Morgan in Nussbaum
2003: 58.

125 *A few hours' command of the sea*   Pares 1950: 45.

128 *Suerly the Deuill*   Colt 1925:

– *international cockpit*   Arciniegas 2004: 216.

129 *The Foreign Legion of the Caribbean*   Arciniegas 2004: 178.

– *They created a style of fighting that had not been seen before*
Arciniegas 2004: 194.

– *When a buccaneer is going to sea*   Exquemelin, quoted in Lewis
2006: 83.

132 *hang them from their genitals*   Exquemelin, quoted in Lewis
2006: 65.

133 *not to call on him in the manner*   Exquemelin, quoted in Lewis
2006: 56.

– *They are very bad subjects*   Jean Baptiste Ducasse, quoted in
Latimer 2009: 109.

135 *If you roast me today*   Beckles 1990: 49.

136 *George Ashby's will*   B. Arch. RB6:13, 3 Oct. 1672, proved
1676.

142 *Almost certainly the exports to England*   Dunn 1969: 58.

– *Like the terraced cane fields*   Dunn 1969: 77.

143 *The houses on the plantations are much better built*   Labat 1957:
171.

– *splendid Planters, who for Sumptuous Houses*   Dunn 1969: 58.

– *the largest trade in the New World*   Labat 1957: 163.

144   *Barbados received between 2,000 and 3,000 negroes*   Davies, cited in Dunn 1969: 72.

145   *One of the great Burdens of our Lives*   Littleton, quoted in Dunn 1969: 73.

–   *Thus sunny Barbados*   Dunn 1969: 75.

Chapter 9

153   *Barbadian character*   Watson, quoted in Jemmott and Carter 1993: 37.

154   *perfectly ravished*   Warren 2001: 6.

155   *The Earth in parts is extremely rich*   Warren 2001: 8.

–   *were the principal cause of the rapid movement*   Abbé Raynal, quoted in Aykroyd 1967: 31.

156   *Sugar, sugar eh!*   Aykroyd 1967: 44.

158   *seemed to be much in a desponding way*   Ragatz 1928: 113.

159   *without any question*   Schama 1989: 57.

160   *The strongest colours could not paint*   Kippis 1784: 5.

161   *The whole face of the country*   Admiral Rodney, quoted in Ludlum 1963: 140–42.

–   *the economic position of Barbados was still poor*   Ragatz 1928: 21.

162   *Children, in these West-India islands*   Greene 2001: 143.

164   *high theatre*   Hochschild 2005: 50.

–   *the lower class of women*   Long 1774: vol. 2, 261–2.

169   *the first great political book tour*   Hochschild 2005: 169.

–   *the prejudices which had been hastily taken up*   The Rev. John Duke, quoted in Handler 2005: 59.

170   *Why ought the slave trade be abolished?*   William Pitt, speech on 'The Proposed Abolition of the Slave Trade' (1792), Slave Pamphlet Collection, Athenaeum, London.

171   *new temper and ideas*   Gaspar and Geggus 1997: 31.

172   *In few other societies can the ideals of liberty*   Gaspar and Geggus 1997: 3.

173   *Have they not hung men*   James 1980: 132.

–   *The white slaves in France*   Gaspar and Geggus 1997: 12.

175   *The God who creates the sun*   Boukman, quoted in James 1980: 87.

176   *Imagine all the space that the eye can see*   Hochschild 2005: 257.

179   *in drinking, gaming and wenching*   Ragatz 1928: 22.

\- *through the most simple forms of life*   Edward Long, quoted in Buckley 1997: 230.

181 *the only issue which seemed to have a unifying effect*   Watson 1998: 18.

\- *cultural action*   Edward Brathwaite, quoted in Buckley 1997: 236.

\- *When I first came into this Country*   Thomas Howard, quoted in Buckley 1997: 236.

Chapter 10

183 *to guard their daughters against dapper braids wearers*   Ragatz 1928: 97.

184 *stuffed to the gills with romantic nonsense*   Moreau de Saint-Méry, quoted in Girod 1959: 31.

190 *I went one day to a sale of Negroes*   Wyville 1975: 24.

191 *Instructions . . . offered to the Consideration of Proprietors*   Quoted in Beckles 1998: 15.

192 *You belong no massa*   Lewis 2005: 69.

193 *Your negroes are giving in to despair*   Desalles 1996: 15.

194 *the flower of all field battalions*   Walvin 1993: 94.

\- *It has often occurred to me that a gang of Negroes*   Walvin 1993: 94.

195 *as if they had never eaten before*   Nugent 1966: 57.

197 *I was one evening*   Wyville 1975: 26.

199 *Caribbean slavery was, by every measure*   Hochschild 2005: 65.

202 *If a stiller slips into a rum cistern*   Pitman 1926: 48.

\- *Managing a sugar estate*   Trevor Burnard, quoted in Walvin 2007: 126.

204 *submission to the state, in which*   Rolph 2009: 165.

\- *after the greatest Captain that the world could produce*   Lewis 2005: 123.

\- *The ceremony was performed with perfect gravity*   Lewis 2005: 124.

206 *the slaves would probably have been better off*   Kenneth Kiple, quoted in Handler and Jacoby 1993: 75.

207 *It was his constant practice*   Lewis 2005: 323.

\- *Two of our sergeants came and informed me*   Wyville 1975: 25.

208 *To be sold a mulatto man*   Wyville 1975: 24.

209 *nowhere does time pass more slowly*   Stuart 2004: 20.

210 *It is a sad society*   Stuart 2004: 56.

Chapter 11

213 *like a vessel traversing the ocean*   Lieutenant Howard, quoted in Hochschild 2005: 274.

– *Black, white, brown, all de same!*   Gaspar and Geggus 1997: 14.

216 *attempts to get another Man into his Absolute Power*   John Locke, quoted in Ball 1999: 31.

217 *every year we had eight, ten, twelve, and fourteen pregnancies* Desalles 1996: 71.

218 *Barbados contains fewer hiding places*   Handler 1997: 190.

– *Lydia Ann, aged 13 or 14 was suspected to be harboured*   Handler 1997: 193.

– *nobody had done anything*   This and the following quotes from Desalles 1996: 143.

219 *They are fully persuaded they will return to Guinea*   Senhouse 1988: 179.

220 *In his very first days on the island*   Walvin 2007: 113.

221 *Had him well flogged and pickled*   This and the following quotes from Hall 1989: 72.

222 *The whip is the soul of the colonies*   Victor Schoelcher, quoted in *Vivre, survivre et être libre* (Fort de France, Martinique), 22 May–22 July 1998: 33.

223 *I was broken in body and spirit*   Douglass 2003: 160.

– *I lay down in at night and rose up in the morning*   Prince 2004: 16.

224 *for over-indulgence to my own negroes!*   Lewis 2005: 236.

225 *conspicuously liberal*   This and the following quotes from Stephen 1824.

– *I arrived in Martinique*   Governor Fenlon, quoted in Cohen 1980: 104.

Chapter 12

228 *The greatest drawback*   Lewis 2005: 150.

– *Certainly, if a man was desirous of leading a life of vice here* Lewis 2005: 150.

– *Both blacks and whites knew each other well*   Watson 1998: 210.

232 *He who should presume*   Edward Long, quoted in Jordan 2003: 647.

– *The slave girl is reared*   Jacobs 2000: 57.

233   *That which commands admiration*   This and the following quotes from Jacobs 2000: 30–31.

234   *sable Venus*   This and the following quotes from Quintanilla 2003.

235   *I have observed many instances*   Waller 1820: 148.

237   *in a vulgar corrupt dialect*   Waller 1820: 120.

Chapter 13

241   *Genealogical trees do not flourish amongst slaves*   Douglass 2003: 30.

242   *For they carry burdens on their backs*   Ligon 1657: 69.

243   *The slave mother can be spared long enough*   Douglass 2003: 42.

–   *The practice of separating children from their mothers*   Douglass 2003: 32.

244   *Men do not love those who remind them of their sins*   Douglass 2003: 46.

245   *Interracial sex was said to be a violation*   Ball 2001: 25.

246   *the crowds of Mullatoes*   Schaw 1921: 112.

247   *The rage of a creole is most violent*   Wyville 1975: 26.

248   *Brothers and sisters we were by blood*   Douglass 2003: 39.

–   *There is not, beneath the sky*   Douglass 2003: 47.

–   *This was the happiest period*   Prince 2004: 7.

249   *born for another's benefit*   Douglass 2003: 37.

–   *I was a slave – born a slave*   Douglass 2003: 37.

–   *What are [Bonaparte] and his ruffians*   James Stephen, quoted in Blackburn 1988: 313.

250   *In 1805 the slave population of the French-controlled Caribbean*   Blackburn 1988: 300.

251   *on principles contrary to justice*   Blackburn 1988: 311.

–   *Let all the Negroes have sufficient provisions*   Clarkson 1807

Chapter 14

254   *be kept in the profoundest ignorance*   This and the following quote from Jemmott and Carter 1993: 36.

255   *Persons live and die in the midst of Negroes*   Clarke 2005: 229.

259   *They have no fellow feeling with the slaves*   Thome and Kimball, quoted in Cummerbatch 2008: 226.

261   *I could grow, though I could not become a man*   Douglass 2003: 224.

262   *a kind of right to be idle*   Watson 2000: 18.

–   *is impossible to generalize*   Orlando Patterson, quoted in Watson 2000: 7.

263   *I have often sung to drown my sorrow*   Douglass 2003: 76.

265   *They avail themselves of the passions and prejudices*   Clarke 2005: 154.

266   *Let him [the slave] be taught to revere God*   Peter Beckford, in Pitman 1926: 64.

267   *Jack, a light-skinned carpenter*   Handler 1997: 195.

270   *not to let a slave be corrected in his presence*   Pares 1960: 122.

271   *To make the negro think about all these ideas*   This and the following quotes from Desalles 1996: 126.

272   *something brewing up in their minds*   Beckles 1998: 10.

–   *I consider my property reduced*   Pares 1950: 121.

–   *Ideologically, the colony was in deepening crisis*   Beckles 1998: 12.

Chapter 15

273   *was remarkable for having yielded*   Beckles 1998: 17.

274   *severe disciplinarian*   Morris 2000: 3.

275   *[It] is those slaves*   John Vaughan, quoted in Beckles 1998: 21.

–   *insurrection was entirely owing to these hopes*   Beckles 1998: 23.

278   *It was about twelve o'clock*   Beckles 1998: 29.

–   *were quickly dispersed*   Beckles 1998: 29.

279   *Large quantities of cane*   Best, quoted in Beckles 1998: 32.

–   *The insurgents did not think*   Beckles 1998: 33.

280   *conflagrations had ceased*   Beckles 1998: 34.

282   *By these means the planters hoped*   Beckles 1998: 38.

–   *The disposition of the slaves in general*   Beckles 1998: 40.

283   *Murder was to have been*   Beckles 1998: 40.

Chapter 16

284   *there existed no plan*   Wilberforce, quoted in Blackburn 1988: 324.

286   *The yearly returns*   Colonial Slaves and Compensation Records, PRO T.71.

288   *A court martial to be held at Town Hall*   *JBHMS* 2: 117.

289   *fees for the relief*   B. Arch. Vestry minutes 1832.

292   *Ladies' Associations . . . did everything*   Hochschild 2005: 327.

293 *By buying sugar we participate in the crime* Heyrick, quoted in Abbott 2009: 251.

– *a colony of wasps had actually built a nest* Henry Bleby, quoted in Hochschild 2005: 330.

295 *Yes and I shouldn't much care if* D'Egville Case, *JBHMS* 8: 125.

299 *Everywhere people are asking me about immediate abolition* Clarkson, quoted in Hochschild 2005: 324.

– *It is dreadful to think after my brother and his friends* Clarkson's deathbed speech, quoted in Hochschild 2005: 332.

– *the demon of procrastination* George Stephen, quoted in Hochschild 2005: 335.

300 *the sun took on a decidedly blue appearance* Ludlum 1963: 140–2.

301 *the best and most economical means* Vestry Records 22/8/1831.

– *late awful hurricane* Vestry Records 22/8/1831.

302 *the most intelligent and remarkable slave* Henry Bleby, quoted in Hochschild 2005: 342–3.

– *I know I shall die* Hochschild 2005: 341.

– *Generally four, seldom less than three* Bleby, quoted in Hochschild 2005: 341–2.

303 *I would rather die upon yonder gallows* Hochschild 2005: 343.

304 *Know all Men by these Presents, That I Robert Cooper Ashby* BDA: Book of Powers Index; 1832 Manumission of Sukey Ann and others RB 7/26.

305 *I feel great sorrow when I hear some people* Prince 2004: 26.

306 *As England is avowedly the author* This and the following quotes from Beckles 1990: 127.

307 *We should like to know* Editorial in *The Barbadian*, from Gopert and Handler 1974.

– *800,000 human beings lay down last night as slaves* William Hart Coleridge, Bishop of Barbados, quoted in Wilder 1994: 32.

Chapter 17

310 *The baptism record* BDA: RL/17 and 18, Box no. 1157931.

311 *Many of our children who are now grown* Newton 2008: 66.

312 *We were kindly invited* This and the following quotes from Thome and Kimball 1838: 61–2.

315 *The monster is dead!* William Knibb, quoted in Abbott 2009: 263.

–   *Died on 18 [of this month]*   The Barbadian newspaper, quoted in
      JBHMS 8: 164.
317 *Robert Cooper Ashby's last will and testament*   B. Arch
      RB4/69:81 dated 4 November 1837, proved 30 October
      1839.
319 *The first wish of my heart*   Jacob Hinds, quoted in Hughes
      2006: 14.
321 *They all carried the badge of colour*   Morris 2008: 5.
323 *One of the most important legacies of the plantation culture*   Morris
      2008: 2.
324 *the home class of ministers*   Ball 2001: 14.

Chapter 18
328 *We are sensitive in Barbados*   Barbados Weekly Herald, quoted in
      Watkins-Owens 1996: 21.
331 *Between 1900 and 1930 some 40,000 immigrants of African
      descent*   Watkins-Owens 1996: 1.
333 *a little fat, black man*   DuBois, quoted in Watkins-Owens 1996:
      119.
335 *On coming to the United States the West Indian*   Eric Walrond,
      quoted in Philipson 2006: 4.
338 *Aframericans who, long deracinated, were still rootless among
      phantoms*   Claude Mckay, quoted in Philipson 2006: 8.
339 *little less than a corner of hell*   This and the next quote from the
      Rev. Charles Morris in Watkins-Owens 2001: 32.

Chapter 19
341 *She was good at it*   Interview with Barbara Stuart née Ashby,
      2008.
345 *She was so glamorous*   Interview with Barbara Stuart née Ashby,
      2008.
346 *Quite early, I felt my father's vulnerability*   Interview with Barbara
      Stuart née Ashby, 2008.
347 *Do you know who that guy is?*   Interview with Trevor Ashby,
      2005.
348 *It's a great life*   Interview with Trevor Ashby, 2005.

Chapter 20

353 *for children of the better classes* Stafford 2005: 272.

– *The school intended to supply* Stafford 2005: 120.

354 *a good knowledge of the Greek classics* Stafford 2005: 256.

– *Colonialism was not just an economic* Carmichael 1996: 198.

– *Turn sideways now and let them see* H.A.Vaughan, quoted in Carmichael 1996: 248.

355 *Today I shudder to think how a country so foreign* George Lamming, quoted in Carmichael 1996: 198.

– *Garvey's politics, more than any other single factor* Beckles 1990: 223.

356 *restrain or subdue the rebels* Beckles 1990: 238.

– *open wounds of colonisation* Beckles 1990: 245.

357 *to provide political expression* Beckles 1990: 245.

– *I suggest that the plantation system is basically the cause of our trouble* Grantley Adams, quoted in Beckles 1990: 250.

– *only if he was white* Stafford 2005: 190.

359 *Throughout the history of this island* This and the following extract from the *Barbados Observer* quoted in Beckles 1990: 254.

Chapter 21

370 *the road to destiny* Hoyos 1978: 242.

371 *Others, notably the South Americans* Hoyos 1978: 188.

– *the colony owes much of its increasing prosperity* The Colonial Secretary, quoted in Hoyos 1978: 188.

381 *the Barbadian economic miracle* Blackman 1998: 61–8.

Select Bibliography

Abbott, Elizabeth. 2009. *Sugar: A Bittersweet History*. London and New York: Duckworth.

Anderson, Virginia Dejohn. 1991. *New England's Generation*. Cambridge: Cambridge University Press.

Anon. 1741. *Some Memoirs of the First Settlement of the Island of Barbados*. Bridgetown.

Arciniegas, Germán. 2004. *Caribbean Sea of the New World*. Kingston: Ian Randle.

Aykroyd, W.R. 1967. *Sweet Malefactor: Sugar, Slavery and Human Society*. London: Heinemann.

Bailyn, Bernard, and Morgan, Philip D. 1991. *Strangers in the Realm: Cultural Margins of the First British Empire*. Chapel Hill, NC: UNC Press.

Ball, Edward. 1999. *Slaves in the Family*. London: Penguin.

Ball, Edward. 2001. *The Sweet Hell Inside*. New York: William Morrow.

Beckles, Hilary. 1989. *Natural Rebels: A Social History of Enslaved Black Women in Barbados*. London: Zed Books.

Beckles, Hilary. 1990. *A History of Barbados: From Amerindian Settlement to Nation State*. Cambridge: Cambridge University Press.

Beckles, Hilary. 1996. 'The Concept of White Slavery in the English Caribbean in the Early Seventeenth Century', in John Brewer and Susan Staines, eds., *Early Modern Concepts of Property*. London: Routledge.

Beckles, Hilary. 1998. *Bussa: The 1816 Revolution in Barbados*. Cave

Hill, Barbados: Department of History, University of the West Indies, and *JBHMS*.

Beckles, Hilary. 2002. *Slave Voyages: The Transatlantic Trade in Enslaved Africans*. Paris: UNESCO.

Blackburn, Robin. 1988. *The Overthrow of Colonial Slavery 1776–1848*. London and New York: Verso.

Blackburn, Robin. 2011. *The American Crucible: Slavery, Emancipation and Human Rights*. London: Verso.

Blackman, Courtney N. 1998. 'The Barbados Model', *Caribbean Affairs* 8.1: 61–8.

Bowden, Martyn J. 2003. 'The Three Centuries of Bridgetown: An Historical Geography', *JBHMS* 49: 3–138.

Bridenbaugh, Carl. 1968. *Vexed and Troubled Englishman 1590–1642*. Oxford: Clarendon Press.

Bridenbaugh, Carl, and Bridenbaugh, Roberta. 1972. *No Peace Beyond the Line: The English in the Caribbean, 1624–1690*. New York: Oxford University Press.

Buckley, Roger. 1997. 'Slave Testimony at British Military Courts', in David Barry Gaspar and David Patrick Geggus, eds., *A Turbulent Time: The French Revolution and the Greater Caribbean*. Bloomington: Indiana University Press.

Bush, Barbara. 1990. *Slave Women in Caribbean Society, 1650–1838*. London: James Currey Ltd.

Campbell, P.F. 1993. *Some Early Barbadian History*. Barbados: Caribbean Graphics.

Carmichael, Trevor, ed. 1996. *Barbados: Thirty Years of Independence*. Kingston: Ian Randle.

Clarke, Erskine. 2005. *Dwelling Place: A Plantation Epic*. New Haven: Yale University Press.

Clarkson, Thomas. 1807. 'Three Letters to Slave Merchants on Compensation'. London: Athenaeum, Slave Pamphlet Collection.

Cohen, William B. 1980. *The French Encounters with Africans*. Bloomington: Indiana University Press.

Colt, Sir Henry. 1925. 'The Voyage of Sir Henry Colt', in V.T. Harlow, *Colonising Expeditions to the West Indies and Guiana, 1623–1667*. Hakluyt Society. London: Bedford Press.

Connell, Neville. 1956. 'Furniture and Furnishings in Barbados During the 17th Century', *JBMHS* 24.1 (November): 102–21.

Connell, Neville. 1958–9. '18th Century and Its Background in
    Barbados', *JBHMS* 26 (November): 165.

Craton, Michael. 1991. 'The Planter's World in the British West
    Indies', in Bernard Bailyn and Philip Morgan, eds., *Strangers in
    the Realm*. Berkeley: University of California Press.

Craton, Michael, and Walvin, James. 1970. *A Jamaican Plantation: The
    History of Worthy Park 1670–1970*. London: W.H. Allen.

Cummerbatch, Cynthia. 2008. 'Out of Slavery: Wealth Creation by
    Free People of Colour in Barbados 1780–1840', unpublished
    PhD thesis, University of the West Indies.

Davies, John. 1666. *The History of the Caribby Islands*. London.

Davis, David Brion. 1966. *The Problem of Slavery in Western Culture*.
    Ithaca: Cornell University Press.

Davis, David Brion. 2008. *Inhuman Bondage: The Rise and Fall of
    Slavery in the New World*. New York: Oxford University Press.

Davis, N. Darnell. 1887. *The Cavaliers and Roundheads of Barbados,
    1650–1652*. Georgetown, British Guiana: Argosy Press.

D'Egville case, *JBHMS* 8 (November 1940/August 1941).

Dering, James. 1959–60. 'A Letter from Barbados in 1640', *JBHMS*
    27: 124–5.

Desalles, Pierre. 1996. *Sugar and Slavery: The Letters and Diary of
    Pierre Desalles, Planter in Martinique 1808–1856*, ed. and trans.
    Elborg Forster and Robert Forster. Baltimore: Johns Hopkins
    University Press.

Douglass, Frederick. 2003. *My Bondage and My Freedom*. New York:
    Penguin.

Dunn, Richard. 1969. 'The Barbados Census of 1689: Profile of the
    Richest Colony in English America', *JBHMS* 33 (November):
    37–55.

Dunn, Richard. 1972. *Sugar and Slaves: The Rise of the Planter Class
    in the English West Indies, 1624–1713*. Chapel Hill, NC: UNC
    Press.

Eltis, David. 2000. *The Rise of African Slavery in the Americas*.
    Cambridge: Cambridge University Press.

Equiano, Olaudah. 1791. *The Interesting Narrative of the Life of
    Olaudah Equiano, or Gustavas Vassa, the African*. London.

Exquemelin, Alexandre de. 1684. *Buccaneers of America*. London.

Fergus, Claudius. 2009. '"Dred of Insurrection": Abolitionism,
    Security, and Labor in Britain's West Indian Colonies,

1760–1823', *The William & Mary Quarterly* 66.4 (October).

Fermor, Patrick Leigh. 1950. *The Traveller's Tree: A Journey through the Caribbean Islands*. London: John Murray.

Firth, C.H., ed. 1900. *The Narrative of General Venables*. New York: Longman and Green.

FitzHerbert, Sir Henry. 1998. 'Journal Kept while in Barbados', *JBHMS* 44.

Foner, Nancy, ed. 2001. *Island in the City: West Indian Migration to New York*. Berkeley: University of California Press.

Forde, Norma. 1975. 'The Evolution of Marriage Law in Barbados', *JBHMS* 35.1.

Fraser, Henry, and Hughes, Ronnie. 1982. *Historic Houses of Barbados*. Bridgetown: Barbados National Trust.

Galloway, J.H. 1989. *The Sugar Cane Industry: An Historical Geography from its origins to 1914*. Cambridge : Cambridge University Press.

Gaspar, David Barry, and Geggus, David Patrick. 1997. *A Turbulent Time: The French Revolution and the Greater Caribbean*. Bloomington: Indiana University Press.

Gaspar, David Barry, and Hine, Darlene Clark, eds. 1996. *Black Women and Slavery in the Americas: More than Chattel*. Bloomington: Indiana University Press.

Gately, Iain. 2001. *La Diva Nicotina*. London: Simon & Schuster.

Gilmore, John, ed. 1996–7. 'A 1789 Description of Barbados', *JBHMS* 43.

Girod, François. 1959. *La Vie Quotidienne de la Société Creole*. Paris: Hachette.

Gopert, David L. and Handler, Jerome, ed. and trans. 1974. 'Captain de Corvette. Barbados in the Post-Apprenticeship Period: The Observations of a French Naval Officer', *JBHMS* 35, no. 4.

Gordon-Reed, Annette. 2008. *The Hemingses of Monticello: An American Family*. New York: W.W. Norton.

Gragg, Larry. 1996–7. '"Concerning Mr Huncks": Barbados Governors as "Tough Guys" in the Early English Empire', *JBHMS* 43: 1–14.

Gragg, Larry. 2003. *Englishmen Transplanted: The English Colonization of Barbados 1627–1660*. Oxford: Oxford University Press.

Greene, Jack P. 2001. 'Changing Identity in the British Caribbean: Barbados as a Case Study', *JBHMS* 47 (November): 106–65.

Hall, Catherine. 2002. *Civilizing Subjects: Metropole and Colony in the English Imagination 1830–1867*. London: Polity Press.

Hall, Douglas. 1989. *In Miserable Slavery: Thomas Thistlewood in Jamaica, 1750–86*. London: Macmillan.

Handler, Jerome, ed. 1967. 'Father Antoine Biet's Visit to Barbados in 1654', *JBHMS* 32 (May): 56–76.

Handler, Jerome S. 1991. *Supplement to A Guide to Source Materials for the Study of Barbados History, 1627–1834*. Providence, RI: John Carter Brown Library.

Handler, Jerome S. 1997. 'Escaping Slavery in a Caribbean Plantation Society: Marronage in Barbados, 1650s–1830s', *New West India Guide*, no. 71, vols. 3 and 4: 183–225.

Handler, Jerome S. 2002. *A Guide to Source Materials for the Study of Barbados History 1627–1834*. Newcastle: Oak Knoll Press. (First published 1971.)

Handler, Jerome S., ed. 2005. 'A Rare Eighteenth Century Tract in Defense of Slavery in Barbados: The Thoughts of the Rev. John Duke, Curate of St. Michael', *JBHMS* 51: 58–65.

Handler, Jerome S., and Jacoby, JoAnn. 1993. 'Slave Medicine and Plant Use in Barbados', *JBHMS* 41: 74–98.

Harlow, V.T. 1925. *Colonising Expeditions to the West Indies and Guiana, 1623–1667*. Hakluyt Society. London: Bedford Press.

Hartman, Saidya. 2007. *Lose Your Mother: A Journey Along the Atlantic Slave Route*. New York: Farrar, Strauss & Giroux.

Hill, Christopher. 1972. *The World Turned Upside Down: Radical Ideas During the English Revolution*. London: Penguin.

Hochschild, Adam. 2005. *Bury the Chains: The British Struggle to Abolish Slavery*. London: Macmillan.

Hottens, John Camden, ed. 1982. *The Original Lists of Persons of Quality; Emigrants; Religious Exiles; Political Rebels . . . Who Went from Great Britain to the American Plantations 1600–1700*. Repr. Baltimore: Genealogical Pub. Co.

Hoyos, F.A. 1978. *Barbados: A History*. London: Macmillan Education Limited.

Hughes, Ronnie. 2006. 'Jacob Hinds (?–1832), White Father of a Mulatto Clan', *JBHMS* 52 (December): 12–16.

Jacobs, Harriet. 2000. *Incidents in the Life of a Slave Girl*. London: Penguin.

Jaeffreson, Christopher. 1878. *A Young Squire of the Seventeenth Century*. London: Hurst & Blackett.

James, C.L.R. 1980. *The Black Jacobins: Toussaint L'Ouverture and the San Domingo Revolution*. London: Allison & Busby.

Jemmott, Ralph, and Carter, Dan. 1993. 'Barbadian Educational Development: An Interpretive Analysis', *JBHMS* 41: 32–50.

Johnson, H., and Watson, K., eds. 1998. *The White Minority in the Caribbean*. Kingston: Ian Randle.

Jordan, Winthrop D. 2003. 'American Chiaroscuro: The Status and Definition of Mulattoes in the British Colonies', in Gad Heuman and James Walvin, eds., *The Slavery Reader*. London and New York: Routledge.

Kippis, Andrew. 1784. *The Annual Register or General Repository of History, Politics and Literature in the Year 1781*. London.

Labat, Jean M. 1957. 'Father Labat's Visit to Barbados in 1700', trans. Neville Connell, *JBHMS* 24. 160–74.

Lambert, David. 2005. *White Creole Culture, Politics and Identity during the Age of Abolition*. Cambridge: Cambridge University Press.

Lamming, George. 1987. *In the Castle of My Skin*. New York: Longman.

Laslett, Peter. 1965. *The World We Have Lost*. London: Methuen.

Latimer, Jon. 2009. *Buccaneers of the Caribbean: How Piracy Forged an Empire 1607–1697*. London: Weidenfeld & Nicolson.

Levy, Claude. 1980. *Emancipation, Sugar and Federalism: Barbados and the West Indies, 1833–1876*. Gainesville: University Presses of Florida.

Lewis, Colleen. 2004. 'Pictorial Depictions of the West Indian Landscape in the 18th Century and 19th Century: The Sublime, the Picturesque, the Romantic', *JBHMS* 50: 129–53.

Lewis, John E. 2006. *The Mammoth Book of Pirates*. London: Robinson. (First published 1833)

Lewis, Matthew Gregory. 2005. *Journal of a West-India Proprietor, Kept During a Residence in the Island of Jamaica*. London: John Murray.

Ligon, Richard. 2000. *The True and Exact History of the Island of Barbadoes*, ed. Howard Hutson. Bridgetown: Barbados National Trust. (First published 1657.)

Long, Edward. 1774. *The History of Jamaica*. London: T. Lowndes.

Ludlum, David M. 1963. *Great American Hurricanes 1492–1870*.
　　Boston: Boston Meteorological Society.

Marshall, Woodville. 2009. "'For the Better Ordering of Negroes":
　　The Barbados Slave Laws'. Unpublished lecture delivered to
　　The Barbados Museum and Historical Society.

Mintz, Sidney W. 1986. *Sweetness and Power: The Place of Sugar in
　　Modern History*. New York: Penguin.

Morris, Robert. 2000. 'The 1816 Uprising: A Hell Broth', *JBHMS*
　　40: 1–15.

Morris, Robert. 2008. 'The Ashbys: A Prominent Oistins Family'.
　　Unpublished lecture delivered as part of a series on the local
　　area, Oistins.

Naipaul, V.S. 1970. *The Loss of El Dorado*. London: Deutsch.

Newton, Melanie J. 2008. *The Children of Africa in the Colonies:
　　Free People of Colour in the Age of Emancipation*. Baton Rouge:
　　Louisiana State University Press.

Nugent, Maria. 1966. *Lady Nugent's Journal of her Residence in Jamaica
　　from 1801–1805*, ed. Philip Wright. Kingston: Institute of
　　Jamaica.

Nussbaum, Felicity, ed. 2003. *The Global Century*. Baltimore: Johns
　　Hopkins Univeristy Press.

Oldmixion, John. 1708. *The British Empire in America*. 2 vols.
　　London.

O'Shaughnessy, Andrew Jackson. 2000. *An Empire Divided: The
　　American Revolution and the British Caribbean*. Philadelphia:
　　University of Pennsylvania Press.

Pares, Richard. 1950. *A West-India Fortune*. London: Longmans.

Pares, Richard. 1960. *Merchants and Planters*. Cambridge: Cambridge
　　University Press.

Parker, Matthew. 2011. *The Sugar Barons*. London: Hutchinson.

Parkinson, Wenda. 1978. *'This Gilded African': Toussaint L'Ouverture*.
　　London: Quartet Books.

Patterson, Orlando. 1982. *Slavery and Social Death*. Cambridge,
　　Mass.: Harvard University Press.

Philipson, Robert. 2006. 'The Harlem Renaissance as Post Colonial
　　Phenomenon', *African American Review* 40.1 (Spring): 145–60.

Phillips, Anthony. 1990. 'The Parliament of Barbados 1639–1989',
　　JBHMS 38.4: 422–51.

Pinckard, George. 1806. *Notes on the West Indies*. 3 vols. London.

Pinder, Richard. 1660. *A Loving Invitation to Repentance and Amendment of Life, unto all the Inhabitants of the Island Barbados*. London.

Pitman, Frank Wesley. 1926. 'Slavery on British West Indian Plantations in the Eighteenth Century', *Journal of Negro History*, 11.4 (October).

Prince, Mary. 2004. *The History of Mary Prince, A West Indian Slave* (1831). London: Penguin.

Puckrein, Gary. 1974. 'The Carlisle Papers', *JBHMS* 35.4.

Puckrein, Gary. 1984. *Little England: Plantation Society and Anglo-Barbadian Politics, 1627–1700*. New York: New York University Press.

Quintanilla, Mark. 2003. 'The Domestic World of a Vincentian Planter and his Sable Venus', cavehill.uwi.edu/BNCCde/svg/ Conference papers.

Ragatz, Lowell Joseph. 1928. *The Fall of the Planter Class in the British Caribbean, 1763–1833*. New York: Century.

Ramsey, Andrea Butler. 2008. 'Documenting the Life of a Barbados Slave Ancestor', *JBHMS* 54: 207–12.

Rediker, Marcus. 1997. *The Slave Ship: A Human History*. London: John Murray.

Rolph, Dr Thomas. 2009. 'Excerpt from a Brief Account, together with Observations Made during a Visit to the West Indies' (1836), *JBHMS* 55: 137–76.

Rous, John. 1656. *A Warning to the Inhabitants of Barbados*.

Sale, Kirkpatrick. 1992. *The Conquest of Paradise*. London: Papermac.

Schama, Simon. 1989. *Citizens: A Chronicle of the French Revolution*. New York: Knopf.

Schama, Simon. 2005. *Rough Crossings: Britain, the Slaves and the American Revolution*. London: BBC Books.

Schaw, Janet. 1921. *Journal of a Lady of Quality*. New Haven: Yale University Press.

Schomburgk, Sir Robert H. 1847. *The History of Barbados*. London: Longmans.

Schwartz, Stuart B., ed. 2004. *Tropical Babylons: Sugar and the Making of the Atlantic World 1450–1680*. Chapel Hill, NC: UNC Press.

Senhouse, Joseph. 1988. 'Diary of Joseph Senhouse', *JBHMS* 38: 179–95.

Shepherd, Verene, Brereton, Bridget, and Bailey, Barbara, eds. 1995. *Engendering History: Caribbean Women in Historical Perspective.* Kingston: Ian Randle.

Sheridan, R.B. 1974. *Sugar and Slavery: An Economic History of the British West Indies 1623–1775.* Barbados: Caribbean University Press.

Smith, Captain John. 2006. *The Travels and Works of Captain John Smith.* Whitefish, MT: Kessinger Publishers.

Spoeri, Felix Christian. 1961. 'A Swiss Medical Doctor's Description of Barbados in 1661', *JBHMS* 30.1 (May): 3–13.

Stafford, Patricia. 2005. 'The Growth and Development of the Brown and Black Middle Class, 1838–1988, and its Role in the Shaping of Modern Barbados'. Unpublished PhD thesis, University of the West Indies.

Stephen, James. 1824. *The Slavery of the British West India Colonies*, vol. 1. London: Butterworth.

Stuart, Andrea. 2004. *Josephine: The Rose of Martinique.* London: Pan.

Thirsk, J., ed. 1967. *The Agrarian History of England and Wales 1500–1640.* Cambridge: Cambridge University Press.

Thomas, Hugh. 1997. *The Slave Trade: The History of the Atlantic Slave Trade 1440–1870.* London: Picador.

Thome, J.A., and Kimball, J.H. 1838. *Emancipation in the West Indies: A Six Months' Tour in Antigua, Barbados and Jamaica in the Year 1837.* New York.

Thomson, Ian. 2009. *The Dead Yard: Tales of Modern Jamaica.* London: Faber and Faber.

Tree, Ronald. 1972. *A History of Barbados.* London: Hart-Davis.

Trouillot, Michel-Rolph. 1998. *Silencing the Past: Power and the Production of History.* Boston: Beacon Press.

Tryon, Thomas. 2009. 'Thomas Tryon's Letters from Barbados', *JBHMS* 55: 65–101.

Uchteritz, Heinrich von. 1969. 'A German Servant in Barbados in 1652', *JBHMS* 33: 3–13.

Waldrick, T. 1947. 'T. Waldrick's Letter from Barbados, 1710', *JBHMS* 15.1 (November): 27–51.

Waller, John. 1820. *A Voyage in the West Indies.* London.

Walvin, James. 1993. *Black Ivory: A History of British Slavery.* London: Fontana.

Walvin, James. 2007. *The Trader, the Owner, the Slave: Parallel Lives in the Age of Slavery*. London: Jonathan Cape.

Warren, Jack D. 2001. 'The Significance of George Washington's Journey to Barbados', *JBMHS* 47: 1–34.

Waters, Mary C. 2001. *Black Identities: West Indian Immigrant Dreams and American Realities*. Cambridge, Mass.: Harvard University Press.

Watkins-Owens, Irma. 1996. *Blood Relations: Caribbean Immigrants and the Harlem Community, 1900–1930*. Bloomington: Indiana University Press.

Watkins-Owens, Irma. 2001. 'Early Twentieth-Century Women', in Nancy Foner, ed., *Island City: West Indian Migration to New York*. Berkeley: University of California Press.

Watson, Karl. 1997. 'The Barbadians Endeavour to Rule All', *JBHMS* 43: 78–95.

Watson, Karl. 1998. 'Salmagundis vs. Pumpkins: White Politics and Creole Consciousness in Barbadian Slave Society, 1800–34', in Howard Johnson and Karl Watson, eds., *The White Minority in the Caribbean*. Kingston: Ian Randle.

Watson, Karl. 2000. *A Kind of Right to Be Idle: Old Doll, Matriarch of Newton Plantation*. Barbados Museum and Historical Society in conjunction with the Department of History, University of the West Indies.

W.B.W. 1789, 'Description of Barbados', ed. John Gilmore, *JBHMS* 43: 125–42.

Welch, Pedro L.V. 2003. *Slave Society in the City: Bridgetown Barbados, 1683–1834*. Kingston: Ian Randle.

Whistler, Henry. 1900. 'Extracts from Henry Whistler's Journey of the West India Expedition', in C.H. Firth, ed., *The Narrative of General Venables*. London: Longmans, Green.

Wilder, Rachel. 1994. *Insight Guide to Barbados*. New York: Houghton Mifflin Co.

Williams, Eric. 1944. *Capitalism and Slavery*. Chapel Hill, NC: UNC Press.

Wyville, Richard. 1975. 'Memoirs of an Old Army Officer', ed. Jerome Handler, *JBHMS* 37: 21–7.

Yetman, Norman R., ed. 1984. *Voices From Slavery: 100 Authentic Slave Narratives*. New York: Dover.

Index